# MEMOIRS *of a* Showgirl

# MEMOIRS of a Showgirl

### Shay Stafford
with Bryce Corbett

**Author's note:** These are my memoirs. Some of the names of people in this book have been changed to protect their privacy, some of the characters have been blended. It's possible others will have experienced events differently – this is but one woman's account. It is all written with the greatest respect and deepest affection – Shay, 2010.

Published in Australia and New Zealand in 2010
by Hachette Australia
(an imprint of Hachette Australia Pty Limited)
Level 17, 207 Kent Street, Sydney NSW 2000
www.hachette.com.au

10 9 8 7 6 5 4 3 2 1

Copyright © Shay Stafford and Bryce Corbett 2010

This book is copyright. Apart from any fair dealing for the purposes of private study, research, criticism or review permitted under the *Copyright Act 1968*, no part may be stored or reproduced by any process without prior written permission. Enquiries should be made to the publisher.

National Library of Australia
Cataloguing-in-Publication data

Stafford, Shay.
Memoirs of a Showgirl/Shay Stafford with Bryce Corbett.
1st ed.

978 0 7336 2487 2 (pbk.)

Showgirls—Australia—Biography.
Corbett, Bryce.

792.8082092

Cover, text and picture section design by Christabella Designs
Cover photographs by Carla Coulson, www.carlacoulson.com
Inside front cover photograph courtesy Iko Ouro Preto, www.ikoouropreto.com
Inside back cover photograph courtesy Lido, Paris, www.lido.fr
Typeset in 12.5/16 pt Bembo by Bookhouse, Sydney

*For Flynn and Rose*

*Être Parisien, ce n'est pas être né a Paris, c'est y renaître*
SACHA GUITRY

(To be Parisian is not to be born in Paris, but to be reborn there)

## Prologue

### Paris 2009

It's late at night on the Champs Élysées. I'm standing in the wings, backstage at the Lido, preparing to make my entrance. A line of dancers, bedecked in feathers, file hurriedly past me onto the stage. As the music builds to a crescendo, I take my cue and step into the light. I'm wearing a sumptuous showgirl costume, a barely there confection of sequins and jewels. Despite a cumbersome feather backpack, tonight I feel light, weightless. The choreography comes effortlessly, seems to flow out of me. I am floating.

I'm determined to commit to memory every second of this evening's performance – soak it all up. I've danced this routine more times than I can remember, but this one is special. I want to make it count.

All around me now the stage is full. A mad crush of feathers, sequins, legs and breasts. I feel my heart beating faster as the number comes to an end. This is it, my grand finale. My last curtain call. On the final count, the lights explode and the company strikes a pose. The audience erupts – whistling, cheering, holding their champagne flutes aloft. I am beaming. A rush of adrenaline shoots through me and I tingle. Before I know what's happening, a large bouquet of roses is being thrust into my hands. And then I start to cry. Showgirls flank me on either side, clapping and wiping tears from their eyes. I feel the heat of the spotlight, drink in the spectacle of a packed auditorium in the midst of a standing ovation and I feel like the luckiest girl alive.

Down in the dressing-room there are more flowers and more tears. A parade of semi-naked colleagues files by. They take it in turns to hug me – telling me how much they will miss me. The feeling is mutual. For twelve years I have been here in the City of Light. Twelve years as a Paris showgirl, first with the Moulin Rouge and now with the Lido. Almost a third of my life spent draped in jewels and festooned with feathers, performing two shows a night, six nights a week. Fighting off injury, surviving backstage politics, building lifelong friendships and navigating the nether world of Paris by night. All to arrive here: I'm thirty-four and on the brink of retirement.

Emotion runs high as I sit down to pack up my dressing-room table. Leaning in to the mirror to remove the eyelashes and scrape off the pancake one last time, I glimpse the woman beneath, and she looks tired. Exhilarated and happy, but oh so tired. It's definitely time to hang up the heels.

The street is deserted when I step out the stage door and climb aboard the Vespa. It's well past 2 a.m. as I sputter onto the Champs Élysées and set a course for home. The early summer's air is still warm, despite the hour. Certainly warm enough to warrant taking the long way home, down by the river and along the *quai*. As the bike hums along beside the Seine, the Musée d'Orsay flashes by, floodlit and majestic. The river appears not to be moving at all tonight: the lamps that crown the Pont Neuf are reflected in the water's glassy surface. My heart catches as I think about how much I am going to miss this view – how much I am going to miss this remarkable city, my home for more than a decade. I think back to when I first arrived, scared and alone. I think back further to where it all began – in a church hall in suburban Brisbane with a gaggle of similarly uncoordinated six-year-olds in tap shoes and tutus.

Arriving home, I park the Vespa, take the lift to the sixth floor and turn the key quietly in the lock. From behind the closed bedroom door I hear the soft sounds of sleeping. The living room is a jumble of boxes, suitcases and bubble wrap. I pick my way to the kitchen and quietly prepare a cup of tea. I throw open the living-room window and lean on the railing, staring out across the darkened Paris skyline, listening to the hum of the slumbering city. And I start to think about how my life is about to change.

# ACT I

# Chapter One

## Suburban Brisbane, 1980

Mum turned off the ignition. We both sat quietly and stared straight ahead. The only sounds were the ticking of the engine as it cooled and the muted chatter of a group of little girls swinging from the railings of the stairs leading up to the Annerley church hall.

Dressed in leotards, their hair scraped back in loose ponytails and buns, a few hung listlessly off the rails in the late afternoon heat. Skinny, bony, angular little slips of things.

'Well, this is it, Shelb,' Mum said, breaking the silence. 'Do you want me to come in with you?'

I shook my head and tried my best not to look nervous. Starting ballet class had been my idea. I'd been pestering Mum about it for months – ever since my best friend Julie Ann, or 'Chick', as everyone called her, had come up to me bouncing with excitement about the fairy dance she had learned. She'd been attending dance classes for a couple of years. We had been friends since our first days at school – but she had this whole other world that I wasn't a part of. Mum had finally given in and today I would be starting out in the beginners' class. But now that I was here, I wasn't sure I wanted to do it anymore.

'Come on sweetheart, it will be fun.'

I nodded, but didn't budge.

'What about if you just go in and do one class? If you don't like it, you don't ever have to come back. Deal?'

I looked at Mum and nodded again.

'Come on, I'll come with you.'

As we crunched across the gravel car park, I felt suddenly very self-conscious. Dressed in a pair of mint green terry towelling shorty-shorts and a pink T-shirt, my honey-blonde hair in pigtails, I didn't look the same as the others. The gaggle of girls fell silent as Mum and I climbed the steps and walked into the hall.

A tall, fifty-something woman looked up from the tape player she was hunched over at the opposite end of the hall. 'Hello, can I help you?'

As she walked towards us, I took in the room. It had a wooden floor; two rows of windows ran the length of the building and a dusty portrait of the Queen hung on the far wall. A couple of battered ceiling fans turned lazily above us, seemingly too exhausted to beat back the heat. On the off-white fibro walls, secured with strips of yellowed sticky-tape, were a couple of dog-eared, sun-faded posters of ballet dancers, pirouetting on stages belonging to another time and another world.

After baking all day in the Queensland sun, the hall felt more like an oven than any incubator of budding dance talent.

'I'm Jill Casey, you must be Mrs Stafford.' The woman stepped forward and offered a heavily tanned hand. 'Which would make you Shane?'

'Shay', my mother corrected. 'S-H-A-Y. Shay.'

'Well, welcome to our dance studio, Shay, I'm sure you're going to love it.'

I emerged from that initial class, if not in love with dance, at least sufficiently intrigued by it to shrug in a noncommittal way when, later that night, Mum asked if I wanted to go back the next week.

In retrospect, it would be a bit of a stretch to describe what we did in those classes each week as dancing.

Mrs Casey did her best to teach us the basics we'd require for the end-of-year examinations, but we were only interested in running around in circles, pretending to be fairies. For the first few months, armed only with a pair of Jiffies, a set of knobbly knees and a growing enthusiasm, I struggled to wrap my mind and skinny frame around the basics of ballet, tap and jazz.

As I made friends with the girls in my class and my confidence grew, I began to really enjoy my visits to the church hall. Each week, Mrs Casey would add a new dance movement to our repertoire. One week we would do *pliés*, the next a simple tap step. Jazz ballet was squeezed into the off-moments we weren't outside the hall playing elastics or seeing who could hang upside down from the stair railings for the longest.

By some miracle, when the end of the year rolled around we apparently knew enough to take the Commonwealth Society of Teachers of Dancing official examinations.

Leading up to the exams, the church hall was abuzz with activity. There were leotards to be road-tested, hairstyles to rehearse and even the prospect of our first smear of make-up.

When the big day arrived, we assembled outside the hall in our brand-new regulation pink leotards: fifteen little bundles of nerves and excitement barely contained within ill-fitting strips of musk lycra.

Mum had bought me a pair of ballet shoes for the occasion and I couldn't wait to show them off, though I was terrified about having to perform in front of an official examiner (a woman who had driven to Annerley all the way from the next suburb). A local hairdresser had been brought in to tend to our locks. She pulled my hair back into a bun and sprayed it with a wholly unnecessary, but absolutely thrilling, amount of hair lacquer. The air was heavy with the sickly sweet chemical stench of it.

We waited outside until our names were called, ran into the hall, curtsied before the examiner and handed over our paper – the form that she would fill out to assess our performance.

I don't remember how I fared. Between the new shoes, the smudge of lipstick I was proudly sporting and the helmet of hair lacquer, it was all I could do to focus on the exam. Not that it mattered whether we passed or failed. Come what may, as fully paid-up members of the junior class of Mrs Casey's Annerley Church Hall Dance Studio, me and my pint-sized peers were destined to take part in the end-of-year recital.

And so it was that in the December of 1980, I fronted up to the Schonell Theatre at the University of Queensland in my recital costume, ready for my first-ever public performance.

For a little girl like me, obsessed with pink, the costume could not have been more perfect: a pink printed dress (with puffed sleeves, of course), a pink tutu, pink satin bow tied in my heavily hairsprayed hair, long white socks and pink ballet shoes. We had some basic steps to perform, and what we lacked in dance talent we more than made up for in pure cute factor: who wasn't going to be charmed by fifteen six-year-olds in pink tutus?

As I took my bow and stood under the spotlight before the gaze of hundreds of proud parents, I felt exhilarated. There were no nerves, there was no fear – just pure excitement. How much of that excitement was to do with the concert and how much was to do with the imminent, post-concert arrival of Santa Claus with gifts, it's hard now for me to say.

What I do know is that when I ripped open the wrapping paper around the gift Santa gave me (one Mum had bought, wrapped and labelled clearly with my name) and discovered a cassette-book, I was pretty sure this day was about as close to perfect as I had ever had.

After the concert, we went to my grandparents' house. Ma and Pa lived not far from us in a beautiful old Queenslander on Longueval Street. The weatherboard house stood on stilts, raised high above the ground. In the backyard, next to Pa's incinerator, stood a huge poinciana tree.

Pa grabbed his instamatic, took me out into the garden and shot a whole roll of film of me posing in my recital costume. Cassette-book in hand, I struck a series of poses: me under the poinciana tree, me next to the Hills hoist, me pointing my toe in front of the laundry door.

I was only too happy to indulge Pa's sudden attack of the shutterbugs. At the time, I thought nothing of the fact he was beaming with pride. But looking back, I wonder if my little turn on the stage and pretensions of being a ballet dancer didn't affect him more deeply than I was able to appreciate. After all, it was Pa who had taken me earlier in the year to see Rudolf Nureyev. The legendary Russian ballet dancer had been touring Australia and alighted briefly on the Brisbane stage for one performance.

I was too young to understand the significance of Nureyev being in Brisbane – which in the early 1980s was not exactly the world capital of culture. I was equally too young to really appreciate the masterful display of ballet to which Nureyev treated us. But for Pa, a man whose poet's soul had remained unhardened, despite prolonged exposure to the harsh elements of Queensland, the experience must have been magical.

For me, it was just a fun day out with my Pa. I'd be lying if I said I'd had some kind of epiphany sitting there in the dark, while one of the greatest dancers to ever take to the stage floated in front of me. I was six years old. The packet of Jaffas at the interval made just as much of an impression. While other little girls routinely cite the classic dance movie *The Red Shoes* as their inspiration for strapping on ballet slippers, I can honestly say I never saw it. With two brothers and a footy-obsessed dad, the TV in our house seemed to be permanently tuned to sport.

And yet, thanks to Ma and Pa, dance had always been part of my childhood, a kind of wallpaper to my early years in the Brisbane suburbs. Leo and Iris, as my grandparents were known to their churchgoing and bowls-playing circle of friends, were Brisbane's answer to Fred and Ginger. Both of them loved to dance. Back in 1940s Brisbane, when they were courting, my grandparents used to dance the night away in the city's music halls. Later in life, they loved nothing more than settling down in front of the TV on a Saturday night to watch the old musicals. *High Society, Singin' in the Rain, An American in Paris*. On a sideboard in their living room sat a framed photo of Broadway actress and Hollywood musical starlet, Joan Blondell. I always assumed she was some long-lost relative: a bohemian, other-worldly aunt who had somehow managed to escape suburban Brizzy and tap dance her way to a more glamorous life.

I remember as a child I would watch Ma and Pa slow dance occasionally in their living room, both of them happily transported by the music, lost in memory and in each other.

With the exams done, the recital over and photographs taken, my six-year-old brain assumed that I had gone as far as I could go with this whole dance caper. I'd learned how to *plié*, I'd mastered a basic time-step tap movement. And when it came to running in a diagonal line across a church hall in a pink leotard, or running in a circle before an auditorium full of parents, I felt I'd demonstrated I was more than capable.

So that night, with the lacquer washed from my hair and the last remnants of lipstick scrubbed from my mouth, I stood in the kitchen next to Mum as she washed dishes and told her I didn't plan to go back to dance class.

'But I thought you enjoyed it?' she asked, taken aback.

'Oh I do', I replied. 'But I've learned everything.'

With the patience and forbearance that comes with being a mother, Mum just smiled, kept on scouring and didn't say a word.

She would tell me years later that Mrs Casey had scolded her for allowing me to give up dance classes. 'It's a waste of good potential,' Mrs Casey had apparently said. But at the time, I was well and truly done with dance and ready to take on weightier challenges. Chick was moving to Muswellbrook and I had bigger fish to fry.

# Chapter Two

The Mary Immaculate Primary School sports carnival was a highlight of the school calendar. The rest of the year was a blur of recesses and lunches – sessions of handball and elastics, intense bouts of schoolyard politics and Vegemite sandwiches – bookended by the sputtering pursuit of academic achievement. The annual sports carnival always stood out for me as a major event. I was a skinny child and taller than all the other girls in my class – in some cases by a foot. I spent a good part of my school days walking with a self-conscious stoop. But when sports carnival day swung around, my height came into its own and for that one day I stood up straight and revelled in my athletic build. My favoured event was the high jump.

I loved every moment of competing. I'd take the first few qualifying jumps with a scissor kick, sailing effortlessly over the pole. As the bar was raised, I'd switch to the Fosbury flop, flinging myself backwards up and over the pole. No-one Fosbury flopped quite like I did; I was the undisputed Fosbury flopping queen of Mary Immaculate Primary School. Not that sporting prowess was anything unusual in the Stafford household.

My older brother, John, was one of those infuriating people for whom every sport came naturally. It didn't matter whether he picked up a golf club, a football or a cricket bat – he was instantly annoyingly good at wielding it. I worshipped the ground John walked on, and he exploited this fact mercilessly in the way older brothers are wont to do. When he was going through a pentathlon phase, I would dutifully follow him down to the oval every day after school and help him practise his javelin throw: he would throw the javelin and then instruct me to run and fetch it. Back and forth I would sprint, a willing slave in his quest to become the sportiest kid in the greater metropolitan Brisbane area.

Later in life, John would play schoolboy cricket for Queensland and become a kind of rugby prodigy. He donned the Australian Schoolboys' Rugby jersey, was selected for the Queensland Reds, played under-21s for the Brisbane Broncos and ended his brief but brilliant rugby career playing for a team in northern Japan.

My younger brother, Adam – five years my junior and possessed of the same natural sporting prowess as our older brother – would also grow up excelling at every sport he turned his hand to. When he wasn't surfing like a pro, he played representative cricket and rugby, and went on to play club rugby in Scotland and Ireland. Every memory I have of Adam as a small boy involves him with a ball of some sort or other. He was constantly bouncing, throwing, catching – it was like a nervous tic. He was also unusually skilled at breaking bones, especially his own.

To Dad, a former rugby league player, it was a source of constant joy that the house was a hotbed of sporting activity and that the Hills hoist was constantly creaking under the weight of freshly washed jerseys and football socks. Mum, being of a famously gentle nature, was less excited. She was happy to encourage our every sporting endeavour, and took no small amount of pride in our successes on the pitch, but she was an old-fashioned woman at heart who loved the fact she had a little girl to counterbalance a house full of men. She made sure that when I wasn't tearing about the Little Athletics oval I was surrounded by all things pink and girly.

I was born on 21 August 1974 – a Wednesday. To confound the morbid poem that contends that Wednesday's child is full of woe, I was, by

all accounts, a happy little baby. To Dad, from the first moment he set eyes on me, I was always his 'little ray of sunshine'.

From the very outset of her pregnancy with me, Mum had decided that if I turned out to be a girl, I would be called 'Erin'. But postnatal hormones being what they are, she had a sudden change of heart when finally I entered the world. Shayleen Ann Stafford was the name she bestowed on me. Even in 1970s Brisbane, Shayleen was an *unusual* choice. If it had come to her in a moment of inspiration, it may have been excusable. If she had borrowed it from a noble historical figure or even a well-loved, if unfortunately named, older relative, it might have been okay. But in her postnatal funk, she had decided on Shayleen just because she overheard the woman in the next hospital bed calling her visiting niece by that name. That my Dad didn't insist they stick with their original choice was one thing. That family services or the hospital's social workers didn't intervene and veto the name was, I would conclude later in life, a complete dereliction of their duty. And so Shayleen it was.

Of course, as a little girl, it was my name, pure and simple. It never occurred to me that it was unusual in any way. Besides, my Nana thought it was a lovely name. And it rarely got a work-out anyway, as family members opted to call me by several nicknames including Shelby, Shelly, Strawb and Tweetie. Only as I got older did I self-consciously shorten Shayleen to Shay.

My childhood was notable for how unremarkable it was. Mum was a nurse: she worked the night shift at the Mater Hospital where she cared for newborn and premature babies. Dad was a welder by trade, first building coaches and then later trucks working for a waste company. If anyone asked him, he said he was a garbo – but over the years his personable manner and easy way with practically everyone saw him move from the factory floor to the sales office.

We lived in an old Queenslander in Tarragindi – a suburb to the south of Brisbane city centre. Brisbane was still a sleepy backwater of a city in the early seventies; people had locks on their doors, but rarely used them. In our backyard, a space that doubled as a cricket pitch, we had a big old German shepherd called Zeke, the trusty Hills hoist and a trampoline. In summer we used to run the hose across the top of the trampoline and launch ourselves onto it from the back balcony (and yes, it was one of the ways my brother broke a bone). My weekdays were spent at Mary Immaculate Primary School up the road, skipping rope and swapping sandwiches in its sun-baked asphalt playground. I was a good student, kept my head down (despite always being taller than every other girl in my year) and *almost* avoided the schoolyard taunting directed at less fortunate members of my class. If it hadn't been for our weekly swimming lesson, I would have been safe. But out of uniform and in a swimming costume there was nowhere to hide, and I was teased for being so skinny.

My weekends were a whirlwind in which I was ferried from my brothers' football games on dust-blown, brown-grass paddocks to my Little Athletics meets or netball games. Like parents all over Australia, mine woke up at the crack of dawn on Saturday mornings and between them performed a finely choreographed tag-team dance to ensure the three of us got to our weekend sporting activities. Dad thought nothing of getting up at 6 a.m. on a Saturday to go down and mark the football oval, and Mum sat stoically in the blistering Brisbane heat through more never-ending cricket matches than any mere mortal should have had to endure. They never complained. They were working with the theory that as long as we were kept busy with hobbies and sports we'd be off the streets and well and truly out of trouble, and they seemed happy enough to play their part.

Besides, sport and the enthusiastic playing of it was a part of the fabric of life in Brisbane in the early eighties. In 1982 the Commonwealth Games came to town, and the city went sports-mad. I remember watching in rapt pleasure when, during the televised opening ceremony, the 13-metre-high games mascot kangaroo, Matilda, rumbled around the stadium and turned her head to wink at the crowd. When her pouch opened and schoolkids dressed as joeys poured out to jump on mini-trampolines, I thought I was going to burst. It was a month in which Robert de Castella, Raelene Boyle and Tracy Wickham became household legends – and one in which I dared to dream that, one day, my famed Fosbury flops might yet see me stand on a podium to receive a medal from the Queen.

# Chapter Three

Life was busy and I was content with school, sport and death-defying trampoline feats, so I was ten years old before I set foot back inside a dance studio. Four years had passed since my star turn at the Schonell Theatre.

It was another friend, Catherine, who pulled me back into the world of dance again. She had started going to jazz ballet classes, so I went along one afternoon to watch. The classes were held at the Annerley church hall; as we settled at the back of the room it all seemed reassuringly familiar.

The teacher was a young woman, Kim Bowkett, who had recently gone into partnership with Mrs Casey, teaching jazz and ballet while Mrs C concentrated on tap. Barely an adult herself, Kim had a passion for dance that was infectious. She was tall, pretty and blonde. And, to top it all off, she had a red Disco Robo – a ghetto-blaster in the shape of a robot. I was smitten.

The music was contemporary and the dance style was like something off the television. I ran home to Mum at the end of the class and told her I wanted in. She didn't seem surprised at all.

It was the *Fame* era – when the kids from New York's High School of Performing Arts were the coolest thing on TV. I distinctly remember going to class on a Friday night and then running home to watch *Fame*. Leroy was my favourite character, closely followed by Coco. In fact, I'm pretty certain the first schoolgirl crush I ever had was on Leroy.

I loved jazz classes with Kim, despite the fact I was among the worst in the class. When it came time to pair off and do a jazz run (an overly dramatic prance requiring the dragging of alternate feet) down the hall, the best girls would go first. It was a natural selection of sorts: the further down the line you went, the worse the dancers tended to be. At the top of the queue you had the girls who had been dancing for years. They were impeccably dressed in the latest dancewear, from their powder blue Bloch leotards right down to their barely scuffed jazz shoes. The further down the line you went, the scruffier, clumsier and more oddly shaped they would get. By the time you reached me, there were girls dancing barefoot, or in terry towelling shorty-shorts, girls who were a little on the plump side and others who were simply uncoordinated.

As well as being new, I only came to class once a week, compared to the front-of-the-queuers who did three classes a week, so I was cast into the daggy group. When the end-of-year recital came around, this meant I was stuck up the back of the stage – to provide colour, movement and a sense of depth, but certainly not to be featured.

For Kim, the recital was an annual exercise in parental diplomacy. Of course she wanted to show off the best kids, whose skills were testament to her talents as a dance teacher, yet she knew she was obliged to showcase even the dowdiest dancer to satisfy each and every fee-paying parent. She cleverly got around this conundrum by sticking the daggy group right up the back and bringing them downstage mid-performance to do a brief, and very simple, combination of moves before consigning them back into upstage obscurity.

As members of the daggy group, even though our moment in the spotlight was destined to be brief, the build-up to each concert was long and full of melodrama.

Weeks before the recital everyone in the class was handed a sheet of paper detailing the exact specifications of the costume we had to wear. I took it home and presented it to Mum. The costumes had to be made from scratch, and each mum had to purchase the exact same coloured lycra and regulation-issue sequins and tulle. To minimise any variations, parents were instructed to buy the components of our costume from the same haberdashery – Queenie's of Annerley. During a one-week period at the end of each November, forty-odd mums beat a path to Queenie's to swell her coffers and humour their daughters.

Queenie was a large, middle-aged Greek woman with an ample bosom. She may have had legs, but in all the years I visited her shop, I never saw them. She sat immobile behind her counter, waiting to serve the bedraggled ranks of stressed-out stage mums, bestowing on them reams of lycra, countless thousands of sequins and bolt upon bolt of tulle, taffeta and organza.

It was the job of Queenie's long-suffering husband Cyril to cut and dispense the lycra. My eternal memory of Cyril is of a kindly, cardigan-sporting, slightly balding, scissor-wielding man scurrying about the store as his wife yelled instructions.

Once we had our costume components from Queenie, Mum and I would troop off to Faye Lewis's house. Because of her prowess with the sewing machine, Faye was one of the designated costume-making mothers. I stood to be measured in the corner of Faye's living room while her son and the Lewis family cocker spaniel watched footy on TV.

The final stop on the recital preparation tour was Lisa Chesterfield's house. Lisa's mum was the local Nutrimetics saleswoman and, according to the instruction sheet, we all had to wear the exact same make-up for the performance. It was always the same: pink blush, red lipstick and periwinkle blue eyeshadow – a combination that never failed to look fetching on a motley collection of nine- and ten-year-old complexions.

A week before the recital, Mum took me into town to buy my first pair of jazz shoes. After I'd been treated to a milkshake in an aluminium tumbler at the Myer cafeteria, we wandered across to the Brisbane Arcade, which housed a beautiful dancewear store called Paul Wright. The arcade was a step back in time to a more refined era of shopping, and the Paul Wright store was a jewel in the arcade and a shrine to dance. I stood awestruck before the window display of tutus and dusky pink ballet slippers. An entire store dedicated to dance! That was the first moment I sensed that the world of dance extended beyond Annerley's church hall, beyond even the end-of-year recital. If a man called Paul Wright could maintain an elegant store in the stately Brisbane Arcade and sell, with such solemnity and refinement, the shoes I was going to need to perform in Kim Bowkett's interpretation of 'Believe It or Not I'm Walking on Air', then perhaps there was a whole lot more to this dancing caper than I had previously imagined.

The fitting of my shoes was a serious process – both for me and for the Paul Wright staff. I took a seat while a shop assistant knelt at my feet and tried out various types and size of jazz shoe. When I emerged with Mum half an hour later, clinging tightly to the box containing my new white leather shoes, I felt like they were my most precious possession. I couldn't wait to get on stage and show them off.

When the day of the concert arrived, I went to school with my hair in rollers. As with the costumes and make-up, we were all required to wear exactly the same hairstyle for the performance. A high ponytail, hairsprayed and teased to within an inch of its brittle life.

My hair, which I had famously inherited from my Nana, was brown, thin and lank and had always resisted any attempts at styling. And yet Mum and I refused to admit defeat. I skipped off to school that morning with a ponytail in pink foam rollers clumped at the back of my head. I felt very showbiz.

When it finally came to showtime and the rollers were removed, the curl held for all of three minutes. Not that I cared. I had my sequinned lycra costume, my periwinkle blue eyeshadow, my white leather jazz shoes and my moment in the spotlight on the stage of the Schonell Theatre.

I don't remember much about the recital itself. I had been so caught up in all the preparation that I didn't have the energy to care all that much about the performance. Even so, after that concert the dance bug was well and truly under my skin. I was hooked.

It was about this time that Chick and her family moved back to Brisbane following an extended stay in Muswellbrook. Our friendship picked up from where it had left off, like she'd only been gone a weekend.

She came to see me in the recital, and on account of it being a big night out, donned her First Holy Communion dress for the occasion.

Chick and I decided that when the new dance year began, we would not only do jazz class together, but would up the ante and throw in a bit of tap as well. I was so excited. I couldn't wait for the Christmas school holidays to end so I could get back in the dance studio.

I went into that second year with more confidence.

Mum bought me a pair of second-hand tap shoes during a sale at the dance school. We were all growing fast and dancewear cost a small fortune, so there was a steady trade among my classmates in used dance shoes. The only ones Mum could find that fitted my feet were old, flat, tired-looking ... and bright red. In what must have been the first stirrings of teen fashion-consciousness, I remember thinking they were easily the daggiest shoes in the whole school. Not that it stopped me from tapping. From the very beginning of classes, I fell in love with tap dancing. I took to it straight away and practised at every available opportunity.

That year, as if my parents didn't have enough on their Saturday morning roster, I also started playing netball. Because of my height and the fact I couldn't shoot, I was relegated to the roles of goal defence or goal keeper, which meant I was only involved in the game sporadically. Whenever the ball was down the other end of the court, I would use the lull to practise my steps. I lost count of the times I was midway through a dance routine when the ball came sailing down the court towards me. The coach would be screaming herself hoarse. 'Shay Stafford! Stop dancing, for the love of God, and watch the ball!'

Meanwhile, Dad transformed the space under our house into a mini dance studio, erecting a wall of mirrors, welding a ballet barre into place and creating a space for me to tap my little heart out. It was a gesture motivated as much by concern for the living-room carpet as it was by devotion to his daughter.

It didn't matter whether I was at the dance studio, in the shower cubicle at home or in line at the school assembly, I was always tapping. When called for dinner I would tap up the concrete stairs from the backyard to the dining-room table. I would forward slap down the cereal aisle at Woolworths, tap out a routine on the back deck and use the car park at my brothers' cricket matches to get in some extra practice. Even when sitting in the pew at church during Sunday morning mass, my feet would silently tap out a combination on the stone floor. For almost two years, there was hardly a smooth, hard surface in the whole of Brisbane that was spared the frantic, compulsive tapping of my perpetually moving feet.

The red tap shoes were daggy in the extreme, but they were more than made up for six months later when Mum finally gave in to my constant nagging and bought me a weightlifter leotard – a low-cut affair designed to be worn over the top of a T-shirt. Chick's mum had bought her a blue one a few weeks before and I *had* to have the same.

Chick and I would troop off together to dance class in our weight-lifters thinking we were the bee's knees. I always liked to team mine with a pink T-shirt emblazoned with 'FAME', a pair of pink and white leg warmers and my jazz shoes. If it was a weekend and I had to walk to class, I liked to complete the look with a pair of pale pink reflector sunglasses. I would even sometimes wear the sunglasses around the house, to the delight of my older brother who – not unreasonably – said I looked like a pink stick insect.

Over the next couple of years, I gradually increased the number and frequency of dance classes I took, so that every moment I wasn't at school, I was busy with one dance class or another. Chick and I were encouraged by Kim and Mrs Casey to start taking part in eisteddfods. We'd practise for weeks, and then our parents would drive us to the furthest corners of greater metropolitan Brisbane to compete in such dance hotspots as Redcliffe and Wynnum.

Mum had distinguished herself as a stage mum by caring enough to indulge and encourage me, but not so much that I ever felt any pressure. This possibly had less to do with her easygoing personality and more to do with the household she had to maintain, the two boisterous, overactive sons she had to wrangle, and the night shifts she was working twice a week in the intensive care nursery at the Mater Hospital. For his part, Dad was always supportive but constantly wondered aloud if there was a point to all this prancing about on stage.

'But what will it all *lead* to, Kim?' he could often be heard asking at the conclusion of yet another eisteddfod.

I'm not sure Kim ever answered Dad's question to his satisfaction, but to further expand our performance experience, she started producing pantomimes to be performed at local shopping centres during school holidays.

In my first public performance for which the audience wasn't just a collection of long-suffering parents, I played a crow in a production of *The Wizard of Oz* at Westfield Shoppingtown Indooroopilly. If the role didn't quite live up to my expectations, I took comfort in the fact that I was also the understudy to the Tin Man (played by a girl, because there were never any boys in our dance classes).

My little brother was intrigued. 'Mum,' he said thoughtfully one morning over breakfast, 'if Shay is the understudy, wouldn't that mean that if we gave the Tin Man a poisoned Popper, Shay would get to do it?' I never did get to go on as the Tin Man, despite my brother's cunning plan, but having to languish at the back of the stage as a crow turned out to be just fine with me. The excitement of performing on a shopping-centre stage and wearing a full face of make-up to the food court to eat potato gems between our 11 a.m. and 1 p.m. performances was more than enough for me. I was only eleven, after all. The simple things still meant a lot.

When the next school holidays rolled around, Kim announced that the school would be presenting *Snow White* as its next shopping-centre panto extravaganza. The afternoon came for the cast list to be posted, and we all scurried to the noticeboard. I had been cast as Snow White. Overcome, I stood there for a full minute. I ran outside to Mum, who was waiting patiently to collect me, the brown station wagon idling in the car park.

'Mum! Mum! You have to come and see this!'

I dragged her into the hall and led her to the cast list.

'Oh Shelby! That's wonderful! I always knew you were the best,' she said, in what would become her standard refrain. In the car on the way home, it was all I could do to contain myself. Then Mum dropped a bombshell.

'When did you say the performances would be?'

I told her the dates.

'You haven't forgotten that you're getting your braces two weeks before that?'

I felt like I had been winded; my world came crashing down.

'That will be okay, won't it?' Mum continued, glancing nervously in my direction.

Okay? Okay?! Didn't she realise this was the worst possible disaster? Here I was, on the eve of my greatest theatrical triumph to date, and the gods of adolescence were conspiring to ruin it all by forcing me to perform with an unsightly mouthful of metal. It was about as far from okay as it was possible to be. I started to cry.

The next day, Mum paid a visit to Kim Bowkett. I never found out exactly what was said but without making a fuss, Mum informed me that she had moved the dental appointment back by a month.

For weeks leading up to the performance, I sat on my bed with Dad's little black cassette player, listening over and over to the tape Kim had given me. The entire show was to be performed in playback, meaning the dialogue and songs had been prerecorded and would then be mimed on stage. I listened to that tape until I had almost worn it out, determined to make sure every song and every sentence was drilled into my head. Play, rewind, play, rewind, play, rewind.

Much to my family's relief, the date of the panto finally arrived and for two glorious weeks over the September school holidays, I took to the centre stage of Westfield Indooroopilly as Snow White. We did two shows a day, and there were always hundreds of kids in the audience. My opening solo called for me to listlessly sweep the carpeted stage with a twig broom while miming 'Someday My Prince Will Come'. At one point in the song, I would gesture dramatically to the mums and kids hanging over the shopping centre balcony, doing my best to look forlorn – drawing on the vast acting range and profound emotional depth my eleven years on the planet had given me.

It wasn't exactly Shakespeare at the Globe, but I threw myself into the role with gusto, singing and dancing for all I was worth. I was a little rake of a thing in an ill-fitting black bob wig, miming and overacting in the neon glare of the Lowes menswear, Goldmark jewellers and David Jones signs. The heady scent of cinnamon and boiling fat wafted on the air from the nearby Donut King as I performed my heart out.

More than anything else, the experience was a whole lot of girly fun. Pre-show we were all crowded into a tiny dressing-room under the stage, and in between performances we would roam the shopping centre spending what little pocket money we had in the food court, or on glitter bath gel balls and novelty erasers at Mr Timothy's.

After the show we'd go back to someone's house and play pool ponies and have a sleepover. It was as near to perfect as an eleven-year-old girl's life can be.

Sadly, the school holidays came to an end, and the spectre of braces once again loomed large. I couldn't put them off any longer. For the subsequent school holiday pantomime, I was cast as the ugly stepsister in a Kim Bowkett original, made-for-Westfield-centre-stage production of Cinderella. Too proud to acknowledge the ugly (sister) truth, I consoled myself with the belief that the lesser role of an ugly sister required much greater dramatic range. That, and the fact that Chick was cast as the other ugly sister, which meant we could get up to all sorts of mischief on stage, was enough to keep me happy and my focus off my metal mouth.

In the few hours of my school holidays when I wasn't doing star turns on shopping mall stages, I was darting into town to attend holiday ballet school. I had been a latecomer to the art of ballet, so I had a lot of catching up to do. I was determined to make up for those lost years – and thankfully Mum and Dad had realised my obsession with dancing was not a passing fad and allowed me to take as many classes as I wanted.

Graduating to high school meant changing uniforms and walking down the hill from Mary Immaculate Primary School to Our Lady's

College. My dedication to the dance cause did not waver. My first year in high school coincided with my first solo performances at eisteddfods. All those extra classes were paying off. And just to round out the onstage experience, I decided to add singing to my repertoire of performance skills.

If my extracurricular life in primary school had been dominated by dance and performance, now it was completely dictated by it. I seemed to constantly be in a state of rehearsal for one concert or another. Four afternoons a week I would finish school and go straight to dance class. The mini dance studio Dad had built under the house was getting an intense work-out as I tapped, *pliéd* and jazz-balleted myself into a frenzy. He no doubt began to wish he'd added soundproofing when I started singing up a storm as well.

Once I was in high school, there were eisteddfods on the occasional weeknight, meaning my Dad could no longer use the excuse of my brothers' football matches to avoid attending. After being dragged to one of my performances, he sat in a moody silence in the car on the way home, finally declaring that I needed to 'have a good feed'. He had a point. I was twelve years old and still painfully skinny. On the brink of puberty, I was about as ungainly and awkward-looking as it was possible to be. My beanpole figure was accentuated by a set of gnashing silver braces which, when I was at home, were set off by the head brace I was required to wear for twelve to fourteen hours a day.

I hated that head brace with every ounce of my being. It was a nasty metal ring that attached to my braces and was held in place by a purple foam strap. As a concession to my mother, who was always reminding me to wear my brace, I used to put it on in the brief hour between school finishing and dance classes starting. I would sit in the church hall in my wet-look lycra tights, my limp hair in a ponytail, self-consciously sporting my head brace while trying to do a spot of maths homework. It was a good look.

It was about this time that Mum decided my hair needed a bit of body and that it would therefore be a good idea for me to get a punch perm. They were all the rage at the time. All over Australia, perfectly attractive young girls were lining up to undergo the punch-perming procedure – we were, for a mercifully brief time, a nation of pubescent poodles. Except for me. Stubbornly opposed to any kind of styling as it was, my hair held the perm for about a day before falling back into its natural state of limpness. It didn't matter how many bottles of mousse I applied or how many times I used the diffuser on the hairdryer, my hair, like my body, remained distinctly shapeless.

But being of a famously determined (some would say deluded) nature, I dispensed quickly with the punch perm and concentrated instead on cultivating a bird's nest fringe. To achieve this most enviable of hairstyles, I went to bed each night with pink foam rollers in my hair. To complete the look, I would put on my head brace and daub calamine lotion on the colony of spots that had taken up permanent residence on my chin, before sliding beneath the covers to get my beauty sleep.

I was so serious about dance and so eager not to waste a moment, even when sleeping, that I went to bed one night and lay on my stomach with my legs in frog position in an effort to improve my turnout – the outward rotation of the legs from the hip sockets that is so important in ballet. I thought I would lie in that position for an hour or so to stretch my pelvic muscles. But I fell asleep, and when I woke a couple of hours later, I couldn't move my legs at all. I had to yell out to Mum and ask her to help me get up. She came in, turned me over, massaged my legs and stretched me out. There I was, her only daughter and the fruit of her loins, legs akimbo, face plastered with calamine lotion, head brace attached and rollers in my hair. It was definitely a sight only a mother could love.

Despite our waking hours already being stuffed to overflowing with dance, Chick and I would use any spare time we had together to choreograph our own routines.

In summer, during family barbecues at Chick's house, we'd often be happily playing Marco Polo in the pool when we'd realise we had a captive audience. We'd run, dripping, inside the house to hurriedly choreograph a routine. Chick would lower an extension lead out of a back window of the house and connect it to the cassette player, and a perfectly pleasant backyard barbecue would suddenly be interrupted by two wet, bikini-clad girls demanding everyone push back their plastic garden chairs to make room for a stage. Our brothers would watch the performance in silent contempt; our parents would applaud politely. As soon as the routine was finished, we'd jump back in the pool and pick up the Marco Polo game where we left off.

But the life of a twelve-year-old dancer wasn't all pool parties and living-room concerts. As our ballet studies progressed, we were obliged to take exams, run by the Royal Academy of Dance and held in a big studio in the city. For weeks beforehand, Kim would have us drilling our ballet exercises. As far as I could make out, the exams were not just about how well you performed, but also about how you carried yourself, how gracefully you moved and how disciplined you could be. They had a reputation for being very tough – and the examiners had a reputation for being scary old ballet mistresses whose sole purpose in life was to intimidate teenage girls.

The ritual of exams was always the same. I would receive a letter, summonsing me to the big dance studio in the city on a certain day at a particular time. In the waiting room we would gather, our hair scraped back into a perfect bun, wrapped with a regulation-sized ribbon and all wearing the regulation black leotard and ballet shoes.

Upon hearing my name, I had to run in, holding my point shoes in my right hand at just the right angle and my exam paper in my left hand. Silence was of the utmost importance.

Girls (and it was almost entirely girls) would come from all over the state. We were made to perform a set of exercises at the barre to the accompaniment of a pianist, who was usually invisible in the far corner of the room. The examiner would look on with what appeared to be complete indifference. We would then field a series of questions about ballet theory, mostly about the French phrases common in ballet and what they meant. I was always so nervous, I could only squeak the answers.

It was close to torture. We worked so hard all year for that one-hour exam. The pressure was enormous, and yet, I never questioned why I voluntarily put myself through it. Whether it was my competitive nature, an inherited family tendency to want to be the best at whatever sport I undertook, or the simple pride of knowing I had given it my all, I kept going back year after year for my annual dose of abject terror and ritual humiliation.

Some girls from other dance schools who went through the ballet exams couldn't get away from them fast enough once they finished high school. Some of them developed eating disorders, many developed body image problems and a good proportion of them were so burned out by the experience that they never set foot in a dance studio again.

But luckily for me, Kim's school was more about performance and having fun than about exams, meaning that when I eventually emerged from schoolgirl-aged classes, I still had the love of dance in me.

# Chapter Four

In Year Ten, I was knocked out by a severe bout of glandular fever. It's often referred to as the kissing disease: I must have been the first teenager to contract it immaculately. Attending an all-girls' school by day, an all-girls' dance class by night and girl-dominated eisteddfods during weekends, the opportunities for me to meet boys, much less kiss them, were severely restricted.

After languishing in bed for weeks, I returned to the eisteddfod circuit a couple of months later carrying an extra seven kilos, much to the delight of my father, who was pleased that I was finally starting to look healthy. It may not sound like a lot, but on a fifteen-year-old stick-creature, the weight gain was noticeable. Almost overnight I was chunky.

I dyed my brown hair blonde in preparation for the upcoming eisteddfod season. Determined to emulate the big, curly, teased hair that was so fashionable at the time, I invested in a set of Breville Hot Sticks and a family value pack of VO5 hairspray. Then, with my hair back-combed, I travelled all over Brisbane belting out Broadway standards such as 'Memory' from *Cats*, 'Wind Beneath My Wings' and – my personal favourite – Whitney Houston's 'One Moment in Time'. On stages as far afield as Strathpine and Ipswich, I would wail into tinny PA systems to a crackly instrumental backing tape.

Enamoured of my bouffant blonde locks and determined to give a full diva performance, I took to wearing a pink strapless taffeta dress, a pair of giant diamanté earrings (kindly lent to me by Mrs Casey) and the shiny flesh-coloured stockings known as redanza tights.

Sadly, no amount of VO5 or Breville Hot Sticking could draw attention away from my newly acquired back fat. In the grainy video footage of my performances, which were faithfully recorded on Dad's Super 8, you can still make out rolls of pasty white flesh spilling over pink taffeta. Somebody should have staged an intervention – if only to spare the poor parents of the other performers. After spending thousands of dollars on their daughters' dance tuition, they quite possibly didn't want to have to sit through the likes of me warbling Whitney.

In my sixteenth year, thanks to my continued obsession with dance, I managed to shed the extra kilos I'd gained. Also – mercifully for everyone on the eisteddfod circuit – I sensibly realised I wasn't going to become Bette Midler or Whitney and dropped the singing. I'd still warble on the odd occasion when the pink taffeta mood took me, but for the most part I concentrated on honing my dance skills.

At one eisteddfod, a judge commended my performance and added that with my height and dance ability, I should consider a career as a Bluebell. I stood on stage and smiled graciously, despite not having the faintest idea what she was talking about. Kim later explained to me that a Bluebell was a member of the celebrated troupe of leggy, topless female dancers at the famous Paris cabaret, the Lido.

'Topless?' I replied, unsure if I was supposed to feel offended.

'It's part and parcel of Paris cabaret,' Kim assured me. 'You have to see it in context to understand.'

Intrigued that an eisteddfod judge would recommend I join a dance troupe in Paris, I did a bit of research. At the local library, I found a photographic book about the city. It was an old 1960s travel book in which the fashions made all the women look like Audrey Hepburn. I flicked past images of the Eiffel Tower, Notre Dame and the fountains of the Place de la Concorde lit up at night, and fell eventually upon a double-page spread dedicated to Paris nightlife. And there, striking a leggy pose of sublime elegance, in exquisite costumes, was a line of Lido Bluebells. I was transfixed. The stage seemed so huge, the costumes so elaborate and the dancers so uniformly beautiful. It looked far more glamorous than any Schonell Theatre or Westfield shopping centre production. I was bewitched by the idea of dancing at the Lido. But I knew it was completely out of my league.

Throughout my early years as a dancer, the one constant had been the ever-reliable presence and friendship of Chick. So when she announced she was giving up eisteddfods to set up her own dance school, I didn't know whether to be elated for her or disappointed for me. But we had reached a crossroads of sorts. We were almost seventeen; the end of school was in sight and there were big decisions looming about what we would do with the rest of our lives. Kim Bowkett's fledgling school had gone from strength to strength so, tapping her inner entrepreneur, Chick decided there was a living to be made helping to train the next generation of aspiring Cyd Charisses. She rented a hall, printed some flyers and launched what in time would become a very successful dance school.

Not long after, Reebok — which at the time was one of the biggest sports shoe companies in the world — approached Kim looking for a handful of dancers to do a spot of promotional work. I was among the few Kim chose to become Reebok girls. After all those years of effort, and of Dad asking where it would all lead, I finally had a paying gig. Admittedly, we were largely required to dress in tight lycra and stand around looking sporty in sneakers — hardly the best use of the dance skills I had carefully honed over almost a decade. But a gig was a gig.

The job required us to dance at corporate and public events, including a big Reebok launch party in Sydney. Sparing no expense, the multinational corporation bundled us all onto an overnight coach, in the company of a couple of chaperone mums, and sent us down the Pacific Highway on a four-day adventure.

We were all so excited. It was the age of Reebok high-tops, and ownership of a pair — usually black and usually worn with big, thick white socks — was deeply fashionable. I was in heaven.

Once in Sydney, official duties saw us perform at a Reebok corporate function in a downtown nightclub. We did a series of short routines, each one a high-energy, high-kicking affair worthy of the high-tops on our feet. We threw everything we had into the performance – only to be received with a kind of studied indifference from the corporate crowd.

Once our dance obligations had been fulfilled, we had a couple of days spare to explore Sydney. I put the time to excellent use by having a musical theatre epiphany.

Kim organised for us to see the Sydney production of the tap-dancing Broadway musical, *42nd Street*. The male lead was played by an up-and-coming young dancer who was well-known in the Queensland dance community, thanks to his impressive talent and his mother's regionally renowned Gold Coast dance studio. His name was Todd McKenney. I remember sitting in the dark at Her Majesty's Theatre, spellbound by the spectacle, carried away by the colour and movement, obsessively watching every move Todd made. His feet tapped furiously, he danced with a fluid grace and he radiated a kind of energy that meant you couldn't take your eyes off him. My only other experience of musical theatre had been a touring production of *Cats* that passed through Brisbane. This was something else entirely.

The next day, still floating from our theatre experience, all the Reebok girls fronted up to an inner-city dance studio where Kim had arranged for us to have a private class with Todd McKenney. When he sauntered into the studio, I couldn't speak. The other girls were mildly awestruck, but I was completely dumbstruck. Here was the star of the show we had seen the night before. He was a Queensland dance world celebrity, he was male and, to top it all off, he was relaxed and lovely. We spent the afternoon learning a routine that was much more mature than any we had done before.

For the first time I could see that this hobby that had overtaken my life might actually become a career. Up until then, the tapping and the ballet and the singing and jazz had just been enjoyable extracurricular pastimes. It had never really occurred to me that they could also amount to a job. To me, a job was something like nursing or teaching or law – a nine-to-five existence with an office, a desk and a water-cooler. But this trip to Sydney revealed that there was an entire nocturnal world of work out there, completely removed from most people's workday reality. And it didn't look half bad.

# Chapter Five

At the end of Year Twelve, and with passable grades, I bade farewell to high school. Like most of my school-leaving peers on the Australian eastern seaboard, I beat a path to Surfers Paradise for schoolies week, to drown myself in West Coast Coolers and contemplate my future. As it turned out, there was more Cooler consumption than career contemplation, meaning that when the Christmas holidays rolled around and the prospect of a new year and university loomed, I didn't have the faintest idea what I wanted to do. I'd applied to do a nursing degree and was waiting to find out if I'd got in. Nursing had always seemed a natural choice. Mum had made such an admirable, relatively comfortable career out of it, and while I didn't know exactly what I wanted to do with my life, I felt it should probably be something that would help people.

When Kim phoned midway through the holidays to tell me about an audition at the Tivoli Theatre in Brisbane, I jumped at the opportunity. After all, entertaining people could surely be considered a kind of help. Or so I reasoned at the time. Besides, I didn't expect to get the job.

The Tivoli was a venerated cabaret venue in Brisbane's Fortitude Valley. Once a seething den of inner-city sleaze, in the 1990s the Valley was starting to clean up its act. The theatre had recently been purchased by a local entrepreneur, a woman who had purchased the dilapidated but charming old premises and given it a face lift. She had taken the hangar-like space – a cavernous former bakery warehouse – and completely renovated it using the Paris cabaret theatre Paradis Latin for inspiration. Designed by Gustave Eiffel (of tower fame) and built in 1889, the Paradis Latin had been playing host to a feathers-and-sequins showgirl spectacular for decades. On the outside, the Tivoli might have been a former warehouse stuck between a forklift factory and the Brisbane showground, but on the inside, she was a little patch of Paris in Brizzy. An elegant wrought-iron balcony wrapped around the horsehoe-shaped dress circle. A long zinc bar ran down one side of the auditorium, lit by crystal chandeliers and framed by a set of beautiful antique mirrors. White linen-topped tables with green velvet chairs were packed into the dining area in front of the stage, where a heavy red velvet curtain hung. Throughout the room, old Ricard and Pommery champagne posters were mounted on the walls. It was a tasteful, refined splash of old-world glamour.

I will always remember walking into the building for the first time. Stepping out of the blazing heat of a Brisbane summer's day and into the cool of the darkened theatre, I made my way to the office. It was empty, but I lingered there, staring at the walls. A framed set of posters advertising old Lido shows was the only decoration. They were artfully rendered cartoon images of men in top hats and girls with improbably long legs, skimpy costumes and a profusion of colourful feathers. It all looked wonderfully sophisticated and enchanting.

By pure coincidence, Todd McKenney and his mother had been hired by the Tivoli to stage the show for which I was auditioning. Todd remembered me and the audition went well. Three other girls from Kim's school and I sailed through the routines and were offered jobs on the spot.

I was taken aback. I'd never expected to actually get the job. This wasn't part of the grand plan: I was supposed to be going to uni and studying nursing. Yet here I was being offered a full-time job, that paid real money, to dance for my childhood hero. It was too exciting to be real.

When I broke the news to Mum, she was a little less enthusiastic. She was worried I was going to scamper off into the flighty world of showbiz without anything to fall back on, and suggested I study nursing for a year and go to night school to improve my grades. At least then

I'd have the backup of a more conventional, more secure career path. I didn't want to ignore my mum's advice – but I was seventeen, and all those antique mirrors and Lido posters had seduced me. I deferred my university degree and accepted the job.

Six weeks later, we started rehearsals. I was nervous as I lined up on stage with my fellow castmates to meet the lady owner of the Tivoli. She wafted into the auditorium and came up on stage to introduce herself. My first boss.

'Oh,' she said, as she came upon me. 'You must be Shay. You're the one with the big face and the big bum.'

I didn't know what to say. I stood dumbfounded, my face flushing with embarrassment. It was the first day of my first real job in the showbiz industry, and already I was being held up, scrutinised, judged and found wanting.

Throughout my entire life, up until this point, I had been supported, loved and encouraged by a family for whom I could do no wrong. I may never have been the most stunning natural beauty, but neither was I grotesquely deformed. And yet, standing there on that stage, after a relative stranger had dismissed me with a cursory remark about my face and my bum, I had never felt smaller or less adequate. Were it not for the state of shock I was in, and a deep-seated sense of pride, I would have dissolved into tears.

The remainder of the rehearsal period mercifully passed without further incident – or insult. The cast was small, the show was compact. But what it didn't have in scale, it more than made up for in professionalism and spectacle. The McKenney mother–son duo choreographed a show that to this day still rates as one of the best I have done.

We'd rehearse all morning, then break for lunch and sit together in the dining room, eating whatever the chef had prepared for us. There was a collegiate atmosphere; we were building a little backstage family. And the frontrunner for the position of all-singing, all-dancing, high-camp big brother was a young guy from Sydney; Brett Mills.

Brett and I clicked from the moment we met. He was quick-witted, with a wry sense of humour and an encyclopedic knowledge of TV-related pop culture. Raised in Sydney's western suburbs on a steady diet of *Laverne & Shirley*, *Prisoner* and *The Love Boat* (to name but a few of the TV shows from which Brett could quote entire slabs of dialogue), Brett had found his way to the Tivoli via a couple of dance contracts in Asia. At 22, he had moved to Brisbane with his fiancée for the Tivoli gig.

My other great friend in the cast was Tamra. We'd performed together at Kim's dance school and it gave me a bit of a buffer to have her there.

When the show opened, amid a modest amount of fanfare in the Brisbane media, the whole cast was brimming with excitement. The first few months had sellout performances every night. Couples on dates, large tables of businessmen on corporate nights out, groups of elderly folk and families all made their way to the Valley's factory quarter, filing through the door of the former warehouse to take in an evening of Paris cabaret–inspired entertainment.

I found it utterly glamorous. The costumes seemed the essence of elegance. The show itself was a musical theatre, Broadway-inspired affair. There was a New York tableau, a Hollywood tableau and a finale with showgirl feathers. Because we were such a small cast, the singers had to dance and the dancers had to sing. All my eisteddfod appearances meant I was well and truly ready to do both.

There were two big tap numbers in the show, which I loved. It was a really energetic piece with great choreography – or 'chorie', as it is known in the industry. There was hardly anything in the way of sets, there was no multi-level stage magic, and while the costumes impressed impressionable me, they were hardly the most elaborate to ever grace the boards. All of which meant that when the lights came up and the curtain was pulled back, it was just us and our dancing feet to distract and entertain the audience. For a young girl fresh out of dance school, it was the best training imaginable. The learning curve was steep and the work was hard – but I thrived.

More than anything else, this first job taught me what it meant to be a professional. We performed five shows a week for forty-eight weeks a year for two years. There was no chorus line to hide in, we had to go out there every night and give 100 per cent. The most important skill I developed at the Tivoli was that of endurance: the ability to dance as if every night was my first.

Also, because we were such a tiny cast, and there were no understudies, swings or replacements, there was never any question of calling in sick for any reason. In two years, no-one ever pulled a sickie. It just wasn't done. We would dance when we were sick, we would dance when we were injured. You could be on death's door, but the show had to go on. That gig instilled in me a work ethic that would serve me well for the rest of my professional life.

It also gave me my first taste of the sometimes startling but always entertaining nocturnal world in which showfolk live. After a performance, the cast would troop en masse down into the Valley proper. Renowned for being an open-all-hours, slightly seedy late-night precinct, the Valley never failed to disappoint. When we weren't living it large in Café Society, ordering potato wedges with sour cream and sweet chilli sauce (a dish considered positively gourmet in early nineties Brizzy), we were squeezing ourselves into tiny pubs to take in drag shows.

Tamra and I had just turned 18. From the comparatively straitlaced confines of Our Lady's College in Annerley to the anything-goes hedonism of Fortitude Valley's gay bars was quite a leap for our little heads to make. 'Eye-opening' is perhaps the best way to describe the experience.

There were occasional nights when I would skulk back home just before sunrise, usually to receive a verbal flogging from my dad. But I'd spent the better part of my teenage years stitched up tight inside a pair of ballet shoes – suddenly I had a taste of freedom, I was a woman of independent (albeit modest) means and I had an exciting new group of showbiz friends. All these factors were busy conspiring to make me lose my head just a little. Fortunately, my family were always there to ensure my feet stayed firmly on the ground. Living at home and sharing the same roof as a down-to-earth mum and dad and two salt-of-the-earth, no-nonsense brothers meant I could never get too carried away with it all.

Apparently I wasn't the only one undergoing a period of personal growth and discovery. One afternoon over coffee on our back deck my dance partner-in-crime, Brett, matter-of-factly informed my mum that he had called off his engagement.

'So it turns out I'm gay, Marie,' he said.

To her credit, Mum just kept on sipping her coffee, trying hard to hide the look of surprise on her face. As she would tell me later, it was not the announcement that he was gay that threw her, but the fact that he so coolly tossed it into a back-deck conversation over Tim Tams and a cup of International Roast. Brett's announcement didn't completely surprise me. Ever since he'd told me about his teenage afternoons in front of the TV, wearing a towel on his head to simulate long hair while learning the choreography from the opening sequence of *Xanadu*, I'd had an inkling.

Brett, Tamra and I weren't just refining our performance skills in the Tivoli show – we were discovering who we were. I honed my stage smile, perfected my stage presence and fell deeper under the spell of the showbiz life.

During the second year of the show, much to my mum's delight, I started my nursing degree at university. I had to attend classes by day and dance by night, and it was exhausting to maintain the double life. The late-night finishes at the Tivoli did little to sharpen my concentration at 9 a.m. lectures, but I was determined to prove to myself, and to my parents, that I was capable of excelling at both dancing and studying.

By the end of my Tivoli contract, the theatre owner had warmed to me, showing me a sort of affection – in her own unique way.

'Our Meryl!' she'd exclaim, each time she clapped eyes on me. She thought I had a nose like Meryl Streep, and thought it appropriate to draw everyone's attention to it at every given opportunity. At least she'd stopped telling me my bum was big.

The thick skin I had developed thanks to a life of relentless teasing from my brothers did deflect the barb somewhat, but it still used to get me down. It was true that I didn't have the most slender nose in the world. And while it would probably have gone unnoticed on someone in another occupation, I increasingly found myself heading down a path towards a career that placed a premium on conventional beauty.

I knew I was a good dancer. I also knew that there were much prettier girls out there who would always get cast before me as long as I had my current nose. And I wasn't prepared to let one thing get in the way of any success I might otherwise have. I loved to dance and had a chance to make a career out of it – and while in a perfect world, if I danced like an angel it shouldn't have mattered what my nose looked like, showbiz was far from perfect. I came to the decision that if I was serious about making a living out of dancing, I had to do something about the nose.

Mum and Dad knew what was going through my head. During a rare Sunday afternoon at the beach with them, Dad took advantage of a quiet moment alone with me on our beach towels to tell me that he and Mum would be supportive if I wanted cosmetic surgery. It fell on receptive, appreciative ears.

The operation was painful, and I spent the recovery period hiding indoors waiting to discover whether it had been a success. It seemed an agonisingly long time before the bandages were removed and the swelling had gone down, but when my new profile was finally revealed it was universally agreed to be something of a small triumph. Even my cosmetic surgeon seemed pleasantly surprised with the outcome. Most importantly, it was a nose I knew I could learn to love.

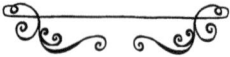

As the end of my Tivoli contract loomed, I dreaded the prospect of not being on stage every night. I was going to miss my backstage family, I was going to miss the Fortitude Valley drag queens, but most of all, I was going to miss dancing. There was no getting away from the fact that I felt more energised and alive when I was on stage dancing than anywhere else. No matter how repetitive it was to perform the same show every night, dancing made me happy in the most fundamental way. It definitely made me happier than the practical work my university studies had required. By night I danced cabaret in feathers and sequins; by day I studied and worked in a nursing home cleaning bedpans. Something had to give.

# Chapter Six

## Japan

With the Tivoli show coming to an end, and my only other prospect of gainful employment being as a giver of sponge baths to nursing-home residents, I began the search for another dance gig.

It turned out I didn't have to look too far. In fact, I only had to look a couple of seats down in the Tivoli dressing-room. One of my fellow dancers had a friend who'd just accepted a contract to choreograph a show for a club in Japan. She was looking for three dancers.

If I had been wavering in my decision to pursue dance full-time rather than finish my nursing degree, the lure of overseas travel proved to be the decider. That and the thought of a future filled with bedpans.

Without even having to audition, I was offered the job.

Japan, a country I knew little about, was very exotic to a nineteen-year-old girl from Tarragindi. The contract was for three months, dancing in a club in the seaside resort town of Kashima, east of Tokyo. It sounded so adventurous. Here was a chance to combine work with travel, to experience another country and another culture. Though I was a relative newcomer to the Australian entertainment industry, I already understood that work for dancers was scarce, competition was fierce and a stint overseas was an almost inevitable inclusion in any aspiring professional's CV.

For three weeks Jody, the choreographer, put me and the other two dancers through our paces rehearsing in a studio in Brisbane. The show required us to do three twenty-minute sets, with short intermissions in between. We three dancers would perform while the singer, Linda, sang a medley of songs. Jody had come up with a show that ran the gamut of musical kitsch – from the *Dreamgirls* musical to En Vogue's 'You're Never Gonna Get It' and the Blues Brothers' 'Shake Your Tailfeather'. One of my new dancing colleagues was Danielle, a feisty Brizzy girl with a wicked sense of humour. We got on like a house on fire.

Mum and Dad came to wave me off at the airport. I know they had reservations about me flying to Japan to dance in an unknown club, but I was nineteen years old and bent on adventure. They knew there was no stopping me. They had little choice but to watch me go and wish me well.

When we arrived in Tokyo, we were met at Narita airport by the manager of the club and escorted to a mini-van for the three-hour drive to Kashima. It was my first trip to Asia and I spent the whole drive with my face pressed up against the window, taking in the scenery as we sped through it, mesmerised by how different from Brisbane it all was. In truth, the road from Tokyo to Kashima passes through undulating miles of industrial estates and nondescript outlying Tokyo suburbs, but it was all new to me and wildly exciting.

Once we got to Kashima, Danielle and I were dropped off at the one-bedroom apartment we were going to be sharing. The building was a grey concrete box in a street lined with grey concrete boxes. We lugged our suitcases up a narrow flight of stairs, opened the door and stood for a moment in shock. To describe the place as a broom closet would be unfair to broom closets. It was so tiny there was barely room for our luggage, much less the two of us.

Our room, such as it was, had two futons rolled up in the corner; when they were unfurled they took up the entire floor space. Perhaps to avoid making it seem cluttered, there wasn't another scrap of furniture in the entire apartment. The kitchen was a cupboard off the hallway with a one-ring electric element, a bar fridge and a mini-sink – the only equipment was a single fork and a plate. And the place was filthy. Every surface seemed to be caked with grime and dust: it obviously hadn't been cleaned in years.

That we didn't turn around and catch a taxi straight back to the airport was testament to how young and inexperienced we were. Instead, we bought some heavy-duty cleaning products, donned rubber gloves and got down to some serious scrubbing – determined to make our cramped new quarters at least vaguely habitable.

Kashima, we were to discover, was a dump of a place. The local council did its best to present it as a seaside resort – a holiday-maker's paradise – but in truth it was little more than an industrial, satellite community of Tokyo. Kashima Beach was a narrow strip of grey sand wedged ingloriously between the pale green sea and an uneven wall of dull concrete buildings that hugged the coastline. The town existed only to service the two industries that dominated it – an enormous petrol refinery and a huge shipping port. Glamorous it definitely was not.

The club in which we were to work was called PC Marina, despite the fact it was a good fifteen-minute walk from the water. PC Marina (or 'Pus Club Marina' as we would come to affectionately call it) was the city's premier *kyabakura* – hostess club. Distant descendants of the geisha house, hostess clubs belong to a rich cultural tradition in which Japanese men pay to spend a couple of hours in a bar in the company of young women. They exist all over Japan, providing lucrative short-term work contracts to girls from Australia, Canada, the U.S. and the U.K. Hostesses are employed to pour drinks, light cigarettes and feign interest in the usually tedious conversation of the country's businessmen, or 'salarymen', as they're called.

The Pus Club was really little more than a glorified karaoke bar. It was a poky place, with a small dance floor and tiny stage. We'd been contracted to provide musical entertainment on stage while our hostessing colleagues kept the clients company at the tables and booths. We had three twenty-minute performances a night. With only four of us on stage and without fancy sets or lighting for backup, we worked bloody hard. In between shows, we had to slip into the management-supplied evening gowns (worn in rotation by the hostesses) and join the other girls on the floor, chatting to clients and singing karaoke with them.

The PC Marina workforce was made up almost exclusively of girls from Brisbane and the Gold Coast, and it was the second or third tour of duty for some of them. No-one especially loved the work, but each of us saw it as a good way to make some quick money in a town where the complete lack of anything to do or buy meant you saved every penny you earned. The girls who had been to Kashima before spoke passable Japanese and had developed a devoted clientele. And I mean 'devoted' in the most innocent of senses. There was nothing untoward about the club or its clients, never any suggestion that hostessing duties should extend beyond keeping the salarymen company in the bar. It was all purely platonic.

The club was run by a man called 'Master'. And while it's fair to assume that wasn't his real name, my almost total lack of Japanese and his corresponding lack of English meant I never found out for sure. He and his son Kenji managed the bar; Kenji's Filipina wife, Jane, and her mum, Maria, toiled in the kitchen. It was pretty much a family affair.

The clients were mostly regulars and salarymen. They each had their own bottle of Hennessy V.S.O.P. cognac behind the bar, labelled with their names. Depending on the frequency with which they came and their alcohol tolerance (in my short time there, I learnt this was notoriously low among Japanese men), it took each client anywhere between a week and a year to get through their bottle.

The regulars would file in every night, take up a position at their favourite table and settle in for the evening. I suppose they had families, but few seemed inclined to spend much time with them. They went from work to the club and only then, finally, home.

We were all under strict orders from Master to encourage the clients to order food: clearly that's where he made his money. Being dancers with fast metabolisms and relatively modest pay packets, we didn't have to be told twice. And as long as the clients had their whisky and a Caucasian girl in an evening gown at their table, they were happy for us to order whatever we wanted. So fifteen Aussie girls, all madly trying to save money, would order entire pizzas and plate-loads of gyoza and wolf down as much as we reasonably could without looking completely inelegant. Every now and then, however, one of the clients would assert themselves and take charge of the food ordering, which meant you'd have to politely nibble on a bit of seaweed.

Each night as the whisky and boredom set in, the hostesses would take to the karaoke machine to belt out Madonna, *Fame* and *Flashdance* numbers. Danielle and I did a nightly rendition of Patsy Cline's 'Crazy', which we thought was fabulous even if no-one else did. It was hard to tell if the clients agreed. Those who weren't too drunk to clap were quite often asleep facedown in pizzas they hadn't ordered. At the end of the night, the bar would be buzzing with roaring drunk Australian girls ready to party, while businessmen slumbered around us.

When the club shut, we'd all pile into the back of Kenji's mini-van and he'd attempt to drop us off at our respective apartments. But we'd have none of it. The night was young; we wanted to paint the town red. Unfortunately, the town was a stubborn dull grey, with nothing to speak of in the way of night-life. We'd end up trawling the fluorescent-lit aisles of the local 7-Eleven, buying our bodyweight in chips and chocolate and stocking up on phone cards. Then we'd stand in public phone booths on the street, calling home and wishing we were there, before walking the deserted streets of Kashima back to our tiny apartments, dressed to the nines in evening gowns and heels.

As the third month of our contract approached, we all started to go a little stir-crazy. Prolonged, relentless exposure to one another at work and at home was starting to take its toll.

The fact that we only had one night off every three weeks meant that when that night came around, we were primed and ready to take full advantage of it. We would travel as a group to Tokyo on the bullet train and spend the day shopping – mostly trying in vain to find shoes big enough to fit us. We'd then descend on the Hard Rock Cafe or some other similarly non-Japanese eatery and stuff our faces with as much non-Japanese food as possible – onion rings, burgers, milkshakes. At night, we'd head to the club district, Roppongi, and spend the evening hopping from one club to the next, shamelessly flirting with

American bond-traders, Canadian teachers, English bankers and U.S. marines. It was just so nice to see new faces and hold full conversations. At the end of the night, we'd all pile back to whatever cheap little hotel room we'd rented and sleep five to a bed until it was time to catch the bullet train back to the coast.

Our final month in Kashima seemed to drag, the days and nights passing with bone-crushing tedium. To deal with it, Danielle and I slept for as long as possible on the futons in our shared cell. We'd get up only when we had to, go to the mall to buy groceries, come home and get ready, and then go to work. The soundtrack to our Kashima home life came courtesy of Carole King and Lionel Richie – the only two CDs we had. To this day, I can't listen to 'Dancing on the Ceiling' without wanting to climb the walls.

When it finally came time to bid farewell to Kashima, few tears were shed. I flew home to Brisbane and almost kissed the ground when I stepped off the plane. I certainly had no regrets about my Japanese adventure, though. I had learned to speak a bit of the language, experienced a fascinating new culture, seen a bit of the world, had an enormous amount of girly fun and saved a fistful of yen into the bargain. But I was very glad to be home.

## Chapter Seven

### Brisbane

Within a week of being back in Brisbane, I was on the job hunt and devastated to learn I'd just missed a big audition for a new show at Jupiters – the casino on the Gold Coast. But the devastation didn't last long. I was in luck: a new show was about to open at the Tivoli. Even better, Todd McKenney was once again choreographing it. He offered me a spot in the cast and I signed on for the three-month run, grateful to have found a job with a minimum of hassle.

The Tivoli gig was fine. Good show, great choreography, fun cast. But I couldn't help but feel I was right back where I started. My eyes remained on the Jupiters prize – and the gods of dance appeared to be on my side. As well as devising the Tivoli show, the industrious Mr McKenney was choreographing the new show at Jupiters. It was called *Tropical Nights* and starred club-circuit regular and all-round lovely person, Chelsea Brown. I told Todd that I was ready to step up and audition should anyone drop out or if a position became available.

When an English dancer failed to get her work visa, I got the nod. I was flown to Sydney for a day of costume fittings: each member of the cast had their hats, costumes and shoes custom-made. It felt so professional and so very glamorous. Once that was done I packed my meagre belongings and headed to the Gold Coast for rehearsals.

The show opened in the casino auditorium, which packed in the pensioners, honeymooners, visiting Japanese tourists and families on Gold Coast package holidays. My finest moment in the production was when I came on stage as a large bunch of bananas. Five other girls and I were dressed as various pieces of fruit. We would make our entrance, perform whatever dance steps our enormously bulky costumes allowed and merge upstage to form a huge Carmen Miranda fruit hat. A bunch of grapes, a pineapple, a slice of watermelon, an orange, a mango and me. At the end of the number, the grapes and I would take a place on either side of the huge hat, go down into the splits and form the earrings.

During rehearsals, I distinctly remember Todd complimenting me in front of the entire company for my convincing banana portrayal. 'It's really beautiful what you're doing with your bananas,' he told me. 'You're really making them work.'

I stood there beaming. Todd McKenney thought I gave good banana. I was so proud.

The pineapple, Jenny from Newcastle, had a tougher job to make her piece of fruit work. It was bigger and more unwieldy than my bunch of bananas and lent itself less to showy displays of the dancing form. But what Jenny didn't have in fancy fruitwork, she more than made up for in backstage personality and presence. She had legs up to her eyeballs, a smile that seemed to take over her face and an easy, ready laugh. She danced like a demon and partied with at least as much gusto. We became friends instantly.

Jenny was a hyperactive presence in the dressing-room, an all-talking, all-laughing ball of perpetual motion. The head dresser, Anne, used to constantly scold her for raiding the biscuit tin and eating all the Monte Carlos. The semi-permanent sugar high meant there was never a dull moment backstage when Jenny was around.

Providing the yin to Jenny's yang was Amani – a dark, half-Persian beauty, also from Newcastle. Amani was softly spoken, gentle and unfailingly sweet. We formed an unlikely but inseparable threesome.

But it was another dancer in the show, Corina, who captivated me the most. At twenty-seven, she was the oldest dancer in the cast. At the tender age of twenty, I was the youngest, and thought Corina was so mature and so worldly. She took me under her wing.

Corina had recently returned from Paris, where she had been a principal dancer at the Lido. In the dressing-room she was indistinguishable from the rest of us; a down-to-earth Australian girl with a no-nonsense approach to her work. But the moment she stepped on stage and into the spotlight, she transformed into a creature of grace and beauty. She carried herself with an elegance I had never seen before. She moved with a confidence that bordered on haughty. Her every move was utterly feminine and effortlessly seductive. I was spellbound.

Corina taught me how to properly apply stage make-up, using the techniques she had learned in the dressing-room of one of the world's most famous cabarets. She would talk about Paris, about her years living in the City of Light, and I used to sit and listen in a state of rapture. She told of walking by the Seine, strolling along the Champs Élysées, shopping in bustling street markets and devouring *croissants* and *baguettes* by the armload. The shows she danced in at the Lido seemed to belong to another universe. Massive in scale compared to anything in Australia, with costumes and sets that were out of this world, they came to inhabit a kind of dream realm for me. A dream that lodged somewhere in the back of my mind and started to take root.

Midway through the *Tropical Nights* contract, a group of male tap dancers started making a name for themselves in showbiz. They hailed from Newcastle (Jenny and Amani's home town) and were partial to tapping out a tune in a pair of Blundstones and a flannelette shirt.

When the Tap Dogs came to Brisbane, they performed at the Tivoli. Jenny and Amani knew a couple of the steelcapped toe-tappers and dragged a bunch of us up from the Gold Coast to watch the show. As an avowed tapper from way back, I loved it. But even if I'd had two left feet, as a single girl with a pulse I couldn't help but be moved by the sheer physicality of the dance. Not to mention the dancers.

Gavin was a charming, polite, easy-on-the-eye tap dancer. He was tall with beautiful green eyes; a mop of dark brown hair crowned a cheeky smile. During drinks after the show, he also proved to be highly entertaining company. I was instantly attracted.

When the Tap Dogs returned the favour and drove down to Jupiters to watch a performance of *Tropical Nights* some weeks later,

I was one very excited bunch of bananas. During another bout of post-performance drinks, Gavin and I spent the entire night talking. Not long after that, we began seeing each other.

Gavin had deferred a law degree to tap his way around Australia. He figured the Tap Dog phenomenon probably only had one national tour in it before public interest waned and it was forced to retreat into the kennel from whence it came. (That Dein Perry's group still performs to packed houses all over the world is testament to the enduring, unexpected appeal of grown men dancing on metal girders.)

While Gavin toured around the country we maintained a steady stream of correspondence. It was back in the days before email, when people wrote letters, licked stamps and waited patiently each day for the postman. The waiting and longing made it all very romantic. We didn't spend that much time together, but when we were in the same town we made the most of it.

It was a lovely few months. By the time the curtain finally fell on *Tropical Nights*, Gavin had already packed up his tap shoes to head back to Newcastle and to university – and so we continued our long-distance relationship.

On the work front, I barely had time to hang up my bananas before auditions began for the replacement show, *Mystique*. I was offered a place in the cast, but the travel bug had begun to bite again. A dance gig in Malaysia was in the offing, via the Sydney dance institution that was Di Heaton. Di produced shows for a variety of South East Asian resort complexes – including the Genting Highlands resort, an hour's drive east of Kuala Lumpur. Jenny had worked previously for Di, and heard that she was looking for girls. So Jenny, Danielle and I decided a five-month stint in Malaysia was as good a way as any to pass the time, and promptly signed on. The distance between Gavin and I was about to get bigger.

# Chapter Eight

## Malaysia

The Highlands are renowned for their lush tropical jungle and stunning scenery. The surrounds were undeniably magnificent: the Genting Highland resort itself was anything but. An awful concrete monstrosity plonked unceremoniously on the top of a beautiful mountain, it was an ugly scar in the jungle canopy. The resort was popular among Kuala Lumpur locals largely because of its sprawling casino. A fun park had been added to the rambling complex to distract children temporarily orphaned by roulette wheels and blackjack tables. On public holidays, the queue of cars snaking its way from the resort back down the hill towards Kuala Lumpur stretched as far as the eye could see.

Danielle, Jenny and I were to stay in the staff accommodation which, in a disturbing case of deja vu, comprised a filthy room furnished with stained single mattresses and a grotty kitchen decked out with a single paper plate and one slighty melted plastic cup. Steeled by our experience in Kashima, Dan and I shrugged our shoulders and started cleaning. Jenny was less sanguine about it all. 'This is bullshit,' she muttered over and over in typically colourful form as she cleaned.

Half the time, the show took place in the resort's main auditorium, which doubled as a Chinese restaurant. Most performances unfurled in the fog of burnt-chicken smoke emanating from the kitchen, while people queued for dim sum, scoffed down plates of noodles and chatted loudly among themselves. Every second day, we'd be trucked out to the main outdoor stage in the middle of the fun park. Because of the altitude, we often performed in a heavy shroud of low-lying cloud. Visibility was barely over two metres, meaning we had no idea if there was anyone watching. The audience (if indeed it existed) could only have been standing there staring into a white-out and listening to the music, forced to imagine the spectacle.

On our days off, relieved not to be competing for attention with lemon chicken or dancing to clouds, we would make a beeline for Kuala Lumpur and seek out fellow expats. Or we would lock ourselves in our apartment, draw the curtains and settle in for an afternoon of trash TV, courtesy of the *Melrose Place* videos Mum routinely recorded and dispatched in bi-weekly care packages. I thought Kashima had been tedious, but this was far, far worse. Still, at least I had two good friends to endure it all with.

When the producers of *Mystique* happened through the highlands on a business-drumming mission, I threw myself upon them. When they told me one of the cast members back on the Gold Coast had fallen pregnant and another was preparing to leave, I all but begged them to take me home with them. Which is how, several weeks later when the Genting contract ended, I found myself back on stage at Jupiters, performing in a show that was four parts cabaret, six parts magic show. Swedish magician Joe Labero had been imported to do his smoke and mirrors thing while dancers provided the musical interludes.

Living in Surfers Paradise and taking part in a show about levitation felt like a return to normality – testament to how desperate things had become in our little Malyasian hillside fantasyland.

It didn't take me long to settle back in to life at home. I moved into a shared house in Broadbeach and began teaching dance to kids during the day for a little extra pocket money. I was happy to be home and close to my family, whom I'd missed terribly. I was also pleased to be back on the same continent as Gavin. We took turns travelling up and down the east coast of Australia, from Newcastle to the Gold Coast and vice versa, but I think we both knew the relationship wasn't destined to work. The distance eventually took its toll and we went our separate ways. I was sad to say goodbye to my first real romance, but I was so crazy busy, I didn't have time to mope about it for long.

Jenny had started a side business choreographing shows for Gold Coast nightclubs. By day I would put aspiring young dancers through their paces; by night I would perform in *Mystique*, then head straight to one of the Gold Coast's myriad nightclubs to hit the stage and entertain the masses. Blessed with the bottomless reserves of energy unique to a 21-year-old, I lived for six months like this. 'You want to be careful not to burn the candle at both ends,' my mother would regularly advise. But I was having too much fun to take any notice.

Towards the end of the *Mystique* contract, I did a job with Jenny at a Surfers Paradise nightclub and was introduced to the club's promoter, Steve. He was a high-school teacher in training and more than a little bit charming. There was something dark and seemingly dangerous about him and, like many girls my age, I couldn't help but be attracted by the borderline bad boy. He came across as the quintessential romantic slacker, one who just happened to have a penchant for Gold Coast nightlife and smoking a whole lot of pot. I no doubt felt he needed rescuing and that I would be the one to redeem him. And so my mothering instinct flared and I was hooked. Of course, it didn't hurt at all that he was cute, in a lost puppy kind of a way. After a couple of weeks, we were together.

Three months passed: months in which my routine of teaching during the day, dancing at Jupiters in the evening, then performing at nightclubs until the small hours of the morning and partying until sunrise started to become drearily monotonous. I began to feel as if the Gold Coast was closing in on me. The neon lights, the high-rise apartments, the out-and-out gaudiness of it all – which I had previously loved – were starting to grate. Mum had been right. I was tired and growing tired of it all.

I kept thinking about Paris. My only knowledge of the city was what I had gleaned from travel programs on TV, stories from friends who had been backpacking around Europe and Corina's starry-eyed recollections of her time at the Lido. It wasn't much, but certainly enough for me to start weaving elaborate daydreams of sipping wine in smoky bars in between star turns as a showgirl on the Champs Élysées. I hadn't let go of the idea that I might one day live and work there. So when Brett phoned from Sydney and told me he'd landed a job at the Moulin Rouge, I took it as a sign.

'You're kidding me! The Moulin Rouge!' I screamed down the phone. 'But when did you apply? How did it happen?' Barely able to contain his own excitement, much less deal with mine, Brett explained that he'd sent off his showreel and photo portfolio to the ballet mistress at the revered Paris cabaret, never expecting to receive a reply. When he received a letter some weeks later summoning him to Paris to take a place in the boys' line, he couldn't buy a plane ticket fast enough.

'Margaret, you have to come over, you have to come and audition. If I can get a job there, so can you.' Since our early days dancing at the Tivoli, we had assumed the M*A*S*H-inspired monikers of 'Frank' and 'Margaret'. I was Margaret 'Hot Lips' Houlihan to his Frank Burns.

I didn't share Brett's optimism. Despite years of training and a steady accumulation of onstage experience, I was convinced that making the grade in Paris, at the world's most famous cabaret venue, was going to require a lot more natural poise, grace and dance talent than I had in me.

Still, with Brett about to start performing at the Moulin Rouge, the dream of dancing in Paris seemed to hover tantalisingly within reach. So I resolved that, come what may, I would get myself to Paris and audition. And though I knew it was unlikely a skinny kid from suburban Brisbane would cut it against the world's finest, I didn't want to go through life knowing that I'd never given it a shot.

Despite the daydreaming and the fact Brett was off to Paris, I still had to deal with the here and now and think about work and paying the bills. As my second Jupiters contract drew to a close, I was contacted by a Sydney-based dance company asking if I knew any dancers interested in going to Japan for a six-month gig. The company was producing a show for a large seaside hotel south of Tokyo. Having established that the town was nothing like Kashima and that the venue was a bona fide holiday resort and not another glorified hostess bar, I put my hand up, with the proviso that I would only do it for three months, and that instead of a return ticket, I wanted a one-way ticket to Europe.

I figured three months of yakisoba and performing to slumbering holiday-makers was a small price to pay for the chance to make enough money to hotfoot it to Paris. I didn't want the trip to only be about the Moulin Rouge, though, and so made plans with Steve to backpack around Europe. But if I was honest with myself, the real motivation for the flight to France had more to do with feathers than footslogging.

In the months leading up to my departure, I submitted myself to the daily rigours of ballet class, determined to improve my technique. It had been a long time between *pliés*, and I was convinced a successful audition at the Moulin Rouge would depend on strong ballet technique. I also visited a professional photographer and updated my portfolio with a series of showgirl-inspired photos, posing in costumes borrowed from a friend who had a small production company. Corina helped me refine my make-up technique and showed me how to strike a Paris showgirl stance. I remember standing in full showgirl regalia in a makeshift photo studio in an industrial estate on the outskirts of Nerang while a photographer called Trevor snapped away, wondering who the hell I was kidding. Paris was thousands of miles and another world away.

With ballet classes under my belt and my photo portfolio updated, I only had my parents left to deal with. Even if they weren't always convinced I was doing the right thing with my life, they had remained stoically, steadfastly supportive. Now, as I planned to head off to Europe with only a backpack, a skinny sheaf of traveller's cheques, a not-so-motivated boyfriend and the vaguest glimmer of a chance that I would maybe, *possibly*, get an audition at the Moulin Rouge, they faced their greatest test as parents.

They flew with me down to Sydney, where final rehearsals for the Japan show were to take place. It was supposed to be a happy farewell – and in many ways it was – but hanging like a cloud over proceedings was the spectre of me heading out into the big bad world with no real idea of where I was going, what I would be doing or when I would be coming home.

'So you have an audition at the Moulin Rouge then?' Mum asked hopefully on the eve of my departure.

'Not exactly,' I replied sheepishly.

Silence.

'But Brett can help you get one?'

'Well, hopefully. I mean, he can't guarantee anything, but the fact he's there makes it more likely.'

Mum didn't look convinced. 'And Steve? He's going to join you in Japan and travel with you to Europe?'

'That's the plan.'

I thought it best not to burden her with the news that Steve wasn't sure he'd have the money. She already had a low opinion of him: there was no point compounding her disapproval and giving her even more cause to worry.

'Well, you know your father and I are always here for you if you need anything. You just have to pick up the phone and we'll get you on the next plane home.'

It was Dad's cue to pipe up.

'Shelly love, take this.' He handed me an American Express card. 'Keep it with you at all times. If you need it for any kind of emergency, don't hesitate to use it. You can buy a plane ticket home from anywhere in the world if you need it. And don't forget how much we love you.'

Mum brushed away a tear. 'We're very proud of you, love. Now just go out there and be yourself.'

# Chapter Nine

## Japan

The Japanese seaside town of Atami lies some two hundred kilometres to the south of Tokyo. It's renowned for its *onsen*, the hot spring baths to which Japanese tourists flock in their thousands every year. It's considerably less renowned for its Elvis impersonators, which is why an Australian one had been shipped in for the staging of an Elvis revival show in the beachside hotel resort in which I was to perform.

Accompanying Elvis on stage every night were myself and fifteen fellow Australian female dancers. Variously dressed through the hour-and-a-half performance in spangled flares, orange-feathered backpacks and oversized Dolly Parton wigs, it was our job to provide the onstage colour and movement while Elvis belted out tunes and gyrated his pelvis.

Because it was a spa resort built around the hot springs, people would check into the hotel, don a *yukata* (dressing-gown) and slippers, and shuffle about in this dressed-down state for the remainder of their stay. The only time they stepped out of their dressing-gowns was to slide into the hot baths. They ate in their *yukata*, drank in their *yukata* and quite possibly slept in their *yukata*. The never-ending streams of businessmen who descended on the hotel for company-ordained weekends of team-building exercises even attended seminars and played 'trust games' in their *yukata*.

From backstage, we could always tell when a performance was about to begin. You could hear the shuffle of a thousand pairs of slippers as the audience filed in and took their seats for a quick meal and an obligatory glass of Hennessy V.S.O.P. Following a day spent being parboiled in hot springs and feigning enthusiasm in workshops designed to make the supply chain more efficient, it was all most of them could do to keep their eyes open beyond the opening number.

It was pretty disheartening for us. Somewhere between 'Suspicious Minds' and 'Hound Dog', we'd generally lose even the most attentive audience member to the land of Nod. I would have cared more if I hadn't already made the mental shift to Paris. Despite telling myself it was foolish to get my hopes up, I couldn't help but hold out for the Paris option. Wedged uncomfortably each night between a pretend Elvis and a room full of slumbering tourists, the only thing that kept me going was the knowledge that my CV and photos might just be sitting on the desk of the Moulin Rouge *maitresse de ballet*. Any day now she might pick up the phone and invite me to Paris for an audition. I had sent my portfolio to Brett, figuring it was less likely to be ignored if it was handed over by a dancer already in the show. Now all I could do was wait.

Steve was also waiting. He was back on the Gold Coast ready to book his flight and pack his bags for our European odyssey. He'd ended up with an unexpected financial windfall from the Australian Taxation Office, and so was uncharacteristically flush with cash and ready to head to the airport. We'd made a plan for him to come to Paris a couple of weeks after I arrived. That would give me plenty of time to hang out with Brett and make a concerted attempt to convince the Moulin Rouge to hire me.

The only thing that made those three months in Atami bearable were the girls I danced with and the friendships we forged. We were a motley crew of Amazons from Down Under who towered above the local populace, and by virtue of our height and generally brash demeanour, we quickly became known around town. At first, being called 'Tokyo Tower' by a cheeky local had been amusing, but after a few weeks, the skyscraper jokes had started to get old. When my three-month contract was up, I was definitely ready to move on.

I packed my suitcase, farewelled the girls and spent my final hours in Japan strolling the concrete boardwalk above the beach, taking stock. For the first time in my adult life, I was leaping blindly into the unknown. I was travelling halfway across the world with no job to go to and no real idea about what I would do once I got there. Steve and I had talked about travelling wherever the whim took us. We wanted to head south, to Spain, and then on to Italy. It was scary but also exhilarating.

On Atami beach, I resolved to embrace my newfound aimlessness and to simply take each day as it came. I had to suppress my hardwired instinct to lock in each new job long before the previous one had ended. If nothing else, I would finally be going to Paris to live out a few French fantasies, spend a bit of time with Brett and then go backpacking with Steve. Anything that happened above and beyond that would be a bonus. I was going to be swapping sleepy Atami for a city that was vital and dynamic. A place where things happened. Magical, romantic, exciting things.

As I ducked back to my hotel room to collect my suitcase and call a cab, the phone rang. It was Brett.

'Margaret. Thank God I caught you.' In the background I could hear music and an announcement in French over a loudspeaker. 'I've been ringing for the past hour. Listen, I'm just about to go on stage so I have to be quick. I gave your photos and CV to Janet. She said she wants to see you when you get to Paris. She wants you to come and audition when you arrive. This is it, Margaret! We're going to be showgirls together!'

# ACT II

## Chapter Ten

### Paris

As the plane slipped silently across the top of the planet and its passengers slept around me, I cursed the unsuitability of showgirl legs for long-haul air travel. Pulling them awkwardly towards me, I resigned myself to an uncomfortable flight. All I could think about was the Moulin Rouge audition, anyway, despite my best attempts to force it from my mind. I'd done plenty of auditions before: there was no reason why this one should be any more difficult, and yet the stakes were so much higher. To have the chance to dance in Paris – it hardly seemed real. Even though Brett had walked me through the show on the phone the previous night, and despite his assurances that I could dance circles around many of the Moulin company, I had butterflies in my stomach.

I fumbled for the TV control and started channel-surfing. Suddenly, the screen was filled with feathers. A vast spray of white feathers enveloping a small, heavily made-up face and a pair of long, slender legs. I scrambled for my earphones.

'The Lido has been the personification of Paris cabaret glamour since it opened in 1946,' intoned a silky male voice. I watched transfixed as the camera pulled back to reveal a stage filled with dancers wearing enormous pink and orange feather backpacks. Then a succession of leggy women, each as elegant as the next, glided gracefully about the stage, trailing a large train of pink feathers. They wore jewel-encrusted G-strings, necklaces of white stones and not much else. Each dancer had an enormous stage smile plastered to her face.

'Located on Paris's most famous avenue, the Champs Élysées, the Lido has played host to the famous Bluebell dancers for almost sixty years.' For forty minutes I stared at the tiny screen and soaked it all up. The grandeur of the spectacle was astonishing. The sets were enormous, the costumes like nothing I had ever seen. And the dancers seemed like the most beautiful creatures God had ever put on a stage.

I thought back to my days at Jupiters Casino, how Corina would sit at the mirror next to me, applying her make-up and regaling me with tales of her time as a Bluebell and how her sister was now dancing at the Moulin Rouge.

When the program ended, I flicked through the channels to find the in-flight map. We seemed to be hovering somewhere over northeastern Russia, with ten more hours before we were due to touch down in Paris. I could feel the muscle relaxant I had taken start to work its magic. I stuffed a pillow between my seat and the ice-cold window frame and leant back to fall asleep. Outside, a little red light blinked on the tip of the plane wing – a tiny red blip against a night sky blanketed with stars. I watched the light flash until I felt myself drifting off to sleep, visions of Paris cabaret swimming in my head.

'*Mademoiselle, mademoiselle*,' the voice seemed miles away, barely able to penetrate a heavy fog of sleepiness. I felt a hand grab and gently rock my shoulder. '*Mademoiselle*, you must sit up and fasten your seatbelt.'

It was a flight attendant. I opened my eyes to a pretty set of rouged lips and dark brown eyes, and sat up with a start. I had been asleep for almost ten hours. My stomach grumbled – I had obviously missed a meal or two. Down on the ground, the fields of France were unfurling as we hurtled towards Paris.

I stretched my legs out and thought about Brett, and how good it would be to see him. I thought about all the fun he must be having as a single gay man in Paris. I wondered if he had found what my mother would refer to as a 'special friend'.

With a high-pitched whine, the plane came thudding to the ground and glided to a halt.

'*Mesdames et messieurs*,' came the voice of the captain over the PA, '*Bienvenue* à *Paris Charles de Gaulle*. The local time in Paris is 6.15 p.m.

It's seven degrees Celsius and, as you can see, we have a bit of rain. Thank you for flying with us and we hope you enjoy your stay.'

Disembarking, I was hit by a cold blast of air. I pulled my coat around me, wrapped my scarf around my neck, and followed the shuffle of my fellow passengers into the airport terminal. For a moment, I wondered if I had arrived at the right destination. Was this Paris? Could the international capital of style and fashion really have an airport terminal this ugly? It was a drab, grey, concrete shell.

As I stepped off the moving walkway I hit a wall of people. The multitudes who had poured off their respective planes were now being funneled towards just two immigration officers, glass-encased in individual booths and summoning passengers one by one with a look of supreme boredom. Two other immigration officers stood casually to the side, smoking cigarettes and sipping on small plastic cups of coffee, apparently unconcerned by the sea of human restlessness building up before them.

When I finally made it to the top of the queue, I strode forward and presented my passport with a huge smile.

'*Bonsoir!*' I offered, excited to be uttering my first words in French. The officer glanced up at me, glanced down at my passport, scowled at it, stamped it and handed it back without a word or even making eye contact.

'Welcome to France,' I mumbled as I headed towards the baggage claim.

Pushing a trolley laden with my luggage, I negotiated my way through the crowds and followed the signs for the Air France bus. Brett had told me the bus was the easiest way to get from the airport into town – and given that I had used up my entire French vocab with the immigration official, I figured it was best to follow his advice.

I looked nervously around me. In my money pouch was the entire three months' worth of salary I had earned in Japan. It weighed heavily on me as I pushed past a group of men offering taxi rides into the city. Mum had spent a good part of our last phone call warning me to watch out for pickpockets at Paris airport.

'You speak English? Good price, *mademoiselle*. Straight to your hotel.'

On guard, I moved away quickly to join the huddle of people at the Air France bus terminal waiting for the coach to arrive.

When we finally boarded the bus and pulled away, we coasted along a freeway past fields of mud, squat airport motels and vast, hulking warehouses. After a while the relatively featureless landscape in the immediate vicinity of the airport started to yield to tall, grey apartment blocks seemingly built on top of one other, crowding in around the road. Rain-slicked and slowly being swallowed by the night, the scene was grim. It didn't at all resemble the Paris of my imaginings.

The bus hit traffic and crawled its way towards the city limits. As we rounded a bend, I sat upright in my seat. On a hill in the distance, the floodlit domes of Sacré Coeur shone like a beacon. I felt a thrill pass through me. At last – the Paris of picture postcards. As we inched closer to the city centre, the foreboding tower blocks began to thin out, giving way to smaller buildings – cafes and brasseries with flashing red neon *tabac* signs, people standing at bars, sipping small glasses of red wine. The buildings gradually became more elegant. Soon the bus was flanked by grand, fawn-coloured stone buildings with ornate wrought-iron balconies. Through tall French windows I glimpsed spacious *salons* with elaborate ceilings and beautiful crystal chandeliers.

I imagined the wonderfully French lives being played out in each of the buildings we passed. An elderly couple might be preparing their *foie gras* and *baguette* for dinner. A family sitting down for a meal of snails and frogs' legs. A young couple making passionate love, their half-smoked cigarettes smouldering in the ashtray beside the bed.

A frisson of excitement passed through the bus, jolting me from my reverie. Everyone seemed to be sitting upright in their seats, straining to see something up ahead. I peered over the top of the seat in front of me, and through the rain-dappled windscreen saw the Arc de Triomphe. She stood tall and dignified at the end of the boulevard, a bank of floodlights dutifully casting her in a flattering, golden light.

I was unmistakably, completely and utterly in Paris. And I couldn't have been more excited.

The bus pulled up on one of the cobbled streets that ran like a spoke from the wheel that was the infamous Étoile roundabout – a mess of cars, motorbikes and vans spinning wildly around the base of the Arc de Triomphe. The rain had stopped and I wheeled my suitcase across the road and stood for a moment under a street lamp, staring up at the famous monument. I had seen it countless times in books and on TV, but nothing had prepared me for its grandeur. Perfectly positioned, perfectly in proportion with its surroundings, and perfectly showcased by the amphitheatre of uniformly beautiful buildings that encircled it.

To my left, the Champs Élysées spilled down a gentle slope. The trees lining the avenue had all shed their leaves, and through the naked branches, I could just make out the obelisk in the Place de la Concorde. I knew the Lido was on the Champs Élysées, and briefly entertained the idea of dragging my suitcase down the avenue to go and stand before it. But the bag was heavy, and besides, I was unwashed and smelly after twelve hours on a plane. I felt far too shabby to set foot on the world's most famous boulevard. No, it would have to wait until I had a chance to glam myself up a bit.

My fellow passengers were collecting their luggage and dispersing into the night. Some disappeared underground into the Métro, while others started forming a line at a nearby taxi rank. With neither the French nor the fortitude required to take on the Métro, I joined the taxi queue and plonked myself down on my suitcase.

I used the wait to dig out the scrap of paper on which I had scribbled Brett's address. In the weak light cast by the street lamp, I could barely make out the words. God only knew how I was going to pronounce them. The queue dwindled rapidly, and soon a taxi pulled up for me. The driver jumped out and together we hauled my case into the boot of his car.

'*Vous allez où, mademoiselle?*' the driver asked as he opened the door and got back behind the wheel.

'Rue Dautancourt', I offered meekly.

'*Quoi?*' he replied aggressively. I didn't dare try again and simply handed him the scrap of paper.

He held it up to the car's interior light. '*Ah, Rue Dautancourt,*' he declared. My pronunciation had not even been close to the mark. '*C'est à La Fourche.*'

'If you say so,' I replied.

We set off into the evening traffic. As I fumbled in the dark for the seatbelt, the driver looked into his rear-vision mirror and started laughing, apparently at my attempts to buckle up.

'*Ah, les Anglais!*' he said. 'Always with the seatbelt. Is not necessary. Just sit back, relax.'

As the taxi drove, I pressed my face to the window, soaking up Paris by night as it flashed by. Neon signs reflected off the still-wet footpaths; cafes filled with people sitting down to dinner; couples in long coats walking arm in arm under umbrellas. We coasted by ornamental entrances to the Métro. We idled at traffic lights in front of *boulangeries* and I watched as well-dressed women whisked inside and emerged moments later with golden *baguettes* under their arms. We passed a sign announcing the Place des Ternes, where a florist wrapped a large bunch of flowers and handed it to a man in a suit. In a brasserie across the street, a waiter in a black coat and tie showed an elegantly dressed elderly couple to a table.

I felt like I was in a film.

We hummed along a cobbled street lined on one side by a tall black iron fence. Where previously there had been a row of stunning buildings, now there was just darkness. I could make out trees and bushes in silhouette against the night's sky.

'*C'est le Parc Monceau,*' the driver informed me, glancing into the rear-vision mirror. '*Très, très beau.*'

I had no idea what he was saying, so uttered a noncommittal 'Ah' and resumed my staring.

The meter clicked over to 120 francs as we came to a roundabout. A statue of a woman in flowing robes with a defiant stance stood high above the traffic, looking down impassively as it surged at her feet. Crossing a busy street, we turned into Avenue de Clichy and arrived in the *quartier* called La Fourche. Where previously there had been quaint cafes and *pâtisseries*, now there were kebab shops and discount shoe stores. Gaudily painted shopfronts advertising cheap phone calls to third-world countries competed for space with run-down bars lit by fluorescent lighting. Groups of black men loitered on street corners. It all suddenly looked much less romantic, much less Parisian.

Rue Dautancourt was a run-down affair, too. The taxi driver pulled up in front of a dimly lit building and jumped out to unload my suitcase. I paid him, thanked him in broken French and hurried to the front door. I had no reason to think the neighbourhood wasn't safe, and yet it distinctly felt like the kind of street you wouldn't want to linger on after dark. Punching in the security code Brett had given me, I pushed against the heavy door and fumbled my way inside, dragging my suitcase behind me.

Brett's apartment was on the second floor, so I was relieved to see a lift at the end of the corridor. But when I flung open the door, I stopped dead in my tracks. The inside of the lift was tiny, barely big enough for two adults to stand side-by-side – a vertically travelling wardrobe. I jiggled the suitcase down onto the lift floor and straddled it awkwardly, reaching around behind me to press the button for the second floor. The doors closed and the lift started climbing, creaking ominously all the way.

Brett shared his apartment with another Australian dancer, Megan. She hailed from Queensland and had been dancing at the Moulin for over a year. Both she and Brett would be at work, but Megan's family – mum, dad and little brother – were visiting Paris and staying in the apartment. Brett had assured me they would be home when I arrived. And sure enough, from behind the door I could hear the unmistakeable twang of the Australian accent.

Megan's kid brother answered the door, his mop of blond surfie hair looking out of place in this wintry, determinedly Parisian setting.

'G'day,' he said. 'You must be Shay. I'm Ryan. Come in.'

I rolled my suitcase across the threshold and down the short hallway, the wheels clacking on the parquet floor. Megan's family were splayed around the living room, a space that was clearly struggling to contain their broad Aussie proportions.

'Don't get up,' I said. 'There's barely enough room for me out here. I'm Shay. Lovely to meet you all.' We exchanged a few pleasantries, during which I learned they were a family of horse breeders on their first trip to Paris. In France for three weeks in total, they were all sleeping in Megan's room.

'I suppose I'd better get freshened up,' I said.

Megan's mother pointed at a door across the hall.

'That's Brett's room there. I put a fresh towel on the bed. Go and get yourself settled, love.'

I opened the door and switched on the light. Brett's room was tiny: a double bed took up most of the space. I shimmied around the bed to the window and pulled back the curtain, hoping for a Parisian vista. It had a view straight into the neighbour's toilet window.

I plonked down on the bed and lay back to stare up at the ceiling, my arms stretched above my head. From the TV in the living room, the muffled sound of French voices came floating across the hallway. The initial rush of excitement at arriving in Paris was starting to ebb, and in its place, a tide of loneliness started to swell. I knew it was mostly the result of exhaustion and hunger, and that once Brett came home and the sun rose the next morning the excitement would well up again – but at that moment I felt very alone and very far from home.

I jumped in the shower, threw on my pyjamas and hopped into Brett's bed. It would be a good three hours before he returned from work: there was no way I could sit up and wait for him. I curled up and within minutes was fast asleep.

'Shay, are you awake?' The whispered voice seemed far away, yet sounded familiar. I creaked open an eye and waited for the face to come into focus.

'Margaret, it's me, Frank. Are you awake?'

Though he was backlit by the lamp in the corner of the room, I could still make out Brett's familiar features. That broad smile, that handsome face. 'Frank!' I croaked groggily. 'Is it you? Is it really you?'

He let out a quiet scream. 'You're in Paris! You're in Paris! Ahhhhhh!'

I flung back the bed covers and jumped up into his bear hug. 'God, it's good to see you!' I said. 'You look great! So thin! All that cancanning is doing wonders for you.'

'Don't talk to me about the cancan. I swear it will be the death of me,' Brett shot back melodramatically. 'God, I can't believe you're actually here! We have so much to catch up on. How was your flight? Did you have trouble getting here? You look great. And oh my God, I've met someone!'

Words seemed to spill out of him. We talked for a good half an hour almost without a breath, each of us speaking over the other, dizzy with excitement. He told me how much he was loving Paris and that he'd recently started seeing a fellow dancer, Matthew.

'He's really nice. English, fun, gorgeous. You're going to love him.'

I gave him the lowdown on Japan, Steve and our European travel plans. Once we'd calmed down a little, I confessed I was nervous about the next day's audition.

'You'll be fine, honestly,' Brett assured me. 'Wait until you see some of the tragedies still high-kicking in there every night. It's embarrassing.'

We sat up and talked for hours. At one point, Brett went to the kitchen, returning with a block of chocolate and a bottle of red wine. 'It's medicinal, darling, it will help you sleep.'

We gossiped about mutual friends, exchanged news about our families and stifled screams and guffaws out of deference to Megan's family sleeping in the room next door.

'Does she have an enormous room?' I whispered. 'I mean, how do they all fit in there?'

'Oh don't. You should see it in there, it's like a refugee camp. Bodies everywhere. Her room is the same size as mine. It's madness.'

I grilled him for information about the Moulin Rouge – the show; the acts and solos; the ballet mistress, Janet; and, of course, the company. He gave me a rundown, sparing no details of in-house gossip, and I listened intently. I was determined to soak up as much of it as I could, convinced that if I immersed myself in Moulin lore I would be better prepared to tackle the audition. At 4 a.m., we decided it was time for sleep and turned out the light.

I woke five hours later, feeling remarkably refreshed. Megan's family were already awake, and her dad had been to the *boulangerie* and returned with a pile of fresh *croissants*. I gorged myself, smearing the pastries with a generous dollop of raspberry jam. They were my first genuine French *croissants*, and they certainly lived up to the hype.

After a shower, I stood at the bathroom mirror and put hot rollers in my hair. After all these years I was still an optimist, even though I'd be lucky if the curls lasted the walk from Brett's place to the theatre. It didn't matter: it gave me something to do and distracted me from obsessing about the audition. When Brett finally woke up he opened his eyes to see me resplendent in leotard, fishnets and curlers, stretched out in the splits on the floor of his bedroom.

'Jesus, that's a sight to wake up to,' he moaned. 'What in God's name are you doing?'

'I'm warming up for the audition.'

'How many times do I have to tell you? You will be fine. You should see some of the brick-eaters who show up for these auditions. I remember there was this one girl who stood up on stage and when they asked her what training she'd had, said she'd never had any training but whenever she went to a club her friends were always telling her she was a great dancer. I mean, can you imagine?'

'I suppose you have to admire her for giving it a go.'

'Admire nothing. She was rubbish. Leave the show-ponying to the professionals, that's my motto.'

I leaned forward, grabbed my ankles, and with no small amount of effort, stretched out along my legs.

'I'm nervous, Frank,' I said. 'Now that I'm actually here, I realise how much I want this.'

'Okay. Get up, Marge. You've never been loose, so no amount of last-minute stretching is going to make a difference to those hamstrings of yours. Besides, you only need to be really flexible if you want to be a cancan dancer. And trust me, you definitely don't want that.'

I maneouvred myself around to sit cross-legged on the floor in front of him.

'It's much better to be a nude, then you can just swan around being beautiful every night – and maybe even learn soloist.'

Ah, yes, the whole topless thing. It wasn't that I was prudish, but it was still going to be a big deal to go on stage and perform topless to a room full of strangers every night. I figured it was a bridge I would cross if and when I came to it.

'What do you mean?' I asked. 'What do the nudes do?'

'I could show you some of the chorie, but it's so camp you wouldn't believe me,' he said. 'The best thing you can do is just go in there and be fabulous. That's my other motto.'

Brett explained how all the girls had to be at least 175 centimetres tall and that for a girl to be considered for one of the plum nude or soloist roles, she also had to have the right assets.

'So today, you'll be auditioning for Janet, the ballet mistress,' he continued, warming to his theme. 'She's an old diva herself. Danced at the Moulin for years. She's been running the show for almost a year now. She's in her early forties and still has a fantastic figure, which is probably why she's so tough on everybody about the way they look. Let's just say she has an uncanny knack of noticing if you're carrying even an ounce of fat. And she's not afraid to tell you about it.'

'So it's true then', I said. 'Everyone gets measured and weighed when they start work?'

Brett nodded.

'Oh God, now I'm even more nervous.'

'You'll be fine. The thing to remember about Janet is that her bark is worse than her bite. She's from northern England, she speaks French with the heaviest accent and she watches the show each night from a little booth at the back of the *salle*, calling through corrections from a little black phone. She lives and breathes cabaret. She can pick a showgirl from fifty paces. The one thing I remember from my rehearsals with Janet, she was all about teeth.' He mimicked a Yorkshire accent: 'More teeth, I want more teeth!'

I let out a laugh.

'Right,' Brett said, standing to leave the room. 'I need a caffeine fix before I do anything else today. And you'd better get moving, your audition's in an hour. I'll walk you in.'

I dashed into the bathroom to apply my make-up.

'What kind of make-up?' I yelled through the door. 'Heavy or natural?'

'Heavy natural!' came the reply from the kitchen, followed by a self-satisfied laugh.

I applied a light foundation, eyeliner, shadow and mascara. A little lipstick – but not too much. I made a last-ditch attempt to fluff up my hair, hoping to gain a couple of inches in height, and gave it a light spray to hold it in place. I took one last look in the mirror and took a deep breath.

Brett and I stepped out onto the street. If Rue Dautancourt had been forbidding by night, it was plain grotty by day.

'So what's the name of this area?' I asked as we passed a run-down bar and stepped around a pile of broken furniture dumped on the footpath.

'This is La Fourche,' Brett replied. 'The arse end of Paris.'

'So this is not a typical Paris area, then?' I asked.

'It's a pretty shitty neighbourhood. But it's close to work and the rent is cheap.'

'So I'm guessing that this job I'm about to go for is not exactly well-paid?'

'Put it this way, you won't be buying a villa in the south of France any time soon.'

We came over a rise and walked a short way down a gentle slope. As we turned the corner, I stopped.

'Oh my God! There it is! The Moulin Rouge!' I let out a little squeal. Up ahead, the famous red windmill spun slowly atop the entrance to the theatre. It looked smaller than I had imagined. In the daylight, you could make out the cheap yellow lighting-tube that had been tacked onto each of the windmill's four red-painted balsawood sails. It looked tawdry. And yet here it was, one of the most recognisable landmarks in all of Paris, perched above the most famous cabaret venue in the world.

As I stood on the street before it, I realised that this simple red windmill had been the wallpaper of my entire dance career to date. The church hall in Brisbane, the Tivoli, Jupiters and even the little karaoke club in Japan – all had had some rendering of this famous Parisian *moulin*.

'I can't believe I'm actually here! I can't believe this is happening!'

Brett laughed. He grabbed my arm and pulled me, running, towards the theatre entrance.

'Here she is, Margaret,' he said, stopping me outside the wide entrance lobby. 'The Moulin Rouge. Now let's get in there and do the Tivoli proud.'

# Chapter Eleven

Brett took my hand and led me inside. Beyond a set of red upholstered vinyl doors, a staircase led down to the auditorium. I floated past framed posters from Moulin shows dating back to the music hall's inception. The iconic names of former luminaries and *habitués* flashed by in a blur: Jane Avril, Mistinguett, Toulouse-Lautrec. As if I wasn't nervous enough, each poster served to reinforce the rich heritage of the theatre and the distinguished place it held, not only in the history of Paris, but in the history of the cabaret itself. Brett pushed open the doors to the auditorium and I stepped inside.

I was momentarily taken aback.

'Is this it?' I asked.

'What do you mean, "Is this it?"' Brett retorted.

'I mean, I guess it's just smaller than I expected.'

The *salle* looked tiny compared to Jupiters, and wasn't even as big as the Tivoli. A small stage seemed to be pushing back against skinny rows of tightly packed tables. At the back of the auditorium, three rows of balconied seating were crammed in, rising steeply towards the ceiling. Chairs were stacked on the stripped-back tables and a lone cleaner moved lazily between the long rows of furniture, the whine of her vacuum echoing in the empty chamber.

'It's the Moulin Rouge,' I continued, by way of explanation. 'I guess I was just expecting something a bit more – I don't know – spectacular.'

'The building is heritage-listed,' Brett explained. 'They can't renovate it even if they wanted to. It looks small now, but trust me, with eight hundred audience members in it, it fills out.'

'Oh, no, don't get me wrong – it's intimate. I like it. It's just a bit of a surprise.'

There were a group of girls on the stage, some sitting and stretching, others standing in groups, chatting among themselves. One woman, older than the rest, appeared to be lecturing one of the dancers.

'That's her,' whispered Brett. 'That's Janet. They're rehearsing one of the new girls today. Come on and I'll introduce you.'

As we stepped up onto the stage, I took a deep breath to try to calm my nerves.

'Janet,' Brett said, as we moved into earshot. 'This is my friend, Shay.'

Janet turned from the group of girls to look at him, then looked me up and down and burst into a wide smile.

'Shay, lovely to meet you,' she said. 'Welcome to the Moulin Rouge.'

I smiled back, suddenly aware the eyes of every dancer in the room were on me, sizing me up.

'Alison, can you pick it up from here with these girls?' Janet said. 'I'm going to pop upstairs with Shay and put her through her paces.'

A girl with short brown spiky hair stepped forward to take over the rehearsal. Janet winked at me. 'Come on, love. This way.'

I turned to follow as she made for the wings.

'Break a leg, Marge!' mouthed Brett.

Backstage was musty and dim. We climbed a set of rickety old spiral stairs to a mirrored rehearsal room, harshly lit by rows of fluorescent light bulbs. 'So, let's get started then, shall we?' Janet said, moving towards the tape deck in the corner of the room.

'Um, sure,' I replied. 'So we're not waiting for everyone else?'

'Who else would that be, dear?'

'The others? The other girls auditioning today?'

'There are no others. It's just you.'

'Oh.' I stood rooted to the spot. This was news. I had assumed the audition was a general call, and had imagined I would be trying out with a pack of other hopefuls. It certainly added an unexpected layer of pressure to proceedings.

'Okay, get yourself ready while I cue the tape,' Janet instructed.

I stripped down to my fishnets and leotard and swapped my trainers for chorus shoes – my lucky pair of dance heels.

'Right,' Janet said as I walked back into the centre of the room. 'I'm going to walk you through a combination from the show, then I'll get you to do it.'

The tinny sound of cassette-recorded cabaret music echoed around the room and I copied Janet as she counted out the steps, mentally recording the sequence. It was a fairly simple combination with lots of flowery arms and poses. She went through it a few times and asked me if I thought I had it. I nodded in reply.

'Good, so let's see you do it. And remember, I want to see performance quality,' Janet said.

Five years of smiling my way through shows at the Tivoli and Jupiters and in front of slumbering audiences in Malaysia and Japan stood me in good stead. I lifted my head, pulled back my shoulders and pasted a huge smile on my face. I was showgirl-ready. I did the combination easily.

'Very nice,' Janet said. 'Now let's see some ballet. It says on your résumé that you've had classical training. It goes without saying that all of our dancers need a strong classical foundation. Let's see what you can do.'

She walked me through a ballet sequence.

'Right foot front in *croisé*, arms in *demi* second, and *coupé, chassé, pas de bourrée*, double *pirouette* and down. *Posé, arabesque, glissade, grand jeté*.'

On her count, I repeated the routine, throwing everything I had into my *grand jeté* and landing as gracefully as my high heels would allow.

'Excellent. Well done,' said Janet. 'Now I need to see your *battements* – your kicks. Go to the back of the room please, and give me a series of cancan kicks on the diagonal.'

I dutifully retreated to the far corner and, on her count, high-kicked my way down the room. Flexibility had never been my strong point: I sensed I was going to pay for each kick the following day.

'Very good. I see you've done this before,' Janet said. 'Now finally, I'm going to need to see you cartwheel. Starting in the back corner again, I want you to cartwheel in a diagonal down the room towards me.'

Brett had told me this would be part of the audition. As the famed home of Paris cabaret's most celebrated dance, the cancan, Moulin dancers were required to high-kick and hurl themselves about the stage with acrobatic abandon in every performance.

I cartwheeled down the room and came to a halt beside Janet, red-faced and puffing.

'That's lovely. Just lovely.' She paused to look once again at my CV. 'Now, it says here on your résumé that you're 177 centimetres tall. Is that right?'

I nodded and pulled myself up – keen to cover up my two-centimetre fib.

'That's interesting, because I'm 178 centimetres and you look quite a bit shorter than me.' She gave me a knowing grin. 'Pop on over here to the measuring tape, take off your shoes and let's take a look.'

My stomach lurched. A wooden measuring stick had been nailed to the wall, its sliding crossbar ready to make a liar of me. I slipped off my heels and reversed into the wall. As Janet slid the crossbar down, I elongated my neck and gently lifted my heels off the ground as subtly as I could.

'Heels flat to the floor, please,' Janet said, pushing the crossbar down to meet the crown of my head. 'I'd say you're 176 at a stretch, my dear.' She pulled back to gauge my reaction. I did my best to look surprised.

'It's uncanny how every dancer shrinks at least two centimetres between measuring themselves for their CVs and showing up to audition for me,' Janet said, winking. I just smiled back, feigning innocence.

'At any rate, you're definitely tall enough to join the company. You have lovely lines, nice technique and I can see that you like to perform. I do like a good smile. If you're interested, I'd like to offer you a job.'

I couldn't believe my ears. I stood and stared at her, my eyes wide, my mouth agape. 'I'm sorry,' I stammered. 'You mean that's it? Just like that? I got the job?'

Janet nodded. 'I have a place coming up in about six weeks. If you want it, the job's yours.'

I wanted to scream, I wanted to jump up and down, I wanted to reach out and hug Janet – but I just stood there and beamed.

'So is that a yes?' Janet ventured.

'Absolutely!' I shot back. 'I'd be delighted! I mean, I'm honoured – I mean, thank you!'

Janet smiled. This was clearly a part of her job she enjoyed.

'Now, do you want to dance nude or covered?' She looked at me expectantly, and though I was determined not to blanch at the question, I could feel my face flushing. Scared that a wrong answer would scupper the deal, I heard myself replying that I didn't mind – that I would be pleased to dance in either line.

'Well, if you're going to join the nude line, I'll need to see you topless,' Janet said, almost apologetically.

'Now?' I said. 'Here?'

She nodded.

'Right, of course. No problem.'

I turned to face the back of the room and slowly started peeling off the straps of my leotard. Behind me, I could hear Janet lighting up a cigarette. I rolled the leotard down to my waist, took a deep breath, put my hands on my hips, struck a showgirl pose and turned slowly and self-consciously around. Janet looked up. She took a long drag on her cigarette and stared at my naked chest for what seemed like an eternity.

I felt exposed. I felt cold. I started to think about how absurd it was that I was standing topless in front of a relative stranger in a dingy rehearsal room in Paris. I became suddenly aware of a draft coming from the open door, and shivered. But I held my pose and maintained my showgirl smile.

'Smashing,' Janet said finally, exhaling a large plume of smoke. And with that, I had the job.

'That's all I need from you today,' Janet continued as I hurriedly pulled my leotard back up. 'I'll let them know in the office that we'll be taking you on in six weeks. In the meantime, you'll have rehearsals, costume fittings and we'll have to sort out your working papers.'

I could hear her speaking and I could see her mouth moving, but my mind was racing too fast to take any of it in.

'I'll need you to pop back in tomorrow to sign your contract, at which point I'll weigh you.' She stopped and looked at me. I was wide-eyed and trembling. She moved towards me, put a hand on my shoulder and looked into my eyes.

'Congratulations, Shay. You're a Moulin Rouge dancer.'

Unable to stand still any longer, I thanked her and ran out of the room, skipping down the stairs, across the stage and up to the back of the auditorium where Brett was waiting.

'Well?' he asked, a grin already starting to play on his face.

I nodded excitedly. 'I'm in! I got the job!'

Brett's scream was louder than mine. We hugged each other and jumped up and down on the spot.

'Come on, we're going to celebrate,' he said. 'We'll walk down to Opéra, grab a bite to eat and do a bit of shopping.' He grabbed my hand and dragged me back through the lobby, up the stairs and out into the daylight. We linked arms and skipped across the street.

My head was still spinning, trying to process what had just happened. I'd just been offered a job at the Moulin Rouge. I was going to become a famous Doriss Girl and join the hallowed ranks of some of the best-known cabaret dancers in the world. Moreover, I was going to live in Paris – this remarkable city, which on this wonderful afternoon, bathed as it suddenly was in a burst of autumn sunshine, seemed laid out exclusively for me.

'I can't believe this is happening,' I said. 'I'm moving to Paris!'

We walked arm-in-arm, chatting excitedly about all the things we would do together, the adventures we would have.

'But what about your trip around Europe? What about Steve?' Brett asked finally.

He was right. I had been so focused on the audition, I had completely forgotten about Steve. He knew I was going to audition for the Moulin, of course, but I had so convincingly talked down my chances of getting the job that neither of us had really believed it would happen. He was looking forward to backpacking around Europe with me – what was I going to tell him? It was a dilemma that would have to wait. I was too happy. I was determined to savour the moment, and to soak up the beauty of my new surroundings.

As Paris's newest would-be resident, I let myself be carried away by the city's magic. People marched along the footpath in finely tailored coats. The sun reflected, golden, off rows of proud-looking Paris apartment buildings, uniformly elegant and capped with soft-grey lead roofs.

As we walked down Rue de Clichy and came upon the Casino de Paris, a look of horror came across Brett's face. 'Oh Jesus!' he exclaimed. I followed his gaze to a homeless man slumped against the brass doors of the theatre. He had unzipped his pants and exposed himself to us.

'Welcome to Paris, Marge', Brett intoned. 'The most beautiful city in the world.'

# Chapter Twelve

As a dancer, it's impossible to sit passively in the audience of a live show. If you tread or stomp the boards for a living, you can never go and see theatre or a musical or even a rock concert and just sit back and let it wash over you. Like it or not, your brain has been hardwired to notice everything about the production and you can't help but dissect the spectacle: analysing choreography, passing judgement on dance-ability and assessing the quality of costumes, sets and lighting. Ask any professional dancer and they'll tell you that, instead of looking at faces during a show, they watch feet, hands, the extension of limbs and the line of bodies. They also perform the choreography in their heads as the show plays out on stage. Engrossed in a performance, I have often been caught out performing the choreography in miniature, my feet shuffling silently under my seat as I count out the beat and shadow the steps.

At Janet's invitation, and having just been ordained a Doriss Girl, I used my second night in Paris to go and see the Moulin Rouge show. I was beyond excited – hankering to see Brett perform. But I was also burning with curiosity to see firsthand exactly what I had gotten myself into.

Each night the Moulin dished up two servings of heavy confectionery Paris cabaret – a first show at 9 p.m. and a second show at 11 p.m. Janet had arranged for me to come and see the second show. It was just after 10.30 p.m. when I came up the Boulevard de Clichy and took my place in the long queue of people outside the gaudily lit entrance to the theatre.

Pigalle, the neighbourhood over which the Moulin presides, is famous for its nightlife. Where other parts of the city have cornered the market in classy nocturnal after-dark distractions, Pigalle has spent the better part of its existence forging a reputation for unabashed seediness. At the turn of the century, the *butte de Montmartre* had been the primary haunt of Paris's ladies of the night, and courtesans had entertained well-heeled gentlemen clients at the Moulin Rouge with risqué displays of provocative dancing, and more. The Pigalle of yore had been a grotty, impoverished *quartier*, and as I looked about me now it seemed as if not a great deal had changed. There were semi-respectable bars and nightclubs along the boulevard, but they competed for space with a neon-festooned strip of seedy sex shops and downmarket strip clubs.

The footpath in front of the Moulin was crowded with middle-aged couples who'd piled out of a convoy of tour buses. The women wore sequin-encrusted blouses and pushed self-consciously at their short, older-woman hairstyles, set especially for their big evening out in Paris. The men wore sports coats over chinos. Neither the men nor the women seemed especially comfortable in the middle of Pigalle. Further back in the queue was a group of Japanese tourists, huddled together around a little flag held aloft by their tour guide.

At the front of the queue, a gorilla-proportioned bouncer stood staring out into the street, absentmindedly lifting and dropping the red velvet rope to regulate the flow of guests into the lobby.

'*Excusez-moi*,' I said in my best French accent. 'My name is Shay Stafford. The ballet mistress, Janet, has organised a ticket for me for tonight.'

Without looking at me, the bouncer lifted the rope and indicated with a barely perceptible tilt of his head that I should wait inside the lobby. I went in and hovered obediently, scanning a wall filled with photos from the show. I couldn't believe how nude some of the dancers were. I knew Paris cabaret involved topless dancing, but some of the girls in the photographs were wearing nothing more than a G-string and a necklace. They looked so bare, so exposed. There was no doubting they had spectacular bodies, but I was taken aback at how little was left to the imagination. My perception of Parisian cabaret was clearly a lot tamer than the reality.

I told myself that I was in Paris, that the rules were different here. Above all, if I was going to join the chorus line at the Moulin and become a Paris cabaret dancer, I was going to have to lose the prudishness.

'Shay?' came a voice from over my shoulder. I turned to see a smiling older gentleman, dressed in a tuxedo.

'My name is Monsieur Henri. Welcome to the Moulin Rouge.' He extended his hand and gave a slight bow. 'Please, there is no need for you to wait here. Come with me.'

I sailed past the patrons waiting patiently for the padded double doors to open. As I walked down the stairs into the inner vestibule, I was struck by the transformation the theatre had undergone since my visit earlier in the afternoon.

With the overhead chandeliers casting a soft golden light, the red-carpeted and red velvet-walled room looked like a sumptuous, glamorous boudoir. Monsieur Henri delivered me to the entrance of the *salle,* where a middle-aged French gentleman stood waiting, beaming as I approached.

'You must be Shay,' he said, extending his hand. 'I recognise you from the photos on Brett's dressing-room mirror. My name is Thierry, the company manager. Welcome to the Moulin Rouge! We're delighted to have you. Brett has told me so much about you, I feel like I know you already.'

As welcomes go, it could not have been more warm. I hadn't even signed my contract and already I was being made to feel like part of the family. Thierry pushed open the doors to the theatre and led me to a table. He motioned for a waiter to bring me a glass of champagne and handed me a program.

'Enjoy the show. It's been lovely to meet you, I look forward to working together.'

The last of the audience members from the first show were filing out of the auditorium, talking excitedly among themselves. A team of waiters in white-pressed tunics buzzed hurriedly from one table to the next, stripping them back, replacing linen tablecloths and slamming down champagne flutes for the next round of clients. Tiny red lamps with gold fringing glowed on every table. A string of multicoloured party lights and lanterns hung in a lazy loop across the breadth of the *salle*, setting off the candy-striped circus-tent faux-ceiling and faintly illuminating a series of oversized Moulin Rouge posters from shows gone by. It evoked a Paris of a bygone era, and it all looked so magical.

A little card standing upright on my table declared, 'Welcome to the Moulin Rouge – the world's most famous cabaret! La Famille Clérico are proud to present *Formidable!* Now in its tenth successful year!'

Ever since the Clérico family had taken over the Moulin Rouge in 1962 (adding the venue to their high-kicking portfolio of Paris properties, including rival establishment the Lido), they had named all their Moulin shows with a word beginning with the letter 'F'. It was one of those showbiz superstition things. Between 1963's *Frou Frou* and this latest offering, *Formidable!,* the Paris cabaret-going public had been offered up *Frisson, Fascination, Fantastic, Festival, Follement, Frénesie* and *Femmes, Femmes, Femmes*. Most shows had run for between two and five years. *Formidable!* had been running for over ten years. As Brett had been at pains to point out – in what I suspect was an attempt to manage my expectations – in the fast-moving world of showbiz, *Formidable*'s ten-year run meant that the show was anything but. On the contrary, according to those who danced in it, it was dated, tired and way past its use-by date. But sitting there in the moments before the curtain came up, I was buzzing with anticipation.

Once the *salle* was ready, the doors were flung open and the audience herded to their seats. There was a manic bustle of activity as people took their places, willingly accepted proffered bottles of champagne and settled down to take it all in.

When the lights dimmed and the music started up, I instantly recognised *Formidable*'s signature tune. It was music that I knew well, having performed to it in various productions over the years, yet hearing it in the venue for which it had been composed was something else again. Through the darkness, I could just make out the curtain beginning to rise. As the music reached a crescendo, the stage lights burst on, illuminating a flamboyant mass of showgirls decked out in orange feathers. The audience gasped. I sat in the darkness, wide-eyed and tingling with goosebumps.

The opening number was classic cabaret – lots of leggy, smiling girls, high kicks and artfully exposed breasts. Try as I might to focus on the costumes and choreography, I just couldn't seem to get past the nakedness – the raw, screaming, nudity of the whole spectacle. Certainly the feathers and jewels did much to distract the eye, but for at least half of the twenty-eight girls on stage, a sequinned G-string was the only thing between them in all their glory and an audience of eight hundred complete strangers.

When the boys made their entrance halfway through the first number, it was all I could do not to laugh out loud. Dressed to a man in full-length, electric blue sequinned jumpsuits, they came hopping and skipping onto the stage performing some seriously dated choreography. It was a kind of jazz ballet that had gone out of fashion with leg warmers. Performed by a troupe of six-foot-tall muscular men, it was plain comical, and all the more so for their seriousness. I sat in the dark and giggled, hoping Brett found it as amusing as I did. What if, after the show, I had to pretend to have loved watching him leap around the stage like some bad, blue-sequinned eighties throwback?

Once they had finished convulsing, the boys parted to reveal a singer centre stage. Dressed in a long-sequinned white and gold dress with massive shoulder pads and wearing a wavy auburn wig that seemed to eat up her heavily made-up face, she brandished a diamante-encrusted microphone. It was all very *Dallas*. As she opened her mouth to sing, a backing track kicked in and she proceeded to lip-sync the lyrics. I couldn't believe it. Here I was at the world's most famous cabaret venue – watching a woman mime. In all the shows I had worked in, there had been a live singer. I was disappointed.

But then, with the arrival on stage of the principal dancer, I was entranced. She looked divine. And familiar. I scrambled for the program and looked up her name. Marissa Burgess – Corina's younger sister. I watched, transfixed, as she moved about the stage. She had perfect lines, precise execution and a compelling stage presence. Newly inspired, I sipped on my champagne, settled into the show and resolved to try to let it wash over me – in all its kitsch, high-camp, lip-synching glory.

As I watched one tableau after another I started studying the different groups of girls and their choreography, visualising myself performing. Some of the numbers didn't require dancing per se, but rather a whole lot of elegant walking – the cumbersome feather backpacks rendering all other movement impossible.

Of the twenty-eight female dancers in the chorus line, most were excellent. They had loads of energy, fantastic figures and big smiles. There were some among them who had obviously been beautiful ballet dancers in their time, too. But you didn't have to search too hard to find the tragedies. They were the ones with a look of abject boredom pasted to their faces, the performers who were simply marking the choreography rather than dancing – a limp wrist here, a half-hearted kick there. I thought of all the dancers I knew back home who aspired to one day grace the boards of the Moulin Rouge. I thought of all of the girls who worked so hard on tiny Japanese karaoke bar stages or gave their all each night in Elvis revival shows for slumbering Japanese tourists. So many dancers – good, young, energetic, talented dancers – would give their right foot for a chance to live in Paris and dance at the Moulin Rouge, and here were a handful of the company appearing to take it for granted.

And then there was Brett. Good old Frank. Each time he made an entrance, ridiculous costume or improbable choreography notwithstanding, he brought the stage alive with his energy and electric smile. Whether by virtue of his relative youth or of his utter professionalism, he seemed to give everything he had to every second he was in the spotlight. I felt a surge of Tivoli- and Aussie-inspired pride.

In between each tableau, while sets and costumes were hurriedly changed out of sight behind them, a variety act would take to the stage. These 'attractions', as they are known, are a staple of modern-day Paris cabaret and part of a vaudevillian tradition. Attractions are renowned in cabaret circles for being of vastly varying quality. Some are excellent: their acts can lift an entire show. Some are just cheesy. *Formidable!* had its fair share of both kinds. The man who played the drums by spitting ping-pong balls from his mouth was not so hot. The couple of bouncy, elastic Portuguese brothers who threw each other into the air in a good old-fashioned balancing act were very entertaining.

A chintzy glitter curtain formed the backdrop for each act and the sound effects guy underscored each feat of physical or comical prowess with a drum roll and a *Ba-da-ching!* noise. I couldn't help but feel I was in Rooty Hill RSL.

At one point during the show a horse came trotting onto the stage. He seemed to do little more than a brief circuit and an enormous poo, requiring one of the dancers to sweep the manure off into the wings. And then there was the python. It made its entrance draped artfully around the neck of one of the dancers, who writhed about in the spotlight before setting the snake down on the stage. It began slithering towards the audience, causing a ripple of excitement down in the stalls before being scooped back up by its handler and transported offstage.

The second section of the show had an Arabian Nights theme. The nudes came out on stage dressed as slaves, or rather, dressed as a costume designer at the Moulin Rouge had imagined slaves might appear. Wearing nothing but a G-string and a pair of Roman sandals, and sporting dirty, matted cave-woman wigs, they drifted on stage shackled to one another and wafted aimlessly about as a male singer stood centre stage cracking a whip. Quite apart from looking unflatteringly naked, they looked lost, clearly unsure what narrative arc of the performance they were supposed to be interpreting. I sat in the dark and started to feel nervous. Was this what I had just signed up to do? Could I really do this twelve times a week for the next twelve months?

Towards the end of the show, Janet appeared out of the darkness, pulled up a chair and sat down at my table. She raised her glass of champagne to clink with mine. 'Welcome aboard,' she said, leaning across the table, the underside of her face illuminated by the red lamp. 'So, what do you think? Are you excited about joining us?'

What was I to say? I was excited, yet I definitely had reservations. It wasn't as if I didn't appreciate the time and effort that had gone into the show's creation, but it was just so dated.

'It's great,' I said. 'Some of the costumes are amazing.' It served the dual purpose of being truthful and diplomatic. There was a minute's silence between us as we sat and watched the performance. I wondered if Janet really believed this was the pinnacle of dancing. Was she really pleased with the overall quality of the performances? I couldn't help myself. 'Some of the girls are wonderful dancers,' I ventured. 'They have so much energy. But there are a couple up there who look like they'd rather be somewhere else. Are they okay?'

In the darkness, I could just about make out Janet's eyebrows rising. 'Well, yes, Shay. There are a few who've been here a bit too long and have lost their sparkle. But don't worry, I'm on to them.'

I figured I was on a roll. 'How come the singer doesn't sing live? Is she sick?'

'Oh no,' came Janet's reply. 'We haven't had live singers here for years. Miss Doris decided singers were all divas and too much hard work. It's much easier to get a dancer to mime.'

Onstage, an upping of the tempo marked the start of the cancan – the dance that had made the Moulin famous and which every audience member had come to see. People sat upright in their seats as, with a flurry of catcalls, squeals and whooping, the cancan dancers came rushing onto the stage. The famous dance had a rich heritage, originally being performed by the local girls of Montmartre – amateur dancers whose energy and bawdiness more than compensated for any lack of dance technique.

Now the dancers came thundering downstage in a series of cartwheels, flips and turns. Offenbach's rousing tune echoed through the auditorium, its catchy riff and insistent beat compelling the audience to start clapping along. From a cartwheel the girls would fall directly into the splits: I sat there wincing, thanking my lucky stars that as a nude I wouldn't be required to cancan. The dancers formed a line and kicked in unison, stopping occasionally to lift their skirts and show off the red and white ruching underneath. They formed a circle and each raised a leg into the centre, creating a kind of spinning human maypole. I was shocked by the violent physicality of the dance, how each dancer's boots thudded heavily on the wooden stage with every step. It was fast and furious and left the audience breathless with excitement.

When the number reached its climax, the auditorium exploded. People jumped to their feet and gave the dancers a standing ovation. Onstage, and spread evenly about it, dancers were in splits on the floor, one arm thrown dramatically over their heads, chests heaving as they tried to catch their breath. I stood up and joined the ovation, marvelling how a single number had the power to carry an entire show. The *salle* was buzzing, and slowly I felt the excitement start to surge in me once again. I was going to be a part of a show that people travelled from all corners of the globe to see. I made a mental note to stop being critical and instead count my blessings.

As I walked back out onto the street, surrounded by shiny-faced audience members grinning from ear to ear, I felt a small surge of pride. I wasn't yet part of the show that had transported these people, but I soon would be. And what a privilege it was going to be to give so much pleasure to so many people every night.

I went to the stage door exit and waited patiently for Brett to appear. It was 1 a.m. and the streets of Pigalle were heaving. A light shower had fallen; the flashing lights of the Moulin Rouge and its sex-shop and nightclub neighbours reflected off the rain-slicked bitumen. I watched as dancers came pouring out onto the street, either charging off purposefully into the night or lighting up cigarettes to wait for their colleagues. They stood in basketball caps, jeans and bulky winter jackets, the heavy stage make-up scraped from their faces and their hair still wet from hurried showers. Whatever glamour they had had on stage had clearly been left behind in the dressing-rooms.

'Marge!' Brett shouted as he pushed through the door. 'So what did you think?'

'Frank!' I exclaimed 'You were fabulous! I'd recognise that two-finger stage smile anywhere.' I placed two fingers between my teeth, measuring out the desired mouth gape required for an exaggerated onstage smile. Frank fell about laughing.

Then he reached around behind him. 'Marge, there's someone I want you to meet.' He put his arm around the shoulder of a tall, blond, good-looking dancer.

'This is Matthew. Matthew, this is Shay.'

I proffered my hand. 'Nice to meet you. Brett has told me so much about you.'

'Likewise,' said Matthew with a soft English lilt, flashing a pair of huge blue eyes. 'It's lovely to finally meet you.'

I recognised him from the cancan. He'd appeared to have legs up to his armpits and superhuman flexibility. 'Impressive effort in the cancan. I don't know how you guys do it every night.'

'With a lot of after-hours physio,' Matthew said. 'Don't worry, I'll be paying for that tomorrow.'

We decided to end the evening with a nightcap.

'Follow me,' Brett said. 'I know just the place.'

We walked around the corner from the Moulin, picked our way through the mob lined up outside the panini and crepe kiosk, and crossed Rue Lepic.

'This is Jimmy's Bar,' Brett said as we walked up a darkened alley.

'And it redefines the word "dive",' Matthew whispered to me out of the corner of his mouth.

Jimmy's turned out to be not so much a bar as a glorified hole in the wall. From the outside, it looked like nothing much at all, the only thing marking its existence was a rainbow flag hanging limply above the door. There were iron bars on the blacked-out windows and the door was closed. We rang the doorbell and waited to be admitted. Once inside, I was amazed how tiny the place was. There was barely enough space at the bar for four stools. At capacity, it might have held fifteen people, but they would all have had to be standing and would want to know each other quite well. The walls were covered in leopard-print velvet and the tiny space reeked: a nasty combination of stale cigarette, rising damp and air-freshener.

'Welcome to Jimmy's,' Brett said as we took our places at the bar. 'Let me get you a Kir Royal. You need to try one.'

Cyril the barman poured a splash of cassis into a flute, then filled it with champagne.

Brett was beside himself with post-show excitement. It was obvious he was proud of *Formidable!* and had relished every second onstage. His enthusiasm was infectious.

Matthew proved to be delightful company. He shared Brett's quick wit and they riffed off one another like a two-person comedy act. He'd come to cabaret from the Royal Ballet in London, having left his home in Bristol at the age of eleven to take a scholarship at the Royal Ballet School. It was all very *Billy Elliot*, and accounted for his technique being so clean and his lines so impeccable. Perhaps because of the years of exacting classical training he had undergone, Matthew seemed more willing than Brett to acknowledge the shortcomings of *Formidable!* and its smattering of bored showgirls.

'What about Paulina? Isn't she awful? I have to lift her in the Viennese waltz. It's like throwing a sack of potatoes around. Could she be less interested?'

As we dissected the show, more Moulin dancers started trickling into the bar. A tall black girl I recognised as one of the dancers came up to Brett and Matthew and air kissed them both.

'This is Big Nic,' Brett said. 'Nic, this is my friend Shay; she's starting work with us in a couple of weeks.'

Matthew helpfully explained that she was called Big Nic because there were two Nicoles in the company, and she was the taller of the two. She moved with a considered, feline grace.

'*Ciao*,' Big Nic purred, offering a limp hand for me to shake. She ordered a 'baby Leffe' – a beer served in a tiny glass – and proceeded to smoke a skinny, elongated cigarette. The baby beer and mini-cigarette looked ridiculous in the hands of someone so tall.

Despite hailing from Miami, Big Nic had been in Paris long enough to be more than slightly chuffed with the French she had picked up, and peppered all her conversation with as much as she could. She started telling Brett a story liberally laced with obscure French words and expressions. I could tell by the look on Brett's face that he, like me, didn't have a clue what she was talking about, but we nodded politely and laughed on cue at the end of it.

Big Nic was accompanied by Dimitri, a friendly but not especially talkative Russian dancer. As Brett and Nic chatted, Matthew gave me the Dimitri run-down. Now pushing forty, he was the oldest male dancer at the Moulin. Like Matthew, he had come to cabaret via ballet; in Dimitri's case, he had trained at the Kirov. As a very young man and somewhat of a USSR dancing prodigy, he had defected from the Soviet Union and joined the French national ballet. After twenty-odd years of gruelling effort in the French corps du ballet, he had defected once again, this time to the comparatively cushy world of cabaret; the hours were easier, the job less physically demanding and the money was better. Like many of his Eastern bloc colleagues scattered about the various Parisian cabaret venues, Dimitri would send home as much money as possible to his family for as long as his legs could keep high-kicking.

As we chatted and I sipped my second Kir Royal, Brett's flatmate Megan breezed into the bar and did the air-kissing rounds, bestowing a 'Salut chérie, ça va?' on each person as she went. Brett waited until she got to him before turning to introduce me.

'Megan, this is Shay.'

'Lovely to finally meet you,' Megan said, planting a kiss on my cheek. 'We keep missing each other at home: even my mum met you before me! Brett talks about you all the time.'

'Nice to meet you too,' I replied. 'Your family are lovely.'

'They flew out tonight', she said. 'I'm going to miss them.'

She was dressed in a miniskirt and a pair of towering high heels. Through her heavy make-up you could tell she was a natural beauty. Despite her newly acquired French affectations, she was clearly a Queensland girl at heart; there was an earthiness about her that no amount of *salut chéries* could hide.

'I can't stay kids, I'm just here for a glass of champagne and then I'm off. There's a private *soirée* at Queen for Johnny Depp tonight. He's here for the Paris premiere of his new film.'

I watched, fascinated, as she downed her champagne and floated back out into the Parisian night.

'Excellent,' Matthew said as she disappeared. 'She'll come rolling in tomorrow morning at ten-thirty with some great stories for breakfast.'

When we finally spilled out of Jimmy's, it was 3.30 a.m. and bitterly cold outside. We pulled our coats around us and hurried back down the street to Boulevard de Clichy.

Pigalle was still brightly lit and humming with activity. Drunken tourists were falling in and out of strip clubs, packs of young men squashed into cars were cruising up and down the boulevard. The Kir Royals had done their job, ensuring I was ever-so-slightly, comfortably drunk. As we walked under the big red windmill, still illuminated and spinning, we passed a group of tourists posing tipsily for a group shot in front of the famous landmark. And in that moment, with my arms interlocked with those of my dear friend and his lovely new boyfriend, I knew Paris and I were on the brink of a grand adventure together.

# Chapter Thirteen

I woke late the next morning, having slept deeply – so deeply that I sat up disoriented, unsure of where I was. And then it all hit me. Unless the last forty-eight hours had been a dream, I was in Paris and had just landed a job at the Moulin Rouge. A shiver of excitement passed through me, followed immediately by a feeling of dread.

It was all well and good that I had myself a job, but where was I going to live? And what about Steve? He didn't have working papers for France or any job prospects in Paris. He was arriving in a few weeks and I was going to have to drop a bombshell.

But first things first, I told myself. I had to go to the Moulin Rouge to sign my contract and formalise my employment. Once the job deal had been sealed, the rest would surely fall into place.

I fronted up at the Moulin at midday, as per Janet's instructions. A wizened old man at the stage door pointed me in the direction of Janet's office. By some miracle, I successfully negotiated the backstage warren of corridors, costumes and dressing-rooms and soon found myself sitting opposite Janet as she rifled through a pile of papers on her desk.

The office was a poky little space that stank of stale cigarette smoke, and was buried deep in the Moulin's backstage maze. Janet's desktop was piled high with the CVs and photos of dancers from all over the world. Reading upside down, I could make out a couple of aspiring Moulin dancers from Russia, another from England, two from the U.S. and one from the Ukraine. In a cupboard behind Janet, shelves heaved under the weight of videotapes, the showreels of a similarly hopeful army of would-be showgirls. I began to marvel at my good fortune at having landed the job.

By way of making conversation, I asked Janet what had brought her to the Moulin Rouge and how long she had been here. She seemed genuinely pleased at the chance to talk about her eighteen years at the famous venue.

She'd come to Paris to dance at the Lido. She'd earned her showgirl stripes as a Bluebell for several years before moving to the Moulin Rouge, where she worked her way through the ranks, eventually becoming dance captain.

When Miss Doris, the Moulin's ageing ballet mistress – den mother to the famous Doriss Girls – announced she was leaving Paris to while away her twilight years in Monaco, Janet was chosen to replace her. Her ascension to the role of *maîtresse de ballet* had been recent, and she was clearly relishing it.

'Here's your contract then,' Janet said, passing a sheaf of papers over the table to me. 'Have a read through and let me know if there's anything you don't understand.'

It all looked pretty straightforward. I was to join the Moulin Rouge as a '*danseuse*', and would be expected to perform two shows a night, six nights a week. My contract was '*un CDD*' (*contrat à durée determinée*) or fixed-term contract of twelve months. I was to serve an initial thirty-day probationary period, during which time the Moulin could terminate my employment if they felt I wasn't working out. A clause specified that I was to be weighed at the signing of the contract and was not allowed to gain or lose more than two kilograms. To do so would constitute a breach of contract and provide the Moulin with grounds for dismissal. The final page of the contract was headed '*Fiche de Physique*' and required a series of my measurements: weight, height, chest, waist, thighs, calves, arms.

'Right then,' Janet said, standing up and pulling a set of scales out from under a sideboard. 'Let's get you weighed.'

I stood up and removed my shoes and jacket.

'So, according to the terms of your contract you have to stay the weight you are now. Don't get fat, don't get skinny,' Janet said, throwing me a smile.

I stepped up onto the scales.

'Fifty-nine kilos,' Janet said, scribbling onto the *fiche de physique*. 'Height we did yesterday, didn't we? It was 175 centimetres, from memory. That's real height, as opposed to dancer's CV height.'

I gave a sheepish nod. She smiled.

With a measuring tape in hand, she then set about taking stock of my other vital statistics. I felt like a cow in a competition at the Easter Show. She ran the tape around my waistline, across my hips and around an upper thigh. She noted the size of my arms and took an especially long time getting exact measurements of my chest. I'd never given my breasts an enormous amount of attention, but here in Paris, they were being scrutinised like never before.

Finally, she got down on her haunches and wrapped the measuring tape around my knees.

'This is how you can really tell if a woman has put on weight,' she told me.

It was the first I had heard about knees acting as some kind of weight-gain bellwether. But I figured she had been doing this longer than me and probably knew what she was talking about. Once measured, I set about getting redressed and realising we hadn't yet talked money, I started searching through my contract.

I flicked to page two and read down the page, skipping the French and skim-reading the sketchy English translation. For my two shows a night, six nights a week, plus the four rehearsals a month and any promotional and publicity work required of me by management, I was to be paid the princely sum of 515 francs a night.

I did a quick mental calculation. It converted to approximately 120 Aussie dollars. Brett had explained to me that there would be all manner of deductions for social security, retirement funds and of course income tax. In all, I could expect to hand over at least 40 per cent of my salary each year to the government, meaning my take-home pay each year would be just over 30,000 Australian dollars. Translated into French francs, it didn't look like much.

Janet must have read my mind.

'The soloists and principal dancers are of course paid more, so there are ways and means of increasing your income,' she said. 'And as a nude, you'll also receive a supplement. It's another fifteen francs per night.'

Fifteen francs? A whole $3.50 extra to dance each night with my breasts exposed? I tried my best to look enthusiastic.

'Besides, we're not in this for the money are we? If we wanted to be rich, we would have become lawyers and bankers. Having said that, Shay, if you're smart, you'll be buying your own apartment in Montmartre before you know it. Or you'll be like some of the others,' she continued with a knowing smile. 'Working here for twenty years and barely a cent to their names. But they've got their memories, and that's what's important.'

I gave a wan smile, wondering how exactly memories were going to help pay the rent.

It was true that I hadn't become a dancer because I wanted to make a pile of money. God knows Mum had worried herself sick about the wisdom of my career choice, concerned I was always going to battle to make ends meet. But it was what I loved. I couldn't imagine doing anything else. And this was the Moulin Rouge; I was about to realise a long-held dream of dancing on the Paris stage. A glance at the pile of CVs on Janet's desk was proof, if any were needed, that if I didn't take this job, there would be plenty of others who would happily put their hand up for it.

I signed on the dotted line and handed back the contract.

'So that's it,' Janet said, brandishing the contract. 'You're officially one of us. Rehearsals start in three weeks. Congratulations and welcome aboard.'

With my contract signed, and the prospect of an income on the horizon, the next item on my agenda was finding somewhere to live.

While the Moulin was more than happy to employ bright-eyed young dancing *ingénues* from all over the world – some as young as eighteen – when it came to finding a roof over their heads, it was every showgirl for herself. Not even the fact that the Moulin company comprised 60 per cent foreigners, the vast majority of whom couldn't speak a word of French when they arrived, appeared to make a difference.

I sat down and worked out a list of must-haves for my new Parisian abode. It had to be close to Brett, as he was the only person I knew in Paris. It had to be within walking distance of the Moulin, as we would be finishing each night at 2 a.m., long after the Métro had stopped running. The modest salary meant paying for a cab out of my own pocket was out of the question. The apartment should also ideally be big enough to receive the inevitable stream of guests from Australia and should be tastefully furnished, saving me the hassle and expense of having to buy my own furniture.

My Paris daydreams had always featured an elaborate rendering of my ideal Paris apartment. I'd imagined living on the top floor, among the Paris rooftops. There would be a couple of rooms, a pair of big double doors leading from the parquet-floored *salon* to the bedroom, and a set of large French windows looking out on the Eiffel Tower.

It only took a day of apartment-hunting for me to realise my dream was destined to remain a fantasy.

Armed with my contract and a couple of rudimentary French phrases, I had fronted up to an estate agent's office on the Avenue de Clichy, not far from Brett's apartment. The woman tending the office looked sceptically at me as I walked in the door, but brightened noticeably when I handed over my contract and blurted the phrase Brett had taught me: '*Je cherche un appartement à louer. Je suis danseuse au Moulin Rouge.*'

She was clearly impressed by the contract. It was my first lesson in French bureaucracy: bits of official-looking paper emblazoned with the word '*contrat*' put people like estate agents visibly at ease. With the guarantee of a regular income, I was a relatively safe bet as a tenant.

It was only later I would learn that I was also considered an attractive prospective tenant because I was a foreigner and therefore blissfully unaware of my rights as a tenant in France. With tenancy laws weighted very heavily against owners; the fact that I would be relatively easy to get rid of if the agent or owner wanted the apartment back was a valuable attribute in a city renowned for its squatters.

The kind of glamour associated with Moulin Rouge dancers clearly didn't hurt either. As the agent's mood switched suddenly from taciturn to obsequious, I got my first taste of the fringe benefits of being a Moulin Rouge showgirl. Yes, she had some apartments for me to see. And yes, she would be happy to show them to me now.

Thus began what became a two-week, utterly disheartening search for a home. If I had been hopeful of finding a cosy little corner of Paris to call my own at the start of the flat-hunting process, two weeks and fifteen hideous apartments later I was starting to become desperate. Coming from Australia, where space is a commodity in ample supply, I was used to rooms being slightly larger than your average cupboard. Even the accommodation in Kashima and Atami had been better than what I was being shown. Here in Paris, it was apparently acceptable for humans to live in spaces that were so small as to be uninhabitable, had no windows, no natural light and no bathroom. At home, you wouldn't have kept your lawnmower in them.

True, I was only looking for a studio apartment, and my budget was very definitely on the modest side. But even so, the agent would have had to pay *me* to live in some of the places I visited. One apartment was on the fifth floor of a ratty old building. The spiral staircase was narrow, dark and stank of urine. The higher we climbed, the more narrow and steep the steps became; by the time we reached the top, I had to stoop to stand on the landing. The agent bent low to insert a large brass key in a tiny door and stepped inside. Feeling like Alice in Wonderland, I ducked under the lintel and followed her. The ceiling was so low, there wasn't a spot in the apartment in which I could stand upright. At nine square metres, nestled under the eaves of the old building, the place was really just a skinny rectangle of lino-covered floor space. A sink cut into the wall constituted the kitchen. The only light in the apartment came from three tiny square windows that had been punched through the sloping roof.

'Where's the bathroom?' I asked. *'La salle de bain?'*

The agent motioned back over her shoulder at the landing outside. Sure enough, on closer inspection, there was a forlorn, filthy toilet on the landing – the common toilet for all *les misérables* forced to live up in the roof, where clearly no self-respecting plumbing pipe had ever dared to venture. I almost gagged at the sight and smell.

'You share it with the other tenants,' the agent explained in faltering English.

'And the shower?' I asked. '*La douche?*'

The agent shook her head. '*Les bains douches,*' she said. 'You use the public baths and showers.'

Another apartment, this time on the ground floor, looked promising on paper. But it took me less than ten seconds to step over its threshold and realise a prison cell would have been more accommodating. It only had one, heavily barred window, mysteriously positioned high up in the far-right corner of the back wall. The white-tiled floor was stained with what looked like grease, and the 'sleeping area' – a raised platform above the kitchen sink that could only be accessed via a dirty white ladder – was furnished with a single, badly stained mattress.

I also visited a studio that sat directly above a kebab shop on Avenue de Clichy, but decided the battle against the constant stench of chip fat wafting up through the floor was never going to be won by me.

'What's with this no-bathrooms business?' I asked Brett one night. He explained that many upper-floor apartments in the city used to be servants' quarters, or *chambres de bonnes*. Not even the encroaching twenty-first century had managed to deliver plumbing to these rooms. I was in another country and fully prepared to accept cultural differences, but this was one compromise I couldn't cope with. It was beyond depressing.

And then, just when I was about to give up hope, I stumbled upon a third-floor studio that was neither too small, too dark, too smelly nor devoid of bathroom facilities. It didn't have a scrap of furniture, the floor sloped vertiginously from one corner of the room to the other and the carpet was old, blue and synthetic. But it was bright, it looked out across a nondescript but essentially inoffensive courtyard and – crucially – at 3000 francs a month, it was affordable. It also happened to be two streets away from Brett and within stumbling distance of the Moulin, which sealed the deal. It was a relief, as Steve was due to arrive any day. I was looking forward to seeing him and keen to have our own space.

I signed all the necessary paperwork, handed over all the money I had in the world for a bond and deposit, and took the keys for my first Parisian home. The following day, I packed my bag, bade farewell to Chez Frank and moved in.

When it comes to unfurnished apartments in Paris, you pretty much get what's on the label. No furniture *or* white goods. In my case, my new home also had no curtains or lamps – the previous tenants had left with the light fittings, leaving a tangle of wires dangling precariously from the walls and ceiling. The kitchen was just a narrow benchtop with a single sink in one corner of the room, its pipes exposed thanks to the complete lack of surrounding cupboards or drawers. There was no stovetop, no oven, no fridge and no shelves. And the place was freezing. The estate agent had explained how to crank up the heating, but I couldn't for the life of me remember the complicated procedure. So there I was, shivering in the winter cold in an empty little room. Home sweet home.

Thankfully, however, Brett had helped me buy a mattress and doona earlier in the day, which now sat forlornly in the centre of the room. I took a shower, crawled under the covers and lay awake in bed, staring out the windows.

Two days later, Steve arrived in Paris. I was so happy to see him. Despite its humble beginnings, my new life in Paris was starting to take shape and I couldn't wait to show it off. Steve was genuinely excited that I had landed my dream job. He also loved our little bedsit and declared it the perfect base from which to launch two-person excursions into the world's most romantic city.

He brandished the French phrasebook he had bought back on the Gold Coast and proudly demonstrated the three sentences he had learned by heart: '*Où est le Métro?*', '*Une bière, s'il vous plaît*' and 'How much does the pig cost?'

Free of the onerous task of apartment-hunting, I was finally able to enjoy my surroundings and happy to have someone special to share them with. For a week we ran about the rain-soaked city together, taking in the tourist sights and escaping the cold by drinking coffee in bustling cafes, their windows fogged up by the steady hum of conversation between the wine-sipping locals.

We'd strike out from our gritty corner of the seventeenth *arrondissement* and lose ourselves in Paris – surfacing from the Métro at the Eiffel Tower or Arc de Triomphe giddy with the excitement of being in such a beautiful city. We paid a visit to the Mona Lisa and joined the queue for Notre Dame, happily letting Paris cast its spell over us. To be in the City of Light, with my boyfriend on my arm and an exciting new job on the horizon, felt close to perfection.

In phone calls home to Mum, I sensed the relief in her voice as I relayed the news of my gradually solidifying life on the other side of the planet. Job, apartment, boyfriend – it was all coming together.

As the countdown for rehearsals began, Brett kept me abreast of the rolling home furniture sale taking place backstage as showgirls came and went. Before long, our apartment was decked out in a slightly worn, mismatched collection of furnishings. Mum had packaged up curtains and mailed them from Australia; we also had a pre-loved couch, a lamp I found in the street, a second-hand TV and a slightly rickety old chair. The little studio started to seem more like a proper home, albeit a very small one.

Also helping us to settle in were the friendly neighbourhood Brazilian transsexuals. By night, dressed to the nines in lurid lycra miniskirts, crop tops and platform heels, they worked a dark strip of the *Peripherique* – the ring road that encircles Paris, whose northernmost arc passed not far from our *arrondissement*. By day, they moved in packs up and down the street, buying their groceries at Franprix, walking their little dogs or doing their laundry at the laundromat. Even when not on duty, as it were, they were on parade. They all had superskinny legs, huge fake boobs and fried blonde hair, a look that was nicely complemented by their tattooed eyebrows and lipliner. When I first saw them, I thought they were simply a group of very tall, well-endowed, heavily accessorised women. But on closer inspection their Adam's apples, broad shoulders and, if it was late in the day, five o'clock shadows gave the game away.

One afternoon, two days before rehearsals began, I was sitting at the table in Brett's poky kitchen. Steve had begged off for the afternoon to go out and look for a job. He was headed to Corcoran's, the Irish pub near the Moulin Rouge, figuring that an expat bar would be the best place to start. Corcoran's had Guinness on tap, so I wasn't sure there'd be a whole lot of job-hunting going on, but I figured he needed a little space to himself. Plus, any attempt by him to develop a social circle independent of me had to be encouraged. As tolerant of the show-world as he was, there was only so much showbiz talk he could take.

Brett was making tea, Matthew was pottering about in his pyjamas and I was midway through a *pain au chocolat* and a story about the Brazilian transsexuals when there was a knock at the door. Brett looked up from the tea bag he was jiggling and threw me an exaggerated look of surprise.

'Who can that be?' he asked melodramatically, bouncing out of the kitchen to answer the door. I heard the lock turn, the door creak open and a loud scream as a reunion of some sort took place. I looked at Matthew. He shook his head and shrugged.

'Come in! Come in!' I heard Brett say, followed by footsteps down the hallway. He re-entered the kitchen with a broad smile on his face, and a head poked around the doorframe.

'Shayleeeeeeeeen!' came the cry of a familiar voice. It was Jenny. It took a moment to register.

'What?' I finally stammered. 'What are you doing here?'

Jenny laughed, clearly delighted at having surprised me. Brett stood triumphantly beside her, pleased with himself at having been party to the surprise.

'Oh my God, Jenny!' I said, launching myself at her and throwing my arms around her neck. 'You're in Paris! What are you doing here?'

She gave me a big toothy grin. 'I got a job at the Moulin. I sent my tapes across to Janet, she liked what she saw – she's only human after all – and here I am! I start rehearsals in two days. We're going to be Moulin Rouge dancers together!'

We both let out a scream as Jenny started doing cancan gallops down the hallway.

'Can you believe it? I'm going to be a Paris showgirl!' Jenny hollered.

Matthew gave the new arrival the once-over. An oversized beige trench coat hung shapelessly from her shoulders. On her head she wore a black and white leopard-print pork-pie hat, clearly something she had picked up in a flea market. Unruly shoots of frazzled yellow-blonde hair sprouted from under the hat. A pair of heavy black boots and tortoiseshell reading glasses completed the bag-lady ensemble.

'And you look the part too,' Matthew deadpanned.

Jenny had arrived that morning and made straight for the Ibis Hotel at Place de Clichy, where the Moulin had agreed to put her up for three nights. It wasn't explained to her exactly how she was expected to find somewhere to live within three days, without a word of French, while starting rehearsals.

'Talk about knowing how to make a girl feel welcome,' she said.

Suddenly the prospect of starting rehearsals seemed less daunting. With Jenny by my side, things were destined to be entertaining, if nothing else.

## Chapter Fourteen

The first day of rehearsals for a new show is always nerve-wracking. It doesn't matter how long you've been in the business, how many shows you've performed or how many times you've proven yourself capable, you always walk into the first day of a new rehearsal period hoping you'll measure up. Hoping that you can produce the goods. Worried you won't.

After years of dancing, the brain and the body develop a kind of shorthand. The eyes see a routine performed, they send signals to the brain, the brain processes it and the limbs perform it. It requires concentration, for sure, but at a certain point, you have to abandon yourself to your body's intuition. You have to trust that all those years of jazz classes, all those ballet exams and all those hours spent tapping on the concrete floor of the makeshift dance studio under the house will come together and see you through. The trick is not to think too hard about it.

That, at least, is what I told myself as I fronted up to the Moulin for day one of rehearsals. It was midday on a cold, grey November afternoon. I'd collected Jenny from the Ibis Hotel lobby and we'd walked along Boulevard de Clichy to the panini and crepe kiosk on the corner of Rue Lepic. A ham and cheese crepe had been ordered, not so much to calm the butterflies in my stomach as to completely drown them in butter and cheese fat. It seemed to work. Jenny, true to form, had kept up a steady patter of lighthearted banter, which went some way to taking my mind off the nerves. Yet as we entered the stage door, I still felt a mild rush of fear.

It wasn't as though I hadn't started new jobs before – it's just that none of them had been my dream job. This was the Moulin, this was Paris. It was important that it all went smoothly.

We wended our way through the backstage corridors to the stage, where a group of girls were variously stretching, chatting in small groups or standing nervously at attention. I cast a quick glance over them, sizing up the competition. It was true that we'd all been offered jobs and hence were not competing for a place in the show, but we'd entered a new phase of rivalry – that of jockeying for prime position on stage. There would be friendliness and camaraderie between us new girls for sure, but just beneath the surface, smouldering, would be the fire of competitive spirit that had gotten us here in the first place.

A small group of girls downstage were seated on the floor with legs spread in front of them, stretching their torsos down along each limb, talking loudly and laughing among themselves. From their accents and general boisterousness, I recognised them as fellow Aussies. Eavesdropping on the muted conversation of a pair of tall and beautifully pale girls standing just off stage right, I was able to pick them as Russians, the telltale inflections of their language giving them away. There were also two English girls, one with mousy brown hair scraped back on her head into a tight bun, the other with an impressive Rubenesque figure barely contained in a grey leotard. A tall, curly-haired blonde girl of indeterminate nationality seemed to be floating between groups, chatting amiably to everyone. There were eleven of us in total. As I scanned my new colleagues, I thought of the pile of unanswered CVs on Janet's desk.

'So we're the lucky few, eh?' I whispered to Jenny as we took a place on the stage and started stretching.

I got chatting to two girls – Melissa and Kelly – one from Sydney and the other from Adelaide. Like Jenny, both had been offered jobs on the strength of showreels they had sent. They'd met with Janet just the day before for the contract signing and weigh-in.

'She told me my thighs were too fat,' said Melissa. 'She's got me on a thirty-day trial. She told me not to go near a *baguette*.'

'Are you serious?' I asked, incredulous.

'Oh, she was very sweet about it, it was nothing nasty. But I just sat there dying.' She bent forward and laid her chest on the patch of stage between her outstretched legs, and then sat up again. 'I mean, it would be fine if I hadn't sold everything I owned and given up a job at home to come here.'

Janet came walking onto the stage, cigarette in hand.

'Okay ladies, everyone upstairs to the rehearsal room. We need to figure out who's doing what.'

We all sprang to attention and started trooping upstairs. As we went, I stole a glance at Melissa's thighs. They were slightly heavier than those of the rest of us, but they looked fine to me.

At the top of the rickety spiral staircase we emerged into the dank dance studio in which I had performed my private audition for Janet. It seemed like an age ago – so much had happened since then. I noted that the room had not improved in my absence. The only thing that appeared to have changed was the ambient temperature: it had got much, much colder. Heating was apparently a luxury we were going to have to live without.

'So, I'm going to need four nudes and the rest of you will be doing cancan,' Janet announced. 'Shay, Jenny and Jean, I'd like you three to be in the nude line. And I need a fourth . . .'

She scanned the room, looking each girl up and down, analysing legs, bums, height, faces and breasts. 'Natalia, what about you?'

One of the Russian girls looked up, a wide-eyed look of terror on her face, and stepped forward dutifully. 'Da,' she replied in Russian. She was clearly unsure of what had been said and what she was expected to do.

'I think you might be a nice nude, Natalia,' Janet persisted, apparently unfazed that her conversational companion spoke not a word of English. 'Before I make a decision, though, I'll need to see your boobs.'

The entire room cringed: the moment couldn't have been more awkward. There was a long pause while Natalia looked beseechingly to her Russian companion for a translation. There was an exchange in Russian. None of us spoke or understood a word of the language, but the look on Natalia's face as she realised what was being asked of her needed no translation.

'Well?' Janet asked. 'Can you take your top off for me?'

We all looked at the ceiling, the floor, our feet – anywhere but at the poor girl slipping her leotard straps over her shoulders to stand topless in the centre of the room. Janet stood back and studied Natalia's chest like an art aficionado analysing a canvas. Natalia shifted awkwardly on the spot, staring straight ahead, until Janet finally broke the silence.

'You,' she said, pointing and nodding at Natalia. 'Very nice, but you need to eat more.' She mimed the act of eating. 'You need bigger boobies,' she smiled, miming a pair of large breasts.

Jenny and I exchanged looks of disbelief, and stifled giggles. What *was* this place? Emphasis on a presentable, attractive body had always been a part of my job, but this was something else again. Signing contracts not to gain or lose more than two kilograms? Girls being warned their thighs were too chunky? Russian ballet princesses baring their breasts to a room full of strangers and then being told to eat more? I felt I'd arrived at some kind of bizarre body image boot camp. But then again, it wasn't as if people were paying top dollar to come to the Moulin Rouge to see dancers with nice personalities. It was part and parcel of the gig. Auditions were cruel at the best of times; even in my brief career I'd seen girls reduced to tears while trying out for jobs. The Moulin selection process was no more ruthless than other auditions I had been to – but it was definitely much more surreal.

'Well, maybe further down the track,' Janet said to Natalia, scanning the room for her next candidate. 'Katie, what about you?'

The slighter of the two English girls looked up. She looked terrified.

'From what I saw yesterday at your contract signing, I think you'd be perfect. But you said you weren't sure about being topless. What do you think?'

In her pale pink leotard and black tights, Katie looked as if she'd come straight from an after-school ballet class. She gave a slight shrug before nodding sheepishly, wide-eyed with fear and nervousness.

'Good, then it's settled,' Janet said.

With her nudes duly selected, Janet sent the remainder of the girls downstairs to start learning the cancan.

'I'm going to leave you nudes in the capable hands of Nicole,' Janet said, motioning to Big Nic, who'd just entered the room. 'Nicole, they're all yours.'

The curly-haired blonde we'd noticed before sidled up to Jenny and me. 'Jesus, Mary and Joseph, would you look at that?' she said in a broad Irish accent, nodding at Katie, who now stood alone on the far side of the room, arms folded across her chest. 'The poor thing looks petrified. She must be seventeen if she's a day.'

Big Nic busied herself at the stereo, cueing music.

'I'm Jean, by the way. It's grand to meet you both. So what do you make of all this, then? That business with the boobs, I mean I wouldn't have believed it if I didn't see it with my own two eyes.'

Speech seemed to pour out of Jean like water from a fountain. We would soon learn that keeping up with everything she said wasn't entirely necessary in order to partake in a conversation with her. Your presence may have been a catalyst for her words, but your input certainly wasn't vital.

Jean was from Dublin and had come to the Moulin direct from an extended stint on various cruise ships in the Caribbean. (It was written into showgirl lore that if you wanted steady employment as a sequin-sporting high-kicker, you either had to perform on cruise ships, dance in Vegas or take to the stage in one of the Paris cabaret shows.) She was tall, and had wonderfully smooth skin. I too had Irish heritage, but clearly our ancestors had not swum in the same gene pool – where I had blue eyes and pale, freckled skin, Jean had a set of dark brown eyes and golden tanned skin, crowned by a mop of unruly blonde curls. She spoke with a melodic Irish accent that was lovely to listen to, which was just as well, as she tended not to draw breath between sentences.

Jenny and I stood and nodded for a full five minutes as Jean gave an unsolicited account of her life story. For Jenny to have been rendered silent took some doing. She had met her conversational match.

Then Big Nic proceeded to put us through our nude line paces. Because we were to be dancing topless for much of the show, our choreography was less energetic than that of the cancan girls. Being a Paris showgirl, we were told, was all about line and form – celebrating the female form, to be specific. As such, our choreography was restrained, in order to limit the potential for excessive onstage breast movement. The moves were long and graceful and considered. There was to be little or no jumping. Some of the numbers we were taught that afternoon with Big Nic were hardly dancing at all – more like wafting.

'Why do I get the feeling these dance moves are more about the costumes than about the dance?' I asked Jenny midway through one routine.

'Glorified coathangers, honey, that's all we are. Glorified coathangers. We might as well accept it now.'

The music, however, was exactly what we had signed up for: kitsch and camp and utterly cabaret. The show's signature tune, *'C'est Formidable'*, was straight out of the 1970s cheesy cabaret vault. It exploded in a frenzy of horns and strings followed by a choir of session singers belting out lyrics, heavy with *la-la-la*s and mindless repetition of *'C'est formidable!'*

As we followed Nic's instructions and performed a showgirl walk in formation, a wide grin spread across my face. The music was so high-camp it was impossible not to be transported by it. I closed my eyes and strutted proudly across the rehearsal room, imagining myself on stage before a capacity audience. It didn't matter that the show we were to perform was already ten years old and utterly dated. It was Paris cabaret. And it felt so good.

The showgirl walk, Nic explained, was the most important step in our entire cabaret dancing repertoire. It was also Janet's pet obsession. If she was going to haul us up over one thing, Nic assured us, it was going to be our walk.

The walk usually required your arms to be outstretched in second position, your hands held in an elegant, controlled drape. Hips had to be thrust forward and swung in an exaggerated but graceful way, one foot always on demi-point while the other dragged behind, stretched long and pointed.

We also learned a Viennese waltz, a number we would eventually perform with male partners and which required us to float angelically about the stage. It was easily the prettiest, most classic of the numbers. Then there was the slave number that I had been so unimpressed with when I saw the show. It required us to come on stage shackled together and undulate listlessly.

'Glad I brushed up on my ballet technique for this,' I whispered to Jenny.

For the next few days, from one to five in the afternoon, we were taught our show. At intervals, when our respective shows had to be enmeshed, we'd join the cancan girls downstairs on the main stage. Janet sat up the back of the *salle* for the most part, occasionally giving corrections or pulling up a girl on her showgirl walk.

'I want elegance, ladies! You are Doriss Girls now: I want you to own it!'

We would break for afternoon tea, during which half of the girls would scoot outside for a panini and a cigarette. On occasions I would join them for a cheese and ham crepe fix. Melissa would stand by forlornly watching us eat, sucking on a cigarette, convinced it would ward off the hunger pangs.

Four hours a day of dancing and learning the chorie was starting to take its toll on all of us, but the effort was compensated for by a sense that we were beginning to get on top of our respective shows.

For the most part, when it was just the four of us nudes and Big Nic, Katie stood apart from the rest of us. Younger and less confident, she kept her head down and quietly learned her show. In the evenings, when we filed out the stage door, she would be met by her mother and spirited away into the night.

One afternoon, during a nude line session in the rehearsal room, we were joined by Janet. She appeared at the door with a pair of costume assistants, or 'dressers', in her wake. Each of them carried a couple of long, voluminous white gowns.

'Sorry to interrupt, ladies,' Janet said. 'But the time has come for you to try on your waltz dresses.'

The gowns were distributed and we put them on over our rehearsal gear. Janet also donned a dress then stood at the front of the room in a stunning flowing white silk and chiffon gown with a delicate sprinkling of diamantés – pulled on over her jeans, T-shirt and cardigan.

'Ladies, in your whole life, you may never own a frock as expensive as this. I want you to think about that when you are on stage and be beautiful and elegant.' She marched down the length of the studio, demonstrating her take on beautiful and elegant. It was hard, admittedly, to get past her worn black cardigan, coral T-shirt, jeans and trainers in order to imagine her as a Viennese countess, but I tried nonetheless.

The gowns were undeniably beautiful, sitting gracefully on our waistlines and cascading down to the floor in generous folds of white chiffon. Bizarrely, two of the dresses had bodices, while the other two, including mine, were sculpted so as to leave the breasts exposed.

'Now walk, ladies! Walk the room and assume the dress!' Janet commanded, prancing about in front of us.

I glimpsed myself in the mirror. In leotard, trackpants and trainers, with my hair pulled back in a ponytail and not a scrap of make-up on, I felt far from glamorous. I glanced across at Jean, who was still hamming it up theatrically. Jenny made eye contact with me and began to giggle.

Behind us, a cleaner had appeared with his mop and bucket, a cigarette hanging from his bottom lip. There was an unsightly brown stain on one of the studio's brick walls, and an icy draft pushed its way through cracks and holes in the dirty windows. Try as I might, I just couldn't summon nineteenth century Vienna.

# Chapter Fifteen

The next stop in our transformation into Paris showgirls was a visit to Nadine, the Moulin Rouge's in-house wigmaker.

Wigs were worn to ensure onstage consistency across a company whose members had all kinds of different hairstyles. While hats and elaborate headpieces were worn for most of the show, for the numbers that called for hair to be displayed, it was easier to stick everyone in a wig than try to get a line of girls to have their hair done every night in exactly the same style. All that would ever be seen onstage of our real hair was the scraped-back front and sides: otherwise, it was smoke and mirrors.

Nadine had been plying her wigmaking trade at the Moulin for decades. She spoke only French and called everyone, from chorus girls to Moulin management, *ma biche* (a French endearment).

She toiled in a cupboard-sized workshop backstage. When it came our turn to pay a visit to her, Jenny and I had to squeeze ourselves into the tiny space.

'*Bonjour mes biches*,' Nadine said, motioning for us to sit down. The entire room was packed to overflowing with bags of human hair of every hue. It was on shelves piled to the ceiling, in garbage bags all over the floor, on the tabletop and hanging in long ponytails from the back of the door.

Nadine herself was partial to a wig. On this encounter, and every subsequent encounter I would have with her at the Moulin, she was sporting a jaunty little half-wig – a big blonde bob that sat on the back of her head. It should have looked ridiculous, but in this bizarre museum of hair it looked completely at home – artistic even.

Nadine started speaking French at me. I didn't understand a word. So she motioned for me to move my chair closer to her. When I did, she promptly took up a position behind me, pulled my hair from its ponytail and started brushing it. She began humming away to herself and I sank back into my chair, happily reflecting on how pleasant it was to have my hair brushed. Suddenly, and without a word of warning, she whipped out a pair of scissors from her work apron and cut off a swatch of my hair.

'Wait!' I exclaimed, sitting suddenly forward. 'What are you doing?'

Nadine just smiled and continued humming as she held the clump of my hair up to the light and analysed it through her half-moon glasses. I watched in stunned silence as she picked up a bulging, dog-eared exercise book and started flicking through it. Page after page of hair samples flashed by me, each one stuck haphazardly to the page with yellowing sticky tape, a name noted next to it. When she reached a blank page, she pulled off a rectangle of tape and plastered my lock of hair to the paper, scribbling my name next to it in spidery, old-lady handwriting.

We later discovered that the 'hair book', as it came to be known, was one of several that Nadine owned. Her collection held a lock of hair from every girl who had danced at the Moulin for the past twenty years. It was a follicular record of every head that had donned a Moulin wig for the past two decades.

Whenever she needed to make a wig for a dancer, Nadine would refer to the books to match the swatch of said dancer's hair with one of the many hundreds of colours of hair stuffed in bags all over her office. Once she had located a perfect match – or as near to perfect as possible – she would style and fit what Janet poetically described as a 'doggie' – a curly fringe attachment that you secured at the front of your head for certain numbers. It was called a doggie, according to Janet, because of its resemblance to a poodle. Nadine would also create an elegant French roll for the waltz. Once your lock of purloined hair had been matched and a suitable quantity of some stranger's hair had been located, Nadine would start sewing the hair into a mesh base moulded to fit the back of your head. Layer upon layer of hair would be meticulously woven into the mesh frame until it was completely covered with braids and swirls. A transparent hair net would be placed over the hair to keep it neat, and finally a constellation of tiny rhinestones was sewn into the French roll. The end result was a work of art that seemed even more beautiful when you considered its dubious origins: a human hair graveyard in a dimly lit backroom of the Moulin Rouge.

It was Nadine's job not only to make the wigs for each member of the cast, but also to meticulously maintain them, ensuring that the wig colour and hair colour of each member of the cast remained as consistent as possible. For this reason, she was at pains to emphasise that afternoon, in her peculiar Franglais, how important it was that we not change our hair colour.

'You change colour, I must start again,' she intoned, giving us a stern glare over the top of her glasses. But not even the ire of Nadine would prove scary enough to stop Jenny. By her own admission, she was easily bored with her hair, and changed styles and colours every couple of months. It would become the bane of Nadine's existence, as with each colour change Jenny would go trooping back to Nadine's office to sheepishly request a new French roll.

'*Mais non, Jen-ny!*' Nadine would scream melodramatically, upon seeing Jenny had turned once again from a blonde to a brunette. '*Catastrophe!*' She would start rummaging through sacks of hair and piles of old doggies to find new matches for Jenny's colour of the month.

Every now and then, usually when we were midway through learning a new routine, rehearsals would be halted so we could be fitted for costumes. First the head dresser, Monique, would take us backstage to the dressing-rooms – or *loges* as they are called in French – and roughly match us in size to the costumes of one of the girls whose places we were taking. Then we would each be assigned costumes according to the show we would be performing – which numbers we would be in and whether we were nudes or cancan dancers. Fittings would take place, during which it was determined whether hemlines needed lifting, waistlines needed expanding or hats needed stretching. I had one of the biggest heads in the company, so the call went out for all of the show's largest hats to be seconded to my service.

Because *Formidable!* was already ten years old, each costume had been worn every night, twice a night for ten years by an average of six different girls. They were not, therefore, in pristine condition.

One costume, known as 'the doughnut', was a massive feathered collar on a backpack. They came in hot pink or royal blue and swung in a large circle from around our necks to just below our hips. They resembled toilet seat covers and smelt about as fragrant – thanks to ten years' worth of showgirl sweat, they stank to high heaven. Tired from years of faithful service, they had also started shedding feathers at an alarming rate. We quickly discovered you couldn't inhale while wearing a doughnut without accidentally ingesting half a bird.

If wearing the doughnut threatened death by asphyxiation, wearing other costumes threatened death by pneumonia. Some of the costumes were so brief they were hardly there at all. The *maillot* I was to wear for the opening number was a bejewelled backless, frontless G-string leotard – a pair of straps came up over the shoulders and plunged down in a deep 'V' to well below the bellybutton. It looked so old and worn I could only hope the stage lights would work their magic and make it look beautiful. This *maillot* formed the basis of the nudes' costumes for the first three numbers, with various accessories – such as an orange feather boa and bustle or a white flower backpack – added and subtracted.

Altogether, it meant that once on, the costume felt like a much more substantial piece of covering than it actually was.

Nevertheless, as I stood before the mirror in the *maillot* while Monique fussed around me taking note of adjustments that needed to be made, I couldn't help but feel exposed. In three weeks' time I was going to be dancing topless before up to sixteen hundred strangers a night. And I felt self-conscious enough in front of this middle-aged French woman and a couple of fellow dancers. It was clear I was going to have to loosen up a little.

The *maillot* was nothing compared to the costumes for the slave number: a threadbare G-string, a long, matted brown wig and a pair of shackles. And that was it. As we stood backstage, semi-naked, our pasty-white midwinter skin goosebumped from the draft blowing in from the wings, we started to laugh.

'Oh yes,' I said, pushing a rank-smelling dreadlock out of my eye. 'Now I know I've really made it as a Paris showgirl.'

As the costume fittings continued, though, I began to appreciate that many of the other outfits were works of art. On more than one occasion, Monique would dispatch me into the deepest recesses of the backstage warren to an *atelier* where seamstresses toiled day in and day out, maintaining the costumes. The wear and tear they sustained from nightly use over a ten-year period kept six full-time seamstresses busy.

The six ladies sewed hunched over tables in a room lit by low-hanging fluorescent lamps. Their worktop was a mess of fabric, scissors, tweezers and glue pots. Containers spilled over with rhinestones and plastic emeralds, sapphires and rubies. Costumes hung limply on walls stained yellow from years of cigarette smoke, waiting to be tended. I found it hard to reconcile these scraps of jewel-encrusted lycra with the glamorous creations I had seen on stage. It was like pulling back the curtain and discovering the little old man behind the Wizard of Oz: a glimpse of the pedestrian, daily reality behind the nightly fantasy.

Despite the cramped workspace and the less-than-salubrious surroundings, there was something noble about the way these women went about their work. They laboured quietly and methodically; if there had been a clock in the room, you would have been able to hear it tick. And you only had to look at the care with which they applied every jewel and the skill with which they reinforced every hook to understand you were in the presence of artisans.

Waiting patiently for attention on one table in the corner were a couple of hats. It was the job of the *couture*, as the seamstresses were known in-house, to maintain the headgear – along with the Moulin's signature feather backpacks.

The hats had all been handmade ten years ago by a team of local milliners whose house had been manufacturing hats for Paris cabaret shows for as long as showgirls had been around. The feathers had been commissioned, at enormous expense, from the Paris-based theatrical feather supplier that had been wowing cabaret audiences with its creations for more than a century. They came mostly from South Africa, where the birds were hand-reared and their feathers hand-dyed to order.

Once our costumes had all been fitted and adjusted, the only part of the showgirl outfit puzzle left was the shoes. A dancer's shoes are the tools of his or her trade – so of all the items of costume for which we were fitted, the shoes were far and away the most important. An ill-fitting pair of shoes could ruin our feet, leading to injury. With all of the choreography and onstage acrobatics to be performed, the stairs – both onstage and off – to be negotiated, and all of the feathered backpacks and unwieldy headgear to be worn, the shoes were the bedrock of any showgirl's outfit.

Several pairs of shoes were to be custom-made for each of us, from basic chorus heels to thigh-high boots. Working on the theory that the higher the heel, the sexier the leg, each pair of shoes featured a six-centimetre heel. And according to Moulin tradition, each and every shoe was to be handmade by Maison Clairvoy.

'You have to go and see Clairvoy to get your shoes fitted,' Janet said to me one afternoon during rehearsal. 'Go down Rue Fontaine and he's on your right. Tell him Janet sent you.'

I knew better than to ask her to elaborate. That was as specific as Janet's directions ever got.

I had visions of skipping down the glamorously named Rue Fontaine and sweeping into a bright, airy palace of footwear. It would be just like I imagined Audrey Hepburn's 1960 costume fittings at the House of Givenchy. I had no idea where Rue Fontaine was: I thought it must be the ninth *arrondissement*'s answer to the Champs Élysées.

'Oh, that's just near me,' Jean piped up, interrupting my private reverie and bursting my bubble. If the House of Clairvoy was near Jean's place, then it was near the Moulin. And if it was near the Moulin, it had to be in the midst of the sex-shops, kebab shops and seedy bars that seemed to be the only other types of business that flourished in Pigalle.

'Come to my place first thing tomorrow morning and we'll go down together,' Jean offered. 'I'll do you a fruit shake.'

The next morning, I followed my Paris street map to Rue Fontaine. It ran diagonally downhill from Place Blanche, just opposite the entrance to the Moulin Rouge. As expected, the street was lined on either side with a collection of down-at-heel bars, takeaway shops and dodgy saunas. All of them had their heavily graffitied rollerdoors shuttered, their tawdriness only exaggerated by the daylight.

After dutifully drinking my fruit shake, I walked down Rue Fontaine with Jean until we came to a shopfront with a couple of pairs of old shoes and a yellowed, dusty photo of a showgirl from the seventies in the window. There was no sign above the entrance, no indication at all that this was the famous Maison Clairvoy. A curtain hung across the glass door. We knocked gingerly, pushed on the door and made our way inside. A bell rang as we stepped across the threshold.

The interior was dark and cluttered, with shelves rising to the ceiling, bowed under the weight of shoes and large bolts of leather. On a workbench down one side of the room sat a pile of wooden foot moulds. Off-cuts of leather lay scattered all over the floor; an overwhelming smell of glue and shoe polish hung in the air. Old posters from the Moulin, the Lido and the Crazy Horse plastered what little wall space was not taken up with shelfloads of shoes.

In response to the bell, a tall, silver-haired gentleman stepped into the store from a backroom: Antoine Clairvoy, the cabaret cobbler. He had broad shoulders, looked to be in his mid-fifties and wore a leather apron over a white shirt and dress pants.

'Je peux vous servir, mademoiselles?'

'Janet sent us,' Jean responded. 'We've just started at the Moulin Rouge. We're here to have our shoes fitted.'

Monsieur Clairvoy pulled a notebook from behind the counter and started flicking through its pages. He asked our names, ran a finger down the page and ticked them off.

A shoe-fitting session with Monsieur Clairvoy was a step back to another era – a time when bespoke tailoring and shoemaking was the norm rather than the exception. Monsieur Clairvoy clearly treated his *métier* with the utmost respect and went about his job with an impressive seriousness.

I stood in the centre of the room as he busied himself at my feet. Starting with my right foot, he ran his measuring tape around my ankle, from my ankle down to my toes, around my heel and across the bridge of my foot. He measured the height of my instep, the length of my foot, the circumference of my calf and the length of my legs from thigh down to ankle. Between each measurement, he would pause to write detailed notes in his notebook. At least twenty different measurements were taken of my right foot. Then he did it all over again with my left.

'No two feet are the same,' he said by way of explanation.

The process took nearly thirty minutes, at the end of which there were almost two pages of notes in his book dedicated to the particularities of my feet. Monsieur Clairvoy next explained that he would be making six pairs of shoes for each of us: a tap shoe, a sandal, several pairs of high-heeled ballroom shoes, a pair of black ankle boots and a pair of red leather cancan boots.

I had never paid much attention to my feet before, but as I slipped them into my worn trainers and stepped back onto Rue Fontaine with Jean, I looked at them in a whole new light.

With three weeks of rehearsals under my belt, I was desperate for the show to start. We were busy running through the waltz for the umpteenth time when Janet popped her head into the rehearsal studio.

'Shay, your shoes have arrived. Pop down to *couture* and collect them, will you?'

I shuffled off to the seamstresses' workshop to find six boxes piled high on the workbench. The ladies worked in concentrated silence around me as I opened the boxes and took in their contents.

Each pair of shoes was more lovely than the last. When I pulled out one of my ballroom heels, I let out a gasp of delight. It had been hand-stitched in silver leather, with a single rhinestone positioned over the toe and a neat line of tiny diamantés running up the T-bar. There was a solid, elegant heel, a padded arch and reinforced stitching at the tiny silver buckle. It was beautiful. I turned the shoe over to see that my name had been burned into its sole. My very own, custom-made pair of Moulin Rouge shoes.

I paused for a moment to watch the seamstresses at work, and it struck me that they were probably the last of a dying breed of specialised artisans. With the world increasingly turning for amusement either to mega-stadium productions or to their TV or computer screens, the age of the cabaret show was on the wane. I looked at these middle-aged women with their needles and thread in hand and saw for the first time that they were part of an artistic whole – part of a creative vision. I might not have understood the complete vision but I had to give credit to the many talented hands and minds that had gone into conceiving it.

The Moulin, in a sense, was really just a tourist attraction. A tourist attraction with a proud history and a noble heritage, but a tourist attraction all the same. Yet for as long as Paris continued to attract tourists by the millions each year, the red windmill would keep on spinning and the seamstresses would keep on sewing.

On my way back to rehearsals, I stopped to take in a faded, curling poster outside the *couture atelier* showing Josephine Baker striking a coquettish pose. The famous performer had entranced audiences with her lithe body and playfully risqué routines back in the 1920s. She was as big a star in her time as any multi-platinum-selling pop singer was in mine, and she too had graced the Paris stage. The metaphorical shoes I would be stepping into in a week's time, when the curtain rose on my first performance, were huge, filled as they had been through the ages by some of the biggest names in cabaret.

I felt humbled, excited and just a little nervous. Nothing could take away from the fact I was about to take my place in the chorus line of history. No matted slave wig, no tattered costume and no outdated choreography could ultimately tarnish the magic of the experience in front of me. I took a deep breath and vowed, no matter how many performances I did, no matter how repetitive the choreography became, never to forget this moment.

# Chapter Sixteen

'I'm just saying you might find it easier to find work if you actually left the apartment.' I stared across the room at Steve. He looked back at me from his perch on the sofa, where I was certain he had been sitting all day. 'And we have no milk, again. Would it have killed you to go to the shops?'

I hated what we were both becoming. The first flush of excitement at being together in Paris had faded, and after five weeks Steve had made little attempt to find work, even though he kept promising he would.

I knew things were difficult for him, without the language, without the ready-made social outlet I had with my new colleagues, but I couldn't help resenting his complete lack of effort.

This was not how either of us had envisaged our sojourn in Europe. By getting the job at the Moulin Rouge, I had fulfilled a lifelong dream. Yes, our travel plans had been messed up, but Steve had assured me he was happy to stay in Paris – had said he'd get a job and we'd have just as much fun. But this was anything but fun. Paris was expensive and it cost money to enjoy its restaurants, cafes and museums. All my savings had been sucked up by finding the apartment and setting up home in a new city, and my first Moulin paycheck was still a couple of weeks off.

A week before my debut at the Moulin, I felt worn down, and not just by the physical exertion of rehearsals and my frustrations regarding Steve. The mental effort required to deal with French bureaucrats, bank managers and gas and phone company salespeople was draining me on an almost daily basis. In order to get the apartment in working order, I had to spend hours in long queues at service centres and government offices scattered all over the city.

Even when I did have the correct paperwork (which in France, as I was fast discovering, was extremely rare), I would usually stand before the officials and either not be able to understand what was being said or not be able to express myself. I always scanned the dictionary beforehand and practised the phrases I thought I would need in each situation, but as soon as the people behind the counter started speaking back to me, I was generally lost. As a result, it usually took me three attempts to get anything done.

I decided I had to enrol in French lessons if I was going to survive in Paris.

Meanwhile, back at the Moulin Rouge, opening night was drawing closer. Hats were being adjusted to fit us and each of our new pairs of shoes was slowly being broken in. At first the leather was hard and unyielding, causing painful blisters. But after a week, as it softened and the shoes started to mould to the shape of our feet, we began to appreciate the care with which Monsieur Clairvoy had done his job.

In the days leading up to the dress rehearsal, sessions onstage and in the rehearsal studio upstairs became increasingly frantic and panicked. The tedium of rehearsing had started to affect our concentration spans, and more and more silly mistakes were being made.

'Come on ladies! It's really not that hard!' Janet would say, annoyed at having to reblock a sequence for the tenth time.

In addition, while we all knew the steps we were to perform and we'd had glimpses of our costumes during fittings, none of us had a clue how it was all supposed to hang together. Janet tried explaining how a set change would take place around us, but it only added to our confusion.

But before any dress rehearsals could take place, we had a couple of much more important tasks to perform. Tasks that would bring us face to face with the lumbering beast that is French bureaucracy. Tasks so complicated and delicate that they could only be attempted with the help of Madame Jacqueline.

Madame Jacqueline's job title was 'Head of Human Resources'. A much more appropriate title might have been 'Madame Fixit and Chief Wearer of Over-the-Top Furs'. Madame Jacqueline was a former entertainer. It was rumoured that she had been a *chanteuse* who'd graced stages all over the world and made men swoon with her syrupy French ballads. Certainly, though she was no longer in the spotlight each night, she had lost none of the charisma that had made her a star. She was a sixty-something bouncing ball of energy. She bustled instead of walked and every sentence she spoke seemed to burst out of her.

She was short, despite wearing stilettos with every outfit, and would scurry about the backstage area sporting one of several signature fur coats. Her lips were always painted red and her skin was always tanned. As she walked, her cropped bleached-blonde hair would bob atop the coat's fur collar and her shoes would clip loudly on the floor, announcing her arrival in a room long before she actually appeared.

As well as taking care of all the internal paperwork for the Moulin Rouge and its many employees, Madame Jacqueline organised the vital medical checks for all new dancers and helped them to process their working papers. In order to be legally employed by the Moulin, we needed a visa from the French government granting us the right to live and work in France. One of the visa's requirements was a full medical check-up by a government-ordained doctor. To apply for the visa, we either had to make a solo assault on the notoriously impenetrable French administration or clamber aboard the Madame Jacqueline Trojan horse. Given that I was still battling to buy a *baguette*, the decision was a no-brainer.

Of all the accessories that Madame Jacqueline wore – and there were many – easily the most important one was her handbag. It was a well-worn brown leather affair almost as big as she was. It seemed to be permanently attached to her arm, which was probably just as well given that it appeared to contain the entire administration department of the Moulin Rouge. Every document, individual contract, pay cheque and file pertaining to the personnel of the Moulin was rumoured to be inside that handbag. She was, without even knowing it or intending to be, a pioneer of the mobile office.

During the first week of rehearsals, Madame Jacqueline had requested that all new girls bring their passport into work. I'd watched nervously as she collected them and dropped them into her handbag. As my passport sank without a trace into a nest of loose-leaf paper, I figured that was the last I'd ever see of it.

But that was the remarkable thing about Madame Jacqueline: despite her eccentric and occasionally shambolic appearance and the manic way she flitted about the place, she was actually very organised. It defied all laws of effective office management, but not only did Madame Jacqueline miraculously process all the necessary paperwork, the handbag also managed to spew forth 300-odd pay cheques every month. Long before salaries were paid directly into employee bank accounts, Madame Jacqueline would sail about the backstage area of the Moulin at the end of every month dispensing pay cheques from her handbag.

On the morning of our visa application we fronted up to the *Préfecture* to lodge our papers. The *Préfecture* building sat on the Île de la Cité, just in front of Notre Dame. As tourists braved the morning chill to photograph one another in front of the world's most famous church, a long queue was forming at the *Préfecture*'s entrance and snaking around the corner. Immigrants from all over the world stood hunkered down against the cold, waiting their turn to submit applications for residency papers.

I met the other new Moulin girls outside the entrance, just as we had been instructed by Madame Jacqueline.

'Don't join the queue,' she'd told us. 'Wait for me at the front door.'

By the time I arrived there was already a sizeable contingent of dancers in a gaggle near the entrance. A pair of burly policemen stood at the door, shuffling from one foot to another in an effort to keep warm.

'You are waiting for Madame Jacqueline?' one of them asked.

'Yes,' Melissa replied, surprised. 'How did you know?'

The policeman nodded and gave a knowing smile.

Then, across the paved courtyard with the spires of La Sainte-Chapelle rising up behind her, Madame Jacqueline came trundling into sight. She had chosen an especially showy fur coat for the occasion and seemed to be wearing even more make-up and accessories than usual. Her handbag hung heavily on one arm.

'*Bonjour les filles,*' she chirped as she made her approach. '*Vous allez bien?*' Without waiting for an answer, she marched over to the policemen and gave them both a double-cheek peck.

'*Bonjour Antoine, Bonjour Stefan,*' she chimed. The policemen, who seemed genuinely pleased to see her, swung open the door.

'*Allez, allez* – this way, girls,' Madame Jacqueline trilled. 'We don't queue at the *Préfecture.*'

We fell into line and filed inside behind her, not daring to make eye contact with the hundreds of people who had obviously been queueing for hours. As with the medical check-up, with Madame Jacqueline stage-managing proceedings the visa application lodging process didn't appear to require our presence at all. The forms were all filled out by Madame Jacqueline. Questions were answered and assurances provided on our behalf, despite the fact that none of us spoke, read or wrote a word of French.

We all emerged clutching a *recipissé* – a temporary residency card – which would in time be replaced with a permanent residency card. Thanks to Madame Jacqueline, it seemed we had successfully navigated the notoriously difficult French immigration process without even opening our mouths.

As bemusing as this foray into the world of French bureaucracy was, it offered a welcome couple of hours' respite from the pressure cooker of rehearsals. For me, it was also a break from the tension building between me and Steve.

Routines we had rehearsed fifty times were starting to come undone as exhaustion and nerves set in. Despite the fact most of the new girls had had some previous professional experience, there was something about dancing on stage at the Moulin Rouge that made us all a little nervous.

Mercifully, the day of the dress rehearsal finally came around. For the first time we were going to rehearse as a full company and dance in costume, with sets and backdrops on stage. The new girls were instructed to be at work early: for us, full dress rehearsal meant wearing full stage make-up and costumes. The rest of the company, who didn't need practice in applying their make-up or dancing in costume, were scheduled to arrive later in the day.

'The first thing we're going to do is show you where you'll all be sitting backstage,' explained Janet after the new girls had assembled on stage. 'To the dressing-rooms, ladies.'

We followed her up a set of narrow, steep stairs to the low-ceilinged, claustrophobic girls' *loges*. There were a series of poky rooms with the 'nudes' separate from the cancan girls. Each dancer was allocated a seat in their respective room. 'My nudes in here please,' Janet called. We entered and saw that the walls were lined with mirrors, a neat border of light bulbs carving out the portion of mirror belonging to each girl. A collection of eyebrow pencils, mascara and blusher brushes competed for bench space with pancake-encrusted sponges, and hair nets and flesh-coloured G-strings hung listlessly from hooks above each place. To each mirror was pasted a collection of personal mementoes: photos of boyfriends or family members, pictures of sultry-eyed male models torn from magazines, hand-scribbled drawings from faraway nephews, *billets-doux* from lovers and notes of friendly abuse from colleagues. An out-of-date calendar of semi-naked rugby players held pride of place in the middle of the room. It was a typical dressing-room, only older and more stale-smelling than any I had worked in before.

Janet pointed to a chair in a corner. 'Shay, you'll be sitting here. Katie here. Jean, I've got you here and Jenny, over there, love.'

'Now get yourselves settled and let's get some slap on.'

Stage make-up application is an acquired skill. While it uses roughly the same tools as everyday make-up application, the results are vastly different – seen up close or in daylight, a fully made-up showgirl is a frightening thing. The make-up is so heavy she looks for all the world like a drag queen, with false eyelashes, heavy eye shadow, bright red lips and thick pancake. Yet seen from the auditorium, framed by over-the-top feathers and jewels and lit by harsh stage lights, she can look the epitome of glamour. It just takes a deft touch, specific skills and a few make-up secrets to get it right.

Before unleashing us on an unsuspecting cabaret-going public, Janet wanted to make sure we all took to the stage looking sophisticated and not like kids playing with Mum's make-up kit. And so she instructed us to apply full make-up for the dress rehearsal as if we were performing a show. Being a veteran of several professional shows, and armed with the make-up tips Corina had taught me at Jupiters, I had a fair idea of what I was doing.

Katie, on the other hand, clearly didn't have a clue. She looked with bemusement at the pile of make-up in front of me. 'I didn't realise we had to buy our own, I thought it was going to be supplied. And I thought there were going to be people doing our make-up every night.'

'Welcome to the real world of dancing, honey,' Jenny said, taking her seat and emptying the contents of an enormous make-up bag on the tabletop.

Katie looked forlornly at my make-up bag. 'Can I borrow yours?'

'Sure. You've never had to apply stage make-up?'

'Not really. I mean, we used eye shadow and lipstick for the end-of-year recital, but I've never even seen a fake eyelash before. I have no idea how to put one on.'

'It's easy. Here, I'll show you.'

I opened my make-up bag to get a pair of eyelashes, then closed it again for a minute. The best part of the make-up process, I always felt, was the transformation itself. I tried to explain this to Katie first. 'Even if you've had a rotten day and everything has gone wrong, or you feel like a total frump, you can leave it all behind you. If you've done the job properly, at the end of it you won't recognise yourself. Think of it as helping to get into character for the show.'

Recalling the speech Corina had made to me a few years earlier, I went on to explain that good showgirl make-up was all a matter of striking the right balance. 'The lights are unforgiving. If there's a wrinkle or a blemish on your skin the lights will find it, so the make-up has to be heavy. The main purpose of stage make-up is to accentuate your features – to make sure they don't get lost under all those feathers. The bigger and more over-the-top the costume, the heavier the make-up.'

Katie smiled and nodded.

'But you don't want to look like a man in drag. People are paying good money to see beautiful women up on stage. And that *salle* out there is more intimate than most. When we step out on stage, the audience will be so close they'll be able to see the whites of our eyes. So, while the make-up has to be heavy, it should also be subtle.'

Katie looked at me dubiously. 'Heavy and subtle?'

'Trust me. Just do what I do and it will all make sense.'

Daubing a sponge on the end of a large stick of pancake, I started spreading a thick covering of base across my face, throat and neck, blending as I went, evening out my complexion. With each flick of the sponge, freckles and blemishes magically disappeared. Next came a layer of thick powder, to make it all matte. Then, with a large brush, I applied pink blush.

'The blush accentuates your cheekbones', I said, reciting the gospel according to Corina. 'You want to make them look high.'

With a pencil, I got to work on shaping my eyebrows. The trick, I explained to Katie, who was watching in rapt, open-mouthed silence, was to re-draw to make them arched, symmetrical and, most importantly, visible.

'You're going to be wearing great big false eyelashes, and your eyes are going to be so dark and exaggerated by the lashes that you need to make sure your eyebrows are visible or you'll look odd.'

Then came the eyes. A dusting of white eyeshadow up under the eyebrows, more white on the eyelids, and layered shades of light brown, dark brown and black in the creases.

'The idea here is to blend the different colours to open your eyes up as much as possible, to better accentuate your expression onstage, and to make sure your eyes don't get lost amid the costume and eyelash action.'

After painting a thick black line of liquid eyeliner underneath my eyes and across the top of my eyelids, it was time to apply the false eyelashes. I opened my make-up bag again and selected one of my three plastic-encased sets. Then I took a tube of Copydex glue, dipped the tip of a bobby pin into the tube and smeared the white gooey stuff across the base of my lashes.

'What's that?' Katie asked.

'Copydex. It's a wood-modelling glue. Kids use it for craft or to make model planes. We use it because it holds all night but peels off like gum at the end of the show.'

Katie laughed.

'Now, this is the tricky bit,' I said as I carefully applied a lash. 'You have to get these on at the right angle or they hang down like a dead spider.'

I took the mascara brush and blended the false eyelashes with my own, finally sitting back and giving the eyes a blink to make sure everything was in working order.

Next, I painted onto my mouth the outline of a perfect pair of lips with dark red lip liner. 'Lip liner is magic stuff. It makes thin lips full and fat lips even. Just draw on the mouth you want and then colour it in with lipstick.'

The traditional showgirl look was all about false eyelashes and big red lips. It was, I reflected as I painted my face, not unlike decorating ourselves to look like dolls.

'And finally, the lipstick. The redder and brighter, the better.'

On top of the lipstick, I applied a thick layer of clear lip gloss to finish and sat back to stare at myself in the mirror. In the reflection, I could see Katie looking on in wonder.

'Scary, huh? I told you you wouldn't recognise me when it was done. Okay, now it's your turn.'

To the accompaniment of Jenny's out-of-tune humming and Jean's stream-of-consciousness ramblings, I looked on as Katie went through the make-up motions. We had ten minutes before we were due on stage.

Janet came into the dressing-room. 'How are we going in here, girls? Almost ready? Let's take a look then.'

She gave Jenny and Jean a once-over, making generally complimentary comments. 'What colour is that lipstick?' she asked Jenny.

'You need orange-red, love. I don't want any dark reds. We'll have no vampires here. *Pompier* red – think fire engine.'

To Jean, she advised more pink blush and a less obvious pair of false eyelashes. 'Where did you find those? They're enormous. You're a Doriss girl, not a drag queen.'

When she turned her attention to me, I was in the process of applying body make-up – because of the nudity, we were all required to smear ourselves in flesh-coloured body make-up before every performance. It meant applying foundation all over your breasts, stomach, chest and arms. Janet watched as I sat before the mirror, daintily dabbing at my torso with a tiny face sponge.

'Shay, what are you doing, love?'

I stopped and looked at her, confused.

'You'll be there all year with that dinky little thing. Here, allow me.'

Janet took my tiny sponge and threw it on the table. Reaching across me to the next dressing table, she picked up a sponge that looked like something my dad used to wash his car. 'Now this is what you need to get the job done properly. May I?'

Without waiting for me to answer, she up-ended the bottle of body make-up and set about smearing it all over me. Within twenty seconds I was done, covered from neck to hip in flesh paint.

'*Voilà,*' Janet said, holding the sponge in one hand and her cigarette in the other. 'Two francs fifty from Monoprix. Do yourself a favour.'

She turned her attention to Katie, standing to watch for a moment as Katie self-consciously tried to apply lipstick.

'Hmmm. This one is going to need a little bit of work. Katie, you're to come in early and sit watching the girls. You must copy and learn every night.' Then she saw Katie's distraught reflection in the mirror. 'Don't worry, you'll pick it up soon enough. And anyway, that will have to do for now, I want you all downstairs in five minutes. Gold prologue heels, strings and fishnets only please.'

As if meeting the complete company for the first time wasn't nerve-wracking enough, we were going to have to do it in next to no clothing. This was a last chance for Janet to see how we looked semi-naked and fully made-up on stage, to make sure we were ready to be revealed to the world as Moulin Rouge showgirls.

As I pulled on my fishnets and bent to do up the clasp on my heels, I glimpsed a series of tiny stomach rolls in the mirror. I did a mental count of the number of ham and cheese crepes I had scoffed between my initial weigh-in and today, stood up and sucked in my tummy.

Down on the stage, the company waited patiently for the new girls. We knew better than to keep them waiting too long. This dress rehearsal was purely for our benefit. The rest of the company all knew the show; they did it twice a night, six nights a week. You couldn't blame them if the majority were less than excited at the prospect of giving up a precious day off to walk through the show for the benefit of a handful of new girls. I shuffled self-consciously from the safety of the wings out onto the stage, and immediately felt the stares of forty sets of eyes upon me. I tried not to blush, tried to maintain my composure and not to shrink into myself, conscious that everyone was looking us up and down. Without meaning to, the new girls had formed a huddle, perhaps hoping that by sticking together we'd feel less naked.

In hindsight, it wasn't significantly different from other dress rehearsals I had done. The company contained the same cross-section of castmates that I had encountered in other shows. There were those who were simply annoyed at having to come in and rehearse, those who were genuinely excited to have new blood and new faces in the show, and those whose position in the company was so shaky that they saw our arrival as a threat. A good proportion of the eyes trained on us as we waited for Janet to launch proceedings were analysing every curve of our bodies. Were we thinner, younger, more beautiful than they were? How did we compare in terms of height? And what sort of dancers would we turn out to be? I tried not to shrink beneath the stares, looking to Jenny for moral support.

Brett and Matthew came up behind me, and Brett slipped his arm around my shoulders. 'Hello showgirl! Don't you scrub up well?'

I flashed him a nervous smile. 'Why do I feel like half the room is staring at us?' I whispered.

'Because they are, darl. And if you think the scrutiny is bad now, wait until you start dancing. That's when the knives will really come out.'

'Thanks for the words of encouragement.'

Megan broke away from a group of girls stretching downstage. 'You guys look great.'

I smiled at her, mostly out of gratitude for extending the hand of friendship.

'You'll be fine, it's a walk in the park. Get out there and be fabulous!'

Behind her, Marissa, the lead dancer and Corina's sister, came strolling into view, a broad smile on her face. When I'd watched her perform, I'd been mesmerised by her – when she took to the stage she lit up the room. She had been the picture of showgirl elegance, radiant in her costumes and so utterly graceful. Today she wore a tracksuit, no make-up and had her hair tied up with a scrunchie.

'G'day, how are you?' she asked, taking time to shake hands with every one of the new girls. 'I'm Marissa. Nice to meet you. Good luck today. You'll be fine.'

Unaffected, straightforward, friendly: I liked her immediately.

A loud blast of music pealed through the auditorium, followed by the screech of feedback from a microphone. 'Can you all hear me?' Janet's voiced boomed over the speakers. The entire company winced.

'Good, then let's begin. New girls, into your costumes now please.'

It took four hours to block the show. Blocking required Janet or Thierry, the company manager, to count out each number as we walked through our dance steps. There was no music, just the monotonous drone of 'One, two, three, four, five, six, seven, eight, and one, two, three, four . . .' over and over again. The majority of the dancers had done the show so many times they could do it with their eyes closed. For the new girls, however, it was an exhausting four hours of cramming into our heads as much information as possible. We had to perform them while also taking note of which partners we were to perform them with, which parts of the stage we were to perform them on, which pieces of set we were to perform them around and which sides of the stage we were to enter and exit by. It was called learning the 'traffic' of the show. A wrong turn or misstep could earn you a boot in the face.

Katie fared the worst. It wasn't that she couldn't dance: throughout the rehearsal period she had proven herself as capable as anyone else of learning and retaining the chorie. But, feeling the pressure of performing under the unforgiving glare of her new castmates, she messed up in almost every number.

'What's going on Katie?' Janet demanded of her at one point. 'I know you can do this, I've seen you in rehearsals. For goodness' sake, concentrate!'

When the rehearsal was over, after hours of blocking, and of desperately trying to remember my choreography and not get in anyone's way, I was drained. 'See you all back here tomorrow at midday for the full dress rehearsal!' Janet called as we filed out of the building. 'Tomorrow night is showtime, boys and girls! Everyone early to bed tonight please.'

I dragged myself home with the full intention of collapsing on the bed. But as I walked in the door, I saw that Steve was busy in the kitchen: he was leaning over the tiny two-burner hotplate tending to a boiling pot.

'Hey,' he said smiling. 'You're back. Sit down, put your feet up. Dinner will be ready in ten minutes.'

I stood in the doorway looking at him suspiciously. In all the time we'd been together so far, he had cooked for me twice. I should have been touched that he'd made the effort tonight, but instead I was annoyed. I shuffled over and flopped down on the bed, removing my shoes and rubbing my feet. On the TV, the evening news unfurled in rapid-fire French.

'So, how was your day?' Steve asked, pouring me a glass of wine.

It was nice to be looked after and pampered a little, but everything felt forced and not particularly right. That night I lay awake and stared out the window long after Steve had fallen asleep next to me. I knew the relationship wasn't working but I didn't know how to make it better. Or even if I wanted to.

We were back onstage at midday the following day. There was a new sense of urgency to proceedings, a buzz in the air as set and sound technicians, lighting guys, stagehands and dressers raced about the *salle* and dodged one another backstage. For the first time I started to get a sense of the mechanics of the Moulin Rouge. The onstage choreography hardly compared to the backstage choreography: the members of the behind-the-scenes team danced in the dark to make the magic happen.

It was the first time we had worked with the Moulin dressers. With sometimes only thirty seconds between flying offstage in one huge costume and running back onstage in another, the quick change was going to become our stock-in-trade. On this, our first proper run-through, there were disasters galore. If there was a system, it wasn't obvious to me. As best I could work out, at the end of a number anywhere up to twenty-eight girls would dart backstage and hurl themselves in front of a dresser. Backpacks would be removed, zips undone, clasps unhooked and costumes shimmied down over hips so that the showgirl could step out of one costume and be hoisted into the next. Huge diamanté bracelets would be thrust onto outstretched arms and hats unceremoniously shoved onto hairnet-encased heads.

Complicating matters even more was the '*poubelle*' system. Each girl was assigned a square, orange plastic mop bucket, labelled with her name scribbled on a scrap of masking tape. In the buckets, or *poubelles* as Janet called them, were placed all of the accessories needed for the show – earrings, bracelets, anklets, gloves, and so on. The *poubelles* were then lined up backstage, so that when quick changes took place, each dancer could run to her *poubelle* and don the necessary bling. Which might have worked as a system, were it not for the fact that all the *poubelles* were identical in colour and shape and that backstage was not only dark but also the scene of unconstrained chaos. The end result was a stampede of Amazons, reaching across one another, grasping for identical mop buckets. To compound the chaos, the wings of the stage were tiny and cramped. The quick change area was so crowded that dressers were forced to huddle under stairwells and costumes had to be ferried in and out of the backstage area as required.

I somehow managed to scrape through the dress rehearsal without too many hiccups, earning a shout from Janet only once, when, during doughnuts, I turned the wrong way and slammed into one of the older girls, who glared at me and pushed me away violently.

By five o'clock, the rehearsal was over. Thierry had joined proceedings to assist Janet. He sat us down on the stage and together they issued corrections. I was relieved that only half of them were directed at the new girls, with many of the oldies being instructed to give more energy or tighten up their choreography.

As we turned to file off to the dressing-rooms and change, Janet called me over. I approached thinking the worst, worried there was something wrong with my performance – something so fundamental it could only be communicated in private.

'Take a seat, Shay, love,' she said. I felt my heart beating. 'Here's the thing. I'm looking at Melissa up there on stage, and I'm not convinced she's lost any weight.'

A wave of relief passed over me. It wasn't about me after all. I didn't know what to say, or if indeed I was expected to say anything, so I just gave a slight nod.

'A girl's got to look like she fits in the line,' Janet continued. 'If we have a row of beautiful bodies up there and one that's slightly heavier, it ruins the whole line.'

She seemed to be trying to convince me. I found myself wondering why I'd been chosen to take part in this conversation.

'I think she's a lovely dancer, and I think she's a lovely girl, but if the Big Boss sees her on stage tonight, I'm worried he won't be impressed.'

I gave a barely perceptible nod, fearing that to agree too volubly would be to betray Melissa. Was Janet telling me Melissa was about to be sacked? My mind started to race.

'I'm not sure I know what you're saying,' I finally ventured.

'What I'm saying is, I'm not sure it's going to work out with Melissa.'

My heart sank. Was she serious? Was she really saying that this girl, who had moved from Australia, quit her job, packed up her life, forked out her life savings to take an apartment in Paris, rehearsed day and night for four weeks and dieted herself to the point of collapse, was going to be sacked on her opening night because her thighs were slightly too heavy?

'Oh,' was all I could manage in response. 'I see.' And then, processing the information, I sat there wondering what I had done to deserve being taken into Janet's confidence and burdened with this.

'I'm only telling you,' Janet began, as if reading my mind, 'because you seem to be friendly with her, and she might need some moral support. If it's okay, I'd like you to be here in my office at 1 p.m. tomorrow when I break the news to her.'

Excellent. So on top of the stress and nervousness of taking to the Moulin stage for the first time, I was going to have to carry around the knowledge that just when she should be on the professional high of her life, a colleague was about to be devastated.

I slunk back upstairs to the *loge*, plonked down at my place and tried not to think about it. But I couldn't push it from my mind. I couldn't help but put myself in Melissa's shoes and imagine how humiliating it would be to be told you were too fat to perform.

With only three hours to go before we were expected to be back at work, Jenny and Jean and I decided not to go home. Instead, we went outside to grab a crepe. I wasn't hungry, the nerves had seen to that, but I knew I was in for a long night and so I forced myself to eat. We sat, wrapped in our coats, on a park bench in the tree-lined pedestrian section of Boulevard de Clichy, silently munching our crepes. I wanted to unburden the Melissa baggage that had been foisted upon me, but finally decided against it, figuring it was better to preserve the poor girl's dignity for as long as possible.

Early evening peak-hour traffic clogged the boulevard in both directions. Exhaust fumes from idling cars hung in the air. Even through the kaleidoscope of Pigalle neon, the Moulin Rouge stood out a mile, the brightly lit sails of the windmill turning slowly against an indigo sky. I thought of my mum on the other side of the earth. I thought of all of the dance classes she had faithfully driven me to and the eisteddfods she had stoically endured, and wished she could be here now, to see me take my first steps onto the stage of the world's most famous cabaret. And then I thought of Steve, and how he'd shown no interest in trying to come along to my opening night. It was disappointing that he wouldn't be in the audience, but if I was honest, I really didn't care. Deep down I knew that unless things took a dramatic turn for the better, the relationship wasn't destined to last.

'Come on then, showgirl,' Jenny said, jolting me from my thoughts. 'We've got a show to put on.'

## Chapter Seventeen

The opening night of any new show always gets the adrenaline going. As I walked back into the Moulin Rouge after my kerbside crepe, I felt my stomach do a nervous flip.

Determined to be as prepared as possible, Jenny, Jean, Katie and I had decided to get ourselves ready and do our make-up early. By 7.30 p.m., when all the other dressing-rooms were still empty and the auditorium was only just starting to be filled by the first of the diners, the four of us were sitting alone in our *loge* wearing fishnets, heels and T-shirts, showered, hair pulled back and full faces of make-up on. The curtain on the first show was scheduled to rise at 9 p.m., so we had a long and nerve-wracking wait ahead of us.

Thankfully, as our castmates started trickling in, it didn't take long for distractions to arrive.

Faye was the first to come through the dressing-room door. A vision in stone-washed jeans and trainers, her mousy hair pulled back in a ponytail, she looked more like a cleaner than a showgirl. At first glance I thought she was someone's mum, come to drop off some forgotten part of her glamorous daughter's make-up kit.

'Hi, I'm Faye,' she said, plonking herself down on her chair and staring blankly into a mirror decorated with photos of a small boy. It seemed as if that was all the conversation she had the energy to engage in. She had come to Paris to dance ten years earlier, met a French man and settled down. By default rather than design she had become part of the furniture at the Moulin Rouge. She had gradually lost enthusiasm for the work, but French labour laws being what they were, she was impossible to sack and she was never going to walk away from a regular paying gig. Each night she left her five-year-old son at home, shuffled into work, slapped on her make-up and summoned just enough energy to get her through another couple of performances. She was friendly and sweet, but not exactly inspiring.

Next to arrive was Fifi, a stunning black Frenchwoman. She had long black hair swept up in a French roll, great cheekbones and a dazzling smile. Her tiny waist and impressive cleavage were highlighted by a tailored suit, over which she wore a chic black overcoat.

'I'm Fifi – very nice to meet you,' she said, her heavy French accent dripping like honey. 'Welcome to the Moulin Rouge.'

Fifi had been dancing at the Moulin Rouge longer than any of the other girls. No-one knew for sure, for no-one dared ask, but there were rumours she was forty years old. No matter what her age, she was still holding her own in the nude line. She had beautiful, flawless skin and, as I soon discovered, pert, full breasts that would have been the envy of your average eighteen-year-old.

Just then, Megan sailed in. '*Salut, salut. Ça va tout le monde?*'

I was relieved to see a familiar face.

'Are the girls making you all feel welcome?' Megan asked as she took her place in front of her mirror and switched on the lightbulbs. She didn't wait for an answer.

'Big night tonight ladies,' she continued, addressing Jenny and me. 'The Big Boss will be in as usual: he always comes and watches when there are new girls starting. Wants to make sure the new recruits are up to scratch. No-one will be daring to put a foot wrong tonight.'

The Big Boss was a man I had heard a lot about during rehearsals. I had never seen him, though, and so he had assumed a ghost-like persona in my mind, hovering ominously above the Moulin Rouge, watching everything and everyone.

Despite managing Paris's most famous nightspot he only had a minor appreciation of the finer points of dancing. What he did know was exactly what he liked to see onstage, and what he believed tourists paid good money to come and see, and that was pretty girls. He was renowned for coming to watch the show and arbitrarily dismissing dancers who he thought were too fat or too ugly. The mere mention of his name would set fear into the hearts of some of the older dancers, who knew that with every day that passed, their claim to a place in the Moulin Rouge chorus line grew ever more shaky.

From down the corridor, a loud, hacking laugh floated into the dressing-room.

'And that would be Sophie,' Megan said, as she leaned into the mirror and started applying lip liner.

Tall, slim, with long straight blonde hair and a set of blue eyes that sparkled with mischief, Sophie crashed into the dressing-room, laughing loudly. She pulled off a black trench coat to reveal a pair of low-slung, hip-hugging jeans, a designer top and a pair of Gucci heels. Either she was planning a night out after the show, or she hadn't yet made it home from the previous evening's nocturnal activities.

'*Salut!*' she screeched in a broad English accent, throwing down her handbag and dropping into her chair. 'Oh God. I'm not well.' She laughed again.

'Sophie, this is Shay, Jenny and – I'm sorry, I've forgotten your names,' Megan said.

'I'm Jean and this is Katie,' Jean piped up.

'Oh hi, nice to meet you,' Sophie said, turning briefly in our direction before spinning back on her chair to engage Megan in whispered, giggling conversation.

Sophie hailed from London and had been dancing at the Moulin Rouge for a year. She was in her early twenties and a striking beauty, and Paris had taken to Sophie with almost as much gusto as Sophie had taken to Paris. She had embraced the special status afforded Moulin Rouge dancers and used it to her social advantage. There was hardly a VIP *soirée* or exclusive event to which she wasn't invited. According to Brett, Sophie and Megan comprised a two-person party machine. They were not averse to the odd late night and keenly exploited the good looks that God had bestowed upon them.

Sophie stripped naked, pulled on her G-string, fishnets and heels, and sat topless in front of the mirror to apply foundation. With only half her face painted, she seemed to run out of steam.

'Can't cope, need a fag.' She threw down her make-up sponge, wrapped a towel around her waist and marched topless out into the corridor to light up a cigarette.

I threw an amused look at Megan.

'Don't pay any attention to her,' she said. 'She's not well.'

'Not well,' I would later discover, had less to do with your physical health than with how convincingly – or not – you had recovered from the night before.

I sat on the dressing-room floor, stretching and warming up, while nervously watching the clock crawl towards 9 p.m. My *poubelle* was packed and ready to go. 'Is everything okay?' I asked Katie, looking up to the dressing table. 'Do you need any help with your eyelashes?'

She looked back at me with a wide-eyed look of terror. 'God, I'm so scared. What if I stuff up out there again tonight?'

'You'll be fine. I'll keep an eye on you. And besides, we're all nervous. Right Jean?'

'Never felt more terrified in my life,' Jean replied cheerily. 'Sweetheart, you'll be fine. You're going to go out there tonight and wow them.'

At around 8.30 p.m., with only a half-hour to go before the curtain rose, Big Nic sailed casually into the dressing-room and sat herself down.

'*Ciao*, girls,' she purred. '*C'est* opening night. *C'est fabuleux. J'adore.*'

As the nude line dance captain, it was Nic's responsibility to take into account which girls were dancing and which ones were off, and reblock the show accordingly. The dressers then had to be informed of which costumes each girl would be wearing in each number. But Nic didn't seem the least bit hurried. In between the leisurely application of her make-up, she issued the occasional order to a dresser or yelled down the corridor to inform one hapless dancer or another that her show had changed at the last minute.

'Odette, I need you to be Veronique in doughnuts, *chérie*,' Nic would say. 'And Felicity, tonight you're Melinda in the prologue and cancan.' She never received a response, but seemed utterly unconcerned about whether her messages had found their mark.

'Fifteen minutes to curtain,' came a heavily accented voice over the tannoy. 'This is your fifteen-minute call.'

We new girls were starting to pace nervously while Nic was still in jeans and a T-shirt, methodically applying eyelashes.

'Relax, girls,' she said with a smile. 'It's only the fifteen-minute call.'

We retreated to our dressing tables and sat down.

'*Elles sont où? Elles sont où Jennee et Shay?*' Nadine's voice came floating down the corridor towards our dressing-room. '*Et voila! Vous êtes là, mes biches! Montrez-moi vos doggies.*'

We turned to face Nadine and show her that we had properly attached our doggies.

'*Parfait, ils sont parfait.* Good luck tonight!'

Just then, a slight girl with mousy brown hair and a pair of glasses over beautiful blue eyes appeared at the door.

'Shay,' Nic called out. 'Come and meet your dresser, Celeste.'

'*Bonsoir,*' the twenty-something girl said, proffering a cheek for me to peck. 'Welcome.'

'*Bonsoir,*' I replied. 'Thank you. Nice to meet you.'

In broken English, Celeste explained the first few changes she would be helping me through before disappearing.

Nic turned back to the mirror and started pulling on her fishnets.

Seconds later, Janet arrived at the door brandishing a brown cigarillo.

'*Merde* everyone! *Merde* girls!' she said, using the French stage cry for good luck. '*Merde* Shay! And nice make-up too. Now let me see your tights. Make sure the seam is straight. I do like a straight seam.'

And in a puff of smoke, she was gone.

'Five minutes to curtain. This is your five-minute call,' the announcement crackled over the tannoy. Butterflies started fluttering wildly in my stomach.

They calmed momentarily at the sound of Brett's voice outside the dressing-room door.

'Boy in the *loge*! Boy in the *loge*! Is everyone decent?' Without waiting for a reply, he came sailing in. He was dressed in his opening number outfit – the electric blue sequinned jumpsuit with the yellow collar. He looked hilariously camp.

'Oh Marge! Look at you! You look fab.' He bent down to give me a squeeze. 'I can't believe this is happening. To think it all began at the Tivoli in Fortitude Valley.'

'God, I can't remember the last time I felt this nervous,' I said.

'Don't sweat it. You have nothing to be afraid of or nervous about. You're going to be great.' He squeezed my hand. 'I have to run and get into position. See you out there.'

With two minutes to go, Nic lifted herself airily from her dressing table.

'Okay girls, showtime. Let's get that body make-up on.'

The girls who weren't already topless removed their shirts. Jenny, Jean, Katie and I looked briefly at one another before following suit. I did my best to look as if standing topless in a room full of strangers came naturally to me, and followed the others as they filed outside to the trough sink in the corridor. Hands grabbed at a collection of filthy body sponges and started hurriedly dipping them into a collection of dirty discs of pancake make-up.

A male technician wearing a headset ran hurriedly by. 'One minute to curtain!' he yelled as he went.

Nobody seemed to flinch. I fought the urge to cover myself up and instead busied myself with the body make-up, making a messy job of it as my hands jerked nervously from pancake disc to torso. I glanced across at Katie, who was still wearing her look of horror. She daubed at the pancake discs in a mild panic and rubbed the sponge over her chest. Silhouetted in the half-light of backstage, she suddenly looked so young and vulnerable: just a scared little skinny kid, clearly out of her comfort zone.

We rushed down the stairs, *poubelles* in hand, placed them against the wall in the wings and stood still while dressers busied themselves behind us. Celeste appeared from nowhere and strapped me into my feathered backpack.

The backstage lights dimmed and the stage manager began to prowl his domain, indicating melodramatically with a forefinger to his lips for everyone to be silent. As I moved into position on the stairs, a group of stagehands dressed head to toe in black bustled around me. Again, I fought the urge to cover myself up. Through the curtain, I could hear the hubbub of the *salle*: glasses clinking, people talking and laughing, the pop of champagne corks.

'Ladies and gentlemen,' came a sultry female voice over the front-of-house speakers. 'The show is about to start. We remind you there is no photographs or filming allowed.'

The audience fell quiet. The backstage lights faded to black. Just as we'd rehearsed, I stood frozen in position in the dark as the curtain slowly rose. The first bars of music burst across the auditorium. The sense of anticipation from the *salle* was palpable. I could make out the faint silhouettes of eight hundred heads in the darkness, all of them straining, re-positioning, peering excitedly into the blackness up on stage.

As the music blared and built to a crescendo, the stage lights flicked on suddenly revealing a collection of carefully poised, semi-naked, long-legged showgirls, festooned with jewels and swathed in a colour-burst of bright orange feathers. The audience gasped.

Goosebumps rose on my arms and tears began to well in my eyes. Exhausted after weeks of rehearsal, yet exhilarated at finally being on stage, I felt the nerves slide off me and the choreography take hold.

The opening number passed in a blur. When it came time for me to strut downstage towards the audience, it was all I could do not to burst with happiness. The stage lights bounced off an auditorium of faces filled with wonder and delight, so close you felt you could reach out and touch them. While it created an intimate ambience, it also made me feel suddenly exposed. A little bit more distance between my bare breasts and the 800-strong audience would not have gone astray. Still, determined to remain professional, I pasted a showgirl smile to my face and performed. For the next five minutes I felt acutely self-conscious. But then, as I concentrated on the choreography and allowed myself to be carried away again by the costumes, the lights and the feeling of excited anticipation from the *salle*, I lost myself happily in the performance.

At the end of every number, I raced offstage, undoing clips and hooks, and stood in front of Celeste as she ripped one costume from my back and replaced it with another. A mad scramble through my *poubelle* produced whatever accessories I needed for each number. Miraculously, and against all laws of organisation and logic, the *poubelle* and dresser system seemed to be working.

At one point, as I stood in the wings catching my breath and watching the show, Melissa sidled up beside me.

'Isn't this amazing?' she said, her eyes shining. 'I mean, can you believe you're actually here, doing this?'

'Yeah. Amazing.' It was all I could do to look her in the eye.

Other than narrowly avoiding an onstage collision in doughnuts and almost breaking a leg rushing down the stairs from the dressing-room to the stage to make it in time for the tap dance, I managed to survive my first performance without major incident. When the cancan music struck up, I stood in the wings and watched with admiration as the guys and girls threw themselves violently about the stage. In a frenzy of cartwheels and splits and to the accompaniment of their own high-pitched squealing and catcalls, they once again brought the audience to its feet. This was what it was all about. Doing what I loved, dancing on stage, wowing audiences and feeding off their energy.

By the time we performed the finale I was giddy with joy, and walked forward proudly to take my bow. As the stage lights went down and the curtain fell, I felt a wave of elation, followed quickly by one of complete exhaustion.

'Nice job ladies,' Nic could be heard saying as we trooped offstage and started climbing the stairs to the dressing-room. My feet felt heavy, my legs felt like lead and my shoulders sagged. As I entered the dressing-room and sat down to catch my breath, the now-familiar voice came over the tannoy.

'Fifteen minutes to curtain, this is your fifteen-minute call.'

Sophie and Megan chatted animatedly in a corner. Faye started eating a sandwich; Fifi began reapplying her make-up. Jean and Jenny were giggling in a kind of post-show delirium, while Katie just looked shell-shocked. I was struggling to process what had just happened to me and yet the countdown had already begun for the second show. We began to steel ourselves to do it all over again as another fresh-faced group of tourists queued outside, waiting to be herded into the theatre.

While nothing could tarnish the excitement I felt at that moment, I glimpsed the well-oiled Moulin Rouge machine and understood how tiny a cog I was in it. Like the windmill out front, it just kept turning.

I blinked away my thoughts and began touching up my make-up. Before I knew it the backstage lights had faded to black and the curtain was rising again.

As I dragged myself upstairs to the dressing-room after the final curtain call, I could hear the showers running already. The three showerheads in the tiny tiled cubicle just off our dressing-room were spewing forth steaming-hot water; I blanched at the sight of three castmates, naked but for gaudy shower caps, casually scrubbing off their body make-up with soaped-up loofahs and shower flowers. Each girl's G-string hung limply from the tap in front of her. There was a queue of girls patiently waiting their turn, all naked but for a pair of plastic flip flops and a shower cap.

'Fannies and armpits, girls! Keep it quick! Fannies and armpits!' came the cry, in a broad Aussie accent, from one of the dancers in the queue. I winced.

At the long trough sink in the hallway, three girls stood before the mirror, working off their make-up with baby oil. A long flesh-coloured streak of oily water ran the length of the sink and disappeared down the drain.

Sophie and Megan sat just outside the dressing-room, topless, with only towels around their waists, sucking on cigarettes and swigging from a bottle of rosé.

It was too much. I'd had enough gratuitous nudity for one night. I sat down at my dressing table and scraped surreptitiously at my body make-up with a handful of cotton pads. There would be no shower for me at the Moulin Rouge tonight. I didn't have the energy for more self-consciousness. I dressed and made to leave.

As I gathered my stuff, a freshly scrubbed face appeared at the dressing-room door bearing a large bunch of flowers.

It was Alison, one of the older cancan dancers. We had crossed paths several times in rehearsals. She wore a tracksuit top and a pair of jeans; her short, wet hair was pulled back off her face with a headband.

'Is there anyone in here called Shay?'

'That's me,' I replied.

She looked me up and down. It was a look of complete disdain.

'These came for you.' She thrust the flowers into my arms. I glanced at the note and could just make out the words 'Love, Mum and Dad'. A smile spread across my face.

'Thanks,' I said. 'They're from my parents.'

'How nice for you,' she replied. 'By the way, make sure you're faster exiting the stage before the cancan tomorrow. You were in our way tonight. You're not the only person on stage, you know.' She turned and left.

I stood there, stunned, feeling as if the wind had just been punched out of me. I turned to Megan. 'What was that all about?'

'Alison? She's a nightmare. Don't worry, you'll get used to her.'

# Chapter Eighteen

It was grey and cold when I woke, and Steve had already left the apartment. He would come back later in the day and no doubt tell me he'd been out job-hunting, but I knew he was more than likely to have been at the movies. The previous week, while doing the washing, I had found ticket stubs in his jeans pockets.

I dragged myself out of bed, my limbs heavy. The physical exertion and anxiety of the night before had taken their toll: I felt like I had been hit by a truck. The gradual realisation that I had to be in Janet's office in an hour for the dismissal of a fellow dancer did nothing to lighten my mood. I ate a light breakfast and headed out the door, hunkering into my overcoat as I stepped onto the street.

Half an hour later, I was trudging along the wet pavement towards the Moulin Rouge. Pigalle looked typically dirty in the daylight. A couple of black men in green uniforms poked indolently at the gutters with their long plastic brooms, nudging a collection of cigarette butts and kebab remnants into a small torrent of water that was sluicing its way towards the drain.

By the time I reached Rue Lepic and the stage door, Melissa was already there.

'Oh my God!' she exclaimed upon seeing me. 'I thought it was only me!' There was a look of relief on her face.

My heart quickened briefly. I'd vainly hoped she would be aware of what was to befall her. But the searching look in her eyes, the slight nervousness to her tone told me otherwise.

'What do you suppose she wants to see us for?' She looked at me imploringly. It was a fair bet she hadn't gotten much sleep the night before.

Melissa pushed on the stage door and went in. 'Well, if it's about the weight, I've lost five kilos since my weigh-in. I've practically lived on air and water. And I live above a *boulangerie*. It's been torture.'

I nodded and smiled again as we wended our way toward Janet's office.

'Mum's coming to visit in June. I can't wait. She's never been to Europe, she's so excited about coming to Paris. She's been telling everyone how her daughter is a Moulin Rouge dancer. She's so proud.'

At that moment, Janet emerged from her office, saw the pair of us and ushered us inside. 'Take a seat girls, take a seat,' she said.

We pushed aside the piles of paper on the chairs in front of her desk and perched gingerly on the edges. Janet took up position behind her desk, her elbows on the tabletop, her hands making an inverted 'V' under her nose.

'Lovely show last night girls, both of you did very well,' Janet began. I looked past her, fixing my stare on the exposed brick of the wall behind her head. 'But as you know, the Moulin has very high standards when it comes to the girls we employ. People travel here from all over the world to see the famous Doriss Girls in action. Which is why we have to work very hard to maintain a certain standard in terms of physical appearance.'

I glanced quickly across at Melissa. If she was starting to cotton on to the drift of Janet's conversation, she was doing an excellent job of hiding it. I found myself biting my bottom lip.

'Now Melissa, you know that when I offered you a contract, it was conditional on you losing a little bit of weight.'

Suddenly the mood in the room changed. Beside me I could hear the penny drop: Melissa emitted a short, sharp whimper as the truth started to hit home. I didn't dare look at her.

'Now you're a lovely dancer and a lovely girl,' Janet continued, leaning towards Melissa, trying to cushion the blow. 'And I know you've been trying hard to shed some of that weight. But sweetheart, I just don't think it's going to work. Your legs are shorter and heavier than I first thought, and onstage they just don't measure up to the other girls'. They don't look right in the line.'

She sat back in her chair, giving it time to hit home. In Janet's defence, you could tell this was a part of her job she hated. Keen to be approachable and friendly, preferring to be considered one of the girls, she squirmed uncomfortably whenever she had to perform one of the less pleasant duties that her title demanded of her.

Melissa let out a cry. The cry became a sob, and for a good minute I wished for all the world that I could just sink into my chair and disappear. Tears started welling in my own eyes as I reached across and pulled Melissa's head onto my shoulders. She was so consumed by her own grief, she hadn't yet thought to wonder what my role in her dismissal was.

'I'm so sorry, sweetheart,' Janet said, passing a tissue across the desk. And then, for want of anything more appropriate, she reached for a cliché: 'This can be a cruel business. Just because you've not got the right look for this show doesn't mean you won't be perfect for something else. That's showbiz.'

Melissa stood up and Janet made her way around the desk to give her a hug. It was too much for Melissa to take. She melted into Janet's arms and dissolved into tears again.

After a spell, Janet looked at me.

'Shay honey, why don't you take Melissa up to her dressing-room and help her pack her things. Take your time, love.'

I gathered Melissa up and we turned to leave the office.

'And of course if you need a reference,' Janet sang out to Melissa's retreating back. 'I'll be more than happy to supply you with one.'

By the time I had hobbled with a bawling Melissa to the dressing-rooms, the full extent of what had happened had sunk in.

'But I just signed for an apartment! What am I going to tell my family? I left a perfectly good job in Australia to accept this position!'

The dressing-room suddenly seemed stuffy and airless and I was at a loss to know what to say. So complete was Melissa's humiliation, and so utterly shattered was she by it, that I could barely bring myself to look at her.

And then, pausing in the process of packing up her make-up, she turned her red, tear-streaked face towards me and said: 'But you knew, didn't you? How long have you known?'

I fumbled for a response, spitting out a few noncommittal sounds before finally managing, 'Janet told me last night between shows. I don't know why. She thought you would take the news better if a friend was here. I wanted to tell you, honestly I did.'

'But why didn't you tell me? Why didn't you say something?'

'It wasn't my place. And besides, I didn't see the point in ruining your opening night.' I paused, suddenly aware of how inadequate my excuse sounded. 'I'm sorry if that was wrong.'

I was angry at having been involved in her dismissal; angry at the shallow, capricious nature of the business we were in.

'Listen, if there is anything I can do to help,' I offered. 'With the apartment or anything . . .'

Melissa nodded, blowing her nose.

I stayed with her in the dressing-room, trying to make myself useful by handing her bits of make-up, peeling family photos from her mirror, folding her bath towel and helping to stuff her bag. Part of the reason I wasn't coping with the whole situation was that it so easily could have been me.

My livelihood, my continued existence in Paris and in some senses my entire career rested on a knife's edge. Whether it was something as seemingly arbitrary as a pair of slightly heavy thighs, an unexpected injury or the Big Boss taking an irrational dislike to the way you happened to look one night on stage, a showgirl had decidedly shaky job security. The overridingly fickle nature of the industry we had chosen to work in meant that we were only ever as good as our last high-kick.

I walked Melissa to the stage door; she went home to call her parents. Later that day, I helped her start looking for someone to take over her apartment and buy her belongings, figuring it was best to keep her busy with logistics.

To her immense credit, Melissa chose not to be crushed by her Moulin Rouge experience. Instead of buckling and returning to Australia with her tail between her legs, she picked herself up, dusted herself down and got herself a job at the Royal Palace – a large cabaret venue in the tiny township of Kirrwiller, near Strasbourg. And not just any job. She was employed as the lead dancer.

My first month on stage at the Moulin Rouge sped by, and Christmas came and went. This year, however, there was no money for a tree, a turkey or gifts, and with relations between Steve and me increasingly strained, Christmas was a very flat affair.

I worked Christmas night: it was one of the Moulin's busiest evenings of the year. It seemed odd to me that people would come to a cabaret show at Christmas instead of sitting around a table with family.

In the *loge*, under tinsel we'd hung in an attempt to create a festive atmosphere, we threw a small party during the *entracte* (interval). Friendships with my new colleagues had started to solidify and these people were increasingly becoming my surrogate family. We stood around trying to muster Christmas spirit, yet feeling a long way from home.

I was still finding my way through every performance, while backstage I was being entertained by the eccentric cast of characters.

I'd finally conquered my shower phobia and would join the queue of naked girls lining up to scrub down each night. But I noticed that no-one ever wanted to shower next to Fifi, and asked Megan if she knew why.

'Cold showers,' Megan replied. 'She only ever takes cold showers. No matter what time of year. Summer, winter, it's always cold showers. She says it keeps her skin taut and her breasts pert.'

Whether it was the cold showers or a gift from God, there was no denying she looked amazing for a woman in her mid-forties. Even so, I wasn't about to start taking cold showers in an attempt to ward off the ageing process.

I was also starting to notice idiosyncratic behaviour from my *loge* mate Faye. At the end of prologue – the opening fifteen-minute section of the show – the nudes had a ten-minute break, and every night Faye would sit at her dressing table, roll her fishnets down to her knees and start eating a banana. Every night, the same tight-rolling ritual with the same fruit at the same time.

She caught me looking one night and felt compelled to explain. 'The fishnets chafe me up there,' she said, pointing the banana at her groin.

I soon learned that it wasn't just her backstage antics that raised eyebrows. She was also unwittingly providing the boy dancers with free entertainment each time she took to the stage for the opening number. Positioned behind me on the stairs during the show's big opener, she'd often have a group of boy dancers gathered in the wings, imitating her.

'She never moves her feet,' Brett explained when I quizzed him about it one night at Jimmy's after work. 'It's the funniest thing. She thinks that because she's right up the back, she can just do the chorie above the waist, and that no-one is any the wiser.'

It was almost as comical an effort as that turned in each night by one of the other more senior members of the company, an English dancer that Brett and Matthew fondly referred to as 'Sally Fan-kick'. Like Faye, Sally had been dancing at the Moulin Rouge for a whole lot longer than any paying customer should have reasonably been exposed to. She looked great but pushing forty she simply couldn't perform some of the show's most basic choreography anymore. For the Viennese waltz we would perform a sequence of fan-kicks, exposing the multicoloured linings of our ballgowns to the audience in one fluid wave. It was a fast enough maneouvre that Sally was able to fudge her fan-kick. She no longer had the flexibility required to lift her leg sufficiently high, so she opted to simply throw her skirt up in a wide arc using her hands.

These women had a wealth of performance experience and a level of maturity that was often lacking in the occasionally bitchy backstage environment, but it still seemed odd that the Moulin Rouge would be so exacting when it recruited new girls, but so reluctant to put the old ones out to pasture. The fact these older dancers dared to take to the stage each night and turn in a half-baked performance was less astonishing to me than the fact that it was tolerated.

'Faye, I need you to replace Natalia tonight,' Big Nic said one night as we sat doing our make-up.

'Oh no, I can't,' Faye replied matter-of-factly. 'Not tonight. The Big Boss is in. I can't be seen. I have to stay up the back. He's tried to fire me three times already. If he sees me out there onstage tonight he's going to have a coronary.'

And so it became Nic's job to not only rearrange the show, but to do it in such a way that the underperformers were well hidden for each number. The show was blocked around whoever needed to be out of view in order to stop the Boss from going on a firing spree. The conspiracy had seen Faye and Sally evade the cut on more than one occasion, and had allowed them to keep performing long after their high-kicks had run out of oomph.

It just didn't seem fair that Melissa, who had worked her heart out every day in rehearsals, could be dismissed for something as arbitrary as slightly heavy thighs while these oldies fudged their way through each night's show.

One month in and the cracks in the Moulin's heavily made-up *façade* were starting to open up into canyons. Yet in spite of its seemingly illogical politics, there was still enough magic in the old theatre and enough excitement in performing there each night that I was slowly but surely falling in love with it.

Despite my dramas with Steve, life after work started to become fun. Drinks at Jimmy's became an almost nightly ritual. On the evenings we really wanted to push the boat out, we'd troop out of the stage door and head across Boulevard de Clichy to the Le Palmier cafe, where a *croque-monsieur* and a couple of Monacos (pints of beer with grenadine) would be ordered and devoured.

In those first few months, barely a night went by that there wasn't a cast get-together of some description. We were all living in broom closets of varying size and comfort, and most of us were experiencing the culture shock of having moved to France. We were alone, without family support or networks of friends, and we were all high on the excitement of being in Paris and dancing at the Moulin Rouge. On the nights we weren't crammed into Jimmy's or gorging ourselves on *croque-monsieurs* at Le Palmier, we would gather at one another's apartments for impromptu post-show parties. Jean quickly became the queen of the studio *soirées*, relishing the prospect of a captive audience to listen to her steady stream of chat and sample whatever finger food she felt inspired to whip up.

'Come back to mine,' she said one night after a show. 'I've got chickpeas. I'll make hummus.' And so she would, while twenty of us crammed into her tiny 23-metre-squared apartment on Rue Fontaine. We'd lie on her bed, sprawl on her floor or hang smoking from the window, drinking cheap red wine, chatting and listening to her impressive collection of show tunes.

Sophie would invariably spend much of the time on her phone, texting the mysterious forces that seemed to control her post-work life. While most of us were slumming it in jeans and jumpers, she was always dressed to the nines just in case she was summoned to a five-star hotel bar for a late-night *soirée* in the company of Paris's social A-listers – which often she was. Any time she didn't spend on the phone, however, she'd give free reign to her exuberant, exhibitionist tendencies, leading the room in a lusty rendition of whatever musical tune or cheesy power ballad was playing on Jean's portable stereo. But only when she wasn't otherwise holed up in the bathroom.

'What's with that?' I asked Matthew one night.

'I think it's probably safe to assume she's in there powdering her nose, love,' he replied.

I'd been around showfolk and Gold Coast nightclubs long enough not to be shocked by drug-taking. For the rest of that night I was entertained by monitoring the steady flow of traffic in and out of Jean's bathroom. Rather than being surprised at the number of people partaking, I found myself wondering how they could all afford it.

For Katie, however, all of this was new and exotic. She was shocked, but also intrigued. In the two months since we had first taken the stage, she had grown in confidence and come into her own, assuming the height and natural good looks that God had given her. In the dressing-room, she had started to come out of her shell, and flashes of personality soon morphed into more confident forays into bawdy dressing-room banter. It was clear she was fascinated with – even idolised – Sophie. Attracted by the idea of moulding an *ingénue* in her own image, Sophie would come into work with a new outfit, some of it designer wear, and casually hurl a piece in Katie's direction.

'You can have this if you want,' she'd say. 'You'd look better in it than me.'

Katie's eyes would boggle as another piece of vastly overpriced French designer clothing landed in her lap. As the weeks progressed, she would show up at Jimmy's in a pair of low-slung jeans or a tight-fitting shirt, her face artfully made up, her hair down and expertly coiffed.

Sophie set about recruiting Katie to her troupe of nightly merrymakers, inviting her to one VIP *soirée* or another.

Steve would occasionally meet me after work and join in the festivities, but he rarely enjoyed it. He had nothing against showpeople, but their natural exuberance was at odds with his more understated personality. The personality chasm was even more exaggerated when he was stoned, which was pretty much all the time lately. Without a job and with no social outlets other than me, he had taken to numbing the boredom of his day-to-day existence by smoking as much hash as he could get his hands on.

At these parties, in front of my new friends, I did my best to jolly him along and sometimes it worked. But it was exhausting. I tried to encourage him to keep looking for work, but every day that passed in which he wasn't contributing to our household was another nail in the coffin of our relationship.

Jean would end most post-work *soirées* at her apartment by rifling drunkenly through her collection of videos and screening one of her show tapes. She had a recording of every show she'd been in for the past six years, and she wasn't afraid to show them. We'd scream in delight or squirm in embarrassed recognition as troupes of fellow dancers on cruise ships past or in revues long-gone brought to life the camp vision of one artistic director or another. We had come to the Moulin Rouge from different parts of the world, but we were seasoned veterans of more outrageous kitsch than you could poke an ostrich feather at. And we loved it.

In the midst of the show tunes, the bathroom traffic and the hummus, whether hemmed in by the leopard-print walls of Jimmy's or splayed on Jean's bed listening to her Celine Dion CD collection, we became a kind of family. Or at least most of us did.

# Chapter Nineteen

My first encounter with Alison, when she'd thrust those flowers at me with such disdain, should have been a warning. She'd been a dancer at the Moulin Rouge for almost seven years, and in that time had slowly risen through the ranks. As career trajectories go, hers had been mediocre more than meteoric. Certainly, if dressing-room gossip was to be believed, her progression owed as much to the fact she was still hanging around as it did to any degree of talent on her part. Not even the Big Boss was a fan. Apparently, he'd attempted to dismiss her more than once, but by some miracle she'd always managed to hang in there by the skin of her nicotine-stained teeth.

A chain-smoker, Alison had the yellow teeth and dry, pursed lips typical of someone with a pack-a-day habit. She hailed from Scotland, where she had learned her dance craft at one of the many talent schools in suburban Glasgow. She wasn't mean by nature, just a little bitter, a whole lot insecure and – as I would soon discover – paranoid that every new girl who arrived at the Moulin had been sent expressly to replace her.

I'd encountered a fair smattering of eccentrics and highly strung artistic types in my time, but no-one I'd ever worked with had interacted with their fellow dancers in the brutal, abrupt, out-and-out rude way Alison did. As one of the captains, it was her responsibility to ensure that every girl was dancing each night to her full potential. It was a job that required her to occasionally be strict, but it seemed to me

Alison wielded the small amount of authority she'd been given unfairly, to settle petty personal scores and inflate her sense of self-importance. She seemed to believe her principal role was to denigrate, publicly humiliate and generally beat down every dancer in the company. I can only assume that her behaviour was a misguided attempt to command respect. She didn't understand that backstage respect was something that was earned, not demanded.

She was famously anti-nudes, believing we were nothing but onstage fluff. According to Alison, the cancan girls were the real dancers and the nudes were simply window-dressing. So she would make a point of bailing us up in the wings to issue us with corrections as we flew offstage.

'But you can't take it personally,' Matthew counselled one night over post-work Monacos at Le Palmier. 'She's bitter and twisted and you're better than that.'

I knew he was right, and I had dealt with bigger cows than Alison in my life, but she still bugged me. This was my dream, to dance in Paris at the Moulin Rouge, and here it was being tainted by a tired old showgirl.

Early in the New Year, Big Nic told Janet she no longer wanted to be nude dance captain. The nightly hassle of being responsible for fourteen girls, of planning the show, reblocking it when dancers were off, dealing with the costume department, performing administrative duties for the HR department, issuing corrections when required, liaising between the dancers and management and coordinating regular rehearsals had become too tedious. Nic wanted out. The second captain, a Polish girl called Anouchka, was the natural choice as replacement, but she similarly wanted nothing to do with the job. Which meant it was up for grabs.

Janet, apparently keen to underscore her democratic credentials, announced that the decision was up to us girls. The next captain of the nudes would be selected by the dancers themselves – with her reserving the right of veto. Despite the hassle that the added tasks and responsibility entailed, there was enough status attached to the role of captain to ensure a fair amount of backstage lobbying began. Some of it was subtle, some of it quite brazen. There were clearly girls in the nude line who felt it was their due to assume the captaincy, and so the jockeying began.

In the shower one night, Suzanne, one of the older English dancers in our line, asked me my star sign.

'Leo,' I replied. 'Why?'

'Perfect. They're leaders.' And with that, she launched a campaign to have me anointed captain. Despite the fact that I had only been in the company three months – or perhaps because of it – the campaign started to take hold. So riddled was the dressing-room with old alliances and long-held grudges, people seemed to like the idea of having someone new, fresh and relatively neutral taking the job. I would come to it without any baggage.

The vote of confidence from my colleagues was flattering, but I didn't seriously think Janet would consider me appropriate for the gig. I only knew one place in the show – mine. I was barely on exchanging-of-pleasantries terms with the majority of girls in the nude line and I was still feeling my way around the house. Which was why, when I was elected captain in a secret ballot, I was taken aback.

'But I only know one place in the line,' I said to Janet immediately after the vote. 'I'm obviously honoured that people think I would be capable, but how am I supposed to rehearse and correct fourteen girls when I only know my show?'

'Don't worry, you'll learn everything you need as you go along,' came Janet's reply.

Returning home after work that night, I lay awake for hours, staring at the ceiling, a bundle of nerves. The planning and blocking of the show I figured I could learn quickly enough. The administrative duties and liaison with the costume department and wigmaker were going to be more complicated, not least because of my still almost total lack of French. But it was the prospect of issuing corrections to dancers ten and fifteen years my senior who had been at the Moulin for longer than I had been dancing professionally that really terrified me. That and the maintenance of harmony in the dressing-rooms. Fourteen girls from different cultural backgrounds, of different ages and temperaments and with egos of varying delicacy were not going to be easy to manage. While the dressing-room camaraderie had thus far mostly been exemplary, I knew that simmering just beneath the surface was a hotbed of jealousies and grudges and, in some cases, barely disguised contempt. As the clock ticked through to 5 a.m., I finally got myself off to sleep, steeling myself for what I knew was going to be an exercise in diplomacy. I little suspected that my biggest challenge would be managing a prickly personality who wasn't even part of the nude line.

For my first couple of weeks as captain, I shadowed Anouchka as she went about planning the show each night, learning as much as I could. I started to understand where each member of the nude line fitted into the overall show – who their dressers were and what their strengths and weaknesses were. Part of the job was to liaise each night with the other captain to see who was absent. In order for the show to run smoothly, slight adjustments would be made accordingly. The contact with Alison was fleeting – more of a courtesy call than anything else. I would swing by her *loge* while she was busy with her make-up to see if I needed to know of any changes to her line-up.

During the two weeks I followed Anouchka, Alison was as sweet as pie to her while making a point of ignoring me. When finally I was left to my own devices and I had to fly solo, I could barely extract a civil word from her. For the most part, it was little more than general coldness, but every now and then she would let rip. She seemed to reserve her most venomous attacks for when there was a maximum number of dancers around to bear witness. She clearly wanted to be seen to be putting me in my place. In her eyes, I was a little upstart who had floated in and assumed a role of responsibility that had taken her more than seven years to achieve.

I did my best to be sympathetic to her situation and, on a certain level, could understand why she felt the need to put me down. I decided the best course of action was to ignore her.

# Chapter Twenty

Four months into our Paris stay I came home from work one night to find Steve curled up in bed with the television on. He greeted me with a large smile on his face.

'What are you so happy about?'

'I've got a job.'

It was such an unexpected development, and my faith in him had sunk to such a low level, I assumed he was kidding. But his smile persisted.

'Really? You really have a job?'

'Yes really. A real job. I start next week.'

He'd seen an advertisement in the monthly expat magazine, *FUSAC*, for an *au pair* to work with an English family in the French Alps. He'd trained as a teacher at home and figured the gig was perfect for him.

'It's a change of scene, the money's okay, and it will be good to be down in the mountains,' he explained.

During the next few days I helped him prepare to leave, all the while trying to suppress my relief at the prospect of having him temporarily out of my life and off the couch. The relief, however, was short-lived. Steve only lasted a week in the job before deciding that looking after other people's kids was more hassle than it was worth. He returned as if nothing had happened, and I resented him even more.

We began to fight like never before. At first it was over little things, like washing up and his complete refusal to ever clean the bathroom. When he proceeded to spend his last francs on pot, it was more than I could bear.

Steve and I spent the entire night fighting at a post-work fancy dress party at an apartment on the Île Saint-Louis. He eventually stormed out, leaving me crying in a corner. On the Métro later with Brett and Matthew, the mood was sombre.

Under the unforgiving fluorescent lights of a Métro carriage, my face was flushed red, my eyes puffy. Brett sat on the seat opposite in a punk rocker wig, platforms and flares; Matthew watched on in Liza Minnelli-inspired drag – a red-velour flared jumpsuit, short-cropped black wig and full make-up.

'Shelby?' Brett ventured, using my family nickname. 'What the hell is going on? We like Steve, but this is obviously not working out. This should be the best, most exciting time of your life and look at you. You're a mess.'

I stared out the window, unable to make eye contact.

Brett continued, 'Look, don't feel bad. It's textbook stuff. You brought him to Paris thinking you'll set up house and have an exciting time together. You have a new job and new friends in a new and exciting city. He doesn't speak French, hasn't got a job or any friends of his own and it all falls apart. It happens all the time. You shouldn't feel bad about it.'

Liza sat nodding her agreement. 'He's right you know, Shelb. Sometimes you just need to know when to walk away.'

They were right. I knew that Paris had been a disaster for me and Steve. It was my adventure, and to expect him to tag along and get everything I had been getting out of it was unrealistic, even unfair. I would soon have to summon the courage to cut the cord and set the pair of us free.

In the end, the decision was taken out of my hands.

A week later, Jean invited us back to her house for her by-now famous post-show hummus. It was an understated affair, as Jean's parties went – only fifteen or so of us crammed into her studio, a couple of platters of chicken nachos and five bottles of cheap red wine. Steve was being uncharacteristically charismatic on this particular night; at the end of the evening he was even gallant enough to consent to walk Jenny back to her place on our way back home.

It was around 5 a.m. as we stepped out onto Rue Fontaine and headed towards Place Blanche. The Moulin Rouge looked forlorn without any of its bright red neon, the windmill barely discernible in low-lying early morning fog. We hurried up Rue Lepic towards Jenny's place, pulling our coats about us. It was early March and winter was clinging stubbornly.

As we turned into Jenny's street, I noticed in the shadows up ahead the furtive movement of what looked like a group of guys. They broke out of the shadows and started walking down the street in a line towards us, backlit by the streetlamps, each of them wearing jeans and a hooded sweater. Jenny and I instinctively gripped our handbags. I could feel Steve tense up beside me. As they came closer, it became clear they were not intending to break their line and let us pass. We slowed our pace, unsure of whether to stand our ground or turn and run. Before we had time to react, we were encircled and being poked and jostled.

'Give us your money!' came a guttural demand in heavily accented English. 'Give us your money!'

A little tipsy from the wine, and not yet registering the seriousness of the situation, I reacted with incredulity. 'What? Are you serious?'

'Give us your money! This is not a joke!'

One of the gang pulled a gun from his back pocket and pointed it at me. Not even the glint of steel in the streetlights was enough to convince me to comply.

'That's not real,' I heard myself say. My mind raced and my limbs started twitching as the adrenaline kicked in. Another gang member reached into his backpack and pulled out a machete. Its steel blade caught the light and glinted – there was no mistaking that it was real.

Jenny let out a short scream. I stood frozen to the spot, suddenly awfully aware of how serious this was. The machete-wielder grabbed Steve by his coat collars and pushed him up against a nearby wall, pointing the blade at his chest.

'Money! Now!' shouted the guy with the gun, pointing it at me.

'Okay, okay, okay!' Jenny stammered as we both scrambled in our bags for our purses and threw them on the ground. Two of the gang members bent down, scooped them up and pulled out the cash. The machete-wielder demanded Steve hand over his wallet, too.

'Please, take what you want. Just please don't hurt us,' I sobbed, genuinely terrified.

Then, just as quickly as they had appeared, they started running off down the street.

We stood shaking, horrified, rooted to the spot, the only sound the dull thud of their trainers on the street. Jenny was the first to rouse.

'Fuck, fuck, fuck!' she started screaming, starting to run after them. 'You fuckers! That's my rent!' She stopped running and watched helplessly as three thousand francs of her hard-earned money disappeared into the Paris night.

We scurried into her apartment and, still in shock, sat down to take stock.

'What do we do now?' I asked.

'Ring the police, I guess,' Jenny suggested.

We finally decided to go to the nearby police station and file a report. Visibly upset by the experience and failing desperately in our attempt to explain in French exactly what had happened, we were a sorry spectacle for the two young gendarmes manning the overnight shift. They got us to fill out a couple of forms, asked us to look through a photo album of mug shots and made it as amply clear as their limited English allowed that they were neither shocked by our experience nor expected to catch the perpetrators.

By the time Steve and I got home, morning had broken. A grey light from the overcast sky seeped into the studio.

'I hate it here,' Steve said as he collapsed onto the couch. 'This fucking city. I've had enough of it.'

I looked at him slumped in the corner. He looked broken and pathetic and I felt responsible. 'I know you hate it,' I said. 'It's obvious every morning you wake up, and you have no idea how much I hate feeling like I've dragged you here against your will.'

I watched as he sat with his head hung, spinning his lighter around in his hands.

'Look, I think we have to be honest and accept that this is not working,' I continued. 'I think we need a break. I think you should go to London. You've got the visa, you can find work there. Paris is my dream: maybe it's time you go and find yours.'

He looked up at me, weighing my words, unsure how to respond. 'Will you be okay?' he asked finally.

I started to imagine life in Paris without this stress.

'I'll be fine,' I said, beginning to smile and feeling genuine affection for him for the first time in a long while. 'I'll be just fine.'

# ACT III

# Chapter Twenty-one

Once Steve left I felt as if a veil had been lifted. I began to see Paris as a strikingly beautiful new playground. It felt like a chapter of my life had closed and it was now up to me to shape the next part of my story.

We farewelled one another at the bus station on the outskirts of the city. It had been late morning by the time I had tearfully waved Steve goodbye; I had an entire day to kill before work. Rather than ride the Métro, I decided to take the bus back to Clichy. I sat staring out the window as Paris rolled by.

It occurred to me that I had barely seen anything of the city. I lived in Paris, but since arriving, I had done little to explore it. In the first week that Steve had been there we'd gone a few places but once work had started I rarely seemed to jump off the home–work–home treadmill. On my doorstep were museums, parks, monuments and sights that some people dreamed their entire lives of seeing. I had them all at my fingertips and had so far all but ignored them.

As the bus wended its way towards Place de la République and along the Grands Boulevards, I resolved to get out more, to make the most of my remarkable new surroundings. I was, after all, in the City of Light plus I had spent a lot of time worrying about how my modest monthly pay cheque would stretch to feeding, housing and clothing two of us. Now I only had myself to worry about, and it felt good.

From Sophie's dressing-room accounts of whatever hijinks she had gotten up to the night before, I knew that there was a whole world out there under the cover of Paris night for any showgirl who wanted to have a bit of fun. I figured it was time I made a bit more of an effort to get amongst it. But first, I was determined to get a better sense of Paris by day. Who knew how long I would stay? I didn't want to leave regretting that I hadn't made the most of it.

Striking out from Clichy each morning, I would hop on the Métro or jump on a bus and head to a corner of Paris I'd yet to explore, determined to discover a new *quartier*. Sometimes I'd grab a crepe and eat as I ambled. I went through the Jardin du Luxembourg, across the Pont des Arts, around Les Invalides and along the Seine. I'd hop on a *bateau mouche* (open boat) at Pont Neuf and jump off at Notre Dame. I found flea markets in Vanves and fish markets in Bastille. Spring was in the air and, with it, a noticeable change in attitude among the locals. Where winter had forced their manners and powers of social interaction into hibernation, the prospect of spring seemed to trigger random acts of friendliness and sudden displays of extroversion. A market vendor would offer up a cut of cheese, an old woman walking a dog in the park would initiate a conversation and usually aloof bistro waiters would crack a joke.

On colder days, I would set off to a farflung corner of the city, find a local cafe and hole up for a couple of hours with a book. Just me, a *boeuf bourguignon* and a glass of wine. It was bliss. My French had hardly improved since I had arrived, but now I was surrounded by the language and could feel my ear gradually becoming attuned to it. I felt wonderfully free, fantastically independent and ever-so-slightly adventurous.

The only thing that shattered the peace was the constant stream of male suitors who would mysteriously descend each time I stopped at a cafe or bistro or sat on a park bench. They seemed to appear out of nowhere, tripping over themselves to shower me with compliments, offer me a drink or declare their undying love. At first it was disconcerting and I would bat them away like flies, but eventually, once I'd worked out they were harmless, I came to find it all rather entertaining.

After a day spent exploring Paris, I would return to Clichy in the evening and float into work on a cloud of happiness, my head still spinning from the wonderful sights I had taken in, my stomach contentedly full from whatever French delicacy I had discovered over lunch that afternoon.

'*Confit de canard!*' I would exclaim to Brett in the dressing-room, eyes shining, excited to share these gastronomical epiphanies. 'It's duck, cooked in its own fat and served with garlic-flavoured fried potatoes!'

He'd groan as he munched on another lunch box of carrot sticks, fighting his way through whatever fad diet he happened to be on that week. 'There's no need to rub it in,' he would say, brandishing a celery shoot. 'We weren't all blessed with the world's most hyperactive metabolism.'

*Steak tartare, entrecôte* with blue cheese sauce, *blanquette de veau, magret de canard, salade de gésiers, rillettes, foie gras* – each lunch was a new culinary adventure. I would order a glass of wine and sit and observe the lunchtime crowd. Middle-aged men in suits wore their shocks of greying hair in a kind of elaborate bouffant, making them look slightly feminine, yet undeniably debonair. The women were stereotypically elegant, carrying themselves with poise as they nibbled delicately on lunches of goat's cheese salad and '*un Coca-Light*'.

As much as the French food was a revelation, perhaps my greatest discovery on these sorties out into the city was the Musée d'Orsay.

I found myself drawn each time to the fifth floor and the Impressionists. I would stand before Dégas' ballet dancers and be moved almost to tears. There was something about the light in them and his ability to capture the movement of the dancers. The artist had captured their poise and delicacy so perfectly in those soft pinks and blues. My own ballet experience in a sunbaked church hall in suburban Brisbane was about as far removed from these 1870s Parisian scenes as it was possible to be. Yet I still found myself identifying with the spirit of each work, able to imagine myself in the ballet slippers of the girls he painted.

Life at home also started to take on a new shape. I began to relish having my own space, tiny though it was. I enjoyed being able to come home at whatever hour I wanted, without having to creep into bed and worry about disturbing someone. I was free.

Well, free when I wasn't slaving at the Moulin Rouge. Since becoming captain, I found my workload had increased markedly. Not only did I have to manage fourteen dancers every night, I was also responsible for rehearsing any new girls that started. With dancers' contracts finishing every six months or so, it wasn't long until my first new intake of girls arrived. Four of them were new recruits to the nude line, which meant I had to teach each of them their show. The new girls were the usual varied mix of nationalities, personalities and abilities.

I showed up for rehearsals nervous, worried that I didn't know the show and all fourteen of the nude places well enough to be able to teach it to a group of new girls. I had to show each girl the choreography for her ten different routines, and instruct them all how to interact with their boy partners and how to move about the stage in harmony with the rest of the traffic. Each girl had a different track and it was my responsibility to ensure that when they joined the show in three weeks' time, they slotted seamlessly into it. It was terrifying.

Luckily, one of the new girls was Jo – a stunning English brunette from Leeds.

From the moment Jo bounced into rehearsals, introduced herself and started chatting at me nonstop, I liked her. Not least because the woman liked to talk. After only one hour in her company, I was willing to wager that in a one-on-one talk-off, Jo would have even been able to talk Jean under the table. The subjects she touched on were many and varied, and not always related to the job at hand. I learned more about her life in two hours of rehearsals than I knew about the lives of girls I had worked with for six months. She was, it is fair to say, a compulsive sharer. She was also unfailingly sweet and intuitive enough to sense this was my first time taking rehearsals. She went out of her way to make my job easier, doing everything she could to help me – something I noted and appreciated.

Making my life altogether harder was a new French girl, Severine, who quite simply couldn't dance. She had come to the Moulin Rouge from the Lido, where I heard whispers she had been sacked for exactly that reason. I didn't understand how she had been hired and why I was lumbered with her two left feet.

'She can't dance,' I complained as tactfully as possible to Janet one afternoon. 'I mean, forget dancing, she can't even walk. Her showgirl walk is awful.'

'I know, love,' Janet replied. 'But doesn't she have a great smile?'

Miss Doris, on one of her rare visits to Paris, appeared one afternoon during rehearsals to give the new recruits the once-over. I sat with her at the back of the *salle* as the girls went through their paces down on the stage. After a moment's contemplation, Miss Doris leaned towards me in the dark.

'You've got your work cut out for you with that one.'

I was rehearsing new girls by day and dancing two shows by night. With each performance, I was starting to enjoy myself more and more, a process helped along in no small part by Dimitri, whose dry Russian humour kept me entertained each time we waltzed. Every night as I ran across the stage into his arms, he would declare, '*C'est pas vrai!*' feigning surprise and excitement that he had landed me as his partner again. 'Did you change your make-up darling? Because those eyelashes look good on you.'

We'd spend the entire number chatting through our stage smiles, catching up on each other's day or planning drinks after work at Jimmy's.

Dimitri had a passion for perfumes, and dreamed that when he eventually got too old and too tired to cancan, he would rely on his nose for a living, creating perfumes. It wasn't such a bad plan. In France, still the world capital of perfume production, a good nose could earn a person a very fine livelihood.

'Darling,' he would say as we spun about the stage. 'What is that fragrance you are wearing? I smell patchouli and musk.'

As well as being chief post-show entertainer, Jean quickly assumed the role of my surrogate mother. As the captaincy demanded more and more of my waking hours, I would often walk down to her place between rehearsals and the night's performance, where she would run me a bath and cook me dinner. She had recently taken an amateur interest in massage and had bought a massage table for her tiny living room. Some afternoons, after taking my bath and before tucking into whatever gastronomic delight she had whipped up (Jean really was an excellent cook), I'd stretch out on the massage table and allow myself to be pummelled. Even though I knew she had no training and no real idea what she was doing, it felt heavenly.

As my responsibilities as captain started to take their toll, the massages became more and more necessary.

Fifi was proving to be one of the more difficult dancers to wrangle. She worked hard every night, turning in a consistently solid performance; she showed up every night she was rostered to work and rarely went off sick in the middle of a show – which was already more than a lot of people. But she had a fiery temper that she usually waited until she was onstage to properly vent. And nothing raised her ire more than the sight of an audience member brandishing a camera.

It was forbidden for patrons to take photos of the show. Each night a multilingual announcement to that effect was made over the PA system as the lights were going down. Signs were placed on the tables to reinforce the message and waiters were charged with the job of monitoring any surreptitious camera activity during the show and confiscating cameras for collection afterwards. The revue was a copyrighted creation, and photographing or filming the show or any of the girls dancing in it discouraged people from buying the programs. But more importantly, photography was considered disrespectful to the artists onstage. Just because we made a living dancing topless did not mean we were a photographic free-for-all for anyone who forked out the price of admission.

Being partially naked onstage, under the lights, in the costumes and in the context of the Moulin Rouge was one thing. Being photographed by a random member of the audience – having your semi-naked form recorded for posterity on someone's camera, to be printed, shared, passed about – was something altogether different. Yes, we were contractually obliged to pose for photos for the program or for publicity shots for the Moulin Rouge, but that was part of our job and something over which we maintained a certain amount of control.

As long as there was breath in Fifi's body, she wasn't going to become photographic fodder for a bunch of amateur shutterbugs. Not content to rely on the wait staff in the *salle* to search out sneaky photographers, Fifi preferred to take matters into her own hands or, more specifically, into her own size-nine feet. If someone sitting stage-side dared pull out a camera and start snapping away, Fifi would break from whatever choreography she was performing, charge over and discipline the offender. If they were lucky, they got a severe dressing-down from a six-foot-tall black woman in sequins and feathers. 'No photos!' she would scream as the show continued behind her. If they were less fortunate, they would find themselves drenched as one of Fifi's well-trained, perfectly aimed feet kicked a bucket of champagne into their lap.

As captain, it was my job to discipline Fifi. But I was as terrified of her as everyone else in the company – including Janet, who, when I raised it with her, seemed equally reluctant to take her on.

'Oh, that's just Fifi,' she would say. 'Besides, they shouldn't have been taking photos.'

I had never had to manage anyone before, much less manage people from so many different cultural backgrounds. Of course, some problems were easier to fix than others. Two girls having a fight could usually be sorted out by bringing them together in a quiet corner and forcing them to reconcile. Even if I knew the resentment would continue to fester, the edge would be taken off their mutual animosity and a semblance of harmony could be restored, if only briefly.

The management of egos was an altogether more difficult task, as dancers openly competed with one another for the chance to rise in the ranks and become one of the coveted soloists. The soloists were the three nudes who were separated from the pack, highlighted and heavily featured in the show. They had different choreography, generally spent more time in the spotlight and enjoyed a higher backstage status.

There wasn't a girl worth her salt as a dancer who didn't want to be soloist – just as there wasn't a soloist who didn't covet Marissa's job as the principal dancer.

Each girl, no matter what their position, could only work six nights a week and the Moulin Rouge was open seven nights a week, so there always had to be a ready supply of replacements for the soloists and the principal. To be asked to train to become a replacement was an honour and competition for the spots was fierce, in an understated way. We were all friends and colleagues, first and foremost, but we were also competing with one another. None of us had made it onto the Paris stage by being shrinking violets.

As the weeks passed, I started to feel more comfortable in my new role. Even so, there were always problems that I had no idea what to do about.

Vanessa was a Southern Belle in the nude line. She was crazy pretty, in one of those genetic-freak kind of ways: flawless skin, beautiful big brown eyes, perfectly formed and perfectly proportioned facial features.

Which is why, when she returned from a three-week vacation having had a boob job, it took everyone by surprise. Previously she'd had perfectly nice breasts, but post-operation she looked frankly ridiculous. She was top-heavy, and looked as though her slight frame wasn't quite capable of supporting her newly enhanced upper body. And of course, during a performance, Vanessa's new boobs commanded attention. You always knew when Vanessa was onstage, because all the eyes in the audience would be suddenly drawn to her chest. Whether staring in disbelief (the women) or ogling in lascivious appreciation (the men), the reaction was the same every night.

The Moulin Rouge had always prided itself on featuring beautiful women in an untouched, unenhanced, natural state. Dancers with obviously fake boobs were routinely turned away at auditions. Fake breasts in a line of natural breasts stood out a mile. Under the glare of stage lights and in the execution of occasionally rigorous choreography, implants were thought to be nothing more than a distraction. At the most basic level, presenting fake boobs to the hundreds of people who filed into the audience each night to see the Moulin Rouge's renowned line of Doriss Girls was considered to be cheating. People were paying good money to see lovely bodies and graceful dancing, not the handiwork of Paris's most accomplished plastic surgeons.

Surgically altered noses, chiselled chins and pinned ears were all fine, but breasts were not to be tampered with. And like the heritage-listed building in which the show took place, the Moulin Rouge's breasts needed to be carefully protected.

And so each night I had to find a place in the line for Vanessa where her chest wouldn't look out of place. Unfortunately, the fact of the matter was that her presence made the line look suddenly unbalanced. The stupid thing was that the new boobs had done nothing to make her more attractive. She was already one of the most strikingly beautiful girls in the company.

Luckily for me, the problem solved itself. Vanessa went AWOL one night, failing to show up for work and never phoning to report in sick. Two days later, I received a phone call in which she explained she'd had to return unexpectedly to America to visit her ill grandmother, and that she didn't know when she would be back. It sounded plausible enough, even if 'ill grandmother' was the oldest excuse in the book for skiving off work. It seemed less believable when, two months later, she contacted me again to say she was getting married and moving to Israel. She'd met an Israeli millionaire who was apparently unconcerned about (or perhaps even charmed by) her fake boobs. And so off to the Holy Land she went. It was amazing the doors that sometimes opened to a Paris showgirl.

# Chapter Twenty-two

As summer began to take hold of Paris, the city came alive. Chairs and tables appeared on cafe terraces and smiles began to appear more regularly on the faces of Parisians. I had only really known the city wrapped in her winter coat: to see her now shuck off the grey of winter and skip joyously into a new season was a revelation.

The mood of celebration was helped along by the fact that the soccer World Cup was being held in France that summer. Paris threw itself into party mode, the bars and cafes packed every night with festive locals cheering on their national team. It was impossible not to get caught up in the excitement, even for someone like me, who, perhaps as a result of growing up with two sports-mad brothers, had little or no interest in sport. I would walk into work each night and listen to the cheers or groans of frustration emanating from bars along the way, each of them crammed with patriots sporting blue and white jerseys.

As a special World Cup-themed publicity stunt, a team of body painters came into the Moulin Rouge and painted the naked torsos of fifteen girls — me included — to make it look like we were wearing the jerseys of the top teams. The photo was to be featured the following week in *Paris Match*, one of France's highest-selling weekly magazines. I had an Italian jersey painted onto my chest, a process that took two body painters about three hours.

A week later, I collected a copy of the magazine at my local press kiosk. It occurred to me, as I flicked open the page and saw my nearly naked torso in the pages of a mass-circulation magazine, that I had become completely relaxed with nudity. I no longer blanched at the idea of showering with other dancers after the show. On the contrary, I had taken up the post-show ritual of indulging in a glass of wine in the shower with Marissa and the Russian soloist, Vlada, as we caught up on the day's news.

I was becoming very French in this respect. Whereas there was still a certain amount of prudishness in my home country, in France the naked female form was used to advertise everything from ice-cream to *haute couture*. You couldn't walk past a press kiosk without being assaulted by a pair of breasts, whether they were staring back at you from the cover of a magazine about women's health or one about popular psychology. On bus shelters all over the city or on French television in the middle of the day, ads for *camembert* or low-fat milk would feature artfully filmed, lingering shots of female chests.

Of course, this view wasn't always shared by everyone who came to see the show. I had become accustomed to gauging the reactions of different crowds when the curtain went up and the stage was suddenly populated with fourteen sets of naked breasts.

Most of the audience, especially the South Americans and southern Europeans (and particularly the Italians, whose popular media offers a daily diet of scantily clad women), would be enraptured by the spectacle, often taking to their feet to offer up a spontaneous ovation. '*Bellissima! Bellissima!*' they would cry out in chorus.

Others would watch in wide-eyed silence, clapping respectfully at appropriate intervals. You knew they were a little taken aback by the sight but determined not to show it, affecting instead a kind of forced worldliness. Others still were quite plainly unimpressed. These were the ones who would sit with their arms folded, their faces like a shoe, and who would refuse to clap or otherwise show any signs of life.

During one performance, immediately following the opening number, a woman sitting with her husband at the front of the stage turned her seat around to face the back of the auditorium. While her husband took in the show, agog, she sat with her back to the stage for the entire performance.

'Have you seen that woman down the front?' Sophie asked me as we ran offstage after prologue and headed for the dressing-room. 'She's turned her chair around!'

'I know!' I replied as we clomped up the stairs. 'What did she think she was coming to see? It's the Moulin Rouge for God's sake! It's not like she couldn't have known what she was signing up for when she bought the tickets.'

We reached the dressing-room and starting changing.

'Well, I think it's rude,' Sophie said. 'I would never go to her workplace and treat her with such contempt.' She stooped over her dressing-table and started scribbling on a piece of paper, applying a large red lipstick kiss to her note.

'What are you doing?' I asked.

She held up the piece of paper. It had a fake phone number scrawled on it above the words 'Call me'.

'I'm just going to make a special delivery to her husband.'

Sure enough, during our next number, a scrunched-up ball of paper bounced down onto the table in front of the man, catching the eye of his horrified wife.

'That ought to give her something to be upset about,' Sophie said as we came offstage again.

Mischief, I was fast discovering, was one of Sophie's *fortés*. Following my post-Steve daytime adventures, I started to tag along to some of the after-work *soirées* to which she was habitually invited. Megan and Katie would always join the party too.

We would usually start in a bar: always somewhere exclusive, where huge bouncers kept the masses at bay and clipboard-bearing doormonitors granted entry only to a select few. Sophie would normally know the manager or promoter, and once inside, he or she would set us up at a table and send us a complimentary bottle of champagne. It never took long for the assembled Lotharios to start circling. Some would send drinks and respectfully keep their distance at the bar. Others were more direct, inviting us to join their table or accompany them to the private V.I.P. section they had booked. No matter where we went, one thing was certain: we never bought a drink.

From that point, the night could pretty much go anywhere. Sophie nursed her phone, checking it regularly for messages and weighing up the invitations that streamed in.

If it was Paris Fashion Week – which, between the *prêt-à-porter*, *haute couture* and men's collections, rolled around six times a year – there was always a string of V.I.P. parties in glamorous locations all over the city. Sometimes I'd find myself in a private members' bar, other times in a grand *hôtel particulier* (a large private house) or in the sprawling showroom of a big-name fashion house. These were the best parties, packed as they were with gorgeous men (especially during men's fashion week) and featuring famous DJs, free-flowing champagne and lots of manic dance-floor action. Of course, they weren't the kind of parties at which you could hold a conversation with anyone, much less make any meaningful connections – everyone was too busy looking to see who was looking at them. But then conversation was hardly the point.

And then there were the nights I would find myself caught up in the social tornado that accompanied a gala film premiere or a visiting big-name rock band. The parties would usually be held in one of the cavernous subterranean clubs off the Champs Élysées – most commonly Man Ray, the V.I.P. Room or Queen. We'd join the band or hang with the movie stars in the roped-off V.I.P. section, chatting, eating and helping them drink ludicrously expensive alcohol.

As the months passed and I accepted more and more invitations to join Sophie on her wild forays, I began to appreciate that she had stumbled upon a nocturnal alternate universe. The living was high, the alcohol flowed freely and drugs – if you wanted them – were plentiful and readily available. We were frolicking in a world where fashion, entertainment and serious money met: bit players in a nightly bacchanalia that played out in the most exclusive clubs, the trendiest bars and the most expensive hotel suites in the world's most deeply fashionable city. It was easy to fall under its spell.

As the summer flew by I began to get a sense of exactly how easy it was to fall under that spell. If we weren't hanging out with cashed-up French aristocrats – the sons of France's captains of industry or the playboy offspring of some of the country's oldest families – it was Eurotrash jet-set types, music and film celebrities or the spoilt sons of wealthy Arab sheikhs.

The summons to a *soirée* would always come from the same four or five sources – party organisers or club owners who had made it their business to pack their speed dials with a roster of striking young women who could be relied on to come out and party. It was a chicken and egg scenario. Club owners knew that as long as they could ensure a ready supply of attractive women, they would be granted the honour of hosting celebrities and high-rolling, big-spending international players. It was good for business to have a Hollywood star in the house, just as it was good for business to have their venue regularly stocked with eye-catching women.

Which is not to say that every showgirl in Paris was a supermodel. Some of us, without make-up, were as plain as day. But thanks to the nature of our work and the pressure of Janet's eagle eye, we all had good figures, were unusually tall and knew our way around a make-up kit. In the soft light of a Parisian nightclub, the effect could be arresting – especially when we travelled in a pack.

This strange *demimonde* of pop stars, millionaires, nightclubs and neon-lit Parisian streets soon became my natural habitat. I slept by day, worked by night and came out to play in the wee small hours of the morning. There was nothing normal about the job, so it seemed only natural that there would be nothing normal about the social life that went with it. Besides, it wasn't as if there were many other after-work socialising options available to a showgirl. If you were single and didn't want to hang out every night with colleagues or go home alone to your broom-closet apartment, this nocturnal netherworld was pretty much the only choice.

For meeting men, too, it was the only option open to us. Thanks to our unsociable working hours, we found ourselves in the ironic situation of being the onstage objects of fantasy for hundreds of men each night, but never able to meet any of them. How do you form a relationship with someone who works nine-to-five, when your working day starts at 7 p.m. and finishes at 2 a.m.? And it wasn't as if there were rich pickings among our male dancing colleagues. Almost to a person, they were unfailingly sweet, very good-looking and had bodies to die for, but they were also almost all gay. The one or two who were heterosexual were either married or busy making the most of their single status by sleeping with every lonely female colleague they could get their hands on.

If I had learned anything from my seven years of professional dancing – and from my six months of on-the-town action with Sophie and Katie – it was that there were two types of showgirl. Those who were grounded, and those who were either too young or too naïve to see the madness for what it was and allowed themselves to get carried away by it. The former were generally able to take the Paris showgirl whirl in their stride. The latter tended to be much more vulnerable and often got themselves in trouble.

Thanks largely to my age, plus the fact that my brothers had spent the better part of my teenage years making sure my feet never left the ground, I was pretty level-headed. I was happy to enjoy the mad social scene for what it was and dip in and out of the lifestyles of the rich and famous on my own terms. I was able to cherrypick experiences without being sucked into the vortex of Paris by night.

Sophie, too, for all her antics, also knew the game she was playing and, for the most part, where the pitfalls lay and how best to avoid them. While it would be a stretch to say she was in control of every situation she found herself in, she entered each one with her wits about her. To her mind, she was having fun, making the most of her time in Paris, and making the most of being a Moulin Rouge dancer. Though she was occasionally reckless, she was brassy enough and self-assured enough to emerge intact.

Katie, on the other hand, was way out of her depth. Too young and too green to properly understand how to play the game, she had allowed herself to be completely seduced by the Parisian night. The bright lights and big names had made her head turn. She'd undergone a remarkable transformation from the shy, round-shouldered ballet princess of ten months ago, embracing her inner vamp and revelling in the V.I.P. treatment her Moulin Rouge status afforded.

She had taken up smoking, which was in itself no big deal. In Paris, where smoking was still allowed in clubs, bars and restaurants, it really made no difference to your health if you got your nicotine from sucking directly on a cigarette or simply from breathing in all the secondary smoke. She had tarted up her wardrobe so that it seemed to consist almost entirely of miniskirts and stilettos, too. But she had also started dating Bruno, a bouncer at a 'gentlemen's establishment' just off the Champs Élysées – a strip club. A relatively high-end strip club, but a strip club just the same. Bruno was a Neanderthal of a man: short, stocky, shaved head, no neck. He was pushing forty and had nothing much going for him as far as I could see, beyond the fact he seemed to have an inexhaustible supply of money and ready access to a range of drugs. I always suspected he supplemented his doorman duties with a bit of drug-dealing on the side. He was not an especially savoury character.

It struck me as odd that Katie would be attracted to someone as essentially unattractive as Bruno, but whether she liked his protective presence or it was a father-figure thing, she threw herself willingly into dutiful girlfriend mode. For his part, Bruno was insanely jealous and treated her like a possession. Whenever we were all out together as a group, he kept Katie on a tight leash, plying her with alcohol and encouraging her to experiment with cocaine.

'You might want to take it easy on that stuff,' I suggested one night at a hotel suite party, as a clearly drunken Katie hoovered up her fifth line of the night.

Kneeling in front of the coffee table, she looked up at me through a mop of dishevelled hair, her eyes vacant, her eyeliner smudged. 'And you might want to mind your own business.'

By the end of my first summer in Paris, I felt pretty pleased with the way my life was coming together. I was happily single and enjoying my new network of friends and busy social life.

'You sound tired, love,' Mum's voice came down the phone line from Australia. It was just after eleven on a Sunday morning. 'Is everything okay?'

Everything was fine. I had only walked in the door some two hours previously, straight from a nightclub. I stifled a yawn. 'Fine, Mum, everything is just fine.'

'Are you sure, love? I know you're in Paris and it's all very exciting, but you have to take care of yourself.'

'I'm fine Mum. Please stop worrying.'

Phone calls from home were a weekly occurrence. I'd sit and listen to the run-down of family activities and then update Mum on my *vie parisienne*. Dad would usually throw in his two cents worth at the beginning of each call, then retire downstairs to watch the cricket, football or whatever other sporting event he could tune into.

'But anyway love,' Mum continued, 'I've got some good news. Your father and I are coming over for your birthday. We booked the tickets today.'

I let out a squeal of excitement. I hadn't seen my parents since I left home for Japan. It seemed like an eternity. And much as I was loving the independent life in Paris, a little bit of parental love never went astray.

Hanging up the phone, I sat for a moment and thought of all the things we could do in Paris together. I imagined them coming to see me perform – dancing on the stage of the Moulin Rouge. And then I thought of my father in a theatre filled with topless women, one of whom was his daughter, and suddenly I felt nervous. How would he react? How would I feel performing in front of him? I had long ago lost my self-consciousness about stepping out on stage each night in front of an auditorium full of strangers, but dancing in front of my parents was something else again. At least I had a couple of months to get used to the idea.

## Chapter Twenty-three

There are many unsung heroes toiling away backstage at your average cabaret show: people whose hard work make it easy for us show ponies to go out and look as fabulous as we do. Lighting technicians, stagehands, costume-makers and cobblers.

If you were to step backstage during a performance of any show the magnitude of the Moulin Rouge's, you'd be greeted by a scene of barely constrained chaos. While the performance unfurls smoothly onstage, there are scores of people ferreting about in the dark backstage, moving sets, ferrying costumes, fetching animals and dressing dancers. It all requires a finely tuned choreography that seems to work in spite of itself.

Easily the most important unsung hero in any showgirl's life is her dresser. This is a person in whom you need to have 100 per cent faith. You need to believe he or she will anticipate your every costume need, and will be waiting backstage to rip you out of one sequinned folly and stuff you into another.

Dressers mostly fall into two categories. There are the wizened old full-timers who have been scurrying about in the darkness for the better part of their professional lives – among whom there are usually a high number of crazies. Then there are the younger ones, who tend to be aspiring costume-designers or seamstresses: fashion types who study by day and dress showgirls by night. Celeste, my dresser, was one of the younger variety of dressers, and was a complete gem. In her early twenties, she was studying music and worked at the Moulin Rouge to pay the rent. Like many of her generation, she spoke excellent English. From the moment she had greeted me with that huge smile on my opening night, we got on, and she would often join us for our after-work sorties.

One evening she came into work and asked if I would be interested in coming to her music school, where a jazz jam recital was scheduled to take place. Keen to expand my social horizons and spend more time in the company of real-life French people, I happily accepted. Two nights later, I found myself in a part of Paris I had never seen before: the northside of the Butte de Montmartre.

As I emerged from the Métro and looked up, I could see the back of Sacré Coeur. The area, Jules Joffrin, was a mix of stately old stone buildings and ugly, more modern structures. There were supermarkets selling exotic African foodstuffs, phone shops nestled among cafes and florists sitting flush with the ubiquitous kebab shops. Following Celeste's instructions, I found the École de Musique and made my way inside.

It was early evening, and the place was largely deserted. I followed the handwritten notices stuck to the walls that pointed the way to the performance space. I knew I was getting closer to my destination when the doorways of neighbouring classrooms became suddenly populated by chain-smoking music students. All hair, skinny jeans and artfully worn neckscarves, they looked like music students anywhere in the world – aspiring, tortured artists in spindly teenage bodies. I pulled open the door to the auditorium and was hit by a wall of smoke. Through the haze, I could just make out Celeste at the bar.

'You made it!' she cried as I approached. 'Here, I want you to meet someone. This is Olivier, my saxophone teacher.' She turned to the young man standing next to her and spoke in rapid-fire French.

'*Enchanté*,' he said, leaning in to double-kiss me on the cheeks. As his face brushed mine I caught a smell of musky aftershave mixed with tobacco.

'*Enchanté*,' I replied. While Celeste quickly explained to him in French who I was and how I came to be there, I stole a moment to take him in. Tall and lean, with a shock of messy, short brown hair, almond eyes and a gentle-looking face. Very cute.

He looked at me sheepishly, almost apologetically, as Celeste spoke. 'I am sorry,' he finally said in faltering, heavily accented English. 'My English is not terrible.'

'*C'est pas terrible*' was a French expression commonly used to indicate that something was not good.

'No, it's me who should be apologising,' I replied. 'My French is very definitely *pas terrible*.'

He smiled.

As we waited for the jam session to begin, Olivier and I struggled through some pleasantries. The conversation was stilted but not at all uncomfortable, not least because I found myself melting at the sound of his accent.

By the time the concert ended, I was already late for work and so made my excuses and left. As I rode the Métro the few stops to Blanche, I happily replayed the Olivier encounter in my mind, and resolved to make more of an effort to meet Frenchmen.

At work that week there were two developments that put a spring in my showgirl step. Janet asked if I would like to learn the soloist show: they needed a couple more replacements for when the permanent soloists were off work, and Jean and I had been selected. It was all I could do not to squeal with excitement. First the captaincy, now this – I felt like I was on a roll.

'Of course!' I'd said. 'I'd be delighted!'

Less delighted, as it turned out, was Alison. Upon hearing of my imminent elevation up the ranks, she demanded to know how I expected to perform my captain's duties properly if I was also learning a new soloist show. I put it down to sour grapes and gave Alison a wide berth for the rest of the week.

Jean's and my excitement at being asked to learn soloist was only muted by the fact that Jenny had been overlooked. She was a stronger dancer than me, with beautiful ballet technique and greater flexibility. For her part, Jenny couldn't have been happier for us or more supportive, yet I still felt self-conscious that I had been selected. The Moulin Rouge worked in mysterious ways.

The second development to add a touch of spice to work proceedings that week was the kindling of a love interest. With a Frenchman, no less.

As a newly single girl, I was enjoying my freedom too much to jump into a serious relationship, but I was certainly open to a summer fling. Jean-Charles worked as a technician at the Moulin, overseeing the backstage machinations, including sets, lights and props.

He was tall, which already made him exceptional for a French man. He was in his late twenties, had a shaved head, wore a pair of discreet, silver-rimmed glasses and was always dressed in regulation head-to-toe black. He had sparked up conversation with me some weeks before that had since morphed into flirtatious backstage banter. Each night as I prepared to go on stage as a slave, I would make a joke about how ridiculous I looked and he would come back with a witty response.

Soon we were making excuses to see one another in the break between shows. He'd pass by the dressing-room with a cup of coffee; I'd hang around in the backstage area so we could talk. He was a voracious reader, a confirmed Anglophile and an aspiring screenwriter who, conveniently enough, lived in a small rooftop studio apartment around the corner from the Moulin Rouge. He ticked all the boxes. After all, if I was going to have a summer fling with a Frenchman, he might as well be a well-read, English-speaking, starving artist in a Parisian garret.

The ease with which we spoke and the relief I felt at finding someone interesting who didn't just live and breathe the dance world was real. The fact that he was French also didn't hurt, as my entourage to date had been almost entirely composed of fellow expats. It was perhaps only natural, and comforting to boot, but I hadn't come to France just to hang out with other foreigners. With Jean-Charles, I found I suddenly had a window on the French language and culture – and it was, as the French say, *très séduisant*. Besides, I was a girl from BrisVegas. The thought of having an affair with a Frenchman was wonderfully exotic.

One evening, during one of our *entracte rendez-vous*, Jean-Charles asked if we could meet up during the day. I told him we could – but only if he took me somewhere I had never been before. Two days later we met under the fountain in front of the Théâtre Châtelet.

'Okay,' I said as we pecked each other on the cheek in the traditional French greeting. 'I don't mean to be rude, but I *have* been here before.'

'Ah, *les étrangers*, always so impatient!' Jean-Charles replied. 'This isn't it, come with me.' He took me by the hand and walked me along the *quai*, past the *bouquinistes*: old, moustachioed men hunkered in front of their green-metal Seine-side bookstalls. We arrived at the Pont Neuf and stepped inside the Samaritaine department store. As we took the lift to the top floor, I remember thinking it was a strange choice of venue for a first date. We emerged in the luggage department and made our way through displays of suitcases towards a narrow spiral staircase at the far end of the room. At the top of the stairs, Jean-Charles pushed open a door and we stepped out onto a round terrace.

We were on top of La Samaritaine and looking across a stunning panorama of Paris. Below, the Seine made its lazy way under the Pont Neuf, beside Place de la Concorde and on past the Eiffel Tower. I could make out the silhouette of lovers on the Pont des Arts. The sun gleamed off the roof of Les Invalides, and off to our left, the twin towers of Notre Dame stood proudly overseeing the entire scene. It took my breath away.

'So I'm guessing from the look on your face that this is somewhere you haven't been before,' Jean-Charles said, smiling triumphantly.

I couldn't take my eyes off the view.

'It's beautiful,' I said. 'Just beautiful.'

We sat for two hours in the cafe on the floor below the panorama terrace, drinking *rosé* and getting to know one another. Jean-Charles spoke enthusiastically about Paris, about the history of France. He was so passionate about his city, so clearly proud of his country.

Later, we strolled along the bank of the Seine, hand in hand. Whether it was the *rosé*, the magic of Paris that had settled over me or the frisson of a budding relationship, it all felt very, very good.

For the next week, whenever I wasn't in rehearsal, Jean-Charles and I would meet in a different part of the city. He took me to fresh-food markets and gave me a glimpse of the passion every Frenchman I've since met has for food. We wandered the winding backstreets of the Marais and had a picnic in the sun at Place des Vosges. And then, one afternoon, while strolling through the streets of St Michel, we stopped mid-stroll and kissed.

I decided from the outset I didn't want our relationship to be common knowledge at work. I had mentioned it to Brett, Matthew and Dimitri, but otherwise had made very sure to keep any backstage contact as discreet as possible. I liked the fact that our dalliance existed in a context outside of the Moulin Rouge, away from the prying eyes of colleagues. We dancers already lived in one another's pockets as it was: it was nice to have something that belonged just to me.

During the day, I rehearsed to become a soloist and it was such a welcome relief to be learning something new. Performing the same show twice a night, six nights a week was starting to become a grind. The soloist show also involved much more complicated choreography, which I loved sinking my heels into, and required a lot of partner work with the soloist boys, of which Brett was one. With him involved, rehearsals became unusually fun.

When I wasn't at work, my waking hours were otherwise taken up with my French love affair. Sophie and Katie were still hitting the town each night, but while I would occasionally join them, I was mostly content to slip away after the second show to meet Jean-Charles.

He lived on Rue Lepic, just behind the Moulin Rouge. His tiny studio was on the sixth floor, there was no lift and the space was so poky it made my shoebox seem like the Palace of Versailles. But what it didn't have in square metreage it more than made up for in outlook, boasting a most magnificent view onto Sacré Coeur. Tucked away in the Paris rooftops, basking in the reflected glow from the bulbous dome of Paris's second most famous church, the whole scene was very French and fittingly romantic. We'd spend the evenings with the windows thrown open, eating cheese and drinking wine. He would teach me French phrases or show me old French films, and spoke of his grand plans to one day write and direct his own movie. We would wake in the mornings roused by the tolling of bells as the sun rose over a picture-postcard Parisian scene. Bordering on cliché though I knew it all was, it couldn't have been a more perfect introduction to relations *à la française*. I was experiencing the best of everything – a passionate love affair, a crash course in French linguistics and a culinary tour of discovery. I greedily ate it all up.

# Chapter Twenty-four

Two weeks after I had started learning the role, I took to the stage for the first time as a soloist. As I applied make-up that night, I sat in front of the mirror, nervously running through each number in my head. I was still captain of the nude line, so there was the usual barrage of queries and crises piling up as showtime approached. I did my best to deal with each one but mentally batted them to the side, determined not to let anything distract me from giving the best performance possible. I knew Janet and Thierry would be watching carefully, checking to see that the faith they had placed in my dancing had not been misguided.

Side stage before the show, I spent half an hour stretching. I needed to give my recalcitrant muscles as much of a warm-up as possible if I was to get through the soloist show without injury. Julia, the third soloist that night and the company's reigning Russian ice princess, came floating down the stairs ten minutes before curtain.

'You want to try?' she drawled to Brett, who was busying himself with stretches and a series of last-minute push-ups in the wings beside me. It was a pre-show ritual for Julia to practise her lifts just before the curtain rose. Brett, her partner for the night, stood dutifully and braced himself for the lift. Julia took two light steps towards him and leapt. She rose gracefully in the air and held herself in a perfect arabesque, seemingly oblivious to Brett straining below her. I marvelled at how cool she was and wished I could be half as elegant.

'Five minutes to curtain,' came the stage manager's voice over the backstage tannoy. I rushed back to my *loge*, panicking as the choreography began to muddle in my head. I was convinced I was about to make a fool of myself.

With Celeste's help, I slipped into my opening number costume and rushed back down into the wings. Before I had a second more to think, the lights were up, the music was soaring and I was on.

A dancer's body has a mysterious ability to switch off the thinking part of the brain and rely solely on memory and instinct when it comes time to step into the spotlight. During every show I have ever performed, there is a point at which I stop concentrating and let my body take over. Stepping out from behind the curtain, I felt my limbs take control. My feet, responding instinctively to the music, started to glide effortlessly about the stage. The spotlight followed my every move, the eyes of the audience were glued to me and I had that wonderful feeling of weightlessness you get when the choreography comes together seamlessly. A familiar shiver of joy passed through me. I was doing what I loved. I felt electrified and danced my heart out, carried by the waves of applause.

'Lovely show, Shay,' Janet said, sticking her head into the dressing-room during the *entracte*. 'We were all very impressed.'

My cheeks flushed, my face broke into the widest smile and I burned with pride.

As August rolled around, I started counting down the days until my parents arrived.

Jean-Charles and I had been together for just over a month and a half. As the weeks passed, however, I came to realise we had very different expectations from the relationship. Jean-Charles made it clear he wanted to get a whole lot more serious than I did.

Over lunch one day, he told me how much he was looking forward to meeting my parents. The panic I felt was telling.

I thought we both knew this was a summer fling. He was a lovely guy and we got on very well, but I wasn't interested in a long-term relationship and I definitely didn't want to complicate things by introducing him to my parents. It would have created a whole new dynamic in my relationship with him and completely changed Mum and Dad's visit.

I knew what I had to do. One afternoon, a week before my parents arrived, I organised to meet Jean-Charles in a cafe on Rue Lepic and told him how I felt.

'I just want to be on my own for a while,' I explained.

He didn't take it well at all. At first there was a look of shock, followed quickly by one of bewilderment and, finally, hurt.

'But I don't understand,' he said. 'I thought this was going well.'

I did my best to placate him, to soften the blow, but it was clear the announcement had come out of left field and had knocked the wind out of him. He went quiet, shaking his head in disbelief, looking about the cafe and fighting back the tears.

'Okay,' he finally managed. 'Okay. But I'd still like you to have this. For your birthday.'

He leaned under the table and pulled out a paper carry bag festooned with pink ribbon. Inside was a bottle of Jean Patou perfume and a copy of *Moby Dick*, his favourite book. 'I asked Dimitri to recommend a perfume,' he said, disconsolately. 'He said the best fragrance for you was patchouli and that Jean Patou did the finest patchouli scent in all of Paris.'

I felt awful, and sat for a while after he had left the cafe wondering if I had done the right thing.

Mercifully, after a week or so of awkward looks and a few tense backstage moments, Jean-Charles left the Moulin Rouge to take a job working on a film set. I missed him. I missed the intimacy and his easy companionship. But with my parents due any moment, I had plenty to keep me occupied.

We were warming up backstage one night, preparing to go on. The show was in full flight; I was dancing soloist again. The nerves were still there, but having performed the role several times, I was far less anxious. Vlada stood in the wings beside me, kicking her leg backwards over her head to loosen up for the show. She used techniques she'd learned as a child gymnastics prodigy, able to stretch herself into positions that would make a contortionist's eyes water – and all with only the slightest effort. Which is why we were all taken by surprise by what happened next.

If there is a more sickening sound than the snapping of a tendon, I don't know what it could be. Part tear, part pop, the noise shot through everyone within hearing distance. Vlada writhed in agony on the floor, screaming, while the in-house doctor was frantically called and an ambulance summoned.

During the *entracte*, Janet came to see me in the dressing-room.

'Shay, it looks like Vlada is going to be off for a while. She's torn a ligament – it's going to take months for her to recover. We need another replacement to cover Marissa when she's off, and I'd like you to be it.'

I was gobsmacked. I had only recently stepped into the soloist replacement shoes and now I was being asked to understudy Marissa, the star of the show.

'Me?' I replied, incredulous. 'Oh my God! I'd be honoured! Thank you! Thank you so much!'

'Good', Janet said. 'Rehearsals start tomorrow. You're going to have to pick it up quickly.'

After Janet had gone, I sat for a moment staring into the mirror. I wanted to call Mum, to phone home and squeal down the phone to her. I wanted to call Kim Bowkett, my old dance teacher, and tell her the good news. I wanted to jump up and down and yell.

'What's up?' Jenny asked, coming into the dressing room with Jean. 'You look like you've seen a ghost.'

'Janet's asked me to understudy Marissa,' I said, beaming.

'Of course she has sweetheart, I knew it all along,' Jean said, moving to hug me.

'Well done, Shayleen,' Jenny said. 'And to think it all began with a bunch of bananas at Jupiters.'

The next week was taken up with rehearsals as Marissa and Thierry walked me through the principal role. Boys came in to practise partner work as required and at one point Macbeth, the Moulin horse, was trucked in from his paddock on the outskirts of Paris to rehearse the section of the show in which I was to make my exit on horseback.

It had become a recent Moulin Rouge tradition to feature an animal of some kind in each show. Previous shows had featured crocodiles, dogs and even dolphins. Back in the days before animal cruelty laws, a pair of dolphins had lived in the theatre's four metre by five metre watertank, which sat all day and most of the night under the stage. It would be raised during the show's finale so the sad creatures could perform a half-hearted leap. The spectacle apparently thrilled audiences, but incensed animal-rights activists. Mercifully, things had become more humane since then, and the Moulin's current animal performers were trucked in each evening for the performance and then sent back out to their paddock and terrarium at the end of each night.

*Formidable!* had Macbeth, a lumbering, docile but very handsome white-grey stallion, plus a massive, nameless yellow python. Macbeth's sole function in the show was to add wow factor. He got a gasp from the audience each time he cantered on stage – the sight of a live beast on the Moulin Rouge stage, among all the feathers, sequins and over-the-top sets and costumes, never failed to get a reaction.

The python was part of the Arabian Nights scene, and was carried in on the shoulders of one of the dancers. She would set the creature down and it would slither towards the audience while she performed a mini-solo – the people in the front row would all reel back in horror as the snake made its lazy way towards them. Then, at the last moment, the dancer would scoop up the snake and disappear back into the wings.

Any of us could volunteer to be trained to wrangle the snake but it was one gig I never wanted. Snakes make my skin crawl. The thought of having one draped across my neck, wrapping itself around my shoulders and arms each night made me quiver just imagining it. However, for a dancer who was otherwise stuck up the back of the chorus line, a moment in the spotlight with the python gave her a chance to shine. Plus she received a sixty-franc-a-night supplement to do it.

It would have taken a whole lot more than fifteen dollars to get me anywhere near the thing.

I was happy to ride Macbeth, however. I spent hour upon hour with Marissa, practising lifts with her partner and going over and over combinations. I spent at least as many hours with Janet in front of the rehearsal room's mirrors.

'I'll see you at the same time tomorrow,' Janet had said after our first session. 'And don't forget your hairbrush.'

The final tableau of *Formidable!* featured the principal dancer performing a medley of French ballads – miming classics like 'La Vie en Rose' into a rhinestone-encrusted microphone. As I stood before the mirrors with my hairbrush, Janet patiently translated every word for me and told me which emotion I should be feeling and portraying at every stage. I sat on the floor of the studio, projecting to Janet and the mirrors and doing my best to feel like Édith Piaf or Mistinguett, and not like a lip-synching fraud from BrisVegas.

Five days of intense rehearsals later, I was prepped and ready to step up and replace the principal. Marissa, knowing that Mum and Dad were due to arrive the following week, had even kindly offered to swap her day off so I could dance the main role while they were in the audience. I was grateful, but still ever so slightly nervous.

The morning my parents arrived in Paris, I dragged myself out of bed uncharacteristically early to meet them off the Roissybus at Place de l'Opéra.

The moment I saw my mum's beaming smile as she stepped off the airport bus, I began to well up. By the time we were hugging, both of us were in tears.

'Sweetheart, it's so lovely to see you,' she kept saying, over and over, holding me tight and stroking the back of my head.

'Aw Shelb,' said Dad as he pulled me into a bear hug. 'God it's good to see you, love. How's my little girl?'

Dad was renowned for his enthusiasm. With his long-lost daughter under his arm and the magnificence of Paris's Opéra Garnier on a clear summer's morning laid out before him, he was fit to burst. 'Magnificent,' he repeated over and over. 'Just magnificent. How good is this?'

They were both thrilled to be in Paris. We lugged their suitcases down into the Métro and talked nonstop as we travelled north to La Fourche. But when we climbed the stairs and stepped back up onto street level, Mum and Dad fell silent. Deep in the colourful bosom of Avenue de Clichy, it suddenly became clear to my parents that we weren't in Kansas anymore. I could almost feel Dad's hackles rise as we walked down the street towards my apartment.

'Oh,' said Mum, looking for something diplomatic to say. 'It's um . . . different here love, isn't it?'

'Different' was Mum's way of saying she didn't like something.

'It's an acquired taste,' I replied. 'But actually a lot safer than you might think.'

I could tell Dad wasn't the least bit convinced, but he held his tongue nonetheless. They swung back into hyper-enthusiastic mode the minute they crossed the threshold of my studio. I had spent hours rearranging everything, doing my best to declutter the tiny space in an attempt to make it look bigger than it was.

'Oh, it's great love,' Dad said, standing in the kitchen, not daring to move for fear of knocking something over. 'Really cosy.' A hulk of a man, Dad seemed to fold into himself in my apartment, as if the walls were closing in around him.

For five days, we lived on top of each other. But there was so much to catch up on and we had been apart for so long, it felt like one big five-day slumber party. Fortunately, we'd made plans to hire a car and drive south for a couple of weeks after those five days. I had booked my first batch of holidays and had spent many a long-distance phone call plotting a route and booking accommodation through the south of France and Italy.

But before we went anywhere, there was my new Paris life to show them – and the small matter of my performance at the Moulin Rouge. The former I couldn't wait to do. I was so excited about my new home, my rudimentary command of the language and all the Parisian discoveries I had made that I was bursting to show it all off. The latter I had more mixed feelings about. I had never before felt as proud of a job as the one I was now doing: I was a dance captain and a replacement soloist and principal at the world's most famous cabaret. But the thought of dancing topless in front of my parents – especially my dad – made me feel uneasy. I had come to appreciate that nudity was part of the gig and that, in context, it wasn't the least bit remarkable, but would my dad feel the same way?

We spent our five days wandering the streets of Paris. It was late August and the city was empty, as most Parisians had fled south for the summer, leaving the place wonderfully quiet. For my birthday, we tumbled into a cafe next to Notre Dame and celebrated by eating our bodyweight in *tarte tatin*. I loved playing tour guide for Mum and Dad, revelling in the opportunity to show off my French. I took them to the markets, trawled with them through the Tuileries and showed them secret corners of the city that I had discovered but that no guidebook would ever have recommended.

We met up with Brett and Matthew, too, who proudly showed off their new baby – a puppy they had predictably enough called Audrey. Her full name was Audrey Loulou 'Gorge' Harris Mills.

Ever since Mum's back-deck chat with Brett in Brisbane all those years ago, Mum had been holding out for him to meet the right woman, convinced his being gay was 'just a phase'. But after meeting Matthew and seeing how happy they were together, she couldn't have been more pleased.

Then, over coffee with the three of us one day, Brett and Matthew revealed that Megan had decided to return to Australia. She was all out of high-kicks and had started to tire of the showgirl social whirl. She craved the simple life and was hanging up her heels.

'You should take her room,' Brett suggested. 'Why don't you move in with us?'

I could see Mum and Dad nodding enthusiastically. Much as they liked my little studio and approved of the independent life I was forging in this faraway city, it was clear they preferred the idea of Brett and Matthew being there to look out for me each day. From my point of view, it would not only save me a bit of money but also be a lot of fun. And so it was decided. Over *crème brulée* and *chocolat chaud* in a terrace cafe on Rue de Levis, I agreed to move in with the boys.

Walking home from rehearsals one afternoon, while Mum and Dad were resting back at the apartment, I bumped into Olivier, Celeste's handsome, brooding saxophone teacher.

'Shay?' he said, as our paths crossed.

'Oh, hi. Olivier, isn't it?'

He nodded. 'I just finished having coffee with Celeste.'

I was pleased to see that he looked just as cute in daylight. Self-consciously, I pushed a wayward strand of hair behind my ear: in trackpants, trainers and a baggy *Tropical Nights* T-shirt, I wasn't exactly looking my best. We chatted for a few minutes. Or rather, I did most of the talking. He seemed to do a lot of nodding. I wasn't sure if he understood a word until I mentioned I was going to be moving.

'Really? I know someone who might be interested in taking your studio. Maybe I can take your number and pass it on to them?'

If it was a ruse to get my number, it was a smooth one.

'Sure,' I replied, reeling off my number, then reciting it in French – just to be sure.

'Great, well, perhaps he will call you,' said Olivier.

As we made off in opposite directions, I desperately wanted to shoot a glance over my shoulder, but just kept walking.

When the night of my debut as principal finally rolled around, I was so terrified about getting the choreography and lip-synching right, I completely forgot to be self-conscious dancing topless in front of my parents. Not that they appeared the least bit perturbed. As I stepped out on stage at the start of the show and spied Dad in the audience, I realised I hadn't given him enough credit. He was sitting upright in his seat, his chest bursting with pride, waving like a madman while Mum sat next to him beaming.

'Magnificent darlin'!' he declared after the show as the three of us nursed a drink at Le Palmier. 'You were sensational.'

'Oh Shelb, you were the best,' Mum threw in. 'I knew you would be.'

'And what about that show?' Dad continued, about to explode with enthusiasm. 'It's bloody mighty.' He pulled me into a hug and gave a wink. 'And it'll be even better when they make the rest of your costumes.'

After the excitement of my first principal performance, Mum, Dad and I sauntered off south for two weeks, wending our way through eastern France, down across the Alps, into Italy and back again. It was two glorious weeks of being looked after, spoiled and doted on. I had been living away from home pretty much since the age of nineteen, and it felt nice to be the child again for a couple of weeks, to let Dad do the driving and just sit back and take in the scenery. I slept a lot.

I was twenty-four and still resilient; I had an enormous capacity to juggle the work schedule, the responsibility and the social life of a showgirl, and I bounced back from sleeplessness without too much trouble, but a two-week break in which I didn't have to think about work – let alone plan a show or wrangle a dressing-room full of egos – was pure bliss. The aches in my back and pains in my knee joints, which I had come to accept as daily companions, gradually faded, so that when I returned to Paris, it was with a new skip in my showgirl step. And thanks to my father's determination to 'put a bit of flesh on those bones of yours', by the time they packed their bags and headed back to Brisbane, I was carrying an extra kilo or two.

When Mum and Dad went home, summer seemed to leave with them. Autumn slipped into winter; we all scrambled for our coats, scarves and hats, and cranked up the heating in our apartments. The days became shorter and dusk lost its golden-pink hue, to be replaced by day after day of slate grey. The leaves turned on the trees, providing a brilliant last flash of colour in the city, before dropping to the ground and leaving black skeletons of branches. Winter seemed to arrive almost overnight. I pined for the long, languid nights of summer. There were fewer parties after work, with people preferring to scoot directly home and curl up under their doonas.

I was living with Brett and Matthew now, and sharing custody of Audrey. It was lovely to be part of a household again, not least because Matthew – who was an excellent cook – had discovered an old *Country*

*Women's Association* cookbook that Megan had left behind and was slowly working his way through it. There was hardly an afternoon that I climbed the stairs to our Rue Dautancourt abode and wasn't greeted by the smell of pumpkin scones or the unmistakeable scent of savoury mince. 'Have you seen this?' Matthew would ask me as I walked into the kitchen. He was usually sporting a blue gingham apron and up to his elbows in flour. 'It's a recipe for something called coconut ice. Do people really eat that in Australia? I'm definitely trying that one out tomorrow. And make sure you're home on Friday. I'm doing rum balls!'

It may sound counter-intuitive but food and the eating of lots of it was central to my life as a Paris showgirl. People often assumed that my figure was the result of manic dieting and carefully watching what kinds of foodstuffs passed my lips – the reality could not have been more different. Whether I was possessed of an unusually fast metabolism or it was simply that my job was the equivalent of a two-hour gym workout every night, I had never had a problem with my weight. Perhaps if mine had been a desk-bound job, things would have been different. But lifting your leg repeatedly over your head for two shows a night, six nights a week, plus all the onstage running and backstage stair-climbing, will pretty reliably keep your figure trim.

If food appreciation wasn't the defining characteristic of our household, it was most certainly one of its pillars. Matthew and I would routinely bring home cookbooks we had found in obscure second-hand English bookstores about the city – books with titles like *Goose Fat and Garlic* or *Just Desserts*. We'd pore over the recipes, feeling our arteries harden as we read.

It was this shared love of food that also turned us into regular customers of the Cloche d'Or – the late-night eatery across the road from the Moulin Rouge. 'La Cloche' as it was referred to in showgirl vernacular, was a nondescript place that had somehow made a name for itself among the Parisian showbiz community. The proprietors would no doubt maintain it was because of their quality produce and warm hospitality. I suspect it had more to do with the fact that the kitchen was open until 4 a.m., that they served deep-fried camembert as an entrée and that they were tolerant of large parties of showfolk who liked to drink before staging impromptu floorshows.

As winter took hold, it was not uncommon for us to congregate at La Cloche up to three nights a week. But for a few adventurous excursions into the gastronomical wild-side of snails or *tête de veau*, we rarely varied our order. We didn't need to: a deep-fried camembert for entrée, an *entrecôte* with blue-cheese sauce for main and a *crème brulée* for dessert always made for the perfect end to any evening. All of it was washed down with a bottle or two of the house's second-cheapest red.

The walk home in the brisk night air was almost always a welcome chance to digest.

On the nights we weren't at La Cloche, we'd meet up at Corcoran's Irish Pub or the MCM Cafe, a large bar-cum-nightclub next to the Moulin Rouge. It was at the MCM that we farewelled Jenny. She had been dancing at the Moulin for just under a year, and despite her obvious talents, wasn't progressing up the showgirl ladder as fast as she would have liked. So she'd decided to move on.

I was sad to see her leave. She had been a constant in my little Paris universe, a confidante whose friendship stretched back years. As she and I hugged outside the pub and said our goodbyes, we tried to soften the blow of the separation by assuring one another we would see each other again soon: that our paths were destined to keep on crossing. And I was certain they would. It had happened before and it would happen again.

With the onset of winter, I'd made a conscious effort to scale back my exposure to Sophie and Katie's V.I.P. scene, more interested in socialising with my close friends. Living with the boys was turning out perfectly. As long as there were undiscovered culinary horizons for Matthew to explore within the pages of the *CWA* cookbook, I was well fed. With two dear friends ever present and ready to share a laugh over a coffee at the kitchen table, I was also well looked after. And given our shared obsession with Christmas and all its trappings, when the holiday season rolled around, I was happily nestled in the heart of a unique, warm little family unit.

Christmas in Paris is one of the most beautiful times of the year. It's cold, like Christmas is meant to be. There's the smell of roasting chestnuts on every street corner, and the boulevards sparkle with Christmas lights. Grand Parisian spaces like the Place Vendôme and the Champs Élysées are draped with tasteful decorations or transformed with shimmering, elegant lighting displays.

And then there's the food. If Parisians are mildly food-obsessed during the rest of the year, they become unapologetic gluttons in the lead-up to Christmas. Whereas Christmas at home had been as much about the presents as the food, in France it was *all* about the food. Which is not to say we didn't turn in a good effort on the present front. By the time Christmas Eve rolled around, there were fifty-seven presents stuffed under our tree at Rue Dautancourt. In keeping with the over-the-top theme, Matthew had bought a turkey that was so large we had to set our alarm to wake at 8 a.m. (an ungodly hour for showpeople) to preheat our oven and start roasting the bird. Parisian kitchens being what they are, we didn't have a proper oven, and so were forced to place our trust in the toaster oven that served all our baking needs. The turkey barely squeezed inside it.

Jean was joining us for Christmas lunch, and walked ten blocks to our apartment through the eerily deserted Christmas Day streets of Paris carrying her own toaster oven, in which we planned to cook the vegetables. 'Have oven, will travel, sweetheart,' she said as she stepped into the apartment, balancing the oven in one arm and handing over a full-sized white-chocolate cheesecake.

Amid the riot of Matthew's handmade crepe-paper chains and streamers, and the profusion of Christmas baubles and lights, we ate ourselves into a state of immobility. Not even Jean's attempt to get a rousing round of carol-singing going could tempt any of us to move.

Unsurprisingly, work that night was especially painful. The entire company seemed to move gingerly about the backstage area, nursing bloated stomachs and middle-of-the-day-drinking hangovers. Smiles were pasted to faces and stomachs sucked in more rigorously than usual as we took to the stage and went through our showgirl paces, all the while wishing we were at home digesting, curled up on the sofa like normal people.

I struggled through the two shows and spent the whole time wondering what my family was up to back in Brisbane, yet I felt strangely content. I had been in Paris for over a year, and it was finally starting to feel like home.

## Chapter Twenty-five

It was always an enormous delight to come into work every night and see a queue of people outside the Moulin Rouge, patiently waiting to see the show. I was proud to be part of something that so many people wanted to see, and on nights when I struggled to muster the enthusiasm needed to get up on stage and perform, it gave my motivation a boost. However, the Moulin Rouge was open every single day of the year, and while it was nice to be in demand, it meant there was no respite. We dancers had only one night off a week, and the public holidays that most people took for granted simply didn't exist for us. In fact, perversely enough, the two nights of the year we would have given anything not to be onstage were the two nights that management were turning them away at the door. On Christmas night it was standing-room only at the Moulin Rouge. People came in droves. New Year's Eve was similarly popular.

And so I spent my second consecutive New Year's Eve onstage. At the stroke of midnight, as the world ushered in 1999, I was at my dressing-table applying false eyelashes and psyching myself up for yet another performance of *Formidable!*

The show was late to start that night, meaning that we took our final curtain call at almost 3 a.m. As we settled into our post-show routine of make-up removal and showering, Amy, a nude from the other *loge*, stuck her head around the dressing-room door.

'I'm having a party at my place after work, everyone's welcome.'

Amy was having a fling with a member of a visiting American all-male strip revue. His name was Buck or Buff or something equally ridiculous, and he was a walking can of fake tan, had glow-in-the-dark teeth and a mane of painstakingly coiffed, highlighted hair. I was keen for a New Year's knees-up, so I decided to go along. It was the usual scene, with more people squashed into a tiny apartment than it could reasonably accommodate. Champagne, beer and wine were being consumed with typical showfolk gusto and a tiny stereo worked overtime, serving up a steady stream of cheesy pop and thumping dance music. At around 7 a.m., following several complaints from neighbours and a visit from the local constabulary, Amy called it a night and asked everyone to leave.

Jean was not content to let the evening die so easily. 'Come back to mine,' she said. 'I've got fags. We'll sing show tunes.'

I found myself instinctively following the crowd who were wrapping themselves in coats and heading to Jean's apartment. We wandered down Rue Lepic and across Place Blanche, a wan midwinter dawn beginning to lighten the sky. Pigalle was a cesspit of broken beer bottles and discarded fast-food wrappers. Despite the hour, the streets were still crowded with dangerously swaying people who clearly didn't know when to call it a night.

As we walked down Rue Fontaine, I caught a glimpse of my reflection in a window. I looked like death. I had bags under my eyes and, despite Matthew's culinary creations and Dad's efforts to fatten me up, I was as skinny as a rake. I stopped and let my fellow revellers pass. Staring at myself, I made a New Year's resolution: this year, I would scale back the partying. I was twenty-four – which made me middle-aged in showgirl terms. I needed to start taking better care of myself.

With a stable work life and less late-night rabble-rousing, I found I had time to concentrate on other pursuits. So when I received a phone call early in the New Year from Jean-Charles, asking if I wanted to meet for coffee, I was delighted that he had apparently gotten over our break-up and wanted to be friends.

We arranged to meet for a coffee near Opéra; he was already seated at a table at the back of the cafe when I arrived. We chatted amiably, exchanging pleasantries and conducting a brief catch-up. All very friendly and casual.

Then, midway through my account of moving in with the boys, he pulled a paper bag out from under the table and pushed it towards me.

'What's this?' I asked.

'It's a present. For you. Open it up.'

I reached into the bag and pulled out a gift-wrapped parcel. Peeling away the paper revealed a pale blue papier-mâché crescent moon.

'Oh,' I said, unsure how to react. 'It's lovely. Is it a housewarming gift?'

'No, not a housewarming gift. It's a gift for you. I wanted you to know I would have given you the moon.'

I looked at him incredulously. Surely he was kidding. 'This is a joke, right?'

'No joke, Shay. The stars and moon, they could have all been yours.'

I had heard often about French men's tendency to high drama and overblown expressions of love, but this was the first time I'd encountered it up close. He was serious. He was *deadly* serious. My earthy Australian sensibilities reeled at the idea that a grown man who wasn't reading from a Hollywood movie script could sit there and say such stuff. And there was more.

He reached back into the bag, pulled out a cassette tape and a folder, and handed them over solemnly. I eyed the exit and did a quick calculation of how many tables I would have to leap to reach sanctuary outside.

'And this is a screenplay I wrote for you, and the soundtrack to go with it. I wrote and recorded it at home. It's all dedicated to you.'

In some countries, gestures like these would be considered the height of romance. Doubtless there are women in the world who would love nothing better than to receive a papier-mâché moon and inspire a screenplay and its soundtrack. But unfortunately for Jean-Charles, I wasn't one of them. I was a Tarragindi girl at heart, and it was way too much for me.

It was too much for Brett, as well, when I told him the story that evening after diplomatically extricating myself from the encounter and running home. 'He did what?!' Brett howled. 'That's brilliant! That's intense, even for a French man!' The moon henceforth assumed pride of place on top of the fridge. The screenplay and tape, however, went swiftly to the back of my closet, unopened and unplayed.

But my brush with French melodrama wasn't enough to put me off the French male as a species. I had bumped into Olivier at post-work drinks a few times: he would invariably arrive with Celeste, but at the end of the night we always seemed to find ourselves in long conversations.

Once I'd established there was nothing going on between him and Celeste, I found myself making a little extra effort with my appearance post-show if I knew he was going to meet us for drinks. For his part, he stopped pretending he was there as a guest of Celeste and started showing up to see me.

I teased him about taking my number but never calling.

'But it was for my friend who needed an apartment,' he protested playfully. 'Honestly.'

'Sure it was,' I replied.

Olivier was a saxophonist who'd studied at one of Paris's top conservatories. Now he taught by day, played gigs by night and aspired to compose his own album. He was passionate about his art, and even more so about his country – he loved France and all things French. And he couldn't have looked more like a typical French man if he tried. Dark hair, olive skin, brown eyes. He had a lean build and was the same height as me (a definite plus for a showgirl). And he smoked, pouted and flirted as if he had been born to do it. When he spoke English, it was with a gorgeously thick French accent, which I suspect he exaggerated for my benefit. The more time we spent together, the more I craved seeing him. He would sit with me in the corner of a bar and stroke my hair or hold my hand. He would laugh at my attempts to speak French, calling me *'charmante'* and *'mignonne'*. I was swept away by the utter Frenchness of it all.

Olivier took to walking me home. Strolling the artfully lit streets, I came to understand why Paris was considered the world capital of romance: even the grimy streets of Pigalle took on a shiny new look. When, after several weeks of flirting, he pulled me into him under a Montmartre street lamp and kissed me, I melted in his arms.

Over the course of the following three months, we saw each other almost every day. Sometimes we would meet for lunch at one of the myriad rustic little bistros he knew dotted about the city. He took great delight in educating me in the importance of matching wine and food, cringing whenever I ordered an orange juice or a Coke with my *entrecôte*. If we'd slept through lunch and the day was especially cold, we would find a comfortable cafe and while away the afternoon reading and drinking hot chocolate.

We spent all our nights together, either at his apartment or mine; it felt nice to fall asleep in someone's arms again. The fact that my new lover spoke in an accent thick as honey and would sometimes leap from the bed to the keyboard to write down a phrase of music that had come to him – cigarette hanging from his bottom lip – only added to the romance.

We mostly ended up at Rue Dautancourt, for the simple reason that Olivier's neck of the woods was too dangerous for a lone woman to walk at night. The first time I visited his apartment after work, I emerged from the Métro at Goncourt and immediately felt vulnerable. Groups of men huddled menacingly on street corners in the dark. Smoke hung listlessly in ill-lit, run-down cafes. I was used to a certain amount of grittiness in La Fourche, but this was something else again. I flicked up the collar of my overcoat, pulled myself as upright as possible and marched purposefully down the darkened street.

'Are you crazy?' Olivier had demanded when I turned up on his doorstep. 'Don't ever walk out there at night by yourself again. That street is renowned for drug deals.'

As I picked my way around drunks and transvestites in the backstreets of Clichy or hurried with him through the mean streets of Goncourt, it always amused me to consider how different this was from the popular conception of a Paris showgirl's love life. The great myth held that there were millionaires and counts lined up outside the stage door every night to protest their undying love – armed with jewels, caviar and champagne – and eventually carry us off into a south-of-France sunset, to a life of untold luxury.

A few girls did leap happily from the Moulin stage to the lap of a cashed-up suitor. But I had always tended towards the down-to-earth (and down-at-heel) when it came to romantic encounters, and Olivier was no exception.

One of the most attractive things about him was that he had nothing to do with my work. Sure, as a musician he was involved in the entertainment industry, and hence had an interest in what I did and, importantly, an understanding of why I did it. But as a Moulin Rouge outsider he was the perfect antidote to the claustrophobia I had started to feel with Jean-Charles, and still occasionally felt with work colleagues who were friends. I loved backstage gossip and intrigue as much as the next dancer, but I didn't need to talk about work ad nauseum to the exclusion of all else. Olivier had one foot in the normal, daylight world, and spending time with him made for a welcome respite. I liked that my world was changing and opening up a little because of him.

While Olivier was fast becoming an unofficial fifth member (counting Audrey) of the Rue Dautancourt household, there were changes afoot in the Brett and Matthew camp. Tired of languishing in the Moulin's chorus line with no sign of any promotion on the horizon, Matthew had found another job.

Whatever the lot of showgirls, it is far and away preferable to the hand dealt to the showboys. As a general rule, a male cabaret dancer leads a frustrating life – you're vital to the show, but no-one really takes nearly enough notice of you. After all, a chorus line of well turned out, impeccably groomed, sequin-festooned men is not the reason most people are forking out money to see a Paris show.

*Formidable!*'s male company was the usual mixed bag of dancers from France, America, England, Australia and eastern Europe. About 80 per cent of them were gay – the remaining 20 per cent, as I've said before, spent their time getting involved in and then skilfully extricating themselves from liaisons with their female colleagues. In the almost twelve months I had been at the Moulin, one of the male dancers had dated at least half of his female colleagues, leaving a trail of embittered or jealous showgirls in his wake.

For many of the boy dancers, the Moulin Rouge represented a steady job in an industry where precariousness was the norm, and they were prepared to endure their secondary onstage status just to have a regular pay cheque. It was remarkable to me to see Bolshoi- or Kirov-trained primo ballet dancers performing choreography which was clearly a waste of their talent. But as Dimitri explained, 'A job is a job is a job, darling. Besides, have you been to Moscow? It's a hellhole.'

Faced with playing second fiddle to a line of legs, breasts and feathers every night, male dancers usually reacted in one of two ways. Some worked doubly hard to ensure they were noticed; others accepted their lot as bit-players and just went through the motions. Brett had been singled out as a talent and promoted to the role of soloist, allowing him to stretch his performing wings a little more than most each night. Matthew, however, hadn't been so lucky, and had stagnated in the chorus line, falling foul of a new penchant among the powers-that-be for pumped-up beefcake over typically slim ballet-dancing types.

So he applied for, and was immediately offered, a job at the Royal Palace in Kirrwiller – the same cabaret venue in the middle of a paddock near Strasbourg that had been Melissa's salvation. Our household was breaking up, though Brett and Matthew weren't: they planned to become regular commuters on the five-hour train journey from Paris to Strasbourg.

As Matthew packed his bags, tucked the *CWA* cookbook under his arm and hugged me goodbye, I felt a tremor pass through my little Paris universe. I had gotten used to the transient nature of friendships in the showbiz world, but this was different. Matthew was family, and I was sad to see him leave. Nothing was going to be the same.

Not much later, I told Brett I had decided to move in with Olivier: we were spending so much time together that it made sense. Brett was disappointed, but understood. Fortunately, there was always a steady turnover of dancers at the Moulin Rouge and new arrivals were desperate to share a room in an apartment already decked out by a colleague.

I set about the task of finding an apartment for Olivier and I to share. Our combined salaries were modest, so we were looking at the lower end of the market, but I was nonetheless determined to find a place in a neighbourhood where I didn't have to pick my way around a pile of hypodermic needles each time I stepped out the door. I craved a living environment that wasn't heavy with the smell of kebabs and chip fat. Paris is justly famous for being crammed with picture-postcard-beautiful buildings and *quartiers* – I was going to become an inhabitant of one of them if it was the last thing I did.

During visits to my dentist in Villiers, I had come to appreciate the refined qualities of the seventeenth *arrondissement*. It's renowned in Paris as being crammed with old-money, cashed-up nuclear families and grand Hausmannian apartment buildings – a definite step up from Avenue de Clichy, though on a map the two *quartiers* are side by side. Villiers is affluent, clean and looks just like the Paris of popular imagination.

It had the added benefit of being close to work without being right on top of it. I felt like the Moulin Rouge already took up enough space in my life, and I wanted to put a little more physical distance between my workplace and my new home. It would mean forking out for a taxi each night to get home, but I figured it was a price worth paying to have a sanctuary outside the orbit of that eternally spinning windmill.

For several weeks I visited estate agents on the Rue de Levis, a delightful pedestrianised market street in the heart of Villiers. During breaks in my apartment hunt, I'd cross the Boulevard de Courcelles to sit in the nearby Parc Monceau – the same park the taxi driver had assured me was '*Très, très beau*' on my first night in Paris. A new summer was in full swing and the lawns were packed with sunbaking Parisians. It was much more of a traditional English park than the majority of Paris's beautiful but untouchable gardens: a quiet, leafy green haven in the centre of Paris, lined on either side by stately, honey-coloured Hausmannian apartment buildings. I fell in love with it instantly.

Eventually, I found a small one-bedroom place on Rue Légendre, around the corner from Rue de Levis. It was on the second floor and was dark and slightly claustrophobic, wedged as it was between two narrow courtyards, but it was superbly located. Once we had moved in, I set about exploring the neighbourhood further.

Strolling the Rue de Levis and perusing the daily fresh-food market became a morning ritual. French markets are proudly seasonal, and it being July, the fruit stalls were packed with all manner of berries – blueberries, raspberries, wild strawberries. There were also apricots, so sweet you could taste the sunshine in them, and mountains of peaches and nectarines. There were fruits and vegetables I had never seen before – streaky aubergines, green figs and pink grapefruit. The smell of fennel drifted on the air, along with the pungent aromas of thyme, rosemary and tarragon.

The vendors, each one a rotund, apron-wearing hulk of *bonhomie*, would loudly hawk their wares. One in particular, the honey-seller, took an immediate shine to me, asking me all sorts of questions about where I came from and how I came to be in Paris. '*Mademoiselle*,' he would cry each time I wandered by, 'take me to *Australie*! Take me to *Australie*!' I never passed his stall without having a piece of honey cake or a free sample of honey thrust into my hands. I also never saw him sell a single thing. When he wasn't singing the praises of his honey to the world, he spent his time playing tunes on his recorder and games of chess with his fellow vendors.

I was starting to understand that selling wasn't really the point. The markets were all about a celebration of food. The vendors were actors in a daily outdoor soap opera. If they happened to sell some stuff into the bargain, all the better, but it really wasn't the object of the exercise.

Over a two-week period I tested each of the three *boulangeries* on the street. With unwavering dedication to the cause, I threw myself selflessly into the business of taste-testing *éclairs, réligieuses, millefeuilles, croissants, pains au chocolats* – and of course *baguettes* – in order to find the *boulanger* who would be worthy of my regular custom. I settled on the one closest to the apartment, which had the added benefit of a *serveuse* who was unfailingly kind to me, helping me with my faltering French each time I visited.

One morning, I bowled up to the fruit vendors from whom I had been faithfully purchasing peaches, apricots and strawberries all summer. I wanted grapes, but not the variety with seeds inside. Seedless grapes were a readily available commodity in fruit shops all over my homeland, so I assumed you only had to ask to find them in France.

Before leaving the apartment, I had taken the time to look up 'seedless' in the French dictionary. I was quietly pleased with my new vocabulary, and determined to impress the fruiterer with my command of his language.

'*Bonjour monsieur, je voudrais des raisins sans pepins.*'

'*Des raisins sans pepins?*' He looked at me with an amused smile before starting to chuckle. '*Eh Pierre, écoutez!*' he called to his colleague. '*Elle cherche des raisins sans pepins!*' ('Hey Pierre, listen! She's looking for seedless grapes!') The two of them started to belly laugh.

I felt my confidence suddenly deflate, and stood on the spot, waiting to be let in on the joke.

'*Les raisins sans pepins sont pas des raisins,*' lectured the vendor – 'Seedless grapes are not grapes'. He seemed incredulous at the very thought of something so outlandish.

I would learn that the French are nothing if not purists when it comes to their food. Despite the fact they mostly live in cities, they claim a deep and abiding connection to the countryside and all the produce that comes from it. The thought of a grape that has been tampered with so that it doesn't produce seeds offends their sensibilities – it goes against the grand circle of life, the warts-and-all wonder of Mother Nature.

# Chapter Twenty-six

As much as I enjoyed my daily attempts at interaction in the market and my mornings sitting in the sun in the cafe, I couldn't help but feel my lack of language skills meant I was missing out. I relied on the kindness of strangers whenever I had to speak with a shopkeeper, the *concierge* of our building or a taxi driver. The fact that I was living in this vibrant Parisian *quartier* with a real live Frenchman only hardened my resolve to improve my French. While Olivier was extremely patient and fumbled along in broken English, I couldn't help but feel our relationship would plateau unless I made an effort to speak his language. And so I finally enrolled in a full-time French class. Waking early after my two late-night shows, I would mainline a coffee and drag myself to lessons five mornings a week.

The class was held across town, near the Père Lachaise cemetery – it took me twenty-five minutes on the Métro to get there, most of which I spent napping. There were only seven or eight students most days.

At home, I began watching the French TV news religiously and demanded that Olivier only speak to me in French. He would usually oblige until communication became so laboured that he switched back to English out of pure frustration. Even so, bit by bit, my French began to improve. Sometimes phrases would spill out of my mouth that I had no idea were in me. I would surprise myself by understanding the introduction to a TV news story, or picking up the gist of a conversation in a French soap opera. Gradually, I became able to listen to Olivier on the phone to his parents or in conversation with his friends and understand what was being discussed.

To begin with, my accent was awful, but the longer I spent with Olivier, the more I absorbed the French intonation by osmosis. It would be years before I claimed anything even resembling fluency, but the foundations were being laid.

By the end of summer, and after only two months in Villiers, I felt like I had been accepted as a local. I could walk the Rue de Levis and be plied with free honey, the *serveuse* in the *boulangerie* had started to make a point of giving me a *baguette 'pas trop cuit'* (not too crusty), just as she knew I liked it, and even the fruit vendors had moved beyond the seedless grape debacle. But it was only when we began to receive house calls from the *restaurateur* of the bistro at the base of our building that I knew I had really arrived.

Emmanuel ran the quaint little eatery on Rue Légendre next to the entrance of our building. Every month or so he would go to the countryside to visit his mother, and each time he would come back armed with a bag full of snails.

'These are for you,' he would say, standing on our doorstep proffering the bag.

Inside would be two dozen snails in butter, parsley and garlic, ready to be stuck in the oven and devoured. They were heavenly.

Thanks largely to Olivier, but also to my daily adventures on Rue de Levis, my palate was becoming more adventurous and new gastronomic horizons were being opened up to me every week. To Olivier, food wasn't just fuel that got you through the day. For him, it was easily up there with music, smoking and *l'amour*.

His love of food came from his mother, a woman I hadn't yet met, but had heard much about. She was apparently an amazing cook. Her *répertoire* was 'restricted' to classic French dishes (of which there are an impressive number, in any cook's book), but according to Olivier she did each one perfectly.

Being in a relationship with a man who was more excited about new-season potatoes than about any given sporting code was a novel experience for me. I could cook, and had done so for myself for the better part of seven years, but my prowess with pots and pans was nothing compared to his.

I loved that Olivier was passionate about food. I loved that when we went to the market together, he would approach each vendor's wares with a kind of scientific precision. Every melon was prodded or smelled for signs of ripeness. Every nectarine was squeezed gently; every cut of prosciutto, *entrecôte* or *rôti de porc* (pork roast) was examined carefully. And the end result, lovingly prepared and spectacularly presented as it invariably was, never failed to send me into raptures. I could feel my waistline expanding by the day.

## Chapter Twenty-seven

By the autumn of 1999, as the new millennium crept ever closer, *Formidable!* had been running for over eleven years. Even among Moulin revues, which were renowned for their longevity, it was a record.

A new show existed: it had been conceived, designed and scored years previously. It even had a name, *Féerie*. But it had been sitting at the back of a cupboard collecting dust, because management claimed it didn't have a sufficient budget to invest in it. So *Formidable!* just kept stuttering along. The doughnuts were bedraggled and the choreography was dated, but it was still infinitely cheaper to keep the old show ticking over than it was to stage a brand-new one.

If the costumes looked tired to me, they were nothing compared to those dancers who had also been with the show since it opened. It was a feat of staggering tenacity. In my eighteen months onstage at the Moulin Rouge, I'd learned that, as physically demanding as the job was, it was nothing compared to the mental fortitude that was required to go onstage night after night and perform the same show again and again. Audiences deserved and management demanded that every dancer pour every ounce of joy, enthusiasm and life they had into every performance they gave. Which wasn't easy to do when it was the seven-thousandth time you had done it. Endurance was proving to be far and away the most important quality a showgirl could have – that and the ability to smile like you meant it and high-kick your heart out even when you were bored beyond belief.

For as long as I had been at the Moulin Rouge there had been talk of the new show, but nothing had ever happened. By the end of that summer, the backstage rumour mill was working overtime. The new show buzz had become deafening.

'Yes, it's true,' Janet finally confirmed one night. 'There's going to be a new show for the new millennium. If you want to be a part of it, you'll have to audition next month. We'll be recasting the show from scratch.'

In a country where jobs for life were the norm, and in a workplace where complacency had settled in like a rot, the effect of her announcement was electrifying. Dancers who had previously just gone through the motions suddenly started to perform each night like their lives depended on it. Indeed, for some of the company, their lives *did* depend on it. Whether they were single girls from abroad who had established lives in Paris, mothers of three who were the the sole breadwinner, or any one of the numerous eastern European dancers whose Moulin salary supported an entire family back in their homeland – the stakes were high.

Some dancers, myself among them, resolved to return to class to brush up on our skills, convinced that years of performing the same steps in the same show every night had eroded any technique we may once have had. Others, especially the older, less motivated girls, reacted with a sense of fatalism. They saw the writing on the wall. To their credit, they were self-aware enough to realise that their high-kicking days were numbered and that, once subjected to the scrutiny of an audition process, they would come up wanting. Then there were the girls who reacted to the announcement of a new show and a rigorous audition process by going about their business as usual. Girls like Sophie and Katie.

Summer seemed to have ratcheted Sophie's extracurricular activities up a notch. She was out most nights until early morning, and would come into the dressing-room with ever more outrageous tales of late-night excess. Not that her adventures were out of the ordinary. Erratic behaviour among company members was not uncommon, thanks largely to the emphasis that most dancers placed on partying over working. Usually, the first sign that things had gotten out of control was when a dancer's landlord beat a path to the Moulin Rouge offices, demanding that management pay the dancer's months-overdue rent. It was true that our salaries were not huge, but many people in Paris got by on much less, and often with families to feed. A dancer partying too hard had a short shelf life and a high burnout rate.

Unsurprisingly, Katie was among the first casualties.

As captain, I was used to her arriving late, showing up incapable of working, or phoning in sick. But on one particular evening in July, she simply failed to show at all. No phone call, no message, no half-baked excuse – nothing. Thirty minutes before showtime I called Sophie, who had a night off, to see if she knew where Katie might be. The pair of them had been together for the early part of the previous evening, Sophie said, but then Katie had left for a party being hosted by her pop-star boyfriend.

'I haven't had a call from her and she's not answering her mobile,' I said.

'I have a key to her apartment,' Sophie replied. 'I'll go around now.'

I quickly reblocked the show and took to the stage to perform, unable to concentrate properly as my mind entertained all the possible scenarios. At barely nineteen years old, Katie was far out of her depth.

During the *entracte* I checked my phone. There was a message from Sophie.

'I'm here at Katie's place. She's here, she's all right. She won't be coming into work though. Call me when you get a minute.'

I didn't know whether to be relieved or angry. But I certainly wasn't going to absolve Katie of what I sincerely hoped was a whole lot of guilt by calling back immediately.

By the time I came offstage after the second show, I had two meek messages from Katie on my phone, both of them offering an apology, saying her alarm clock was broken and that was why she'd overslept. Oversleeping at seven o'clock at night? I wasn't buying it.

I walked out of the stage door to find Sophie waiting for me on the street.

'Do you have a minute for a quick drink?' she asked.

We went across the road to Le Palmier.

'She didn't oversleep,' Sophie started, as a couple of Monacos were deposited on our table. 'She didn't wake up because of all the gear she stuffed up her nose last night.' She took a sip of her drink and started playing with her coaster. 'You know I'd be the last person to judge, but Katie needs help. She's spiralling out of control.'

For Sophie to be worried meant that something was really wrong.

Three nights later, Katie came into work crying. Assuming it was another of her self-styled, homemade personal crises – the list of which was getting longer by the day – I did my best to ignore her. But when she dissolved into sobs just before the fifteen-minute call, I took her by the arm and led her into the corridor.

'What's wrong?' I asked impatiently.

She stood there crying, shaking her head.

'Katie, I want to help you, but I have a show to put on. Just tell me this. Can you pull it together to go on stage, or am I going to need to re-do the show? I'd really rather know now than in ten minutes if it's all the same to you.'

A flood of new tears and more sobbing.

'Katie, what is it? What's the matter?'

She looked at me, her eyes red and swollen, and for a fleeting moment I glimpsed the nervous young girl who had stood next to me in rehearsals over a year ago. She looked scared.

'I'm pregnant,' she half-whispered, biting her top lip and swiping at a tear as it raced down her cheek. I was speechless. She searched my face for some sign of comfort, but I was at a complete loss to know what to say.

'Oh God,' I finally managed.

She pushed her hair back behind her ear, nodding.

'Look, go home,' I said. 'Just go home. I'll call you later tonight.'

As she made for the dressing-room, her shoulders sunken, her head hanging low, I caught her by the arm. 'You're too young for this, Katie. You should go home to your family and straighten yourself out.'

On stage that night, as the show unfurled around me, I was lost in thought. I remembered the first time I had seen Katie – hair pulled back in a neat ballerina bun, standing awkward and terrified in the corner of the rehearsal room. She was too green to have been left on her own in a city like Paris, too young to have taken a job as a showgirl. The seedy underbelly of Paris had drawn her in, chewed her up and was now unceremoniously spitting her out.

And the worst part of the whole sorry tale was how utterly commonplace it all was. For as long as young girls had been recruited to the cabaret chorus line and Paris-by-night had been able to seduce them, there had always been a Katie in every company. Often more than one. And while she now had to come to terms with the up-ending of her life, the show simply went on. She would be replaced onstage by another fresh-faced dancer. At the hotel suite after-parties, another wide-eyed *ingénue* would seamlessly fill the void she'd left.

Really, the only remarkable thing about Katie's demise was that it hadn't happened sooner. The crash had always been coming, it was only a question of when.

Sophie and I organised to meet Katie at a cafe on Rue Lepic the following day. As soon as she sat down, she started crying.

'How did this happen? How did it all get so out of control? My parents don't know. I've let everyone down! It wasn't meant to go like this.'

'None of that matters, Katie,' Sophie said gently. 'You're going home now.' She pushed a Eurostar ticket across the table. 'We've all thrown in to buy you this. It's time you went back to your family.'

Katie didn't protest. She didn't even seem surprised. She looked utterly spent, and took the train ticket without a word. Tears welled in her eyes as she stood to leave; as we embraced, I felt how skinny she'd become. Whether it was her grief or the months of partying excess, her face looked grey and drawn.

She walked out of the cafe and up Rue Lepic towards her apartment, a lost little girl swallowed up by the Paris street.

Rattled by the Katie drama situation and with auditions for the new show looming, I distanced myself from the Moulin Rouge mêlée and threw myself with gusto into dance classes. I went to work, performed my show and carried out my captain duties, but I was otherwise determined to try to keep the madness at arm's length – at least for a week or two.

Moulin management had engaged the creative team of Miss Doris and Ruggero Angeletti to stage the new show. There was no question they had experience, having created the last several Moulin Rouge shows, but their appointment as creative directors also guaranteed the revue would be about as modern as a Model T Ford. Sprightly as the pair undoubtedly were for their age, there was little doubt that when the new show was pulled from the back of the closet and dusted off, it would have all the hallmarks of a cabaret time capsule.

In an attempt to drag at least some of the show into the twentieth century, renowned American choreographer Billy Goodson was employed to contribute some of his fancy footwork. A veteran of the American commercial dance scene, Goodson had worked with Diana Ross, Michael Jackson and Paula Abdul, among many others. His film credits included seminal teen films including *Electric Boogaloo, Roller Boogie* and *Girls Just Want to Have Fun,* in which he'd had Sarah Jessica Parker, Helen Hunt and Shannen Doherty dancing up a teenage storm.

And so here we were: it was almost the turn of a new century and the Moulin Rouge was shaping up to present a revue conceived by a pair of seventy-year-olds and choreographed by the king of the eighties dance floor. The kitsch queen in me couldn't wait to clap eyes on it.

Prior to tackling our new show, Goodson – or Billy, as he insisted we call him – had agreed to teach a series of classes at the Harmonique dance studios in Bastille. The classes were open to the public, and such was his renown that each was full to overflowing.

I lingered at the back of the class, keen to get a handle on Billy's style without making it too obvious I would be auditioning for him in two weeks' time. But being a foot taller than everyone else in the room, dancing in heels and possessing an unmistakeably upright showgirl posture gave the game away.

Billy, at first glance, was an unlikely choice to choreograph the world's most famous cabaret. Steeped in breakdancing, hip-hop and modern jazz, I couldn't imagine how he was going to adapt to the Moulin Rouge, much less gel with the likes of Doris and Ruggero. *Electric Boogaloo* meets the cancan? It just didn't compute. He was a frighteningly talented dancer, yet he was about as far removed from the Paris cabaret scene as it was possible to be. Which I guess was the point.

From the moment he took to the Moulin Rouge stage and started the audition process, it became clear he was nothing if not versatile. Whatever his background, he obviously loved women and was quite taken by the feathered and sequinned glamour of cabaret.

I wandered into the theatre on the day of the auditions pleasantly surprised at how nervous I felt. A familiar rush of adrenaline coursed through me as I stepped through the stage door and joined the huddle of dancers solemnly warming up.

'Don't wear anything baggy, don't hide your legs,' Janet had advised us the night before. 'We need to be able to see what you can and can't do.'

A small group of American girls were gathered together in one corner of the stage: the fruit of a trip Janet and Billy had taken together to Las Vegas two months previously to find new blood. Another small group of new faces hovered upstage – the lucky ones selected from the open call audition that had been held in Paris a week previously. We old girls eyed the new arrivals with suspicion, aware that for every one of them who was picked, one of us might have to go.

The usual air of jocularity that permeated the dressing rooms each night was conspicuously absent. A couple of the girls joked together, but mostly we kept to ourselves, intent on getting through the audition.

'I'm petrified,' Jo said as she warmed up next to me. 'I know I'm going to get the flick.'

'Don't be absurd,' Brett replied. 'They've been using you for the past three months to model the new costumes. As if they're not going to keep you!'

Billy strolled on stage and introduced himself, touching a little on his experience.

'I want you all to treat this as a dance class,' he said. 'We're all just here to have a bit of fun, after all.'

'Easy for him to say,' said Jo.

We were called on to the stage in one big group and took up position. Without music, Billy walked us through a funky dance combination, followed by a sequence of classic cabaret moves – a couple of *port de bras* and a few turns. All around me, girls and boys were studiously marking the choreography, performing the arm movements and footwork in miniature, their faces a study in concentration.

Once he'd been through the combinations a couple of times, we were broken into smaller groups and asked to perform the chorie to music. Each group had the usual cross-section of auditionees: those who performed it flawlessly without batting an eyelid, those who stuffed up royally, and those who just scraped by, teetering on the edge of disaster.

Billy stood downstage, his arms folded: watching, counting the beat, and studying us all intently. Janet stood next to him, taking notes. Once the groups had performed, we were each asked to perform a series of high-kicks and a pirouette combination solo, so he could see our flexibility and level of classical technique.

As I looked about the room, I was struck by how few of the older girls had bothered to show up. Backstage the previous night, Faye had explained that she had no intention of putting herself through the potential humiliation of a failed audition. 'I've been doing *Formidable!* for ten years,' she'd said. 'It's so ingrained, I'm pretty certain I couldn't pick up new choreography even if I tried. Better to bow out now with what dignity I have left.'

As the audition continued, I was also struck – pleasantly – by the number of confirmed Moulin Rouge wallflowers who were using the occasion to blossom. Dancers who had been put in a box labelled 'chorus-line filler' rose to the occasion, blitzing the audition with unexpected displays of dancing brilliance. You could see the principal dancers from *Formidable!*, myself included, looking nervously over their shoulders. Given Billy's fresh eye, untainted by preconceived ideas about what each dancer was or wasn't capable of, the audition process was a great leveller. It pushed the reset button on all of us and challenged all kinds of long-held perceptions and prejudices.

I found it exciting, as well, to finally be doing some new choreography and to dance without an enormous hat or lumbering backpack. For a brief moment, in the midst of my nerves, I felt myself sailing across the boards – light and free. It was a welcome reminder of why I loved to dance.

When Billy called an end to the audition and we started to walk offstage, Janet took the microphone. 'Thank you all for coming. You'll be notified in the coming week if you've been successful.'

A pall fell over the room. Now there was nothing left to do but wait.

# Chapter Twenty-eight

Within a week of the auditions, Janet began calling us one by one into her office to reveal our fate. She only got through six or seven of us each night, making the whole process painfully drawn out, and filling the dressing-rooms with showgirls even more highly strung than usual. Brett, Jean and I were reasonably certain we would be offered places in the new show; the only question was which places. Would they represent a promotion, demotion or a maintenance of the status quo?

The fate of many of my colleagues was less certain, and as the nights passed and they still hadn't been summoned to Janet's office, they became unbearably tetchy. It was unfortunate, too, that the meetings with Janet usually took place in the *entracte*. On more than one occasion a girl emerged from Janet's office in tears, either incapable or unwilling to perform the second show. Others took to the stage a sobbing mess.

My call to Janet's office came mercifully early in the week. Unfortunately, the news left me less than excited.

'You did a really good audition,' Janet started as I took a seat in her office. 'Billy was very impressed. But unfortunately, you won't be a permanent soloist in the new show.' She stopped and let the news sink in.

I felt winded. I sensed myself wobble, tears welling at the crushing disappointment, but was determined to maintain my composure.

'The thing is, you're doing such a great job as captain of the nude line. And you will still replace the lead girls.'

I sat for a moment, nodding, looking at the wall, processing the information. 'So, I'm a good captain but not a good soloist?'

'No Shay. It's not like that at all,' Janet countered.

I thought of some of the girls who got ahead despite erratic behaviour and inconsistent onstage performances, and I started to feel a flush of anger.

Janet finally explained. 'The other reason is because you're not flexible enough.'

It hit me straight in the gut. A second body blow.

'Vlada is going to be the other soloist and we need someone to pair with her who is at least as flexible, or it won't look right. You of all people should understand that.'

I didn't say anything. I sat in silence, fighting back tears. It was true that I was nowhere near as flexible as a former Russian gymnast, but I still felt as if I was being hard done by.

'As a replacement, you'll get much more variety onstage. You'll get to do all the good roles,' Janet continued. 'But I just cannot make you a permanent soloist.'

I stood to leave, determined to hold back the tears until I was at least out in the corridor.

Then I thought of what my father would have said in this situation. A purveyor of down-home wisdom and a strong believer in standing up for yourself, Dad wouldn't be walking away so quietly. And so I channelled him for a moment.

'Look Janet,' I said, turning to face her. 'Of course I'm grateful to have a job and happy to be in the show. But I'm really disappointed. I've worked really hard, I've always done everything you've asked me to do. I feel like I've earned soloist. I just want you to know that I'm not happy about this.'

Janet raised her eyebrows and shrugged her shoulders. 'I understand, and I appreciate how hard you work. Trust me, it hasn't gone unnoticed.'

I left her office and made my way back to the dressing-room. Vlada searched my face as I walked in.

'Well? What happened? Is everything all right?'

I started to cry, recounting the meeting with Janet as the tears rolled down my face.

'Shayleen,' Vlada said, cradling my head, 'this is not fair! It is not possible!'

And yet there was no denying Janet's reasoning. Next to Vlada on stage, I looked positively rigid.

Brett quickly got wind that I was crying in the *loge*, and came running in.

'Margaret? What happened? Is everything all right?'

When I explained what Janet had said, he hugged me and told me not to worry – that at least we still had jobs and that, frankly, he wasn't sure the Moulin deserved us. 'Besides, it's nothing a *crème brulée* at the Cloche d'Or won't fix.'

By the end of prologue in the second show I had composed myself, and I started to feel embarrassed at how upset I had been, how I had allowed my emotions to get the better of me. I still had a job – and a good one at that. Yet I still had the perception that I had been passed over – a perception that I knew would be shared by the rest of the company. I was nothing if not extremely proud.

After the show, a small group of us gathered at the Cloche d'Or, and I noticed that Dimitri was unusually quiet. As the showtalk bubbled around us, I took him aside and asked if everything was okay.

'They're not keeping me for the new show, darling,' he said, sucking on a cigarette. He looked distracted, nervous.

'What are you going to do?' I asked.

'Oh darling, it's probably for the best. I can concentrate on my fragrances.'

He smiled as he said the words, but I wasn't convinced he meant them. After twenty years of dancing, it was all he knew. It was all any of us knew. To be facing the prospect of redundancy at the tender age of thirty-seven, to be forced to start over again and reinvent himself – it had to terrify him. Not for the first time, I realised that this would be the fate of all of us. The clock was ticking. No matter how good our high-kicks or how indomitable our spirits, our bodies would eventually betray us and, after years of unwavering dedication to the dancing cause, consign us to the scrap heap.

By the time Janet had worked her way through the entire company, either giving each person the nod to start rehearsing the new show or suggesting they start looking elsewhere for work, rehearsals for *Féerie* were imminent. A two-month rehearsal period had been earmarked, culminating with the great unveiling of the new show on New Year's Eve – for the turn of the millennium.

For those of us who were being retained, it meant doing two performances of *Formidable!* every night, getting home at 2 a.m., then turning around to come back in at eleven the next morning to do six hours of rehearsals for *Féerie*.

Rehearsals were broken down into segments, as Miss Doris and Ruggero had been given responsibility for the conception and *mise-en-scène* of alternating sections of the show. The rehearsal day was structured so that Ruggero would work on his cancan tableau for the first part of the day.

Ruggero was an elegant Italian man in his early seventies, and wore a uniform of impeccably tailored dress pants, fine Italian leather shoes and a cashmere jumper over a starched-collar dress shirt. Crowning his perma-tanned face was a head of luxuriant white hair. Miss Doris had recruited him thirty years earlier to help her direct Moulin Rouge shows – and he was still going strong. In fact, for his age, he was impressively sprightly, a little Italian dynamo.

His dance-teaching discipline was old-school and strict, and he would shout out instructions in heavily accented English and French. For two hours every morning, the auditorium of the Moulin Rouge resounded with the sound of his booming Italian voice. 'One, two, three, four *et FIII-E!*' he would scream ad-nauseum, counting out the cancan beat. The cancan was his passion. In every show he had directed with Miss Doris, the cancan had been his baby. He knew how he liked it, he was fiercely proud of this famous French dance style, and he was going to make sure everyone did it justice.

Once Ruggero had put the cancan dancers through their paces, it was Doris's turn to work with us nudes. Then, finally, the entire company would regroup on stage for a session with Billy. His sessions were devised to help us get a feel for his style, to improve our rusty technique and to help us bond as a group. For an hour and a half each day, we'd lose ourselves in Billy's fluid hip-hop style. To the accompaniment of music he chose, we were pushed as dancers to quickly pick up new, inventive choreography – really energetic, dynamic and modern stuff. We would all leave the theatre on a high, lulled into thinking that *Féerie* might actually be a departure from the high-kitsch cabaret that had been the hallmark of all recent Moulin Rouge shows.

However, after a month of hip-hopping excitedly down the path towards what we thought was going to be a hip and happening new Moulin Rouge revue, the show was revealed to us in its entirety. We were all brought crashing back down to earth.

The opening number, titled 'Dance, Dance, Paris Dance', was a pastiche of cheesy cabaret tunes past. The costumes comprised white sequinned baseball caps and matching white sequinned waistcoats over white sequinned, high-cut leotards, with a pair of white sequinned slacks and white ankle boots. The girls' slacks were held together by velcro press-stud seams – at the climax of the number, we were all to bend forward and rip off our pants. It was a new kind of awful.

Our finely plucked showgirl eyebrows were raised even higher when we saw the first full run-through of the show. It was going to take willing suspension of disbelief into new, uncharted territory.

The second tableau, titled 'Nostalgie', brought a change of set and a softening of the musical style. It aimed to remind audiences of the rich heritage of the Moulin Rouge, and to whisk them back to ye olde Paris – the Paris of Toulouse-Lautrec – with girls in flowing white ball gowns and boys dressed as Foreign Legionnaires. For no apparent reason the next tableau featured a stage full of red-feathered, topless dancers – illogical but sublime.

From there, the revue moved into the 'Pirates' tableau. The lead boy appeared in pirate pyjamas and lip-synched a song in French about jewels, cueing a parade of nudes in different primary coloured feather-and-bead outfits, each supposedly representing a different gemstone. Enter the lead girl, an Indian princess dressed in a sari – why Indian, why a sari, and what exactly India had to do with pirates was never explained. Naturally, the two leads fell in love, only to see their courtship rudely interrupted by the appearance of a Medusa-style character – another of the principal dancers, wearing an elaborate headdress of golden snakes. Again, exactly why a famous figure from Greek mythology was moonlighting with a bunch of blown-off-course pirates in India seemed not to have bothered the show's creators.

Medusa, true to unpleasant form, promptly ordered the princess to be hurled into a tank filled with water, where a pair of real-life pythons slithered. The dramatic tension of the sequence was ruined somewhat by the fact that the reluctant pythons wanted nothing to do with the underwater wrestle that was supposed to ensue.

Next, in a dream sequence, the pirate and the princess sang to one another while floating above the audience, attached by wire cables to a ceiling track. In a feat of seriously outdated lighting wizardry, the house U.V. lamps made the couple's specially designed fluoro costumes glow in the dark, their faces illuminated by the pen light torches each of them held. Two glowing orbs, squeaking awkwardly through the darkness towards one another, their paean to love was barely audible over the clackety-clack of the ceiling track. The effect was wonderfully, awfully, unintentionally hilarious.

From the pirate-meets-India-via-Greek-mythology dream sequence, the show lurched headlong into a circus tableau. The stage filled with boys dressed as clowns and girls dressed as lionesses, all in tan leotards. Continuing the circus theme, a line of six girls dressed as majorettes marched onto the stage, each leading a Shetland pony by the bridle. There was then a burst of Russian kalinka dancing and a pair of sideshow freak-inspired 'Siamese twins' (two dancers made-up to look identical and dancing together in one large costume).

At last we were thrust, mercifully, into the *'avant-finale'* section. Set in Montmartre circa 1890, the tableau was homage to the Paris in which the Moulin Rouge had had its origins. Hookers hung out of windows or engaged boy dancers in aggressive bouts of the Java dance as they wandered cobbled rues. The music was heavy with accordion and the backdrop featured the Eiffel Tower. All of which served as a lead-in for the main event – the cancan.

From there it was only a slight imaginative leap then to the 1940s, with an Andrews-sisters inspired bout of boogie-woogie and finally onto a wholly incongruous scene change that saw the three principals appear in bad eighties wigs and thigh-high silver boots, accompanied by the male dancers in skin-tight green leather outfits festooned with silver buckles.

This had been mooted as the boys' big moment on stage. In a departure from previous shows, this number was supposed to showcase the strength and masculinity of the boy dancers – and Janet had chosen especially buff specimens of manhood to add a bit of beefcake to the show. Billy had choreographed a sequence that was hard and strong. Unfortunately, no amount of rippling biceps or pumping choreography could compete with the overall effect of the eight matching sets of skin-tight green leather costumes. And it wasn't like the song, 'New Generation', did anything to harden up proceedings. Written especially for the show, it had initially been so high camp it had been sent back by Billy, who declared it unworkable. The revised version was still a session-singer special. The lyrics had been written by people for whom English clearly was not a first language, and featured such memorable lines as: 'New generation, no isolation, forward salvation, no simulation, we need vibration. You're finding true love, just say yeah!'

The show finale was unapologetic and over-the-top. A sea of pink feathers, pink leather thigh-high boots, mirror-tiled body stockings – for boys and girls – and wild pink feather and silver headdresses. On the theory that too much is never enough, the backpacks were all rigged with fairy lights, which lit up at the show's climax.

Pirates, the circus, Montmartre and eighties leather bars – if there was a narrative theme to the new show, I certainly couldn't find it. But then it was the Moulin Rouge, not Chekhov. Audiences weren't flocking for intellectual stimulation: they wanted an evening of mindlessly fun, high-camp entertainment. As I stood in the auditorium and watched the show, I had to admit that *Féerie* was guaranteed to deliver on that score.

# Chapter Twenty-nine

As Feérie slowly started to take shape, *Formidable!* began the gradual process of fading away. Ironically, as the end of the show drew nigh – and the costumes, sets and lighting grew ever more tatty – the onstage performances became more enthusiastic. There was a kind of sprint for the finish line. With the end in sight, dancers who previously could barely be bothered to mark time suddenly found reserves of energy.

The atmosphere backstage was also warm. Those who were leaving seemed determined to enjoy their last nights onstage; those who were staying seemed determined to savour the dressing-room camaraderie. Even the dancers embittered by not being chosen for the new show couldn't help but get swept up in the onstage joy.

When the final night of *Formidable!* came around, emotions were running high. The second show was an invitation-only performance for management, special guests, anyone who had worked on the show during its ten-year run, and friends and family of the company and crew. There was a long-held Paris cabaret tradition of performers letting their hair down for the final performance of any show.

'Do what you like, play whatever practical jokes onstage that you want, just promise me one thing,' Janet had said before we went on. 'Promise me you'll do the finale as it was set, in the correct costumes, with the correct choreography.'

The whole night was wonderful. Matthew was visiting from Kirrwiller and had smuggled Audrey backstage. She made her Moulin Rouge stage debut during the Viennese waltz, sitting happily under my arm as Dimitri and I danced together for the last time. Boys wore girls' costumes and practical jokes were played throughout.

When the finale came around, however, we all did as Janet requested, donning our proper red and white costumes. As we came on, the auditorium erupted into a sea of shimmering red and white lights. Janet had distributed the lights among the audience members, and they were all now waving them enthusiastically. Onstage, the red and white feathers glowed for one last time, while down in the *salle*, the glimmering lights briefly illuminated five hundred broad smiles and tear-filled sets of eyes. I started crying, and looked around me to see everyone else on stage doing the same. It was a spectacular and emotional end to a chapter, not only of the Moulin Rouge's history, but also of our lives.

It didn't take long for the warm glow of *Formidable!*'s final performance to be replaced by the monotony of daily rehearsals for *Féerie*. With just over a month until opening night, we had lots of work to do. Without *Formidable!* to perform in the evenings, the theatre was now available all day and all night, so we were sometimes there from 10 a.m. one day until 2 a.m. the next. These long days became increasingly common as Doris, Ruggero, Billy and Janet realised how far behind schedule we were.

Mine Vergez, Paris *couturier* to the stars, had been commissioned to bring to life the *Féerie* costume fantasies. When the stage wasn't being used to rehearse, we were all lined up on it being pinned into the most fabulous costumes. After years spent sporting the sad old plumes of *Formidable!*, it was a delight to have brand new backpacks and headpieces that not only looked amazing but fitted perfectly. There were silver beaded necklaces and bodices, outrageously camp red feather skirts, leather pirate-inspired G-strings and corsets, and felt hats with cobalt blue jewels and a spray of blue feathers. Of course, talented as she undoubtedly was in the creation of light, durable and beautiful cabaret costumes, Mine still sometimes came up with outfits that couldn't cope with the dynamism of some of Billy's choreography. Stiff thigh-high leather boots, for example, were not going to work with Billy's instructions to get down low on our haunches – a discovery that was only made way too late. There had to be last-minute changes to either the painstakingly conceived dance moves or the incredibly expensive costumes.

While the long days were mostly hectic, there were still long stretches of sitting around and doing nothing. We would often find ourselves huddled in a corner of the *salle*, wrapped in overcoats and scarves, carefully avoiding the construction workers who sawed, hammered and laid carpet around us. Management had decided to make the most of being closed to the public to refurbish the theatre – including replacing the heating system. It was freezing.

Thankfully, in the down moments, there was usually an attraction or two to divert us.

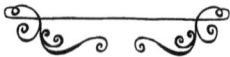

If Paris cabaret had vital components that made it unique and showgirls, feathers and sequins were the top three, attractions would run a close fourth.

Practically speaking, the attractions were used to keep the audience happily distracted while a scene change took place. They were also a cabaret tradition, and had been a feature of the Moulin Rouge for as long as it had been open. When it was a bawdy music hall and Toulouse-Lautrec had joined legions of top hat–wearing counts in the audience, attractions had spanned the gamut of the sublime to the ridiculous.

Cornering the market in the latter variety was Joseph Pujol, better known by his stage name 'Le Pétomane'. Pujol was a self-described '*fartiste*' – a man who had such extraordinary control of his bowels and abdominal muscles that he was able to pass wind on cue. Described in Moulin Rouge history books as a 'flatulist', Pujol's talent, such as it was, took him all the way from Marseille to Paris where, in 1892, the Moulin Rouge snapped him up and made him a star. Audiences flocked to listen to *Le Pétomane*'s backside interpretations of cannon fire and thunderstorms, and his signature renditions of 'O Sole Mio' and 'La Marseillaise'.

Mercifully for those of us who had to share a dressing-room with the show's attractions, tastes had evolved since then and the acts were more of the juggling, acrobatic or feats-of-daring variety. The performers were invariably drawn from the pool of circus folk who made a living touring the European cabaret venues. They hailed either from families – often Italian – who had passed their craft from one generation to the next, or from the former Soviet Union Olympic training programs. For every pair of acrobatic brothers or juggling cousins there was a Ukrainian strongman or Belorussian balancing act. The former eastern-bloc athletes had taken to the European cabaret circuit either because their government-sponsored training programs had dried up after the Berlin Wall had tumbled or (more commonly) because there was good money to be made. They worked like demons, crisscrossing the continent picking up contracts and working as many nights as possible. They were milking it for as long as they could, in the knowledge that it would all end when their act fell out of favour or their bodies packed it in – which was often the case.

For *Féerie*, management had chosen a selection of attractions, including a pair of Spanish brothers who did an acrobatic double act and a comedian who dragged members of the audience up onstage and embarrassed them in five languages.

The fifth apparently vital component of any Paris cabaret show worth its *sel* was, of course, animals. Macbeth the horse and the yellow snake had now been succeeded by six Shetland ponies and two unenthusiastic pythons. The ponies were an obliging little herd who trotted about the stage during the circus tableau.

The pythons were an altogether more recalcitrant pair of performers. Every night their handler applied a water-tight tourniquet of clear masking tape around their nether regions to ensure the water was not befouled mid-performance by a snake call of nature.

The snake act was supposed to be a moment of high drama. The princess was hurled into a tank with writhing pythons, and an underwater wrestle to the death was supposed to ensue. As it happened, the pythons were fundamentally uninterested in writhing or wrestling underwater. They simply wanted out. Each time the tank rose, dramatically lit by the stage lights, they would be huddled in a corner attempting to escape.

'Just pick one up and wrap it around you!' a frustrated Ruggero would bark in rehearsal at the dancer bobbing uselessly in the water waiting to be attacked. And so she would swim across to a python, put it around her neck and simulate an underwater death roll, trying to make it look like the poor creature wasn't trying for dear life to be as far away from her as possible.

December disappeared in a blur of rehearsals, and as opening night loomed, tempers frayed in the company and exhaustion set in. The Big Boss had started to take an interest in proceedings, making everyone even more nervous. With little more than a week to go until opening night, we were all completely drained of energy and enthusiasm.

One day, just before Christmas, Jean and I both pleaded injury and took off to hide for a few hours. We treated ourselves to a long lunch in a smoky *brasserie*, drinking wine and eating desserts into the early evening.

'We've earned this, sweetheart,' Jean assured me as we tucked into *crème brulée* and our second carafe of Brouilly. 'It's a mental health day.'

Christmas came and went amid the last-minute rehearsal scramble. Olivier had shown no interest in celebrating Yule. For months he had promised he was going to get me a kitten, yet I awoke on Christmas morning to find nothing waiting for me under the tree – furry or otherwise. 'I went to collect the kitten, but it turned out to be a full-grown cat,' he offered by way of explanation.

I was too tired to be angry or disappointed. I found myself expecting less and less from him and, despite his company over a huge Christmas lunch, I felt lonely and desperately homesick.

In the week before the grand New Year's Eve gala opening night, it seemed as if our every waking moment was spent at the Moulin fine-tuning the show. By the time we got to dress rehearsals, and at a point where Janet, Doris, Ruggero and Billy might reasonably have expected their company to have the show down pat, it was all we could do to put one foot in front of the other.

Then, with two nights to go, a group of us were sent to perform on one of France's most popular TV variety shows. The appearance had been brokered by the Moulin Rouge's in-house publicist, Fanny, and was considered an excellent chance to advertise the brand-new Moulin Rouge revue. Given that rehearsals were running at fever pitch, Fanny had explained to the TV show's producers that they would only have a two-hour window in which to transport us from the Moulin to the TV studios and back.

So, while the rest of the company paused for a dinner break, those of us required for the TV appearance rushed straight from the stage and out onto Boulevard de Clichy. Sixteen showgirls in six-centimetre heels and full drag-queen make-up clustered under the red neon lights of the theatre entrance, shivering in the December cold. We tried to ignore the stares of passers-by and the wolf whistles from carloads of youths cruising up and down the boulevard. Then a convoy of ambulances pulled up, their blue lights flashing, and the driver of each ambulance bounded out from behind the wheel and threw open the back doors of their vehicle, motioning for us to get inside. A young man with a clipboard and two-way radio came bounding up.

'You are the girls for the TV show, yes?' he asked in heavily accented English. We nodded.

'My name is Jean-Luc. I am one of the assistant producers. We thought these would be faster than taxis or a minivan. *Allez*, hop in!' With lights flashing and cars parting to make way for us, we were taken to a studio lot on the northern outskirts of the city and rushed onto the set.

As we took our places in front of the cameras and waited for our cue, a ripple of excitement passed through the studio audience. People were pointing, sitting upright in their seats and craning their necks to see us. An announcer introduced us as '*les plus belles filles du monde, les danseuses du Moulin Rouge*' – 'the most beautiful girls in the world, the dancers of the Moulin Rouge'.

With a burst of applause from the audience, the lights came up and we were on the air. The choreography that we had laboured over two hours before now came effortlessly. With two hundred sets of eyes in the studio audience and four million sets of eyes in living rooms all over France trained upon us, we suddenly found our rhythm. It lasted barely four minutes, but it was enough to lift all of us out of our rehearsal funk. We were fêted, briefly, like national heroines: it was a timely reminder of the special place the Moulin Rouge holds in the French national pysche. Looking out at the beaming faces in the studio audience, I felt a nation's pride and understood for the first time that in the eyes of the average French person, Moulin Rouge dancers were much more than girls who happened to dance in feathers each night. They were revered custodians of an important piece of French cultural heritage. And I felt humbled.

For the next few days, I couldn't walk down Rue de Levis without being stopped by one local or another, desperate to tell me excitedly how they had seen me on TV. By the time opening night rolled around, I was on such a high I couldn't wait to get onstage. The entire company shared my impatience. We just wanted the curtain to rise and to get on with it.

To mark the occasion, tied as it was to New Year's Eve and the arrival of the new millennium, management had attached a 5000-franc price tag to the opening-night tickets. For a show that would normally have cost 800 francs, it represented quite a mark-up. We didn't realise how poorly tickets had sold, however, until the curtain rose and we found ourselves performing to a half-empty theatre. It was about as demoralising as it was possible to be. Months of rehearsal, massive amounts of hype, another New Year's Eve at work – and for what? For the entertainment of a couple of hundred people, half of whom were so drunk by the time the show kicked off at midnight that they fell asleep.

Champagne was put on by management for the company after the show, but it felt more like a wake than a celebration. As gala opening nights went, it was a bit flat. Not even Janet's attempt to rally the troops and put a bright gloss on the evening could change the fact that this had hardly been the most auspicious start for the new show.

In the cab home that night, as the driver dodged straggling groups of drunken revellers, I performed a quick New Year's Day review of my life. The year 2000 wasn't exactly off to a cracking start.

I was about to discover that it was set to get worse before it got better.

# Chapter Thirty

It was the start of a new year and a new century. If the hype was to be believed, 1 January 2000 was *the* time for fresh starts and new beginnings. It might have seemed more likely if it hadn't also been the day that the month's rent was due.

Waking just before midday, I shuffled into the living-room, where Olivier was busily setting up a desk in the corner. I gave him a sleepy New Year's kiss and parked myself and my fleecy pink pyjamas on his lap.

'*Bonne année*,' I said with a yawn. 'Rent due today. I'll send the cheque if you can transfer your share into my account.'

Olivier came over all awkward.

'Ah. I wanted to speak to you about that, actually.' He seemed to be having difficulty making eye contact. 'I was waiting for the right time to talk to you, but you've been so busy with the show.'

I looked at him expectantly, not sure what was coming.

'The thing is, I've decided to quit my job. I want to concentrate on my album.'

I tried my best not to look shocked.

He started filling the silence with babble. 'You know since forever it's something I've been wanting to do. And I can't be really *concentré* on it if I am teaching all day every day.'

I started to think back. Olivier hadn't been at work for two weeks. I'd assumed he was on Christmas holidays, but obviously he had made the decision to quit his music teaching gig weeks before. It would have been nice if he had told me – perhaps even consulted me, especially seeing as he expected me to support him financially. I felt slighted, but was determined not to show it.

'Oh,' I said, doing my best to rally. 'I see. So you're going to concentrate on your album?'

I was stuck between my love for his passion for music, my heartfelt desire for him to follow his dreams, and my rather more pragmatic wish that he might actually help pay the rent for the apartment we shared. 'So you'll be living for the next few months off savings?' I asked, with a little more doubt in my voice than I cared to acknowledge.

Olivier continued to avoid eye contact. '*Bien sûr*,' he replied. 'Of course. It's just that this month is a bit tight.'

And so I took on the burden of keeping the household afloat, trying to see the romanticism of having a boyfriend hunkered over a keyboard in the corner of the living-room every hour of the day and night. I did my best to accommodate the mini-studio he'd set up in our already overcrowded living space, and told myself his newfound reluctance to leave the house was part and parcel of his artistic endeavour. But as the weeks went by and Olivier became more and more immersed in his work – and consequently more and more disinclined to do anything around the house, much less pay any attention to me – I started to resent him.

Worst of all was the feeling that I was being squeezed out of the home that I was dancing my feet off to pay for. An ever-growing parade of random musicians passed through the apartment, coming in the early afternoon and staying until late at night. I was still in rehearsals three days a week, learning the soloist places and teaching those who would understudy and swing new places. I would often come home with only a few hours to relax between a day's rehearsal and the evening's performances, only to discover my living-room once again full of chain-smoking strangers. A pall of smoke seemed to hang permanently in the apartment. I would take refuge in the bedroom, or eat a hurried meal standing up in the kitchen, craving a quiet moment with my boyfriend or a lazy half-hour with my feet up in front of the television – *my* television in *my* living room!

Another rent day swung around, and still no contribution was forthcoming from Olivier. But some production house had expressed interest in one of his jingles for a commercial, and so, he implied, a river of gold was about to be tapped. I found myself believing him. It was all going to be okay, I told myself. It *had* to be okay.

After the third month of shouldering the entire financial burden of our household, though, I started to panic. My dancer's salary was just about enough to support one, but was hopelessly inadequate to keep both our heads above water. And yet, each time I raised this worry with Olivier in the hope that he might offer to find work, he would spin me a line about a record label being 'really interested' in the album or some crucial meeting that was 'about to take place'.

None of the meetings ever happened, none of the recording contracts eventuated. I tightened my belt and reined in my spending. I stopped going out after work and I never, ever bought myself anything in the way of clothes or accessories. I even shelved plans to return to Australia for my upcoming annual holidays and opted instead to stay in Paris and lie low. And because I had always been independent and fended for myself, I refused to admit to my parents that anything was amiss. During phone calls home, I kept up a cheery banter, determined not to let them worry. Faced with a tightened financial situation, I reacted in the only way I knew how: by working harder.

It was common for girls at work to make a little extra money doing the odd bit of modelling. 'Modelling' meant everything from standing in a department store handing out fragrance samples to taking part in Paris Fashion Week catwalk shows or participating in photo shoots.

One night at work, word spread through the dressing-room that Galeries Lafayette – the big Parisian department store – was looking for tall, well-groomed girls who had a basic command of French to work in their flagship store on the *grands boulevards*. My lessons, plus a year living with Olivier, had lifted my French from barely there to not bad at all, so I went to the casting and was asked to join the ranks of other tall young things promoting Galeries' month-long *Festival de la*

*Mode* (fashion festival). We were given three days' training, in which fashion experts came and explained to us the various trends for the upcoming season. Dressed head to toe in Lanvin and made up each morning by a team from Shiseido, we were to stand near the entrance of the store and provide fashion advice to customers as they poured through the door. In actual fact, we spent nine hours a day on our feet in high heels giving people directions to the toilets. After this I would go straight to the Moulin Rouge to perform my two shows.

Following the Galeries gig, I was put in touch with a French fashion label, which needed someone to work in their design studio doing fittings. They wanted a 'typical size 38' on which to base their designs for tailored trousers. The job saw me take the Métro every other day for a month out to Porte de Pantin, a grotty outer Parisian suburb, where I would stand in the middle of a large sweatshop as the head seamstress and her team pinned pants on me all day long.

Not all of my extracurricular work took place outside of the Moulin Rouge. Occasionally a fashion magazine or photographer would be drawn to the red windmill to use the famous theatre as a backdrop. A couple of dancers were usually required to don full costume and pose alongside the female models, or drape ourselves off male models. One shoot, for French fashion magazine *Jalouse*, featured Kate Moss, who was genuinely fascinated with our profession. She couldn't believe that we did our own make-up and hair.

'And you dance twice a night, six nights a week?' she asked incredulously. 'That's amazing.'

The fashion shoots were always a pleasure to do. Not only was the money good, but the work was usually fun and easy. On top of that, when I looked at the proofs produced by the photographer at the end of a shoot, I would see the Moulin Rouge in a brand-new light and be reminded of how magical it could be. Through the photographer's lens, expertly lit and peopled by immaculately made-up, beautifully coiffed models, the stage, the sets and the *salle* never looked better.

But out of all the moonlighting gigs I took to help pay the rent and keep the household afloat, none were as special as a Cartier job I scored.

The famed French jeweller was doing its annual south of France showcase, taking its latest designs to the Côte d'Azur madames whose

Monaco postal addresses, Swiss bank accounts and profligate spending habits kept the venerable diamond merchant in business. In previous years, Cartier's head office in Paris had taken a bevy of models with them on the south of France tour, but this year they wanted to try something different – to animate their presentation of priceless gemstones by including a couple of dancers in their roadshow. I trooped across the Seine to the Fondation Cartier, a stunning glass and steel construction deep in the Left Bank, where a group of stylish Cartier executives and a choreographer ushered me into a huge boardroom.

'We want to make this presentation more *dynamique*,' explained the choreographer, a small, forty-something man called Jerome. 'We want to give the clients something a bit more *intéressant to* look at.'

I couldn't imagine why a five-million-franc diamond choker would need to be made to look more interesting, but I nodded just the same.

After showing off my portfolio and chatting for a bit in French, I stood against a glass wall as they took my measurements and told me they'd be in touch. Three days later I received a call to say I had been hired, and to ask whether I would be available to travel to Monaco and Cannes in two weekends' time. It was going to mean taking a couple of nights off work, somewhat defeating the fundraising purpose of the exercise, but the chance to travel to the Côte d'Azur and model Cartier jewels was too good to pass up. I told myself that I had earned something special like this.

There were to be a number of dancers 'animating' the jewels. We rehearsed over a few afternoons in Paris, and were told we'd be required to perform two 'shows' – one in a private home in Monaco and the other in a hotel on the Croisette at Cannes. A Moulin Rouge colleague, Elena, was among the group. As well as being tall, blonde and beautiful, she had a bitingly dry sense of humour. It was going to be fun.

It was a one-hour flight to Nice aboard the so-called Air France shuttle. As the plane banked over the Mediterranean in preparation for landing at Nice airport, I could make out the snow-capped tips of the Alps on the horizon. A driver was waiting for us as we stepped off the plane, holding aloft a sign marked 'Cartier', and led us to a minivan which drove us ten minutes down the road to the nearby heliport. Four helicopters sat idle on the helipad.

'Four people per helicopter,' Jerome called out as we tumbled excitedly out of the van. I skipped across the tarmac. It was all so wonderfully James Bond. Under the midday sun, the helicopters took flight and travelled in convoy along the rugged coastline towards Monaco. We raced along the Côte d'Azur, high above multi-level, million-dollar houses clinging to cliff-faces. Sky-blue swimming pools and terracotta roofs flashed by underneath us. As we rounded a peninsula, Monte Carlo suddenly appeared, a collection of chic apartment towers crowded in around a tiny harbour packed with boats. We came in to land on a helipad just near the marina, its collection of massive white cruisers giving the impression of a floating city. A very expensive-looking floating city.

Jerome pointed to a three-storey palazzo perched on its own atop a tall rocky outcrop. 'That's where we'll be doing our show tomorrow night.' Painted cream, the house seemed to glow in the sunlight, and commanded what must surely have been stunning views up and down the coast.

Our first port of call for the day was the Monaco Cartier store, conveniently located across the square from the Casino de Monte Carlo. As our minivan pulled in behind a bright red Ferrari, I took in my surroundings. Perfectly cropped palm trees caught the slight sea breeze. An immaculately dressed older woman walked her primped pooch. A slight, pretty blonde girl in big heels, big sunglasses and a skin-tight miniskirt clung to the arm of a balding, be-suited man, who smoked a cigar as he led his charge into the casino. I felt like I was on a film set.

The Cartier store had been closed to the public for the afternoon; a pair of enormous security guards in black suits and black ties swung open the heavy golden front door and beckoned us inside. A group of models were already being fitted with jewellery – long diamond necklaces, delicate ruby-encrusted bracelets, a huge emerald set in a gold and diamond choker. One by one we were assigned a Cartier sales rep, and carefully draped in the most sumptuous jewels I had ever seen. I watched in the mirror as a multi-chained gold choker was secured to my neck, a delicate web of diamonds woven intricately through the piece. On my wrist was placed a diamond and gold bracelet, and in my ears, a pair of white gold and diamond earrings.

I looked at the trays from which they had been lifted, took note of the price of each piece and performed a quick calculation. I was wearing over seven million francs worth of Cartier jewellery – the overall effect of which was diminished somewhat by the fact I was still wearing the jeans and T-shirt in which I'd flown to Nice.

It was explained that the jewels would only be put on us minutes before the show was due to begin, and if we had to go to the bathroom after that it would be in the company of a security guard.

'Okay,' Jerome piped up once the fitting was over. 'Now off to the house of Lagerfeld for rehearsal.'

Elena and I looked at each other, eyes wide.

'The house of Lagerfeld?' she echoed.

'I think that's what the man said,' I replied.

We piled back into the minivan for the short ride to Villa La Vigie, the palazzo he'd pointed out on top of the hill.

'This house belongs to Karl Lagerfeld,' Jerome confirmed from the front seat as the van wound its way up a steep, narrow road. 'But he is not so often here, and occasionally hires it out for special events.'

A pair of large black gates pulled open as the van turned off the road and into a driveway. We drove up another winding single-lane road to emerge atop a cliff.

The view was magnificent: an uninterrupted panorama out across the Mediterranean. It felt as if we were floating, as if there was nothing but water below us. And the house itself was a model of understated elegance. A simple three-storey villa, it had a vast open-air terrace and a lush, carefully tended garden that spilled down the cliff face to the Monte Carlo Beach Club below.

'I cannot believe we are here!' Elena squealed. 'Karl Lagerfeld's house in Monaco! Can you believe it?'

I couldn't – and so I just stood rooted to the spot, breathing it all in, committing it to memory.

The terrace was a hive of activity. Caterers scampered about laying tables and stocking up bars, while a group of technicians clambered around the low stone balcony setting up lights.

'May I go to the bathroom before we begin?' I asked Jerome. I needed to go, but more than that, I was dying to see the inside of the villa.

'Of course,' he replied. 'One of the catering staff will direct you.'

'Me too! I need to go too!' said Elena, altogether too enthusiastically.

Armed with directions from a tray-wielding waitress, we stepped inside the house and made our way to the bathroom. I pushed open its pair of massive double doors – and froze. A floor-to-ceiling glass wall formed one entire side of the bathroom, affording a stunning view across the sea. Checking to see that no-one was watching, Elena and I clambered into the bathtub and laid back.

'This is the view Karl has when he takes a bath!' I said, giggling as we lay, fully clothed, in a famous stranger's tub.

By the time we got back to the terrace, our dresses had arrived and fittings were taking place. Each girl was given an evening gown – a beautiful piece of *couture* from Chloé, stunning yet subtle, so as not to detract attention from the jewellery. Mine was a soft pink silk and lace robe with shoestring straps. All the dancers' dresses were fitted about the body with plenty of movement in the legs, so that we could still dance easily in them.

Once clothed, we performed a walk-through of the choreography, melding our performance with that of the models. It all went smoothly, so we were given the rest of the afternoon off.

'Go back to your hotel and relax,' instructed Jerome. 'A driver will come to collect you and take you to dinner. Tomorrow you will all have a complimentary day's membership at the Monte Carlo Beach Club.'

There was a murmur of excitement.

'Now go and enjoy yourselves. You'll be collected after lunch tomorrow for hair and make-up. The performance is scheduled to take place just after sunset.'

Following a day spent slumming it at the Monte Carlo Beach Club, we eagerly made our way back to Karl Lagerfeld's eyrie for the three-hour session of hair and make-up.

As the sun started to set and the lights of Monte Carlo began to twinkle down below, guests began to arrive and were ushered out onto the terrace. Bathed in soft light, discreetly populated with tuxedo-wearing waitstaff and set against the backdrop of a stunning cobalt sky, it was a scene of elegance and beauty. A select group of Monaco's most well-heeled residents mingled affably under the starry sky on this balmy summer's evening – sipping champagne from long flutes, dressed impeccably and carrying themselves with the ingrained dignity that comes with old money.

'It could be another half hour before we start,' Jerome informed us as he sailed through the large marble-floored antechamber that served as our dressing-room. 'Cartier have organised a special guest and she's running late.'

We sat in our gowns, nibbled *hors d'oeuvres* and sipped champagne, waiting and wondering what calibre of special guest it would take to outshine the jewels and this magnificent setting.

Eventually, a black Mercedes pulled up at the villa entrance, and the driver leaped out to open the back passenger door. The Italian movie star Monica Bellucci stepped out. Dressed in a fitted, backless black gown, her hair up and her lips painted their trademark glossy red, as she turned to walk into the party, she revealed a stunning diamond necklace. It was short at the front and draped all the way down her back, the long tail of diamonds catching the light as she walked.

While Monica 'performed' outside, mingling with guests and being generally intoxicating, the Cartier reps came into the dressing-room with their security details and armloads of jewels. Clicking open the flat velvet cases and donning white gloves, they began the delicate task of blinging us up. The multi-carat stones in my ears shimmered in the mirror's reflection.

I felt suddenly nervous. Not about the performance – that I could do in my sleep. I was terrified that I was going to walk out onto the terrace, do a *pirouette* and watch in horror as a million-franc diamond earring plummeted down the cliff face and into the Mediterranean Sea. I imagined spending the rest of my life in hock to the House of Cartier. Fortunately, however, all my jewels stayed where they were supposed to and the performance went well. Our V.I.P. audience gave us a round of exceedingly polite applause.

It felt odd to float in choreographed circles about the standing crowd as each pair of eyes we passed scanned our ears, necks and wrists for their next million-franc purchase. The event must have cost Cartier a small fortune to stage. The venue, the catering, the models, the dancers and Monica Bellucci. Whether or not they recouped their investment in sales, I'd never know. If transactions took place, none of the guests was so crass as to engage in them on the spot. Conspicuous consumption was a habit reserved for some of Cartier's *other* clients, as I was soon to discover.

The following day we trooped back down to the Monte Carlo heliport, bade farewell to Monaco and were flown back down the coast to our second engagement, in Cannes. It was my first time in the famed Côte d'Azur town, but thanks to the film festival, it already resided in my imagination as a sun-drenched playground of the designer-clad rich and famous.

At first, as we drove from the freeway into the town past tiny backstreet pizza stores and run-down supermarkets, I wondered what all the hype was about. But as we turned onto the Croisette – that famous, palm-lined stretch of boardwalk above Cannes beach – I took in the strip of regal old hotels standing proudly in line looking out to sea, and the penny dropped. The Majestic, the Carlton, the Martinez – they evoked a more elegant age. I half-expected to see F. Scott Fitzgerald and friends come skipping out the front door in their tennis whites, or a bunch of boater-wearing dandies sipping gin and tonics on the terrace.

As visions of 1920s jet-set glamour swam in my head, we stopped at some traffic lights outside the Dolce & Gabbana store and I was brought crashing back to reality. A woman more plastic than flesh was teetering out of the shop on red patent-leather stilettos. Her fried, dyed blonde hair had been teased into a mop, and she had a pair of pneumatic boobs, and lips stuffed so full of collagen they looked set to burst.

'Welcome to Cannes,' Elena said, looking at her and reading my mind.

That night's Cartier showcase was to take place in the ballroom of the Hotel Martinez. Jerome instructed the driver to drop us at the hotel entrance, whereupon we filed inside for a two-hour rehearsal. The stage was bigger this time, and the room much larger. Hotel staff bustled about the ballroom setting up tables, through which a long catwalk weaved its way from the stage. It was clear there was going to be a much bigger, less exclusive crowd of Cartier clients than had attended *Chez Lagerfeld*.

When evening rolled around, we put on the same Chloé dresses, the same jewels were applied to each dancer and model and the same routines were performed. But after the show, the head Cartier woman came rushing backstage.

'We've had a request for a private viewing of the jewels from an important client. You don't have to do it if you don't want to, but we would really appreciate it. You will, of course, be paid extra.'

One more turn about a room in a designer evening gown wearing more diamonds than we would ever again wear in our lives wasn't going to kill us. We all agreed to one last showing. And so, with our jewels still on and flanked by security guards, we were led from the ballroom through a staff entrance and the hotel kitchen to a service lift. Emerging on the fourth floor, we stepped into the corridor and waited for instructions. I stared down the hallway in both directions. More security guards were posted at regular intervals down the corridor. Black-suited and stern-looking, they stared straight ahead.

'It's the suite down here at the end,' the Cartier woman said, taking the lead and signalling for us to follow. We stopped at a set of double doors guarded by a pair of enormous men, their giant hands clasped together in front of them.

'Here's what's going to happen,' the Cartier woman began to explain. 'You will be called in one by one. You are to go into the room, do a short walk in front of the client to show off the jewellery, and then remain in the room on the sidelines. Okay?'

We all nodded. The whole thing suddenly seemed odd. I began to wonder what kind of client sat in his or her room receiving models one by one and making them perform a private parade. As the first model was called, I craned my neck to get a glimpse inside the room when the door opened. It was dark, the curtains were drawn and a soft light seemed to be coming from a lamp in a corner hidden from view.

One by one girls were called inside. The models wearing the massive stones went first, with us dancers bringing up the rear. As we waited, doors kept opening up and down the hallway and women in Arab dress bustled from room to room. Several walked past us, and we could see that the skin on their faces looked uniformly red, raw and angry. Some of them were peeling. Had they all spent too much time on the beach? Was it some bizarre religious practice? Were we about to parade before the head of some strange religious cult? As my colleagues disappeared one by one into that silent room, my imagination ran wild.

Then a redheaded woman in casual garb came sauntering down the corridor. 'Oh, wow! Don't you all look lovely?' she cooed in a thick Scottish brogue. 'What's the occasion?'

Relieved to have someone to speak English with, I piped up. 'We're not exactly sure. We were doing a Cartier showcase downstairs and someone up here requested a private viewing.'

'Oh, that would be the princess,' replied the redhead. 'I'm her nurse. She's on her twice-annual shopping expedition. We're all here in tow.'

Her employer, a Saudi princess, was travelling with an entourage of two hundred. 'We've got three floors of this hotel and four floors of the hotel next door. It's quite the circus. You've no idea the fuss.'

'And the red faces?' I asked. 'Too much sun?'

'Oh god no! They never go in the sun. Chemical peels. The princess treated all her ladies-in-waiting to a chemical peel in New York. I tried to warn them off it, but they wouldn't listen. I've been doling out Savlon ever since like it's going out of style.'

I started to laugh, only to be interrupted by my summons into the princess's suite. I felt plush carpet underfoot as I stepped into the low-lit room. Against one wall, a group of Arab women stood attentively. Opposite them, with their backs to a set of heavy navy curtains, posed my colleagues, each with a fake smile plastered to their face.

On a large cream sofa in the middle of the room, reclining barefoot in a pair of black trousers and a flowing top, sat a large woman. She looked to be no older than in her late twenties, and was curvaceous without being overweight. Her dark, voluminous hair framed a round face – a pair of brown-painted lips, and dark eyes dramatically painted with too much eyeliner. In the soft light it was hard to be sure, but her face looked at least as red and raw as those belonging to the women scurrying about the hallway.

I performed my walk, turning as gracefully as the mini catwalk and its coffee table obstruction would allow. The princess watched me with a bored expression. Midway through my walk, she muttered something in Arabic to a small woman standing at attention next to the sofa.

'The princess will take four of that necklace and four sets of the earrings,' the small woman translated into French. The Cartier woman nodded and scribbled furiously in a notebook.

Four other girls came in after me. With each model, the princess ordered at least three of each of the pieces on display. When the final girl had made her entrance and taken her place in the line-up against the curtain, the princess asked another question of her translator.

'The princess is asking if that is it? Do you have nothing else?'

The Cartier woman, clearly taken aback, stammered a reply. 'That is all we have to show the princess this evening, but if she would like to come and visit our store tomorrow, we would be delighted to continue the private viewing with many more of our pieces.'

The princess listened to the translation and pulled a face. Then she returned her gaze to the line of tall, skinny models and dancers standing in front of her. After considering us for a moment, she spoke to the translator again.

'The princess would like to know what you eat,' the translator asked, addressing the line of models. There was an awkward silence as we processed the question and wondered what we were supposed to answer. I glanced across at the Cartier woman for guidance. She just glared back, urging someone, anyone, to speak.

'Ummm,' one of the French girls finally responded, shrugging her shoulders, clearly confused, 'just normal, regular food.'

The translator delivered the response, but the princess seemed dissatisfied. Maintaining her steady gaze at us, she motioned with one hand to the ladies-in-waiting behind her. One disappeared silently out of the room.

Within minutes, the double doors leading to the adjoining suite were thrown open and two men wearing tall white chef's hats hurried in, each pushing a trolley bearing huge platters of freshly prepared food. There was smoked salmon, artfully constructed *hors d'oeuvres*, mini-hamburgers and plates of fries.

'The princess would like you to eat,' the translator said. 'She would like you to eat here, in front of her. Now.'

We looked at one another.

The Cartier woman continued to glare, urging us towards the food with sharp nods of her head.

One by one, we leaned in to take a smoked-salmon toast or mini-hamburger and then stepped back into line self-consciously as the princess looked on. We ate in complete silence. All I could hear was the sound of myself chewing. My eyes darted about the room, trying to gauge from the reactions of the ladies-in-waiting whether public displays of eating for the gratification of the princess were in any way usual. It was just so weird.

There was no smile on the princess's face, no indication that she was either impressed or disappointed with the floorshow we were putting on. She just sat and stared at us until every item of food had been eaten. When the trays had been cleared, the princess indicated to the translator that we were free to go.

'The princess would like to thank you for your time,' the translator said.

We couldn't get out of there fast enough, tripping over one another in the short hallway leading to the doors.

On the flight back to Paris the following day, we were upgraded to first class. We were only in the air an hour, but it was enough time to quaff a couple of glasses of champagne. Upon landing, Jerome farewelled us at the arrivals gate, and the Cinderella spell was broken. Elena and I loaded ourselves onto the RER – the grotty suburban train linking the airport to central Paris – and came back down to earth with an ungracious thud. By the time I had negotiated the Métro from the cesspit of Châtelet to Villiers and turned the key in the apartment door, the Côte d'Azur, the jewels and the glamour were already beginning to seem a distant memory.

'*Salut*,' Olivier chimed from the living-room as I walked in. My heart sank. Of course he was home – where else would he be?

'*Salut*,' I replied, not wanting to admit how indifferent I was to him.

After a day back at work, to return to the apartment and Olivier – and his ever-present band of unwashed muso groupies – the glamour of the Côte d'Azur had faded completely.

In a bid to inject something new and exciting into my life, I decided that pet ownership would be my new project. Olivier was still making semi-regular promises to buy me a kitten, but I had long ago dismissed them as hollow. I had learned that if something was to be done, I had to do it myself. So I picked up the phone book and called around to a couple of the local vets. One of them, in Montmartre, happened to have a litter of kittens that needed homes.

I took a tiny grey kitten with yellow-green eyes back to the apartment, walking through the front door and announcing to Olivier, who was hunkered over his computer as usual, 'This is Willy. Merry Christmas to me.'

Olivier looked up, spied the kitten as he began to tentatively explore the room, and fell upon him excitedly. My sarcasm was completely lost. Willy's utter cuteness gave us both a distraction and proved a circuit-breaker that would keep the household together – at least for a little longer.

Meanwhile, back at the Moulin Rouge, *Féerie* had made good use of the first six months of its life and had well and truly come into its own, despite its rocky opening night. The show was proving popular with audiences and, for a period at least, had managed to re-energise the place. The costumes were new and unstinky. The dance routines, though occasionally daggy, required more than a passing thought to perform. The new blood in the cast was refreshing.

For six months, the dressing rooms were interesting again as new eccentrics rubbed up against old ones. But as sure as cabaret features feathers, the glamour gradually began to give way to the grind, and performing *Feérie* twice a night, six nights a week started to take its toll. I began to notice the company settling into a familiar rhythm, and people slipping back into bad onstage habits – going through the motions instead of giving it their all.

Brett had decided to leave. He and Matthew were cruise-ship-bound, opting to take a couple of contracts on the high seas, where at least they could be together.

Jean, too, had declared her intention to bid farewell to Paris. She had spent the first half of the year flying to and from the Caribbean to visit an old flame, Eugenio, who worked as an engineer on one of the huge cruise ships that ply the turquoise waters of Latin America. In another life, pre-Moulin, they had enjoyed a fling, and they'd never quite gotten over one another. After six months of a long-distance relationship, they'd decided to make a go of it. She was headed to Finland, where he was involved in the building and launching of a brand-new cruise ship.

My little Moulin family was dispersing and feelings of restlessness began to stir in me as well. Much as I liked some of my new castmates, it felt like a changing of the guard was taking place at the Moulin Rouge and I was about to be left behind. I also couldn't shake the feeling that I had gone as far as I could go there. I wasn't going to become a permanent soloist or principal, and I could feel my head butting against the Moulin's rhinestone-studded glass ceiling. It was time for me to move on as well.

With the departures of the boys and Jean looming, I sent out my C.V. A couple of cruise ships replied almost instantly, asking when I might be able to start. The Paradis Latin, one of Paris' lesser-known cabaret venues, called me in for an audition. I went along out of curiosity, keen to see inside the famous Gustave Eiffel-designed auditorium and to sharpen up my rusty audition skills. The Paradis offered me a job, but while it was gratifying, I finally decided against making the shift to the less prestigious venue.

The cruise ship offers forced me to consider leaving Paris and made me realise I wasn't ready for that. All of it reinforced what I already knew but had never done anything about – namely, that there was really only one other place in Paris I wanted to work.

And thanks to a chance encounter in the local Monoprix supermarket, it was about to be a step closer to becoming a reality.

# ACT IV

## Chapter Thirty-one

Whenever the fantasy of dancing at the Lido played out in my imagination, it invariably involved a nerve-wracking audition on the stage of the famous Champs Élysées venue first. In my mind's eye, it was always me under a spotlight, being put through my dance paces by a faceless ballet mistress concealed in darkness at the back of the *salle*. Ever since Corina had talked about her time as a celebrated Lido Bluebell, the venue had assumed mythic proportions in my mind. I was convinced that joining the ranks of its elite dance corps, if it happened at all, would only come about as the result of years of fruitless auditioning, months spent haranguing the show's directors and the coming together of a whole lot of factors. Perhaps unsurprisingly, a chance encounter at the Monoprix supermarket on Rue de Levis had never figured as one of them.

As Parisian supermarkets go, the Monoprix at Villiers is nothing special: fluorescent-lit aisles packed to the ceiling with basic French foodstuffs. Waiting in line for the cashier one afternoon, however, I found myself eavesdropping. Two cash registers over, a man was chatting animatedly with his companion in an unmistakeable Australian accent, while a supermarket employee scanned their impressive haul of wine and vodka bottles. His conversation was peppered with references to the Lido.

Dance circles in Paris being notoriously small, and taking into account his age, nationality and the gist of his conversation, I guessed he was Stuart – the Lido company manager.

I made eye contact with him as we were both packing our groceries.

'Excuse me, but are you Stuart from the Lido?'

He raised his eyebrows, taken aback at having been recognised in a Monoprix, then looked me up and down with an amused half-smile. I was dressed in my usual market-crawling outfit of jeans, trainers and T-shirt.

'I could be. Depends who's asking.'

'My name's Shay. I work at the Moulin. I'm from Brisbane.'

'Nice to meet you, Shay.' His faced softened immediately. 'This is Fiona. She was a principal at the Lido back in the day.'

His companion leaned across and shook my hand. She was a tall, svelte woman who held herself with typical dancer poise. The three of us exchanged polite cabaret chit-chat, shuffling awkwardly with our bags of shopping.

'Well, it was nice to meet you,' Stuart finally said, making to leave.

I decided it was now or never.

'I heard the Lido sometimes does shows in Monaco over summer. If you're doing one and you need a few more dancers, I'd be interested.'

'We've stopped doing those shows,' Stuart replied.

'Oh.' I gathered my courage. 'I don't suppose you have any auditions coming up at the Lido?' I looked at him sheepishly, embarrassed at having been so brazen.

'There's nothing at the moment,' he said.

I tried not to look disappointed.

'But we're always on the lookout for good people. Why don't you come by the Lido this week and drop off your photos and C.V.? You never know.'

I knew a polite brush-off when I heard one. I nodded and we bade one other farewell.

Nonetheless, I went through the motions of updating my C.V. Three days later, I set out for the Lido on the way to work.

It was a languid summer's evening. Groups of evening picnickers had set up on the lawns of the Parc Monceau, sprawled on blankets, passing bottles of *rosé*, lying back smoking, and handing around *baguettes* and cheese. I thought how nice it would be to have a normal job with normal hours: to have a social life that didn't start each morning at

2 a.m. To have a social life at all. As I left the park and turned onto Avenue Hoche, the Arc de Triomphe loomed on the near horizon. Backlit by the setting sun, it cut a majestic silhouette out of the hazy pink sky. Summer in Paris was easily my favourite time of the year.

When I reached the Champs Élysées, it was jammed with traffic and its footpaths were packed with people, ambling slowly, stopping to stare at the glittering baubles in the windows of the huge Cartier store and window-shopping their way past the flagship Paris stores of Louis Vuitton, Hugo Boss and Lancel.

The terrace cafes were heaving with beautiful women who smoked and sipped Kir Royals, while their open-shirted, long-haired male companions pouted in designer sunglasses. Across the street, I could make out the famous Ladurée tea house, an orderly line of tourists queuing to sample its famous *macarons*. The chic eatery Fouquet's was also a hive of early evening activity, as Paris's well-heeled set dropped by for an *apéritif*. It was all so wonderfully Parisian – and so very far removed from the strip clubs and kebab shops that surrounded the Moulin Rouge.

The Lido was located on the opposite side of the Champs Élysées from the golden façade of the Louis Vuitton building. From the street, it looked little more than a doorway off the world's most famous avenue. I walked down a long, black-carpeted corridor. Crystal chandeliers hung overhead from a ceiling covered in mauve velvet. Framed photos of scenes from *C'est Magique*, the current Lido revue, were hung tastefully along the wall. A silver-haired, tuxedo-wearing gentleman met me as I stepped through the Lido double doors and into the theatre's vestibule. He was one of the maitre d's.

'*Je peux vous aider, mademoiselle?*' 'Can I help you?'

I explained my mission in my best French, and he took my C.V. and photos and promised to pass them on to Stuart.

Back out on the street, I tried to suppress a rising feeling of excitement. As I sat on the Métro and made my way back up to Pigalle, I told myself not to get my hopes up, but the seed had been sown.

'Are you ready yet? We're going to be late,' Olivier yelled at me from the hallway.

'*J'arrive!*' I replied, hastily applying mascara and straining to check my dress in our tiny bathroom cabinet mirror. I swiped one last coat of gloss across my lips and stepped into the hall. 'Okay, all ready, let's go.'

It was a Saturday night, and I had managed to get the night off to attend the wedding of one of Olivier's muso friends. He was marrying a girl from an Algerian family. The wedding was to take place at a town hall on the southern outskirts of Paris, followed by a reception and a traditional Algerian wedding feast. Just as we reached the front door, the phone rang.

'*Laisse-le!*' Olivier ordered, pointing at his watch. 'Leave it. We're going to be late.'

But I dived back into the living room to pull the receiver off the hook.

'Hello?'

'Hello, may I speak to Shay Stafford please?' The voice was deep, mellifluous and refined, with a definite French accent.

'This is Shay.'

'Hello Shay. My name is Pierre Rambert. I am the artistic director of the Lido.'

I almost dropped the phone. Olivier stood at the living-room door, glaring at me. I waved him away frantically.

'Stuart passed your C.V. and photos to me. He mentioned that you might be interested in coming to work with us.'

I didn't know what to say. I had heard about Pierre – his reputation preceded him in Paris cabaret circles. As the artistic director of the Lido, he was famous for being very particular about the girls he chose.

I was too overwhelmed to respond. There was an awkward moment of silence.

'Are you still there?' Pierre finally said.

'Yes, yes, still here.' I started to pace the room, nervous and embarrassed. What kind of an idiot must he take me for?

'And are you still interested?' I detected a tone of amusement in his voice, as if a small part of him was pleased he had this effect on people.

'Absolutely,' I replied. And then, in an unexpected moment of name-dropping lucidity: 'I used to work with Corina in Australia. She spoke so highly of her time at the Lido. It's been a dream of mine to work there ever since.' Even as the words came out, I cringed.

Pierre seemed even more amused, 'Corina? She was one of our best principals. I remember her fondly. As it happens, a place has just come up. I've recently had to let someone go. I would be very happy to offer you a place at the Lido.'

A rush of adrenaline shot through me. 'I'm sorry?'

'A job. I'd like to offer you a job. If you're interested, of course.'

'Of course! *Of course* I'm interested. Would you like me to come in for an audition?'

'Oh, I don't think that will be necessary. Your C.V. speaks for itself. And I have seen you dance at the Moulin several times. I know who you are.'

Olivier was now standing at the door glowering. 'COME ON!' he mouthed.

I turned my back to him.

'It says here on your CV that you replace principal and work as a captain at the Moulin,' Pierre continued. 'The position I have to offer is as a Bluebell, and the work won't be quite as varied. But if things work out, who knows where it could lead.'

I started hopping excitedly on the spot.

'A Bluebell at the Lido. I don't know what to say.'

'How about, "I accept"?' Pierre joked.

'No. I mean yes. I mean, of course, definitely. Thank you!' I gushed. 'It's just that, the thing is, I'll need to speak to Janet. I can't leave her in the lurch in the middle of my contract.'

'Of course not, dear. Speak with Janet. Take a couple of days to think about it and get back to me. Just know that we'd love to have you on board.'

I hung up the receiver and stood motionless in the middle of the living-room, a look of shock pasted to my face.

'*C'etait qui?*' Olivier asked. 'What's going on?'

'I've just been offered a job at the Lido,' I said. Not even speaking the words out loud could make them seem real. 'That was Pierre

Rambert. He just phoned to offer me a job at the Lido. *He* phoned *me!* I can't believe it.'

'*Mais c'est super!*' Olivier said, rallying. 'This is what you have wanted for such a long time. *Félicitations!*' He moved across the room and pulled me into a hug. 'Now come, we can discuss it on the train. We're running late.'

I sat through the wedding ceremony and most of the reception with my mind racing. Not even the outbreaks of traditional Algerian celebratory shrieking or the sight of so many henna-tattooed hands shook me from my thoughts. It was my one night off a week, and yet I craved to be with my friends so I could workshop the dilemma suddenly before me.

## Chapter Thirty-two

'But I don't see why you're even hesitating,' Brett said the following afternoon as we sat around his kitchen table polishing off a late lunch. 'It's a no-brainer. It's the Lido, Marge. It's the freaking bloody Lido! I went for an audition there once. It was awful. They made me do this really difficult ballet combination. I didn't have a hope in hell. And here you are with Pierre Rambert phoning you at home, offering you a job. And you're hesitating? Are you *mad*?'

It wasn't quite that straightforward. After almost three years at the Moulin Rouge, I had worked my way through the ranks to a relatively privileged position. I replaced the soloists and principals and was nude captain to boot. And while I felt like I'd climbed every Moulin mountain I could, the Lido job would be a step down in terms of seniority and onstage exposure. It would mean working my way up from the bottom again. It also would mean taking a hefty paycut (something I could ill-afford with Olivier still out of work).

Yet Brett was right. Somehow none of that mattered. Above all, it was a new challenge, and that was exactly what I wanted.

'Go for it Marge,' Matthew counselled from the stove as he flipped a crepe. 'It will be a great experience. Imagine having both the Moulin and the Lido on your C.V.'

'But what if I get bored doing the same show? There's no way as a Bluebell I'll have the same variety I have at the Moulin. Plus, the principals there are all so tall, I might never get anywhere.'

'Do it for a year and see what happens,' Brett advised. 'If it turns out to be a dead end, at least you'll have done it. You can always come and join us on a cruise ship.'

I knew that Pierre would have a pile of C.V.s and tapes on his desk from dancers all over the world hoping for a place in his company. I had to decide, and quickly.

Since I'd lived in Paris, I had been to the Lido two or three times. One of the perks of dancing in a show was that you could pretty much get in to see any of the other cabaret revues whenever you wanted.

The show playing at the Lido, *C'est Magique*, was your typical cabaret pastiche of forms and ideas, a loose narrative barely held together by a disjointed series of tableaux whose real *raison d'être* was to show off the high-camp imagination of its creator and the talents of its *costumier*. No-one who saw a Lido show came away analysing the plot.

For me, sitting in the vast Lido auditorium, I had simply been impressed by the size of the production. The stage was so much bigger than that at the Moulin Rouge. The costumes were larger and more extravagant. There seemed to be more feathers, bigger backpacks, more outrageously fanciful headgear. The sets were more detailed, the multi-levelled hydraulics of the stage were more impressive and the lighting more striking.

The choreography was no more or less impressive than what we were doing at the Moulin, but the dancers seemed to be a cut above – not in terms of talent, but definitely in terms of height. Each girl looked impossibly tall. Imposingly, unusually, intimidatingly tall. Was I going to measure up? Next to some of the Lido's Amazons, was I opening myself up to ridicule? Was it better to remain a big fish in a pond full of marginally shorter ones?

To be sure, I mulled the decision over for the full two days Pierre had allotted me. Finally, the desire for change proved too great. Whatever regrets I might have moving to the Lido, at least I would never regret not having tried. I resolved to go into work that night and break the news to Janet.

I performed the first show in a state of high agitation. I'd only caught Janet just before going onstage, and had had to ask if I could see her in the *entracte*. For the next ninety minutes, I went through the motions, barely able to concentrate. Leaving jobs was never easy. Leaving a job that I liked and letting down people who had been so good to me was going to be especially hard.

During the *entracte*, when everyone else piled back to the dressing-rooms or off to have a smoke, I went to Janet's office.

'Come in,' she said, as I knocked on the door.

I stepped into the room, my heart racing.

'Have a seat,' Janet said and smiled warmly. 'What can I do for you?'

Before I could open my mouth, I started to choke up. Tears welled in my eyes. As I began to speak, I could feel my voice wavering.

'Umm, well, the thing is . . .' I paused to swallow and take a deep breath, eyes fixed on my hands in my lap.

Janet looked at me expectantly.

'The thing is . . . Well, you know we've talked before about how I wanted to extend my experience? Well, I've been offered a job at the Lido.' I stopped and looked up, fully expecting my words to have unleashed an almighty wrath.

Janet simply raised her eyebrows and nodded slowly.

'So,' I continued, clearing my throat, 'I, um . . . I wanted to talk to you about it before I accepted.'

I knew I was playing with fire. 'Friendly rivalry' was a major understatement of the relations between the Moulin Rouge and the Lido. They were one another's main rival in the competitive world of Paris cabaret, and every victory for one venue was a slight against the other. I was effectively telling Janet I was off to sleep with the enemy.

Janet took her time answering. 'Well,' she finally began, 'I guess it was going to happen eventually.'

I almost deflated on the spot from relief.

'I'm not going to pretend I'm pleased that you're going,' Janet continued. 'And it doesn't surprise me that you've been offered other jobs. Are you able to say what role Pierre is offering you?'

'I'll be starting as a Bluebell.'

Janet looked puzzled. 'But why would you want to be a Bluebell when you're a captain and first replacement here?' It was her trump card and she knew it.

I shook my head, looking for the words. 'I'm tired of managing all of these girls. Plus, I think the Lido could be a good experience. I'm hoping in the long term it will be a good move.'

Janet said nothing.

'I don't want to leave you in a messy situation,' I continued. 'Of course I'll stay until you find a replacement, and I'll help rehearse the swings and understudies. Whatever is easiest for you.'

I could hear the muffled buzz of backstage sounds through the door. Janet remained silent for what seemed like an eternity.

'Well,' she said, 'I'm not in the habit of forcing people to stay if they've decided they want to go. I'll be sad to lose you. I suppose you can always go and get some experience over there and come back to us when you've gotten this Lido business out of your system.'

We agreed on a month's notice, during which time I was to help out with the necessary rehearsals. By the time it had all been worked through, I was crying again.

'What's wrong?' asked Janet, getting up from behind her desk. 'I thought this was what you wanted?'

'It is. I mean, I think it is. I'm pretty sure it's what I want.'

'Come here.' Janet pulled me in for a hug and I welled up again. 'I can't believe I'm having to counsel *you* to leave *me*.'

We both laughed.

Brett was waiting outside the door. 'What happened? Are you okay?'

I gave him a quick run-down as we rushed back to the dressing-rooms to get ready for the second show.

'It's the right thing to do, Marge,' he said, squeezing my hand as we parted at the bottom of the stairs. 'I can feel it in my waters.'

# Chapter Thirty-three

If I had wanted to indulge in a little nostalgia during my last month at the Moulin Rouge, a frantic new schedule of rehearsing saw to it that I didn't have the energy or the time. Every day I would rehearse my replacements, race to the Lido to do my own rehearsals, and then run back to the Moulin Rouge to perform two shows.

'We'll have you Bluebell-ready in a month, darling,' Pierre had told me when I phoned to accept the job.

The Bluebells were to the Lido what the Doriss Girls were to the Moulin Rouge. Margaret Kelly's celebrated troupe of dancers had originally been formed at the Folies Bergères, where they'd made a name for themselves dancing as the Bluebell Girls. The Lido had featured them since 1946. In dance circles, the name 'Bluebell' was synonymous with the kind of elegant showgirl style that Miss Bluebell, as Kelly came to be known, had pioneered. She built a reputation for only recruiting the tallest and most striking dancers available, ensuring that when they were onstage in nine-centimetre heels and swathed in massive sprays of feathers and lavishly jewelled costumes, they appeared otherworldly.

To say that I was intimidated, as I walked down the Champs Élysées for my first morning of Lido rehearsals, would be an understatement. As I picked my way through the tourist hordes photographing the Arc de Triomphe, I pondered why I had willingly put myself back in this situation. Why had I left the comfort of the known to once again be the new kid on the dance block? If Lido dancers really were the cream of the cabaret crop, they were surely going to have attitudes to match.

I suddenly began to pine for the camaraderie of the Moulin Rouge – the raucous fun backstage, the eccentric characters, the kooky castmates, even the occasional bitchiness. Then I thought of Corina, and how lovely she was. They surely couldn't all be prima donnas. I turned off the Champs Élysées into the Lido entrance. After all, not even the Lido stage was big enough for an entire company of divas.

When I stepped into the softly lit auditorium, it took a moment for my eyes to adjust. Empty, the *salle* looked even bigger than I remembered it. Down near the stage, red-velvet chairs were stacked on long rows of narrow, white-topped tables. Further back, several raised rows of semicircular red-leather booths stretched in a broad arc – seeming to hover in anticipation for the show to begin.

I could make out two figures on the stage, one of whom I recognised as Stuart. I made my way down the stairs towards him.

'Hello again, lovely to see you,' he said, extending a hand. 'I'm pleased it all worked out. Who knew you could pick up a Lido job with your groceries? That Monoprix really does have it all.'

I laughed.

'This is Jane,' he continued gesturing towards a woman in her late twenties with hair in a brown bob and a broad smile on her face. 'She's going to be your captain and will be teaching you your show.'

'Hi there. Lovely to meet you.' Jane spoke with an English accent.

It was too early to be sure, but she seemed relatively un-diva-esque.

'It's great to have you on board. Me and Sarah, the second captain, will teach you the show. It's going to be one-on-one, so it shouldn't take too long. We'll also get you sorted with paperwork, and then you'll need to see Cathy about shoes and hats and things. But you know the drill, you've done this all before.'

I breathed a sigh of relief. So far, so pleasant.

Jane and I spent the afternoon blocking the chorie for the opening tableau. It was a number featuring the entire cast dressed in top hats and capes, in keeping with the show's *'magique'* theme. The choreography called for a jazzy routine with kicks and stylised arms. It was all very eighties, really, but it led into what would become my favourite routine: the panthers. This was the highlight of the Bluebell show, our moment in the spotlight. It required twelve of us to mount a series of rotating podiums and swing provocatively from poles, thrashing our black-feathered headgear and kicking our black lycra–clad legs.

'Just concentrate on each little step and movement for now,' Jane advised as we blocked the panther chorie. 'Once you put on the hat and chain and boots, it's a whole new ball game. I hope you're not afraid of heights.'

The rest of the choreography was classic cabaret. Lots of *port de bras*, lots of flourishes – altogether more posing than any real cardiac-thumping dance moves.

For the next three weeks, Jane and Sarah (another Brit) put me through my paces. There was a lot to remember, and I struggled to retain the two or three dances I was expected to learn each day. Thankfully, *Féerie* was now so deeply ingrained that I didn't need to concentrate on my performances at the Moulin Rouge. All my energies could be channelled into remembering the Lido choreography. In scenes reminiscent of my days tapping down the streets of Tarragindi in my red shoes after dance class, I walked home each afternoon through Parc Monceau practising whatever steps I had learned that day. To the occasional passer-by, the tall girl pirouetting in the middle of the park must have made for quite a sight.

I drilled myself everywhere – in the shower, in the kitchen while preparing dinner, in the living room with Willy as my unwitting dance partner. I willed my brain to take it all in.

In between rehearsals, I was dispatched backstage for costume fittings. Cathy, the head dresser at the Lido, was petite and discreet; even from our first encounter I picked her as the silent and efficient type. She said barely a word as we made our way through various *loges* trying on all of the hats, gloves, jewels and feathers that I would soon be wearing every night.

'*Vous êtes presque la même taille qu'elle,*' she would say, holding up the costumes of the Bluebell I was to replace. 'You are almost the same size as her.' With a few adjustments, they would do just fine.

Considering that the costumes had been worn fourteen times a week for nearly five years already, they were in excellent condition. The feathers were still strong and the beading was flawless. Even the hats were impeccable, despite having probably been modified to fit numerous heads. They were a credit to the team of backstage seamstresses and milliners.

My hat size, as always, drew comment. *'Mais quelle tête!'* ('What a head!') Cathy would exclaim each time she fitted me for a hat. Not even among the Lido dancers, renowned as some of the biggest, tallest women in the dance world, could my cranium be beaten for size and girth. Cathy sent the old hats away to the milliner for adjusting, laughing and mumbling away to herself as I stood there self-consciously.

For each fitting Cathy would take me down into the bowels of the backstage area – a multi-levelled affair that was a warren of passageways, doorways and nooks. Like the front of house, backstage was enormous and at first, whenever Cathy dismissed me, I would get lost, taking ten minutes to retrace my steps and find my way back up to the stage.

'Leave a trail of rhinestones as you go, love,' was Stuart's advice.

One afternoon, while Sarah was teaching me the finale and Stuart was supervising, a man appeared at the back of the *salle* and started making his way towards the stage. I could tell from the subtle change in my new colleagues' body language that he was important. As he made his way down the stairs through the half-light, I could make out a leather jacket, a pair of stylish round glasses, tight blue jeans, an oversized silver belt buckle and black leather boots. He walked with the unmistakeable gait of a dancer. It had to be Pierre Rambert.

Pierre sidled up to Stuart and gave him a peck on both cheeks. I felt suddenly very nervous and clumsily self-conscious, but did my best to focus on Sarah's instructions and not be distracted by this new arrival. By now he'd lit up a Marlboro Red and was standing with his arms crossed, watching me intently. When finally Sarah called a break, he walked towards me.

'Hello darling, I'm Pierre.' He extended a long thin arm and held out a heavily jewelled hand. 'It's lovely to finally meet you.'

I felt an irrational urge to curtsy, and suddenly wished I had worn my good audition outfit and a bit more make-up.

'It looks like it's all going well. Jane and Sarah have nothing but good reports of you. How are you feeling? Is it all coming together?'

'I think I'm getting the hang of it,' I replied.

'Good, very good. If you're done here with Sarah, why don't you come with me and we'll take care of the formalities?'

I followed Pierre backstage. We climbed a flight of stairs and turned down a corridor. Entering a small room and stepping around a collection of dumbbells, we passed the wigmaker's *atelier* and came to a blue-painted door marked 'Miss Bluebell'. Pierre took a key, unlocked the door and invited me into his office.

Inside the tiny room, the air conditioning was set to freezing. Pierre seemed oblivious to the sudden cold as he took a seat behind his desk. I sat opposite him, shivering in my leotard. On the door frame behind me, a tape measure stretched up from the floor. To the right of the desk was a set of scales. Framed photos of principal dancers past adorned the walls, each of them featuring a red lipstick kiss and gushing messages of adoration and appreciation. On Pierre's desk, an ashtray and phone competed for space with piles of C.V.s and videotapes from aspiring Bluebells.

'So, let's see now,' he said, picking up and perusing my résumé. 'Brisbane, Japan, Malaysia, the Moulin. You've been busy.'

He looked up and gave me a friendly smile. He wore his dark, shoulder-length hair in a youthful style belying his fifty-something years. His face was long, tanned and just the slightest bit gaunt. His every movement seemed studied and graceful, almost cat-like. He held my C.V. in one hand while yet another Marlboro Red smouldered in the other.

'I see it says here that you are 177 centimetres tall.' He looked up at me over the top of his glasses.

I froze.

'I don't think that's true, is it?' he asked.

I blushed, dying inside.

Pierre broke into a broad smile, a mischievous glint in his eye. 'If I had a franc for every dancer who lied about their height on their C.V., I'd be a very rich man,' he said.

That night, I went to watch the show at the Lido.

The Champs Élysées was alive with activity. The Arc de Triomphe stood tall, floodlit and majestic, overseeing the streams of traffic that crawled up and down the wide, cobbled avenue. The pavements were packed with aimlessly wandering tourists and locals, making the most of the balmy late summer evening. Well-dressed people stood in a line that snaked out of the entrance of the Lido and down to the corner of nearby Rue Washington.

I felt a frisson of excitement as I walked towards the door, the gold letters 'LIDO' lit up above the entrance.

'*Je m'appelle Shay Stafford, je suis une nouvelle danseuse,*' I explained to a doorman. He was young, bald, black-suited and clearly intent on preventing anyone from entering the building. He looked me up and down, as if well-versed in picking dancers from chancers, and reluctantly lowered the red velvet rope.

Inside, the *salle* had been transformed from the slightly dreary state I had become used to during two weeks of rehearsals. Lit by four large chandeliers and a series of crystal and brass lamps, it looked fabulously seventies. On each table sat a modern red and gold lamp. Champagne flutes glinted in the light. Waiters and busboys dressed in tuxedos, suits and smocks – depending on their level of seniority – bustled about the room, tending to the clients who had opted for the dinner-and-show package.

I felt like I was in Vegas, circa 1975, and that at any moment the red velvet curtain would pull back to reveal a whisky-toting Dean Martin or a fabulously camp Liza Minelli.

The olde-world glamour was ruined somewhat when the audience started to file in. While some, especially the older women, had clearly relished the opportunity to throw on whatever piece of sequinned clothing they owned, many of the younger members of the audience sauntered in wearing jeans and trainers. It was a shame that people had lost the desire to dress up. The success of venues like the Lido depended on them making themselves accessible to the tourist masses but, in the process, the sense of occasion that would once have accompanied a night out on the Champs Élysées had sadly diminished.

As I took my seat, the *salle* was already abuzz with chatter. A waiter swung by my table and deposited a glass of champagne. Within minutes of everyone being seated, the lights dimmed and the show began.

I sat in the dark and made a frantic series of mental connections between the choreography I had been learning and the performances playing out on stage. Pieces of the jigsaw began to fall into place as I watched the Bluebell line move in perfect synchronicity about the stage. Under the table, my feet ghosted out the choreography. I watched carefully which side of the stage the Bluebells entered and exited for each number, doing my best to commit it all to memory. The standard of dance was high but, even within the hallowed ranks of the Lido, there was still the familiar cross-section of those who gave their all, and those who were clearly going through the motions.

Most striking, though, was the average height of the dancers. They all seemed so crazy tall. I was sure I was going to look ridiculous next to them.

The show itself was typical cabaret kitsch – just bigger and more spectacular than anything I had been in before. It opened with a laser show – impressive and cutting-edge ten years ago, now not so much. The opening number, *C'est Magique!* was all top hats and red plumes – big, bold, quintessential cabaret. There was a huge staircase and masses of feathers – it seemed as though, for every feather on a Moulin Rouge costume there were ten on the costumes here at the Lido. It was all so opulent and over the top.

Like the Moulin Rouge, there was a mix of covered dancers – Bluebells – and nudes. The stage was wide and deep. Dancers seemed to keep pouring down the stairs in a never-ending parade of out-of-this-world costumes. In the second number, a male dancer dressed as a bunny jumped out of an oversized top hat, closely followed by six female bunnies. The girls wore a pair of bunny ears, a bow tie, a pair of fluffy-fronted, backless chaps and a fluffy cotton tail. It was a festival of bare breasts and buttocks. I was shocked at how nude the girls looked. The number was risqué in a playful kind of way and, with choreography that required the girls to hop about the stage like rabbits, ensured that all eyes in the auditorium were firmly fixed on six sets of bouncing breasts.

Over the almost two-hour period, the show featured all kinds of high-tech wizardry, including a huge dragon that flew over the audience and the enormous mirror-tiled machine that came up from under the stage and extended hydraulic arms out over the *salle*, on which the Bluebells performed their panther routine. And then, of course, there was the water section.

When it had opened some fifty-five years previously, the Lido had become instantly famous for presenting near naked dancers in a swimming pool. Every subsequent Lido show had featured a water tableau. In *C'est Magique!* the water feature took the form of a stunning series of fountains. They appeared at the back and front of the stage, each one beautifully lit. On staircases that weaved among the fountains, dancers wearing massive sequinned flower hats and diaphanous chiffon capes floated up and down. The effect was breathtaking.

The awe was short-lived, however: a line of male dancers marched onto the stage next, wearing nothing more than G-strings and boots. Coming from the Moulin, where boys were never naked like this, it all seemed shockingly, gratuitously nude.

Leading the onstage action was a live singer, or *meneuse* – a freakishly tall woman who was by turns riveting and distracting. While for the most part she carried the show with her impressive onstage presence, there were moments when she appeared to forget where she was. At times I could have sworn she was lip-synching, not very convincingly, to a backing track.

At one point an ice-skating rink rose up from under the stage and a couple of skaters performed an amazing routine of on-ice acrobatics. Towards the end of the show, there was an arresting Cole Porter number in which a single female dancer, portraying an orchestra conductor with a top hat and baton, performed a beautiful solo. No feathers, no overbearingly massive sets – just her, her body and the music. It was simple, powerful and moving.

And then there was the finale. Down a huge white staircase floated another seemingly never-ending parade of feathered showgirls. I had never seen so many feathers. The lighting, the sets, the costumes – they were all so grand. It didn't seem real that I was going to be a part of it.

By the time the curtain fell, I was exhausted without even having left my seat. My head was swimming with stage directions as I tried to do a mental recap of the entire show and the Bluebells' movements within it.

Stuart, who had been watching the show perched on a bar stool at the back of the room, came to collect me and take me backstage. As we entered one of the dressing-rooms, he explained that he was going to introduce me to Amanda. 'She's going to teach you your track,' he said. 'Amanda is one of our swings. She knows all the places and tonight she's doing yours. Just follow, watch and learn.'

Upon hearing her name, a blonde girl with striking blue eyes looked up from the dressing-room table, on which she had been busily laying out cupcakes and chips. She turned to me with a huge smile.

'Hi there and welcome to our dressing-room,' she said, handing me a piece of chocolate cake. 'You'll be sitting here,' she said pointing to the place covered by the pile of food. 'We're just having a little *loge* party tonight.'

'What's the occasion?' I asked.

'No occasion. I just had a stick of butter in the fridge that was screaming to be used.'

A long line of girls sat at mirrors lit by the usual frame of light bulbs.

'Girlies!' Amanda yelled. 'This is Shay from Australia, via the Moulin. She's going to be starting with us next week.'

A row of girls in various states of undress turned from whatever make-up application they were engrossed in and blurted out hellos.

'Australia?' came a loud voice from the back of the dressing-room in an unmistakebly broad Aussie accent. 'Just what this place needs, another bloody Australian.' A tall girl stood up from her place and made her way towards me. She had long brown hair pulled back in a ponytail. Her striking features were exaggerated with layers of showgirl make-up.

'Hi, I'm Lisa, from Melbourne,' she said. 'Welcome to the mad house.'

We chatted for a few minutes, comparing paths to Paris. She had an easy, open nature and a warm smile, and talked even faster than Jean, peppering her chat with lusty bursts of laughter. I could already see that her enthusiasm was infectious. We discovered we had both come to Paris after dancing in the Elvis show in Japan – Lisa had arrived in Japan only months after I had left. We hit it off immediately.

As the second show got underway, I followed Amanda up to the stage and stood in the wings watching carefully as the Bluebells made their entrance. From my vantage point in the darkness, I could see the faces of audience members illuminated by the stage lights. Most wore looks of wonder and delight, others fought off sleep. The Moulin and Lido shows might be slightly different, but the audiences were the same.

Each time Amanda came floating off stage and thundered in a pack with her fellow Bluebells to the quick-change *loge*, or back down to the dressing-room to cool her heels for a moment between numbers, I followed in hot pursuit. I was starting to feel like the labyrinth of *loges* and corridors were conspiring against me.

'I'm never going to remember where to be or how to get there,' I sighed.

'Trust me,' Amanda replied. 'After a week, you'll be doing it in your sleep.'

'Now this bit is important,' Lisa said as we made our way down another two flights of stairs, even deeper into the bowels of the backstage area. 'For the panther number we have to crawl onto the panther machine while it's here under the stage, so that when it rises up into the *salle*, we're already on it. There's hardly any room to breathe down here, so you can't put your hat on until you've climbed up the ladder, jumped over the gap above the ice-skating rink and pulled yourself safely onto your podium. Does that make sense?'

I must have looked scared and confused.

'Don't worry,' she said. 'It sounds more scary than it is, and after a while you don't even notice the twenty-foot drop down to the ice.'

By the end of the second show, I had run up and down the stairs more times than I could remember. The backstage area, which before had been a maze, was now just a blur. In the taxi home I did a quick recap of the night, retracing my track in my head. In a week's time, I was due to step on stage as the Lido's newest Bluebell. I couldn't have felt less ready.

The night before my debut at the Lido was my final turn on the Moulin Rouge. I spent the afternoon rehearsing with Sarah, in what was my last one-on-one session before a full dress rehearsal the following day with the entire Bluebell line. After blocking each of my numbers one final time, Sarah sent me home. I had been so focused on the Lido rehearsals, I hadn't had time to think about leaving the Moulin.

That evening, as I walked into work along Boulevard de Clichy, I decided to take a moment to sit and reflect. Perching on the edge of the large round vent that sat in the middle of Place Blanche, noisily extracting air from the Métro, I looked up at the red windmill as it cut a lazy circuit through the twilight sky. It seemed funny to think that only three years previously this place had been a mystery to me. The famous Moulin Rouge had enjoyed a quasi-mythical, almost regal status in my mind. But three years of its backstage mania had been more than enough time to burst that bubble.

I smiled, thinking about how oblivious the audiences – and aspiring young showgirls everywhere – were to the chaos that played out backstage every night. How the successful execution of each and every performance was pretty much a twice-nightly happy accident. An accident, ironically, that owed itself to the professionalism and experience of some of the loveliest, craziest, most fabulously eccentric showfolk I had ever had the pleasure of working with.

I watched as the first tour buses pulled up outside the theatre entrance, disgorging their excited passengers. A group of sixty-something women – their hair set for the night, tottering even on their sensible heels, handbags clutched to their ample bosoms – bustled into formation to pose for a group photo. One of the ladies lifted her leg, imitating a showgirl high-kick, a silly, giddy expression on her face. There was a cackle of excited laughter from her friends, who all followed suit, prompting an explosion of camera flashes. A moment of Moulin Rouge-inspired madness captured for posterity. I smiled. In one stolen moment, all the reasons I had begun to be annoyed and frustrated with my lot melted away. She had been good to me, the Moulin Rouge, and I was going to miss her.

I hardly had time to step into my dressing-room before the first of the flowers and bouts of hugs descended. By the time the five-minute call came over the tannoy, I had reapplied my mascara five times. For better or for worse, these people had become my surrogate family. And as infuriating as it occasionally had been to struggle with recalcitrant dancers, the bond that had been forged was strong. When Thierry came in to my dressing-room, hugged me and told me how much he was going to miss me, I barely kept it together. When, minutes before curtain, Janet walked in and followed suit, I lost it completely.

'Oh no, we're not doing this again,' Janet exclaimed, fighting off a tear of her own. 'Go on, get out there and have a good show.'

For my final performance, I was replacing one of the singers. It was as good as it gets at the Moulin Rouge – I was a featured principal, right out front and in the spotlight. It didn't escape me that I was leaving all of this glory behind to go and be a relative nobody in a chorus line across town. Not for the last time, I worried I had made the wrong decision.

Determined to wring as much joy as possible out of my final hours on stage at the Moulin Rouge, I threw everything I had into my last two performances and let myself be carried by the *bonhomie* of my castmates and the applause from the *salle*.

Olivier came to watch the second show with some of our friends. Jo was dancing principal and would wink each time we passed onstage. Brett kept coming up from behind in the wings, when I was about to make an entrance, to give me a big hug. Everywhere I went backstage, there was an outstretched hand, an affectionate smile or a peck on the cheek. Dressers, technicians, fellow dancers: whatever else had gone on between us, we were, at the end of the day, co-conspirators, comrades – colleagues.

As I struck my final pose, I looked out across the *salle*. Whether it was real or just in my head, the audience seemed unusually warm. They broke into rapturous applause. All around me I could feel the eyes of colleagues and friends trained on me, and it was too much. I burst into tears yet again. Jo, Jean and Brett were also crying. By the time the curtain fell, there were rivulets of mascara streaking down faces all over the place.

As I sat at my dressing table and started to pack up my belongings, dressers came in to collect my costumes to take away and adjust for my replacement. I peeled photos of my parents and brothers off the mirror and dropped them into a cardboard box. The *loge* emptied around me as each girl rushed off to a taxi, hurried home or headed out for the night. I had a quick read-through of the *Féerie* poster that the company had autographed in my honour – festooned with lipstick kisses and farewell messages. I took my last shower, not in the least bit troubled by the cold splashes coming from Fifi as she showered next to me.

'We will miss you Shayleen,' she said, as we dried off together. 'I've been here a while and seen lots of girls come and go, but only a few of them have had as much *panache* as you.'

It came completely out of the blue. I didn't know what to say. Returning to the dressing-room, I stepped into my clothes and collected my belongings. Picking up my flowers, I took one last look around before turning off the light and walking out the door.

## Chapter Thirty-four

During the Belle Époque, before the two world wars ravaged Europe, a favourite night-time haunt of aristocratic Parisians was a curious little cabaret called *La Plage de Paris*. Situated on the Champs Élysées in a cavernous basement, the venue served up a nightly spectacle of beautiful women frolicking in a purpose-built indoor swimming pool. Photos from the time show men in top hats and tails, and women in elegant satin gowns sipping champagne at small, round tables, while fresh-faced young girls in barely there swimsuits performed in and around the pool.

At the end of the Second World War, brothers Louis and Joseph Clérico purchased the property. Inspired by the pool and the ornate *décor*, which reminded them of their Italian homeland, they renamed the place 'Le Lido' after the famous beach encircling the lagoon of Venice. They poached a young Margaret Kelly – Miss Bluebell – from the Folies Bergère and convinced her to bring her increasingly renowned Bluebell dancers with her.

In the summer of 1946, while France was still licking its war wounds and Paris was recovering from years of German occupation, the Clérico brothers opened the first Lido show: *Sans Rimes Ni Raison* or 'No Rhyme or Reason'. The feather- and sequin-infused froth catered perfectly to the postwar appetite for light entertainment. The brothers had an instant hit on their hands.

In the fifties and sixties, the Lido was a byword for European jet-set glamour. A night at the Lido was a champagne-soaked affair in which

American movie stars rubbed shoulders with European royalty. Smart black suits and designer dresses were the uniform for audiences, who flocked to be entertained by the Bluebells and a rotating schedule of international talent. Shirley MacLaine, Laurel & Hardy, the Kessler Sisters and even Elvis Presley were among those who made guest appearances on the Lido stage.

In 1955, the Cléricos exported their winning formula to Las Vegas, where a Lido production took up residence in the Stardust Casino. In 1977, having well and truly outgrown its original Paris location, the Lido moved up the Avenue des Champs Élysées into the purpose-built 1200-seat theatre in which it now resided.

The creative flair of American choreographer and producer Donn Arden had had much to do with the Bluebells' early success – but it was ultimately Kelly who could claim credit for creating and maintaining the Bluebell legend.

She'd had an amazing life. Born in Dublin and orphaned at birth, Kelly was raised by a spinster dressmaker, who sent her adoptive daughter to dance class, at a doctor's suggestion, to strengthen the little girl's frail legs. At fifteen, she joined a professional dance troupe and by the early 1930s, she'd joined the Folies Bergères. A romance blossomed with the venue's young resident pianist and composer, Marcel Leibovici, and they married in 1939.

When war broke out and France fell under German occupation, Leibovici and his newly pregnant wife fled to Bordeaux, only to find the last boat out of the city crammed to overflowing. They had no choice but to stay. Leibovici, a Romanian Jew, was arrested and sent to a concentration camp.

With the help of the *Résistance*, however, he managed to escape and make his way back to Paris, where he spent the remainder of the war hidden in an attic across the river from Notre Dame. Kelly visited him regularly, often risking arrest by breaking curfew to see him, and survived multiple interrogations by the Gestapo about his whereabouts.

As a *maitresse de ballet* at the Lido, Miss Bluebell was both a harsh taskmistress and a kind of surrogate mother to the impressionable young things who landed jobs in her company.

Though the Lido lovelies pushed the boundaries of the risqué by night, performing in the skimpiest of costumes, Kelly expected her girls to carry themselves as ladies on and off the stage. Legend had it that at one point she'd insisted all Bluebells travel to and from work in a uniform of heels, skirt, full make-up and a fur coat – to maintain a certain standard. Back in the day, too, after every performance the girls were shepherded by security guards past the stage-door johnnies who hovered behind the theatre, keen to catch a glimpse of their favourite showgirl or thrust a bouquet into her hands.

As I walked down Rue Lord Byron towards the Lido stage door, I found myself pondering how things had changed for the modern showgirl. When I'd signed my contract with Pierre, there'd been no list of prohibited post-work activities or talk of mandatory fur-wearing. At the Moulin Rouge, there had never been a need for crowd control at the stage door at the end of every night. The only people hovering when we came out of the theatre were drunks and the homeless. But then, that was possibly as much to do with the location of the place as anything else.

The Lido was in Paris's exclusive eighth *arrondissement*. Maybe the *clientèle* were different. Maybe the fabled, jewellery-bearing counts or the perma-tanned playboys in sports cars were more likely to materialise here. Maybe the Bluebells were a cut above the Doriss Girls when it came to class and comportment. With four hours of full dress rehearsal with the Bluebells ahead of me, I was about to find out.

The Lido stage was lit from above with bright floodlights when I stepped onto it. Jane was cuing a C.D. on a portable sound system that appeared to have been lugged up onstage for the express purpose of the rehearsal. Stuart sat at a table in the *salle*, poring over paperwork.

'Hello Shay,' Jane sang out, lifting her head from the sound system console. 'Start warming up, the rest of the girls will be here soon.'

I sat down on the stage, off to the side, and started stretching, suddenly overcome with first-day nerves. Thanks to the daily blur of rehearsals and night-time performances at the Moulin, I'd barely had a second to mentally prepare myself for this moment, or indeed the night ahead. Not only was I about to meet and rehearse with my fellow Bluebells for the first time, later in the evening I was going to be making my Lido stage debut. 'And Shay,' Jane said in-between blasts of music, 'I did mention before that it's just you who will be rehearsing in your costumes today, right? The rest of the girls don't need their feathers and hats. They're already perfect.' She winked.

'If only it were true!' Stuart chimed in from his booth, head still buried in a sheaf of papers.

One by one, the Bluebells arrived. I'd met a handful of them the night I'd followed Amanda backstage, but most were unfamiliar. Tracksuit pants and T-shirts seemed to be the order of the day. And where I had been expecting pitch-perfect French and crystal-cut Queen's English, there was only the rough drawl of Northern English accents.

'Awright?' one girl greeted everyone as she shuffled onstage, munching a kebab.

As usual, there were a few natural beauties in the group, girls who looked effortlessly gorgeous without a scrap of make-up. The rest of the girls were pretty enough but I suspected, like me, they were well served by the transformative qualities of stage make-up.

I eavesdropped on conversations, learning about the latest developments on *EastEnders*, hearing that one girl had written home for a new consignment of HobNob biscuits and that another had bought a six-pack of pork pies from Marks & Spencer on the way into rehearsals.

Jane called everyone to attention. 'Girls, I want you all to welcome Shay, she's starting tonight,' she said. 'Do your best to make her feel welcome.'

There was a chorus of 'Hi Shay'.

'We're starting in two minutes,' Jane continued. 'We'll be doing a run-through of the entire show from start to finish.'

There was a collective groan.

'We'll start blocking the show from the start so Shay can see what the formations are and where she fits in.'

I donned my costume for the opening number – a red top hat, red lycra leggings, a red leotard with black sequins and a black sequinned cape.

Everyone took up position for the opening number and the dress rehearsal got under way. Despite feeling ridiculously conspicuous in my costumes while all the other girls danced in casual gear, I felt pretty good about how it was all unfurling. The drilling I had received from Sarah and Jane in my four weeks of one-on-one rehearsals had been so thorough, everything seemed to go like clockwork.

At a certain point in the rehearsal, I felt the company suddenly pull into line. Kicks became noticeably higher, turns became sharper and showgirl smiles were suddenly pasted to faces. Pierre had entered the building.

When it came time to go backstage and charge downstairs en masse to pile onto the panther machine, there was a flurry of instructions from Jane.

'Shay, this is Selina. She's the one you follow down the stairs to the quick-change place for panthers.'

A pretty English girl waved and smiled.

'You're going to be the second girl running down the stairs. Don't dawdle. Remember there are ten girls behind you. Don't hold them up. As you run, start removing your accessories. Whatever you do, don't drop them on the stairs, because someone could trip on them and fall.'

I nodded, fighting off a sick feeling in my gut. And then, cued in by the music, we ran. I hurried my way down the stairs to the thunder of twelve pairs of heels, pulling awkwardly at bits of my costume while trying to keep my balance. Halfway down, the girls helped me with my quick change before we started running again. By the time we arrived at the machine, I had just managed to slide into the black velvet bodysuit and black boots that made up my panther costume.

Hot on the tail of Selina, I clambered up the ladder, hoisted myself across the gap above the ice rink and clambered onto my podium. I knelt down and bent forward to put on my panther hat: five black feather boas sprouting flamboyantly from the top, each held stiff at its base by a steel rod. Lisa took her place in the darkness beside me. We were podium-mates – we had to share the top pole and time our movements so we acted as one.

'Careful with the hat once the podium is up,' Lisa warned as the machine began its ascent. 'It's a death trap. I've lost count of the times my boas have become tangled in the lights.'

As the panther machine rose, rotating, we emerged at stage level to be bathed in a spotlight. As the centrepiece of this impressive piece of hydraulic staging, our podium was pushed up high above the stage to just below the rigging. The number required us to perform an elaborate pole dance with high kicks and thrashing back-bends, flicking our heads about to get maximum dramatic effect from the feathered boas. When the machine had risen fully from the depths below, Lisa and I were so close to the lights I could almost reach out and touch them. The stage looked a long way down. There were no safety lines, no braces, no railings. It was a peculiarly French approach to workplace health and safety.

'Just do your thing and I'll work around you,' Lisa said as the music cranked up and we started gyrating. 'I've been doing this for six months, I'll fit in with you.'

It was absurd to think of anyone as tall as she was fitting in around *me*. Even in my nine-centimetre heels, I felt tiny next to her and was certain it looked comical. She caught my expression.

'Six foot,' she said, reading my mind. 'I know, I know. I'm circus tall.'

I flushed, convinced that Pierre was sitting in the audience shaking his head at the glaring height difference. I spent the entire number – and the rest of the rehearsal – on demi-point.

When it came time to rehearse the tap number, I raced on stage only to discover a massive central portion of it was missing. The ice-skating rink was still making its tediously slow way up from where it was stored under the panther machine, five flights below. I glanced into the hole – the huge drop was lined on two sides by enormous cogs and a whole lot of grinding steel.

'Don't look down,' Lisa said as she stepped carefully behind me. 'Whatever you do, don't look down.'

The tap number had been devised to distract audiences from the machinations of the ice-stage's clunking entrance. It required the Bluebells to line up along the metre-wide strip of stage in front of the gaping hole and tap out a number while pretending to sing to the audience. Carrying a cane, wearing a top hat and nine-centimetre heels with steel taps on the balls and heels, I trooped out gingerly to form the line with the other girls, acutely aware of the twenty-metre drop behind me. I had been tapping since I was a little girl, but never had a pair of tap shoes felt so slippery. I tried to tap unself-consciously, to throw myself with gusto into the lip-synching of the Broadway-themed ditty, but all I could think about was losing my balance and falling backwards to a grisly death on the ice.

Stuart could obviously see my expression of sheer horror.

'Wipe that look off your face, Shay Stafford!' he yelled. 'In my day I had to do eighty-five *pirouettes* with a massive fish on my head. No-one's ever fallen – at least not *back* onto the ice. Trust me, you'll be fine.'

I caught a glimpse of Pierre. He was reclined in the booth, quietly smoking and observing. I was sure he was regretting ever hiring me.

I was relieved when the finale rolled around. It was an elaborately staged affair, featuring all the Bluebells in massive sprays of feathers. We had to start on the stairs, with our backs to the audience, then turn and flow down the staircase to perform a fantastic sequence of choreography.

At the first bars of finale music, Pierre sprang from his position in the booth as if he'd been jolted to life, and strode onto the stage.

'Ladies, ladies, ladies!' he cried, signalling to Jane to cut the music. Cigarette ash scattered across the stage in his wake. 'Ladies, for God's sake, you're Bluebells! I don't want to see any hands like pork chops! If I wanted to see pork chops, I'd go to Les Halles.'

There was an exchange of amused looks and a couple of the older girls rolled their eyes.

'I want *tension* in the wrists. I want the longest fingers possible – they should be *barely* brushing your shoulders. Like this.' He performed a demonstration, exaggerating the movement.

Comical though it was, his intervention had the desired effect. The entire company seemed to pull up, with each dancer suddenly gaining five centimetres. It had only taken one pork-chop reproach for everyone to find their inner Bluebell.

The rehearsal wrapped and we all dispersed to our respective homes for the four-hour break before the first show. The emotion of having farewelled the Moulin Rouge only the night before was still hanging heavily on me, and I was exhausted. Only adrenaline kept me focused on the night ahead – adrenaline and the pure excitement of finally stepping onto the Lido stage and performing.

I picked up a *poulet rôti* and salad in the Rue de Levis and wandered home, determined to put my feet up and zone out with my chicken in front of the telly. As I opened the door, though, I heard the sound of keyboard tinkering and unfamiliar voices coming from the living room. Foiled again. Olivier was perched at the computer, cigarette hanging from his mouth, while two strangers plucked at guitars and smoked on the couch.

'*Salut*,' Olivier said distractedly, without turning his head. Willy was hiding in the bedroom, curled up in a ball on my pillow. I retired, defeated, to the kitchen. Pulling out a folding stool, I plonked myself down by the counter and started picking at my dinner. A pile of unpaid bills stared at me from the kitchen bench. Olivier had collected them from the mailbox and thrown them down carelessly without even opening them: gas, electricity and a reminder to pay the first instalment of our *taxe d'habitation*. Tired, bedraggled, hunched over a barbecue chicken in the tiny kitchen of my increasingly debt-laden apartment, I began to wonder when exactly the famed Bluebell glamour would kick in.

The dressing-rooms were empty when I returned that night. One of my farewell gifts from the Moulin girls had been a brand new make-up case; I set it down at my new place and started to unpack and apply my make-up.

There was something strange about sitting backstage at the Lido applying the same face as I had the night before at the Moulin Rouge: the same combination of foundation, mascara and lipliner, the same powder–pancake–powder routine, the same pair of false eyelashes. I felt as though there should have been something different, something remarkable to set this night apart. And yet, so far it felt like just another night at the office. One or two girls started dribbling in.

Perhaps because I was deep within a well-honed make-up routine, my mind started wandering to the dressing-rooms of Pigalle. I wondered who was off, who was replacing, whether the shoes of the new German girl, Nadia, had arrived from Clairvoy. And then, with a profound sense of relief, I realised I didn't have to care. It was no longer my problem. I only had myself to take care of at the Lido.

Lisa came shuffling into the dressing-room. She took one look at me sitting alone at my place, dumped her bag on her chair and summoned me upstairs.

'Come on, let's go and warm up. I'll walk you through the presets.'

As we went through our pre-show stretches on stage, we started swapping Aussie dance stories. The Australian dance community was a small world. Rather than six degrees of separation, Australian dancers were separated by only two. Originally from Melbourne, Lisa's career as a dancer had always been a given. Both her parents had been accomplished Australian Ballet dancers. Her mother, now the director of the Royal Ballet School in London, had been the iron lady who ran the dance program at Victoria's prestigious College of the Arts. Together with her husband she had also overseen the Australian Ballet School for a while – churning out dance prodigies like a well-oiled machine.

'You're *her* daughter?' I asked incredulously.

'Yes I am,' Lisa replied. 'But as it turns out, there's not much call for six-foot-tall ballerinas.'

At the end of our warm-up, Lisa walked me through the backstage maze, pointing out the quick-change areas and helping me to do my presets. 'Presetting' meant making sure all my earrings, gloves and other costume requirements were gathered together in the quick-change area, ready for when I raced offstage and only had thirty seconds to change costumes.

Lisa was living at La Fourche, not far from Avenue de Clichy, where I had begun my own Parisian adventure.

'It's a complete dive of an area,' she said. 'The other night, to get in the front door I had to step over a smackie passed out on my doorstep – just lovely.'

Back down in the dressing-room, the Bluebells had all arrived and the *loge* was abuzz with chatter and laughter. English was the predominant language. The one or two French girls in the Bluebell line sat quietly at their places applying make-up while the English high jinks carried on around them.

Amanda was treating the *loge* to a high-pitched rendition of a Disney show tune, and adding a flamboyant dance routine.

'Shut up!' Sarah called from her place, midway through the application of her false eyelashes.

'You know you love it,' Amanda replied.

At the dressing-table next to me sat Kirsty. Another of the English crew, she was pretty in an English rose kind of way. A large Tupperware container of homemade pasta sat among her make-up: in between daubs of foundation and the application of lipstick, she would pause to shovel large forkfuls of food into her mouth.

To her right sat Anna. She was a tall Swedish girl, beautiful and with an impressively large bust. Unusually large for a dancer. She had been onstage during warm-up and I had watched with envy as she performed *développés* – stretching her leg up over her head – slowly, effortlessly and with amazing control.

There was a wonderful sense of camaraderie and warmth in the room. I'd been told that the Bluebell line was an especially bitchy, catty group of girls, but nothing like that was evident tonight.

What was evident was a lot of nudity. It was fortunate that the Moulin had long ago cured me of any prudishness, given the ease with which clothes seemed to be peeling off here.

'*Bonsoir* ladies,' Pierre's voice floated down the hall, announcing his arrival in the dressing-room. Amanda scurried to her place while Sarah fumbled with her tights, desperately trying to pull them up.

'Hello darling,' Pierre said, leaning in to perform a pair of air kisses near my cheeks. 'Your make-up looks fabulous. I just wanted to drop by and wish you *merde* for tonight.'

'*Merci*,' I replied.

'Oh no, darling, you must never say *merci* to *merde*. It's bad luck.'
I smiled and nodded.

'Have a good show tonight, ladies,' Pierre sang out to no-one in particular, before turning and floating back down the corridor.

Sarah watched him turn the corner before standing up on her chair, naked but for a G-string. 'Why is it,' she asked the room, 'that without fail the moment I get my gear off and I'm here with my fanny to the wind, Pierre Rambert walks through the *loge*?'

The girls started guffawing.

'I mean what are the chances? It's like the man has a radar or something.'

As Sarah talked, unbeknownst to her, Stuart had rounded the corner to be confronted by her bare buttocks. He stood for a moment behind her – with ten other semi-naked girls in front of him – his arms crossed and a droll expression on his face.

'This is so wasted on me,' he sighed, before turning on his heel and retreating.

With half an hour before the curtain rose, I was fully made up and ready to go. It felt strange not to be running around at the last minute dealing with late-breaking backstage crises. I sat back and took in the dressing-room performance being put on by my exuberant new colleagues. A small, elderly woman appeared at my elbow.

'*Vous êtes Shay?*' she asked. '*Je m'appelle Minnie. Je suis votre habilleuse.*'

True to Paris cabaret form, Minnie, my dresser, stood no more than five feet tall. In almost three years of performing in Paris, I had never met a single dresser tall enough to perform even the most basic tasks required of them.

Being a dresser involved lots of heavy lifting, lots of running up and down stairs and lots of last-minute sewing adjustments to costumes. But more than that, it required reaching up to shelves to retrieve wigs, hats and accessories and reaching up to the heads and shoulders of very tall showgirls to apply large feathered headdresses and sprawling feathered backpacks. Height would have been a definite advantage in such a job.

Minnie had a kind, worn face, framed by a neat bob of impeccably kept white hair.

'I believe you know Corina?' she asked. 'I loved Corina. I dressed her on her first night as a Bluebell.'

I felt a sudden affection for Minnie.

'I'll look after you,' she said with a wink.

At the five-minute call, the nerves I had been successfully suppressing came bubbling to the surface. Staring into the mirror, performing a last-minute touch-up to my make-up, I tried to calm myself.

'Let's do it,' Lisa announced, jumping to her feet and adjusting her fishnets. 'It's time for a little bit of *Magique,* ladies.'

Amanda launched into a faux-operatic rendition of the cheesy opening tune, prompting a volley of fresh insults from her colleagues. If nothing else, I thought as I followed the girls up the stairs to the wings, my Lido tenure was going to be entertaining.

# Chapter Thirty-five

I don't remember much of my first performance at the Lido. Given that it was an event I had been fantasising about for most of my dancing life, it seems remarkable now how little I can recall of it. Perhaps because it *was* so important, because I had built it up so much in my mind, and therefore it was too big to process, retain or recall. I do remember making my entrance in the opening number and being momentarily dazzled by the sight of the *salle* packed with people. The faces seemed to go on forever, receding into the darkness at the back of the auditorium.

I also remember being hyper-aware of the moving bits of stage, convinced I was going to be sucked into a hole or flattened by an automated scene change at any moment. Some of the dancers I had met gave me an encouraging wink or a smile. Most of the nudes and principals were so accomplished that I was sure I would come up wanting in comparison, and that my first show would also be my last.

The nudes seemed to own the stage. Arms outstretched, draped in jewels and with flawless bodies showcased in magnificent costumes, they were the walking embodiment of Paris cabaret. The two principal dancers were both French, and whether they were playing it up for the benefit of the audience or acting out their birthright, they seemed to have cornered the market in haughty. They scared the hell out of me. I did my best to smile and invite an introduction each time I crossed a nude or principal backstage, but they looked straight through me.

By the time the second show rolled around, I had learned the Bluebells' natural backstage allies at the Lido were the boy dancers. As male dancers in a Paris revue, they were used to being marginalised. There was an unspoken understanding – together, we were the worker bees of the Lido and had to content ourselves with playing second fiddle to the show ponies – the nudes and the principals – even if all of us, girls and boys alike, secretly wanted to be one of them.

The second show passed in a similar blur to the first, albeit a slower one. As we took our bow to a polite audience, I remember feeling a great wave of relief that it was over and I had made it through my first night at the Lido without serious incident. I was exhausted. All the adrenaline that had sustained me for the past week seemed to drain from my body, leaving me dizzy and limp.

It was 2.30 a.m. as I trooped down to the dressing-room with the rest of the Bluebells.

'Nice one, Shay,' Jane said, coming up behind me. 'We might need to work a bit on the panther routine, but overall you did a great first show. Well done.'

I was spent and in the mood for a lazy comedown in the dressing-room. I hoped one or two of my new comrades in heels might be up for a debrief – a bit of a chat to help me process the night that had just been. But as soon as we arrived there was a mad rush for the showers. Eyelashes were torn off, hairnets discarded and fishnets hung on hooks as girls scrambled to wash and go.

The Lido provided taxis to its employees, to spirit them all home safely each night. However, because of the complicated logistics involved in getting eighty-odd people back to their various corners of Paris, there was a carefully constructed schedule. If you missed your spot in the tour, you were stranded. Hence the rush. Before I'd even taken off my eyelashes, the *loge* was almost deserted. I looked around and it was just me and a whole lot of swinging, freshly washed G-strings hanging forlornly from hooks above dressing-tables, dripping onto the lino floor.

'You've made it,' I whispered to myself, looking around and giggling. 'You're a Bluebell at the Lido. *Quelle glamour.*'

By the time I walked out the stage door and onto the street, the first taxi tour had long since departed and dancers, technicians and dressers were mingling in groups waiting for the second round. A couple of stagehands sat in the gutter smoking. Three or four of the Bluebells were dressed to the nines, talking excitedly about a V.I.P. party they had been invited to. A few of the boy dancers air-kissed the girls goodbye and told them they'd meet them later at Queen. Some of the older dancers walked off to their parked cars to drive to the suburbs, back to their families.

I took in the dancers near me. They were dressed in tracksuit pants, old jeans and T-shirts. A few wore baseball caps; none were wearing make-up, and after scrubbing their faces clean of the heavy stage make-up, had slightly rosy, just-washed looks. Had you stood each girl in her stage-door incarnation next to her onstage one, you would have been hard-pressed to believe they were the same person.

I recognised these young girls, hair wet from the showers and variously smoking, chatting or staring off into space. I might not know any of them individually yet, but I knew about their lives. They lived alone in tiny studio apartments, where they would return to watch D.V.D.s until the sun came up, eating chocolate sent in care-packages from their distant homes. They would then sleep most of the next day, waking late in the afternoon just in time to get ready and come back in for work. They were living in Paris, but they could have been anywhere in the world for all the advantage they took of their geography.

Only ten minutes before we'd all been fantasy women, shining under the stage lights of the cabaret world's most prestigious stage. Now we were an exhausted, sullen bunch of tracksuit-sporting slouchers. So much for the ermine and pearls, so much for the fur coats and heels. Miss Bluebell would not have been impressed.

# Chapter Thirty-six

In the Paris cabaret world, stories abound about how the pecking order is maintained between showgirls, so the backlash that followed Pierre's announcement that I had been chosen, after only four months at the Lido, to rehearse as a Belle replacement came as no surprise. 'You bitch,' was one of the more playful reactions. I nevertheless kept my head down and did my best to ignore any rumblings of discontent. In any case, the fallout was minor compared to the treatment reputedly doled out to other dancers who had dared to displease their colleagues. Backstage legend had it that one girl who was disliked by her colleagues came running down for a quick change between numbers and reapplied her body make-up only to discover, too late, that it had been replaced with yoghurt. Another story maintained that when a dispute between two principal dancers exploded one night, one of them cut holes in the other's costumes. In *Bravissimo*, a previous Lido show, barely a night had gone by that a long-running feud between the *meneuse* and one of the Belles hadn't played out onstage. The *meneuse* would go out of her way, at the end of one particular number, to strike a pose that caused her massive feather backpack to completely obscure her rival from the audience.

Offstage the squabbling was usually restricted to dressing-room whispering and discreet acts of backstabbing, though occasionally a captain would have to throw herself between two irate showgirls trying to strangle one another. The sight of two six-foot girls in feathers, heels and full stage make-up going at one other was terrifying in the extreme.

While it would be wrong to paint the backstage area as a hotbed of cattiness – the friendships I forged there were stronger and more intense than any I'm likely to experience again – there's no doubt it was a pressure-cooker environment. Sustained exposure to the same people, night after night, did nothing to quell simmering hostilities.

Still, for all the pressure that a showgirl was under from the outside, it usually paled in comparison to the pressure she applied to herself. In a world in which physical perfection was a job requirement, it was all too easy to feel bad about yourself. Being naked in front of forty other girls every night, every inch of your body was under permanent scrutiny – no-one, not even your husband or boyfriend, knew your body like your colleagues did. Every tiny fluctuation in weight, every sign of ageing, every cellulite dimple or stretch mark was noticed – and even if it escaped comment, you knew it had been filed away for future reference.

One evening, I came in to work to find that Anna, the beautiful Swedish girl with the naturally ample bosom, had returned from holidays with a noticeably smaller chest. She had used her four weeks off to return home and undergo breast-reduction surgery. Deemed too large-breasted to ever become a Belle, she had done what seemed necessary to advance her dancing career. No-one in the dressing room said anything to her about it, and she never brought it up.

Each night I would sit next to her as she painstakingly applied layers of body make-up to hide the scars, and I would wonder at the toll this job was taking on us all. Sure, there were the obvious injuries like twisted ankles, torn ligaments and slipped discs, but there were also hidden wounds created by years of worrying that we didn't quite measure up. To the casual observer we were tall, beautiful, slim and self-confident, but you only had to scratch a little beneath the make-up to find the scars. If you believed the hype, a Paris showgirl was the ultimate fantasy woman; in reality, a showgirl's life could be alienating, dehumanising, and occasionally very lonely.

Of course our bodies were in better shape than most people's – but then that was our job. The lights, the costumes and the body make-up conspired each night to make us all look more toned, tanned and perfect than we really were. If you were to stick your head backstage during any quick change, you would pretty quickly come to understand that there really is no such thing as a flawless body. Saggy breasts, inverted nipples, pot bellies, moles, freckles, body hair and wrinkles – they were all there, the whole glorious gamut of human imperfections.

As at the Moulin Rouge, at least a few girls at the Lido had an eating disorder of some kind, but management, as usual, were as strict about weight loss as weight gain. Girls suspected of suffering from serious eating disorders were usually ordered to take time off, seek medical care and not return to work until they had sorted themselves out.

For the most part, though, the average showgirl's relationship with food was a very robust one. Robust in that we ate it. Lots of it. As often as possible.

*Loge* parties seemed to occur every other night at the Lido. Whether it was a girl's birthday or the national day in one of our countries, Easter or Pancake Tuesday or Christmas – there always seemed to be an excuse for everyone to 'bring a plate'. There were plenty of girls like me who loved to bake, too, meaning that on any given night backstage there would be a table heaving under the weight of freshly baked cakes, muffins, biscuits and slices. Bottles of cider, Coke, and occasionally cheap wine were all imbibed with gusto.

As time went on, it became clear that the work and social life of the average Lido showgirl were no different than those of her Moulin Rouge colleagues. All showgirls had the same problems meeting eligible young men.

Lisa, who I had become fast friends with, had had a typically messy personal life. She told me she'd arrived in Paris and taken a job at the Lido a year before without knowing a soul. Alone in a foreign city, she had fallen easily into a relationship with one of the Lido doormen, Fréderic. A guy in his late twenties from the south of France, he'd seemed nice enough and was good-looking in a burly, shaved-headed-doorman kind of way. What she didn't know, until one of her new colleagues brought it to her attention a month into their liaison, was that Fréderic was also dating another dancer – a girl he had been seeing for over a year. It made for an awkward start to Lisa's Lido life.

But I had my own problems with men. Things at home with Olivier weren't getting better, though I was doing my best to ignore the inevitable. Once Brett and Matthew had left for the Caribbean, however, I couldn't help feeling lonely.

From day one, Brett had been there for me – my confidant, my partner in silliness, my rock. And Matthew, more than the boyfriend of one of my closest friends, was like another brother. They planned to spend a year cruising, saving all they could so they could return to Australia and set up house. Audrey couldn't accompany them on the ship, so she came to live with Olivier, Willy and me until they were back in Australia.

Things were even worse since I'd farewelled Jean. As the seasons changed, it seemed, so did everything else.

## Chapter Thirty-seven

As November drew to a close, the skies turned a slate grey and the city began to turn in on itself in preparation for winter. Things on the home front were sliding from lacklustre to lukewarm, so I decided to make a concerted effort to forge new friendships at the Lido.

When Rebecca Clarke arrived to join the Bluebell line, I remember clapping eyes on her and feeling instantly relieved – at last there was someone at the Lido shorter than me! Becky hailed from south London. The daughter of a London cabbie she was that rarest of breeds, a south London princess – a girl whose prodigious dance talent had given her a scholarship at the Royal Ballet School, and whose beautiful face and great stage presence had led to a successful career in West End musicals.

She had danced her way through various productions, most recently carving up the stage in a salsa-dancing duet in *Saturday Night Fever*. The onstage chemistry between her and her salsa partner, John, had been so electric that they had ended up getting married. But in keeping with her princess persona and obsession with all things pink and girly, she had always longed to dance as a Bluebell.

She wanted it so badly, in fact, that when *Saturday Night Fever* went on tour around England, taking her husband with it, she fired off a job application to the Lido and lied about her height. It was clear from the moment she walked in the stage door that her creative-writing skills were more advanced than most but, to his credit, if Pierre was shocked by the height deficit between C.V. Becky and Real Becky, he did a good job of hiding it.

'I'm always prepared to make exceptions for good people,' he had said when she arrived.

Becky was very definitely good people. As I soon discovered, she was a quick study, a sharp wit and hilariously fun company. She and Amanda had worked together before in Disney shows, and picked up almost immediately where they had left off, enlivening the already bubbly Bluebells with regular explosions of laughter and lewdness. Despite her English rose looks – dark brown hair, alabaster complexion, china-doll features and big brown eyes – Becky had a fantastically bawdy sense of humour and wasn't averse to dropping the odd swear word. As the weeks progressed and we got to know one another better, we discovered in each other a kindred spirit, not least because we both loved pink, baking and Christmas.

But sadly, not even Becky could prevent my festive season from falling flat for the second year running. Without Matthew and Brett, and with most of my new friends busy with visiting family members, it was left to Olivier and I to rustle up a bit of Yuletide cheer. Suffice to say, we didn't.

Instead of facing up to the ugly truth about our relationship, I chose once again to lose myself in work. After weeks of rehearsal, I had been stepping in as a Belle replacement from time to time, and was loving doing something different on stage.

Like the nudes at the Moulin Rouge, the Belles were derided behind their backs by some of their colleagues as 'walkers' – the inference being they did little more than appear on stage in stunning costumes and float around. It was true that in some routines not much actual dancing was demanded of the Belles, but as far as I was concerned, the limelight we got more than compensated. And the costumes were simply out of this world.

In one number, the aptly named *Défilé*, we took to the stage in clothes worthy of the most sumptuous *haute couture* fashion show. I wore a fitted, ankle-length, long-sleeved black lace dress. It had a train at the back and a split that ran all the way up the front, exposing my legs. The front panel of the dress was cut low to reveal my breasts, and long strings of pearls hung from just under my armpits to my wrists. And there was an enormous headpiece – a swirling filigree of fine black metal studded with hundreds of black and blue beads. It weighed ten kilograms, so heavy that I couldn't tilt my head forward or back but had to lock it in position and stare straight ahead. With arms outstretched to keep the pearls from tangling, I had to walk around the stage in as graceful and feminine a way as I could, making the practically impossible look effortless.

As winter turned to spring, Olivier had been out of work for almost a year and a half. It had gotten to the point where I no longer even asked him to contribute to the rent, the groceries or the bills – I was a struggling artist supporting a struggling artist. For his part, he had long ago stopped trying to convince me his big musical break was just around the corner, and had withdrawn further into himself and his music.

My brother Adam, who had been playing a season of rugby in Ireland, had spent a few weeks with us at the end of winter. He knew me well enough to recognise things were strained; he also knew better than to ask about it. I'd never told Mum and Dad how bad it was, figuring it was my predicament and my responsibility to get out of it.

One day in spring, Becky and I decided to get out of the city and visit the Monet Gardens in Giverny, seventy kilometres west of Paris. Renowned as the place where Claude Monet painted his famous waterlilies canvases back in the 1890s, the gardens are a high point on many tourist trips to France. In spring, they put on a stunning display of flowers – tulips, daffodils, crab-apple blossom, pansies and irises – a heady mix of perfume and petals.

Possibly because I was away from Paris and at ease for the first time in months, possibly because Becky was so easy to talk to, I found myself sitting on a bench pouring out my heart to her. There were no tears or hysterics, just a rational, calm stocktake of my sorry personal situation. To her credit, Becky sat and listened without judgement.

When I was done, I felt as if I had unloaded a heavy burden. It hadn't occurred to me until that moment how much I had been bottling up and shouldering alone.

Becky took a long time to reply.

'Darling,' she finally said. 'This is not a way to live. I mean, look at you. You're lovely, you're smart – you're in Paris working at the Lido, for God's sake. You should be having the time of your life and you're miserable. You deserve better.'

She was right, of course. I knew my relationship with Olivier had run its course, and I also knew I deserved to be looked after. It wasn't that I wanted to be a kept woman, not by any stretch: I had prided myself on earning my keep and paying my way since I was seventeen. No bank loans, no requests to my parents for financial assistance – just me and my relentlessly tapping feet and high-kicking legs. But just once in a while it would have been nice to come home and find the shopping had been done or the house vacuumed or the dinner prepared. Even a flower picked from the side of the road would have made me feel appreciated, loved and special. It was hard work making my way in the world out here on my own. Every now and then it would have been nice to share the load; to be carried instead of having to carry.

On the train back into Paris, as Becky slumbered beside me, I stared out the window and realised it was time to take back control. There's a line in the movie *Thelma & Louise* that says you get what you settle for. I was tired of settling for second-best.

## Chapter Thirty-eight

As any showgirl will tell you, there's an enormous amount of grind behind the glamour.

The mental exhaustion of performing the same show over and over took a toll that was rivalled only by the physical stress on our bodies. Repetitive strain caused the most damage. Kicking the same leg every night in the same routine, wearing the same heavy items of costume and stupidly high heels, put an enormous amount of pressure on our ankles, knees and hips. The Lido brought in a physiotherapist and podiatrist each week – our feet were, to a person, a gnarled mess of bunions, dead skin and bent toes – and they did their best to mitigate the damage, but they were fighting against forces bigger than them.

It was also not uncommon, if you were replacing a girl who was off for the night, to find yourself wearing a hat that didn't quite fit properly, so the weight was dispersed unevenly on your head. The effort of keeping the hat on while moving gracefully was a common cause of pinched nerves and seized necks.

However, along with the general wear and tear, the threat of serious injury was always present. Each night we negotiated hundreds of stairs – sometimes in the dark – danced in nine-centimetre heels on a metre-wide runway around a four-storey hole, and were lifted and hurled about the stage by boy partners of varying height and strength. Each boy had his own way of lifting and each couple had worked out a shorthand over hundreds of performances together. If you were a swing or replacement, throwing yourself at a boy for a lift, without knowing that shorthand, was fraught with danger. We tried to rehearse lifts pre-show whenever possible, but more often than not it was only dumb luck that saved us from serious accidents.

Occupational health and safety laws stipulated that a doctor had to be stationed backstage for every performance. Unfortunately, more often than not the 'doctor' was a medical student or intern with minimal experience, trying to make a bit of cash to help them through university. The first-aid kit screwed to the wall in the wings contained little more than a packet of out-of-date aspirin and a box of bandaids. Like professional sportspeople, our bodies were our stock in trade and every night we were putting them on the line.

Thankfully, the French social security system was so good that almost every medical treatment was covered. But just occasionally, there were accidents so serious that no amount of health coverage could soften the blow.

As a dancer, you got used to living with pain and developed ways of performing that allowed for it. You might favour one knee, or rein in the high-kicks on a night your hip was acting up: a low-level constant ache of some sort was part of the gig. So when I first started developing back pain, I didn't think much of it. The intensity of the pain would ebb and flow depending on a variety of factors but, for the most part, it was manageable. I just figured that years of dancing with no really long holidays had started to catch up with me.

Being young and convinced of my own invincibility, I kept on dancing. I took an extra ten minutes to warm up before each show and lathered my lower back in heat cream before going onstage – I'd be fine. But then my back started to hurt whenever I bent forward. As the days passed, it became a shooting pain so intense it could take my breath away.

One night in July, as I sat in the *loge* preparing to go onstage, I bent forward to buckle my shoes and found I couldn't straighten up. My back had seized. My attempts to sit upright sent a spasm of excruciating pain rocketing down my legs – pain so intense it made me feel nauseous. In the end I forced myself upright. If I sat completely erect I was okay, but the slightest movement backward or forward was pure agony.

Petra, my captain, came sailing through the *loge* at the five-minute call.

'Shayleen, are you okay? You look pale.'

'It's my back. It's seized up. I don't think I can go on.'

As captain, Petra was used to dealing with last-minute crises like this. She barely batted a false eyelash. 'No problem,' she said with a smile. 'Have a shower and go home. And don't forget to fill out an accident paper on your way out.'

I sat in front of the dressing-room mirror and cried from the pain as I removed my make-up. I knew my body well enough to know that this was serious. And even though Olivier was at home, I felt completely alone and exhausted. I dreaded the prospect of having to nurse myself back to health so far from my family. More than anything else in the world, I wanted my parents to come sailing down the backstage stairs, scoop me up and carry me off to bed. I wanted Mum to stroke my head and tell me it was all going to be okay – and then let me sleep for a month.

I hobbled up the stairs, filled out my accident paper in Stuart's office and struggled out of the Lido to hail a cab.

I spent that night flat on my back on the bedroom floor, unable to get comfortable, unable to sleep. A trip to the doctor the next day confirmed what I had suspected: it was bad. A disc in one of my vertebra had herniated, and when I leant backwards or forwards it pinched the nerve. I came home from the doctor's surgery loaded down with painkillers and anti-inflammatories. I was effectively housebound. Nothing could be done until I had rested and allowed the inflammation to go down; after that I'd undergo physio and whatever else the doctor ordered. I spent days lying flat on my back on the apartment's hardwood floor staring at the ceiling.

The ordeal was made all the more painful by Olivier trying to look after me. He fussed about me, bringing me cups of tea, preparing meals and helping me in and out of the bathtub. He was genuinely concerned and I should have been grateful, but it was too little, too late. While I did my best to be gracious, I just wanted him to go away, to leave me alone to recover in peace. However, even though I was immobile on the bedroom floor all day, he continued to welcome random musicians into our living room. They would smoke and tinker at the keyboard or play the same riff over and over until I felt like I was starting to go crazy. When the time finally came for me to go and see an osteopath, I was incredibly relieved to get out the door. My appointment was at a clinic on the Left Bank, in the fifth *arrondissement*. The weather was glorious and my back was feeling marginally better, so I decided to walk across the river from the Hôtel de Ville Métro station. I was so excited to be out of the house and upright.

Paris Plage, the annual transformation of the Seine-side highway into a beach, was in full swing. Notre Dame was buzzing with tourists. The city was shining and it felt so very good to be out and about in it.

By the time I entered the osteopath's clinic, I was in a buoyant mood. He took a seat at his desk and started reviewing my file.

'If you could strip down to your underwear and get up on the table please,' he said distractedly in French, flicking through my paperwork. He was in his early fifties and sported a mane of flowing grey hair – a style popular with Parisian men of his age. His skin was a kind of orange-brown, clearly the result of too much time on a sun-bed. On his desk were framed photos of him with a couple of small children on a ski slope.

'Okay then, let's get started,' he said a minute later, looking up. I was sitting on the table half-naked, legs dangling over the edge. He stood in front of me, spread his legs wide to brace himself and assumed the back-cracking position – wrapping his arms around me and placing both his hands on my lower back.

'That's great. Just try to relax and let yourself slowly fall backwards. The more relaxed you are, the better this is going to work,' he said as I began to lean tentatively against his clasped hands.

Then he flashed me a cheap smile. 'You smell very nice,' he said.

I stiffened immediately.

'No, no, *mademoiselle*, you need to relax if this is going to work. You have to trust me.'

Was he being sleazy or was I being paranoid? I felt on guard, but the man was a professional. I decided to give him the benefit of the doubt.

'So I understand you're a dancer,' he continued, as I leaned gingerly backward, hesitating to let myself go. 'That would explain why you have such a lovely body.'

I tensed again.

'No, Mademoiselle Stafford. You need to relax,' he protested.

I nodded and gave a tight smile. This did not feel right.

'Would you perhaps like to have lunch with me sometime?'

Delivered in this context, the question was an outrageous abuse of trust and power. I was livid. Ignoring the shooting pain in my back, I sat up, slid off the table and started dressing.

'What are you doing? I haven't started the treatment.' He looked truly surprised, as if he had done nothing to provoke such a reaction.

'I'm sorry. I just don't think this is the right treatment for me just now,' I stammered in reply. I was mad at myself for being flushed and embarrassed. He was the one who should have been embarrassed: why was I apologising?

As soon as I was dressed, I flew out of the clinic and back into the fresh air, fighting back tears, shaken and furious. I wanted to scream – to stand in the middle of the bridge overlooking the Seine and let loose with an almighty, soul-cleansing scream.

And again, more than anything else, I felt overwhelmingly alone. In that moment, all the effort of living as a foreigner in France concentrated into one crushing punch to the gut. As I walked back across the river, I decided that if I was going to continue to survive in France I needed to press the reset button and find my equilibrium – on my own.

By the time I got back to the apartment, I had built up quite a head of steam. I walked in the door to find Olivier sitting on the sofa, smoking and plucking at a guitar. The entire apartment smelled of cigarette smoke. Before I had a chance to start the conversation, however, there was a knock on the door behind me, and Olivier sprang up to let in a guitar-wielding stranger.

It was the last straw. I went into the kitchen to hide.

Olivier came in behind me, concerned. 'Is everything all right? You look like you've been crying.' He went to hug me. I brushed him off.

'Don't, please don't.'

He pulled back. 'What's the matter? What's wrong?'

I turned to look at him.

'I just need some space.' I could hear my voice breaking.

Olivier moved forward and pulled me into him. 'Okay. All right. Don't get upset. Stefan and I will go to a café.'

I looked at him, tears welling in my eyes. The hug felt good and I found myself nodding. 'Can you go to the *pharmacie* while you're out? I need some more painkillers.' I couldn't believe my resolve had evaporated so quickly.

'Of course,' he replied. 'Of course I can.' He seemed to hesitate, then looked at me sheepishly. 'Um. Can you give me the money? I'm a bit short this week.'

It was more than I could bear. I dropped my head and started sobbing silently, tears racing down my cheeks. 'I can't do this anymore, Olivier.'

He lifted my chin, trying to make eye contact. 'Hey, it's okay. Don't cry. We're going to go out. We'll go to a cafe, you'll have the apartment to yourself, you can take a bath and take it easy.'

'No, Olivier, it's not okay. It hasn't been okay for a long time. It's over. I want you to leave. Go and stay with a friend. Just leave, please.'

He stared back at me with a look of total shock.

'What?' he finally managed to say.

'I think you should go. I need some time to myself. Please.'

He was wide-eyed with disbelief. 'But you need me here to look after you. How will you cope on your own?'

I tried not to laugh. 'I'll be fine on my own,' I replied. 'I feel like I've been on my own for two years, Olivier. It's over. Please, just go.'

He took a step back.

'You don't mean it,' he said. 'You're just saying this because you don't feel well. I'm going to go out and I'll come back and we'll talk.'

'There's nothing to talk about,' I countered. 'Why can't you understand? I just need you to leave.'

He took a deep breath. 'You're just upset. You need to calm down and have a sleep. I'll stay at Pascal's place tonight. You get some sleep. It will all be okay in the morning.'

The next day, he showed up at the apartment as if nothing had happened. I watched him go into the living room and turn on his computer to start working.

I walked to the doorway and stared at him.

'I was serious yesterday,' I said, my arms crossed over my chest. 'You have to leave. I can't do this anymore. You need to find somewhere else to live.'

He looked at me, exasperated. 'You're serious?'

I nodded.

'But how can I just move out without any warning?'

'I don't know. You must have friends or family who can help you.' I paused to let it sink in. 'I'm done, Olivier. I've got nothing left. I've been looking after you for two years, it's someone else's turn. I have to look after me now.'

He jumped up from behind the computer and started to walk towards me, a mild look of panic on his face.

'I'm sorry. I'm sorry I haven't been able to pay for anything. I'm starting teaching again soon. I know it's been hard and I know it's been a drag, but I will make it up to you, I promise.'

'No, Olivier, there's nothing more to talk about. It's over.'

I locked myself in the bedroom and listened to him mope about the living room. When he left and I heard the door close behind him, I felt relieved. Drained, but so wonderfully relieved – as if a weight had been lifted. I knew I had done the right thing. That night, as I stretched out on the floor with Willy and Audrey, I felt light and full of optimism. True, I was twenty-seven years old and incapacitated, sleeping on the floor of my bedroom, suddenly single and all alone in a foreign city. But whether it was the painkillers or the glass of red wine I had poured myself before bed – or both – I slept better that night than I had in months.

# Chapter Thirty-nine

Olivier was out of my life, and my back was no longer causing me agony, so I'd returned to work. Paris was stepping out of its summer clothes and winding down a gear into autumn. At the first sign of cooler weather, the tailored coats and artfully arranged scarves beloved of all Parisians – men and women alike – were brought out, and the stony winter faces and perma-pouts along with them. Nothing, however, was able to suppress the feeling of lightness I had. On my nightly walk through Park Monceau to work, I started appreciating the colours and beauty that surrounded me again. It was time to learn what it meant to be a single Bluebell in the City of Light.

In the weeks following my return to work, I had been moved permanently into the Belle line. It was a significant vote of confidence in my abilities, and once and for all I let go of my height insecurities. It seemed as if the universe was rewarding me for making the decision to leave Olivier and go it alone, and I was only too happy to lap it up. From the Belle line it was only a hop, skip and a high-kick to replacing one of the principal dancers. The idea that had bewitched me so long ago was suddenly, tantalisingly within reach.

With the happy combination of extra discretionary income and lots of free time, and after living so frugally for so long to provide for two on my modest dancer's salary, I had more than a little steam to blow off.

Lisa, desperate to extricate herself from her own messy relationship, became a willing accomplice in nightly adventures. She had proven a great support during the latter weeks of my convalescence, not only coaching me through the break-up, but ensuring I remained properly fed and watered – she'd regularly swung by the apartment weighed down with fresh-out-of-the-oven baked goods. If there was a glue that held our relationship together, it was most definitely our shared passion for chocolate cake.

Now that I was well, the two of us made a habit of bringing a change of clothes into work each night so that we could hit the town as soon as the final curtain fell. Some of the boys started to join us; the gay boys even seemed happy to abandon their nightly bar-trawling in the Marais to join me and Lisa on the Champs Élysées.

And so the world's most famous avenue, with its exclusive, pretentious bars and nightclubs, became our nightly playground. While I would never have wanted to set foot in any of the clubs alone, there was something wonderfully addictive about showing up at V.I.P., Etoile, Barfly or Milliardaire with a pack of ridiculously tall, glammed-up girls and designer-clad spunky boys, strolling to the front of the queue and being led to a table inside.

Man Ray, a subterranean restaurant-cum-nightclub on Rue Marbeuf just off the Champs Élysées, became a firm favourite of the gang. One of my new Belle line colleagues, fellow Australian Sabrina, was dating one of the barmen there, giving us an instant in. Part-owned by Johnny Depp, Man Ray was a vast, cavernous, multi-levelled space, all mood lighting, sweeping staircases, balconies and hidden alcoves. Diners ate in the centre of the main room; after midnight, it became a dancefloor where Paris's beautiful people competed for posing space.

The door policy was strict, and strictly enforced by an old woman with dyed red hair and an imperious scowl. Flanked on either side by a pair of muscular black bouncers, she would grant people entry or turn them away with a barely discernible nod or shake of her head. Groups of young men rarely passed muster; anyone wearing trainers or logos or jeans was systematically barred. But a group of Lido girls and well-groomed gay boys, all dressed and ready to play, were welcomed with open arms.

One Friday night in January, the stars and the Lido work roster aligned so that Lisa, Sabrina and I all had the night off. It was such a rare occurrence that we decided to make the most of it by having dinner at Man Ray. We worked our way through a selection of painstakingly over-prepared food, more decoration than substance, and a couple of rounds of Cosmopolitans.

As the evening wore on, the club started to fill, the lights were dimmed and the music became noticeably louder. None of us blinked when a group of four guys were seated at the table next to us.

A Cosmo-and-a-half later, however, Sabrina went suddenly quiet and beckoned us into a table huddle. 'Okay,' she said. 'Don't look now. But I swear the guys at the table next door have been staring at us for the last ten minutes.'

Lisa and I sat up and looked, me craning my neck to get a clear view.

'I said don't look! Jesus!' hissed Sabrina. 'That was real subtle, girls.'

Lisa turned back, her eyes wide. 'Oh my God oh my God oh my God! It's Leonardo DiCaprio!' she exclaimed. 'He's sitting at the table next to us!'

I spun around again for another look. Sabrina kicked me under the table.

'Oh my God, you're right!' I said, turning to Lisa and glaring at Sabrina. 'And they are *so* looking at us.'

Dressed down in a T-shirt and jeans, a baseball cap on his head, Leonardo DiCaprio was indeed at the next table. With a three-person, all-brooding, all-male entourage. Leonardo poured himself a vodka from the bottle on ice in the centre of the table and raised his glass in our direction, giving a slight nod of his famous head. To his left was a smaller guy, sporting a three-day growth, a worn T-shirt and a woollen hat pulled down over his head.

'Who's the little guy with the beard and beanie?' I asked the girls. 'He looks familiar.'

'He's cute,' Sabrina replied. 'But God, he's short.'

'How can you tell he's short? He's sitting down.'

'Oh, they're all short. They look so big and tough up on screen and then you meet them and they're just silly small.'

'Maybe that's because you're a yeti.'

Lisa shooshed us with a frantic waving of her hands. 'Stop it, stop it! They're looking at us.'

'Oh this is ridiculous,' I said. 'I feel like I'm back in high school.' I turned around and caught Leo's eye. He smiled, I smiled back. I turned back to the girls, flushed, and started giggling.

We were suddenly all out of conversation. We pulled ourselves upright in our chairs and played with our drinks.

'So what do we do now?' Lisa finally said. 'Do we say something?'

I started to collect my things. 'Come on, this is stupid. Let's get up and make to go. If they want to invite us for a drink, they'll ask us.'

Trying hard not to look self-conscious, we got up from the table and started to leave.

One of Leo's entourage, an American also in a baseball cap, leant across the table towards us.

'Surely you ladies aren't going already.' He was the fast-talking smarmy type. 'Why don't you join us for a drink?'

The three of us exchanged looks and pretended to weigh up the offer before accepting. The smarmy guy stood up from the booth to allow Lisa and me to slide along the banquette; Sabrina sat down in a chair at the head of the table.

'*Bonsoir*,' the small, bearded guy said to me as I sidled up next to him. He extended his hand for me to shake. 'Guillaume. *Enchanté*.'

From our up-close-and-personal vantage point I was able to take in the full effect of Leo and his French friend's dressed-down fashion sense. Presumably they wore hats in a nightclub to make it harder for people to recognise them, but with their ripped jeans and faded T-shirts, they stood out a mile. It looked to me like they had gone to a whole lot of effort to make it look like they hadn't made an effort. Leo, especially, with his cap pulled down over his eyes, looked very conspicuous in his attempt to look inconspicuous.

'Can I offer you ladies a drink?' he asked, picking the bottle of vodka out of the ice bucket. He poured us each a vodka cranberry before turning to make small talk with Lisa. I chatted in broken French with Guillaume. He was especially interested to learn we were Lido dancers.

'*Vous êtes danseuses du Lido?*' he asked incredulously. 'But this is amazing!' He turned to the other guys. 'They are famous in France. This is an honour.'

We were all completely charmed. The combination of high-voltage celebrity, a spot of French-accented small talk and one too many alcoholic beverages was intoxicating. One vodka and cranberry later, our heads spinning, we stood to leave.

'It was lovely to meet you. We'd love to stay but we have to go and meet our friends after the show,' I explained.

'That's a shame,' Leo said. 'But if you want to meet us for a drink, we'll probably be here again on Monday night.'

The smarmy one added, 'Post-premiere party here on Monday night, it's going to be wild. You girls *have* to be here. And make sure to bring some of your friends.'

As Lisa stood, Leo reached across the table and squeezed her hand. 'It was nice to meet you, Lisa,' he said, looking up at her. 'Hopefully we'll see you Monday.'

Doing our level best to remain calm and not appear as drunk as we were, we said goodbye and threaded our way across the crowded dance floor. We managed to hold it together until halfway up the stairs, and then we started laughing.

'OH. MY. GOD!' I howled, looking at Lisa. 'Did that really just happen?!'

'How funny was *that*?' she replied.

'What about how we meet a Hollywood star and instantly turn into a bunch of giggling teenagers? Have we no shame?'

Sabrina turned to Lisa, 'I'm sorry, but he was totally into you. Leo DiCaprio! Hilarious!'

We ran up the remaining stairs to the exit and stepped out into the night, laughing uproariously.

After a weekend spent milking our Leo story for all it was worth, Monday night finally rolled around – and with it the prospect of our much-anticipated second *rendez-vous* with Hollywood's hottest young star. In the three days since our dinner at Man Ray we had taken the liberty of extending the invitation to the post-premiere party to almost every dancer at the Lido. Backstage looked like a designer dress store, as each girl had trooped into work with her best outfit, eager to launch herself at Leo. The excitement was heightened by the fact that the film premiere was taking place in the cinema next door to the Lido. Coming in to work we'd had to cross the red carpet and fight our way through a jostling crowd of paparazzi and star-spotters, who had been camped out for hours in the hope of setting eyes on their idols.

When the curtain came down, we all rushed to the dressing-room and got down to the serious business of making ourselves beautiful. There were champagne bottles popping, blow-dryers whining and the excited titter of showgirl chat as party dresses were donned and make-up carefully applied.

By the time we got ourselves ready and trooped across the Champs Élysées to Man Ray, there was a crowd ten-deep bustling at the entrance. Some of them waved their invitations, others were trying to talk or bribe their way inside. For the most part, the door staff were indifferent to their entreaties. '*C'est complet!*' I heard a large Algerian bouncer repeat over and over. '*C'est une soirée privée.*' 'It's a private party.'

Making the most of our height and waving hopefully at Man Ray's redheaded gatekeeper, who sat hunkered like a toad on a stool at the entrance, we pushed our way to the front of the queue. She took us in with a glance and we were let inside.

A *maitre d'* met us at the cloakroom as we handed over our coats. '*Vous êtes les danseuses du Lido?*' he asked. '*Suivez-moi.*'

We followed him down the stairs, across the already packed dance floor to a large booth.

'This table has been reserved for you, your drinks have already been organised,' the *maitre d'* said. He fetched a large ice bucket and three bottles of vodka, and started laying out glasses and mixers. I asked him who had organised the table and drinks. He looked at me and gave a shrug.

It was 1 a.m. and the place was heaving. People dressed in film-premiere finery rubbed shoulders with skimpily clad models and artistic types with artfully arranged facial hair. Lisa and I did a quick scan of the place.

'So where are they?' asked one of the younger Lido girls. 'Where are these famous movie-star friends of yours?'

For the first time, it occurred to me that Leo and his mates might not show up. We had only had the briefest of encounters, and for a movie star in Paris there were doubtless plenty of other distractions.

'Come on, let's go dance,' I said to Lisa. We filled our glasses with vodka and apple juice and shimmied onto the dance floor.

At 2 a.m. there was still no sign of Leo. There was a roped-off VIP area, but it was conspicuously empty. We tried not to seem disappointed, and in the process had a few more drinks than was perhaps strictly sensible.

By the time the clock struck 3 a.m., Lisa and I were comfortably drunk and enjoying the party with our colleagues – but no closer to being reunited with the Hollywood heart-throb. It was becoming obvious that the invitation he had casually thrown out had been just that – casual and essentially meaningless.

'Let's get out of here,' I eventually shouted to Lisa over the thud of techno.

We gathered our things and bade farewell to the other girls. But as we stood in line at the cloakroom, one of the girls came bouncing up excitedly. 'He's here! Here's here!' She tugged at Lisa's arm. 'Come on! Leo's here. He just arrived. You have to go over and say hello!'

Lisa and I looked at one another. The vodka made us bold enough to turn on our heels, hurl dignity to the wind and march off to throw ourselves shamelessly at a movie star.

It wasn't hard to find him: he was in the centre of a huge surge of people, making his way slowly across the dance floor towards the exit. Burly minders flanked him on either side, cutting a path through the human crush. He'd only just arrived at the party, but seemed to be on a mission to get out of it as quickly as possible.

We stood on the stairs and watched. When he reached the bottom stair, he looked up and caught sight of us – and his face broke into a broad grin. 'Hey! There you are!' he said, sending our showgirl hearts skipping. 'I was hoping you'd make it.' His minders started moving him up the stairs.

'Listen, the party is moving to Queen. It's too crazy here. You should join us.'

We made an effort to nod coolly – but the vodka saw to it that we just looked like vigorously nodding, madly grinning idiots.

'Great!' Leo finished as he was swept out the door. 'So we'll see you there.'

Stepping out onto the street, we were hit by an icy wind. We pulled our coats around us, pushed our way past the crowd still waiting to gain entry, and tottered down Rue Marbeuf to the Champs Élysées.

It being a Monday night, Queen was packed with revellers in full disco gear. We checked our coats and descended the dark stairs to the dance floor. Peering across a sea of heads bobbing to a seventies remix, we could just make out Leo's entourage, reclining in the half-light of the V.I.P. section. A pair of black-suited bouncers barred our entry, but stepped aside as Leo waved us in.

The dressing-room champagne and Man Ray vodka were starting to prove a lethal combination. While I don't recall every word that was said in the ensuing couple of hours, I know I engaged in lively conversation with Guillaume, slipping in and out of French as we both described our jobs. It took only ten minutes of animated chat before the penny dropped. His face was familiar because he was one of France's up-and-coming young film stars.

Though he was little known outside his home country, he had carved a respectable reputation as a thespian and director in France and his star was very definitely on the rise. We got to talking about a French film I had seen him in on T.V. the previous week, and I was drunk enough to give him a full and frank appraisal. As I finished critiquing his film, I caught myself, suddenly realising it probably didn't play well to criticise a person's body of work while you were drinking his free champagne.

He started laughing. 'You are very direct, *non*? You speak your mind.'

I started to apologise.

'No, please! Don't apologise. I like it. A French girl would not do that.'

We talked spiritedly for the next half-hour, the persistent thud of disco meaning we often had to shout into one another's ears. He was cute, in a boyish kind of way. And he spoke with a heavy French accent that was to die for.

Across the table, Lisa and Leo held hands and chatted. Every now and then I would catch her eye and we'd give one another a look that said 'Can you believe this is happening?'

As the night wore on, champagne bottles were drained and the dance-floor crowd began to thin. I was irretrievably drunk. Not drunk enough that I couldn't stand or manage a full sentence, but not far off. Just as I made a mental note to rein in the alcohol consumption, Leo announced it was time to go.

'Come on ladies. The party's moving to my hotel. There are cars waiting outside.'

'We're just going to go to the bathroom,' Lisa yelled into Leo's ear. 'We'll see you upstairs.' She took my hand and pulled me up the dimly lit stairs that led to the toilets. On the way back down, whether it was the lack of light, the abundance of alcohol or (most likely) a combination of the two, I lost my footing and fell. As I fumbled for a railing, my finger wedged between a strip of metal trim and the wall.

Instinctively, I wrenched it out and felt a sharp shot of pain. A rush of adrenaline surge through me, momentarily clearing my head.

'Are you all right?' Lisa asked, turning on the stairs and looking back at me tipsily. 'You've gone as white as a ghost.'

I stood staring at my hand as blood began to gush from my fingertip.

'What have you done?' Lisa scrambled back up the stairs. 'Jesus! Come on, we've got to get you to the bathroom.'

In the cold, hard fluorescent light of the bathroom, my blood glistened a dark red. Great splotches dripped on the filthy, white-tiled floor. In a mild state of shock – both because of the pain and at the sight of so much blood – I stood at the sink and watched the blood flow as Lisa turned on the tap and forced my finger under the running water.

'It looks bad, hon. I think it's quite deep. We should get you to a hospital.'

The pain started to set in, and I started to cry.

'No, no, it's fine,' I insisted through the tears, trying to convince myself as much as Lisa. 'Let's just wrap it up in paper towels. The bleeding will stop eventually. I'm sure it's nothing.'

Lisa looked at me and scowled.

She wrapped a massive wad of paper towel around my finger: it slowly began to turn red.

'Come on, we are *not* going to miss this party because of a little scratch.' Lisa was clearly getting on famously with Leonardo. It would have been a desertion of my duty as her girlfriend to abandon her now.

'We'll go for one drink, and if it's still bad, we'll leave. I promise.'

A wave of nausea passed over me as we left the bathroom and climbed the stairs to the street. The same icy wind as before cut its way down the Champs Élysées. Our sleeveless, backless, strappy tops put up little resistance as the pre-dawn chill wrapped itself greedily around us.

'The coats! I have to go back and get the coats!' Lisa exclaimed. 'Stay here. Don't move.'

I sank into myself, shivering on the spot as my finger throbbed with pain.

A large black four-wheel-drive with tinted windows pulled up in front of me. The passenger window slid down to reveal Guillaume behind the wheel and Jerome, a member of his entourage, in the passenger seat.

'Shay!' Guillaume called. He clocked the towels wrapped around my finger. 'Ça va? What happened to your hand?'

'Nothing, everything's fine,' I said, doing my best to keep my voice level, hoping to not sound drunk or sick to my stomach – both of which I was.

'Great, then hop in. I'll take you to the hotel.'

Jerome jumped from the passenger seat, took off his coat and put it around my shoulders. As I slid into the back seat, Lisa came bounding up the stairs with our coats and joined me.

# Chapter Forty

The drive from Queen on the Champs Élysées to the Plaza Athénée hotel on nearby Avenue Montaigne takes no more than a minute – not quite long enough for me to thaw out, but long enough for the severity of my injury to sink in. The bleeding appeared to have stopped; the throb of pain hadn't.

At the hotel, the guys left the car with a valet and we walked into the lobby: a regal space with a mottled white marble floor, imposing columns and massive sprays of flowers in enormous vases. A couple of officious, be-suited young men tended the front desk and an elderly Frenchman with a white handlebar moustache sat perched behind the *concierge* counter. Otherwise the lobby was deserted.

Leo was waiting by reception with a couple of his mates and two leggy, scantily clad girls.

'There you are,' he said. 'I was beginning to wonder what had happened to you.' Then he noticed my finger with its bloodstained, tattered paper-towel dressing. 'Oh sweetie, what happened?' he asked. 'Are you okay?'

'Fine, I'm fine,' I said, self-consciously putting my hand behind my back.

'Let Dan take a look at it,' Leo insisted, motioning to one of his minders. 'We'll see you upstairs.'

Dan was a lumbering fifty-something specimen of a man, almost as wide as he was tall. He borrowed a first-aid kit from the *concierge* and led me to the lobby bathroom, Lisa following close behind.

'So what have we done here?' Dan asked in an American accent. His voice was gentle and full of concern. It was all I could do not to start crying again. He peeled off the paper-towel dressing and let out a whistle.

'That's some cut you've got there. It looks to me like you ought to get it seen to at a hospital.'

Lisa harrumphed triumphantly behind me. 'You see?' she said. 'Now will you listen to me?'

I felt a surge of stubbornness and Dutch courage. 'Honestly, I'm fine. We're going to go upstairs for one drink, then you can take me wherever you want. I don't want to make a fuss. Okay?'

Dan shrugged. Delving into the first-aid kit for antiseptic and gauze, he did his best to dress the wound.

I couldn't bring myself to look at it, but tried not to flinch as he sprayed on the antiseptic. The looks on Dan's and Lisa's faces were all the evidence I needed, though, that it was not a pretty sight.

We took the lift to the fifth floor and made our way down a tastefully decorated hotel corridor to the suite. Leo opened the door himself and ushered us inside. There were fifteen or so people variously draped on sofas or milling about. A stereo played R&B; a couple ground their hips together in the corner near a set of bay windows with a view of the Seine and the Eiffel Tower.

The suite itself was sumptuous – very Louis XIV. The living-room area featured a couple of plump, finely upholstered sofas and a gilt mirror above a marble fireplace. The curtains were rich burgundy, tied back in dramatic scoops with gold plaited rope. A pair of double wooden doors led to the bedroom and a huge king-sized bed.

'Is everything okay?' Leo asked doubtfully, pointing to my hand. 'Did Dan sort you out?'

I nodded. 'It's nothing. Dan was great. Really, I'm fine.'

He didn't look convinced. 'Okay then. If you say so. Now, what can I offer you ladies to drink?'

The mere mention of alcohol made my stomach flip, but I didn't want to appear rude, so I accepted one of the two champagne flutes he proffered and sat down in the corner of one of the sofas. After a few moments, Guillaume came and sat next to me.

'How are you feeling? Is everything okay?'

We chatted for a while. He was sweet and attentive and managed to make me laugh. An hour or so later, I had become sufficiently engrossed in our conversation – and pleased by its flirtatious undertones, not to mention numbed by another glass of champagne – that I no longer noticed the pain of my injured finger.

Lisa came over from the other side of the room. 'Shay, I think it's time for us to go,' she said, smiling at Guillaume.

'Already?' I replied, sounding scarily like a petulant child. 'But it's still early!'

Lisa glanced at her watch. 'Honey, it's 7 a.m. We've got work tomorrow.' She leaned in close to my ear. 'It's getting weird over there. We need to leave *now*.'

Taking her hand, I pulled myself up out of the sofa. It took me a few seconds to find my balance. I felt light-headed and the sudden movement had caused the pain in my finger to flare up again.

'Come on Cinderella, the night's over,' Lisa said as she led me across the room. We said goodbye to our host, teetered out into the corridor and took the lift down to the lobby.

'Do we really have to go home?' I asked Lisa after she had ordered a taxi with the *concierge* and led me out onto the street.

It was still dark. Off to our right, and creating a detailed silhouette of the Hausmannian buildings and church steeple on the opposite side of the Seine, the sky was turning a cobalt blue. The sun would be up in an hour. We looked hopefully up Avenue Montaigne for our cab. A black car came around the corner and pulled into the kerb in front of us. The window slid down, revealing Guillaume and his friend Jerome. I could make out Guillaume's impish smile in the soft light from the dashboard.

'Can I offer you ladies a lift? We can drop you home if you'd like.'

I made a squawk of surprise, moving to accept the offer by opening the back door. Lisa grabbed my arm and pulled me back.

'Thank you, that's really kind. But we have a taxi. We'll be fine, thanks,' she said, slamming the car door.

I swayed as she tightened her grip on my arm.

'Come on Shay, we're going home.'

I felt suddenly affronted that the night was being wrapped up, and not on my terms. A taxi appeared and performed a U-turn in front of the hotel.

'I don't want to go home!' I pulled free of Lisa's grip and made a beeline for Guillaume's car. Before anyone, including myself, knew what was happening, I had leaped headfirst into the open passenger window. Jerome sat back in shock as I performed a kind of mid-air breaststroke manoeuvre, trying to worm my way further in.

Over the sound of Guillaume laughing hysterically, I heard Lisa cry, 'Shay! What the hell are you doing? Get back out here now.' She grabbed my protruding legs and started pulling me back out onto the street.

'But I don't want to go home!' I repeated over and over, as I felt myself being pulled backwards. I grasped at the gearstick and handbrake, smearing blood all over the car's cream leather interior. Lisa set me upright on the pavement, apologising profusely to Guillaume and Jerome.

'Get in the taxi!' she ordered me, waving off the boys.

'Wait,' Guillaume called to Lisa. 'Give me your number. I want to make sure you get home okay and that Shay's finger is all right.'

Lisa shouted out her mobile number while she stuffed me into the back of the cab. I waved drunkenly out the rear window as we pulled away from the kerb.

'You're staying with me tonight,' Lisa said as we slipped through the empty streets of pre-dawn Paris. 'There's no way I'm leaving you on your own. You're out of control.'

By the time we got back to Lisa's apartment and I had climbed the five sets of stairs to reach her front door, the numbing effect of the alcohol had begun to wear off. When we crawled into bed, my finger had resumed its throbbing and the first inkling of drunkard's remorse started to kick in.

'What have I done?' I asked Lisa as I sat on the edge of her bed, freshly showered and in borrowed pyjamas, holding my finger aloft.

'Get some sleep, we'll deal with it in the morning,' Lisa said.

It was almost four in the afternoon when we finally stirred. My head pounded with the world's worst hangover and a flush of shame washed over me as the full horror of my behaviour the night before came rushing back. Vowing to never drink again, I performed a mental checklist of my drunken antics. The obnoxiousness, the stupidity and the rudeness of it all seemed almost too much to bear. I was mortified. I was also in a whole new world of pain. The cut on my finger was now infected after more than twelve hours of neglect. I wanted to cry but didn't feel I had the right to self-pity.

'I think I might need to go to the hospital,' I said sheepishly to Lisa when she woke.

She gave me a withering look. 'You think?'

I spent four hours in the fluorescent-lit waiting room of the Hôpital Lariboisière – a run-down hospital on the fringes of the seedy Gare du Nord *quartier* – as a parade of drunks and other unfortunates got treated before me. When I finally got to see a doctor, he peeled back the dressing on my finger and tutted loudly. Shaking his head and mumbling under his breath, he gave me a local anaesthetic and stitched me up.

By the time I got home, I felt sore and very, very sorry for myself. I had been instructed to take three weeks off work to let the wound heal, and then have a couple of months of physiotherapy to get proper function back in the finger. The cut had been so deep that nerves and tendons had been severed, and I would forever have a slightly crooked, permanently numb right forefinger as a memento of my brief brush with Hollywood.

That night, alone in my apartment, I nursed an alcohol-poisoned stomach, a pounding headache, a throbbing right hand and some severely bruised dignity. And I found myself wondering what the hell I was doing with my life. After the Olivier break-up, I had taken to late-night partying again with gusto.

As wake-up calls went, the wash up of my wild night on the town with Leo & Co. could not have been louder or clearer. It was, I decided as I sipped on soup, wrapped in a blanket in my living room, time to rein it in a little.

## Chapter Forty-one

In the first couple of days following my nightclub misadventure, my damaged finger proved far less painful than my bruised pride. I'd been drunk in my time, but never so much as to cause myself bodily harm. As I sat in my apartment with little else to do, I was taunted by flashbacks from the evening – my cavalier dismissal of the gaping wound in my finger, my loud and obnoxious declarations that the night was not over until I said so, and of course the ridiculous way I'd launched myself headfirst into the window of a film star's car. I cringed each time the scene replayed in my head.

It was early evening, three days after our big night on the town when I picked up my phone to hear a clearly excited Lisa on the other end.

'Oh my God! Oh my God! Guess who just called me?'

'The king of the world?' I replied, using our *Titanic*-inspired nickname for Lisa's momentary almost-love-interest.

'Yeah, right, as if,' Lisa shot back. 'Guillaume. It was Guillaume. He called just now to get your number. He said he wanted to call you to see how you were.'

I flushed red at the thought of having to confront the man who had politely rebuffed my attempt to throw myself at him, literally. Either he had extremely good manners or he enjoyed ritual humiliation. A sense of dread settled over me.

'I'm getting off the phone now in case he's trying to call,' Lisa said, signing off.

I put the phone down on the sofa next to me. As if on cue, it started vibrating and its little blue screen lit up, blinking 'Unknown Number' at me. I looked at Willy doubtfully. He gave me one of his disdainful feline looks.

'I know, I know. I have to face the music.'

I picked up the phone, cleared my throat and answered the call in the cheeriest voice possible.

'*Allo?*' said the husky voice on the other end of the line. '*C'est* Shay?'

'*C'est moi,*' I replied, doing my best to seem insouciant.

'Shay, it's Guillaume. We met the other night.'

I bit my bottom lip and closed my eyes. My stomach tightened. 'Oh, hi,' I said. 'How are you?'

'*Très bien, merci.* I just thought I would phone to see how *you* were.'

'Fine, thanks,' I replied, altogether too urgently. 'No, everything's good here.'

'*Génial,*' Guillaume said. 'And the finger? Is it okay?'

I looked down at the wad of bandage around my injured digit.

'Oh, you know. Seven stitches, three weeks off work.' I paused, as a fresh flush of embarrassment washed over me. 'Listen, I need to apologise for the other night. The whole jumping in the car thing. Lisa tells me I got blood all over the interior.'

'And on my friend's coat,' he teased.

'Oh God, I'm so embarrassed.'

'Don't be,' Guillaume laughed. 'It was actually very funny.'

'Funny for you maybe. I've ruined my finger and have to take a month off work without pay.'

With all the suaveness for which his countrymen are renowned, my new film-star friend spied an opportunity and went for it. 'If you have all of this spare time, perhaps we could get together some time – for a dinner or drink or something.'

The fact that he was phoning me at all came as somewhat of a shock. Most men would turn and run if confronted, at the end of a night out, by a blathering Amazon clambering headfirst into his vehicle while bleeding profusely. But, unless I was mistaken, this man appeared to be asking me out on a date.

'Ummm,' I stuttered, utterly dumbfounded. 'Sure. I guess. Why not?'

'*Bon*. I'll be out of town for a few weeks, but when I'm back in Paris, I'll give you a call. Maybe we can – what's the word? – 'ook up?'

''Ook up,' I repeated with a smile. 'That sounds good.'

In normal circumstances, I would have relished the prospect of three weeks off work. But because the accident wasn't work-related, it meant I had no income for the rest of the month. I consigned myself to house arrest, where not even the smorgasbord of *EastEnders* omnibuses on B.B.C. Prime could relieve the boredom that kicked in after only four days. The sooner I could get back to work, the better.

Another factor in my frustration was the imminent arrival of my parents. Dad had booked a trip to celebrate Mum's birthday, so she could spend time with me and watch me perform at the Lido. I was damned if I was going to let them down.

When Mum and Dad arrived from Brisbane, they hopped into a taxi and came straight to the apartment.

'You look wonderful, Shelb,' Mum said tearfully, pulling me into her.

'But what are we going to do about that finger?' Dad interjected playfully. 'Remind me again how it happened?'

As well as relieving the boredom and ending my solitude, my parents' arrival heralded two weeks of unmitigated spoiling. The apartment was spotless, meals were cooked, washing was done and clothes were ironed. It felt so good to be looked after. It had been a long while since I had felt I could just let go and be carried.

'So you never did explain what happened with Olivier,' Mum said one afternoon over tea in the kitchen. 'It seemed like one minute he was there and the next he was gone.'

The temptation to unload was enormous. But I had been so independent for so long, the last thing I wanted was for her to start worrying about me. If there was one thing worse than bottling up the Olivier disaster, it was giving my parents a reason to think that I was far from home and not coping. Besides, the worst of it was well and truly over.

I told her some of what had happened, but chose to leave out the messier details. Being a mum, I knew she would read between the lines anyway. And being *my* mum, I knew she would leave well enough alone.

Over a meal in a rustic restaurant to celebrate Mum's fiftieth birthday, I looked across the table at my parents – their faces glowing in the light from the open fire – and wondered what it was that made their relationship so special. As an example of a happy marriage, it was a hard act to follow. But it was also an inspiration: they were one another's world. I silently vowed that unless I found someone who could make me as happy as my parents so clearly were, unless I found someone I could love without reservation or compromise, then I would remain alone.

My weeks of enforced idleness duly ended, and the big night arrived for Mum and Dad to come and watch me perform. Knowing that dancing at the Lido had always been my dream, they made a huge fuss, taking me to lunch and toasting my success with a glass of champagne.

It was always special to have people you knew in the audience – but having Mum and Dad there meant the world to me. Under the spotlight, and with the smiling faces of my proud parents beaming back at me from the *salle*, I gave it my all.

As we returned home together in a taxi, Dad hugged me to him. 'Shelly, I was so proud of you up there tonight. You were just beautiful, darlin'.' The taxi swung around the floodlit base of the Arc de Triomphe. He was beaming. 'Look at me. Here in Paris with my two beautiful girls. Who would have thought it? My baby girl works on the Champs Élysées! I couldn't be happier!'

# Chapter Forty-two

Whether it was the three weeks of enforced rest, the extra enthusiasm injected into my performance with my parents in the *salle* or just dumb luck, Pierre called me into his office a week after Mum and Dad had returned to Australia and asked me to learn the principal role.

'You want me to learn principal?' I asked, certain that I had misheard.

'Yes,' he nodded. 'We need another replacement for the holidays.' He took in my look of complete shock. 'That is, of course, provided you want to learn it.'

I snapped to attention. 'Of course, yes! Of *course* I want to learn it.'

'Good,' Pierre said, allowing a smile to break across his face. 'Rehearsals start Monday. You'll be on in a month.'

I raced down to the dressing-room and picked up my phone to call home.

'Mum! Mum! You'll never believe it. Pierre just asked me to learn principal! It's happened. I'm going to dance the principal role at the Lido!'

I found myself whispering the news, conscious of the ripple effect it could have in the dressing-room.

'Shelby! That's amazing!' Mum screamed excitedly down the phone. 'Wait until I get your dad!' I heard her yell, 'Graham! Pick up the phone!'

More than anyone, Mum and Dad knew how much this meant to me. From my humble beginnings in a church hall in Annerley, the skinny kid from Tarragindi was getting a shot at the top prize of the Paris cabaret world. Sixteen years of dancing, seven of them professionally, had been leading up to this moment. Dancing at the Lido was a notable professional achievement, but taking the stage as its principal dancer was my dream come true.

After celebrating on the phone with my parents, I hung up and caught my breath. I could feel my stomach start to churn with nerves. It was going to be a long month.

Rehearsals began almost immediately. I trained with Stuart most afternoons, drilling a show that included ten costume changes, several *pas de deux* with boy dancers, a whole lot of lip-synching and one very technical solo.

The *chef d'orchestre* solo towards the end of the show had always been the one piece of choreography in *C'est Magique* that I revered. From the very first time I saw it, I had been enchanted by that solo. In a profession that so often required us to underplay our danceability and serve as mobile, semi-naked clotheshorses for the over-the-top costumes, the *chef d'orchestre* solo was a chance to shine as a dancer. It was as raw and stripped back as the Lido got. Just a dancer and her talent, some music and a spotlight. The prospect of performing it filled me with terror.

During a break in rehearsals one afternoon, I got a phone call from Dad in Brisbane. He sounded excited.

'Love, it's me. It's late here. Your mother doesn't know I'm calling. I need you to keep a secret.'

Dad was famed for his surprises – he was always sneaking around doing a terrible job of hiding stuff from Mum.

'Let me guess. You've bought another van to take the dogs to the beach in and you haven't told Mum?'

'No love. Better than that. Though come to think of it, there is this one Mitsubishi Starwagon I've had my eye on.' He chuckled.

'What then, Dad? What's the big secret? I'm at rehearsals.'

'Right, of course, sorry love. The thing is, I've organised for your mum to come across to Paris to see you dance principal.' He paused, triumphant at having truly surprised me.

'What?' I couldn't believe it. 'But how? You were only here three weeks ago, how can she get the time off work again?'

'I've had a quiet word to her boss and sorted it all out. I bought the tickets this morning. Your mum doesn't know. She's just going to love it.'

'Oh my God!' I was screaming and jumping now. 'Dad! That's amazing!'

'Shelb, I know how much this means to you. I know how hard you've worked for this. And I know how much it will mean to Mum to see you dancing principal at the Lido. She's been there from the beginning. This is the realisation of your dream, love, and at least one of us should be there to see it.'

I started crying. A wave of homesickness shuddered through me. 'I don't know what to say.'

'Don't say a word. She arrives two days before your big performance. Organise her a ticket to the show, will you?'

Three weeks later, rehearsals were over and Mum was back in Paris. With the help of her boss, Dad had managed to keep the trip a secret until a week before her departure. To say that she was excited to be back in the City of Light would be an understatement. Not only had she come to see me perform, she had come to spend ten days in Paris on her own – a state she hadn't really been in since marrying my dad thirty-odd years before.

It had been lovely to spend time in Paris with my parents, but it was something else again to have the chance to spend time alone with my mum. For four days leading up to my opening night as a Lido principal, we strolled the streets of Paris and lingered over long lunches in terrace cafes, talking about everything and nothing in particular.

The words poured out of me. Seven years of coping alone, of managing in a city far from home, had taken more of a toll than even I knew. In buzzy cafes, amid lunchtime crowds and under the first sunny skies of springtime in Paris, I sat down with my mum and shared everything.

It was a recalibration of sorts, a squaring of the emotional ledger, as I detailed the ins and outs and highs and lows of the Olivier experience.

Mum listened, torn by feelings of pride, compassion – and frustration at not having been able to provide comfort, a shoulder to cry on, support, or a solution.

'I could have done something. I could have come over and helped,' she kept repeating.

'But Mum,' I explained. 'That's the whole point. You did help. If it wasn't for the way you brought me up, the independence you instilled in me, I never would have coped.' Just by being them, by getting on with their jobs and providing a roof over our heads and meals on the table, by letting us know that no matter where we went or what we did they were always there for us to fall back on, my parents had given me the confidence to go out and take on the world.

There were tears, but not too many. Being of a famously pragmatic nature, Mum and I were content to deal with the emotional stuff and then put it to one side and concentrate on enjoying the moment. There were too many shops to explore, *pâtisseries* to raid and long walks in spring gardens to enjoy.

When the day of my performance arrived, I woke up a bundle of nerves. I spent the day with Mum and her friend Veronica, a nursing buddy who had interrupted an extended break in England with her husband to come and spend a couple of days in Paris with us girls. I did my best to concentrate on the company and conversation as Mum and Veronica skipped about the city like a pair of giggling schoolgirls, but my mind refused to do anything but go over and over the choreography, stage cues and costume changes that would be expected of me later that night. Eventually, I excused myself and headed back to the apartment, to try and rest before the show. When Mum came home a couple of hours later, she was armed with a huge bouquet of red roses.

'These are you for you, Shelb, from your dad, your brothers and me.'

The card had been signed by Dad, Adam and John. 'Hey Stinky!' John had scribbled. 'Congratulations on becoming principal. Hope you're not as mean as Sister Brenda.'

I started to cry.

'We're so proud of you,' Mum said, giving me a hug, her eyes welling.

I was unable to sit still, much less eat anything, so I decided to walk into work early. The nerves weren't going to abate any, but at least I could distract myself with a lengthy warm-up session and the deliberately slow application of my make-up.

'I'll come with you,' Mum declared. 'Just let me get ready.'

I had reserved two tickets for Mum and Veronica to come and see the show. Pierre had made the booking and seen to it that they had the best seats in the house.

As we strolled along the wide gravel path that cuts through the heart of Parc Monceau, Mum put her arm through mine and gave my hand a squeeze.

I forced a smile, but felt like vomiting. In almost ten years of dancing professionally, I couldn't remember feeling so nervous. It wasn't as if I hadn't done opening nights before. It wasn't as if I hadn't danced principal before – towards the end of my Moulin Rouge tenure I'd replaced the leads all the time. But I had vested so much in dancing principal at the Lido that the prospect of it finally happening filled me with fear, and not just about the performance. What was I supposed to aspire to once I had done this? What was going to drive and inspire me? Wasn't the whole point of a fantasy that it remained forever, elusively, just out of reach?

I thought back to that fateful plane trip to Paris from Japan all those years ago. How, even before I knew I had a job at the Moulin Rouge, I'd sat in the dark and watched scenes from the Lido splash across a tiny screen. I remembered sitting backstage at Jupiters dressed as a banana and listening, awestruck, as Corina talked about being a Bluebell, living in Paris and dancing at the Lido. I thought of the eisteddfod judge from my youth who had invoked the Lido and 'Bluebell dancer' as my destiny. And now here I was.

I kissed Mum goodbye at the stage door.

'Just go out there and do your best, darling,' she said. 'I'm so proud of you.'

# Chapter Forty-three

The curious thing about a first night like this one is that, while the upcoming show means everything to you, for the rest of the cast it's just another night at the office. I existed in my own private bubble of anxiety.

Fortunately, backstage was deserted when I first arrived. I moved my make-up to the principals' dressing-room and started sponging on the body paint. Usually it took no more than two minutes of wide, slap-dash strokes across my torso with a foundation-soaked sponge. But tonight, I made sure my body make-up was smooth and even. I worked just as meticulously to make up my face, then in my warm-up gear, spread my yoga mat on the floor and started stretching. The principal role required me to perform choreography that worked muscles ignored in my regular show, and I needed to be as loose as possible.

With an hour to go before the curtain went up, Stuart came to the dressing-room.

'How are you feeling?' he asked.

'Fine,' I lied.

'Just relax, you'll be okay. You know the show; we have complete faith in your ability to do this. Just enjoy yourself.' He smiled. 'The boys are ready to practise your lifts.'

Brimming with nerves, I went down to the stage. A significant portion of my show required me to be hurled about in the air by the boy dancers. Every lift was a disaster waiting to happen – so each one had to be drilled. Thankfully the run-through went smoothly.

'Fifteen minutes to curtain,' came the announcement over the tannoy.

I rushed back to my dressing-room to find Lisa there.

'Agggghhh!' she screamed in excitement. 'Look at you, principal woman! This is it! Now, I don't want to make you any more nervous than you already are. I just want to wish you luck. You will be fabulous.' She stood up, gave me a hug and ran downstairs to get ready for the opening number.

The principals' dresser, Marie-Laure, arrived bearing my costume: a set of pink bunny ears and a pair of fluffy, pink, bottomless chaps.

'*Voilà, ma chère*,' she said, handing them over.

Natalie, my fellow principal, sat quietly at her dressing-table, flicking through a magazine. I knew better than to expect a glimmer of recognition from her, much less a word of encouragement. I donned my costume and, unable to sit still, went down into the wings to watch the prologue unfurl. As the Bluebells filed upstairs to take their position onstage, I was bombarded with a volley of air kisses and cries of '*Merde!*' and 'Good luck!'

My pulse raced as the opening number started drawing to a close. As I stepped behind the massive top hat from which I was to emerge and make my entrance, the sound of the music was suddenly drowned out in my head by the beating of my heart. I stood looking down, in the darkness. The music seemed to be coming at me through an aural fog – muted and far away.

And then, as the top hat divided in two and pulled back, bathing me in spotlight, I looked up, gave a showgirl smile and felt everything come into focus. With the stage lights trained upon me I felt electrified. Invincible.

My nerves melted away. When the moment comes, you can't see the audience through the glare of the spotlight, but you sense every set of eyes on you. The music feels louder, the lights seem brighter, you have the whole stage to yourself. Thirty seconds into my opening routine I was overcome with joy – and relief. It was happening and it was all okay. It was more than okay, it was amazing! With every step

I felt my confidence grow, and after weeks spent wondering if I really wanted to do this at all, I suddenly never wanted it to end.

In the wings, a small crowd of girls had gathered to watch me. Knowing that my every move was being analysed, I threw myself with abandon into the performance. I could picture my mum sitting at attention somewhere out in the *salle*, nervously, proudly watching me. I tried to savour every second, aware that this was the culmination of years of hard work, years of struggle, disappointment and triumph. As I struck my final pose, the audience erupted in a thunder of applause and my heart sang.

Between each number, I would race backstage and ask Marie-Laure to photograph me in costume. There was a fiercely guarded pecking order among replacements, so I had no idea when I would dance principal again – or if I ever would. I wanted to preserve every moment for posterity.

The show seemed to fly by. In what seemed like no time at all, I was running backstage to change hurriedly for the finale. Flanked on either side by the entire company, and dressed in a pair of thigh-high black suede boots, a black sequinned G-string, a spray of black feathers about my neck and a black sequinned hat in the shape of a serpent, I strode forward singing my heart out. I was only required to lip-synch, but I was damned if I was going to waste the opportunity to belt out a tune. The entire show leading up to this moment had required varying levels of concentration and stress – now all I had to do was relax, give it full, over-the-top cabaret cheese and enjoy the moment. Wielding the outrageously camp rhinestone-studded microphone, I strutted to the front of the stage and hammed it up.

When I glanced into the audience, I saw Mum staring back in wonder and pride. Her hands were clapped to her mouth and her eyes were moist. Before I knew it, there were tears in my eyes too.

Because it was the last night before the intense summer period of fourteen shows a week, management had organised post-show drinks. Having showered and changed, I walked down onstage to a cheer from a group of my Bluebell friends. Mum and Veronica were hovering on the fringe of the crowd, sipping flutes of champagne.

'Shelb,' Mum said as I walked towards her, beaming. 'You were wonderful. Just wonderful. You're the best.'

She pulled me into a hug, and I felt I could have stayed there forever. I was deliriously happy, but so very tired. And in that moment I knew if I never got to do principal again, it wouldn't matter. It had been as close to perfect as any night I had ever been on stage.

# ACT V

# Chapter Forty-four

'Remind me again how we got invited to this?'

Lisa walked alongside me as we crossed the street to enter the Australian Embassy. The roads surrounding the Eiffel Tower had been closed to accommodate the thousands who were descending on the Champ de Mars to watch the Bastille Day fireworks. It was a typically steamy July evening and the sun was hovering on the horizon behind us, casting a golden light over the row of regal, honey-stoned buildings that hugged the river near Trocadéro.

'My brothers know James, the sports attaché,' I replied. 'They played rugby together in Brisbane.'

'The Australian Embassy has a sports attaché?' she asked. 'Is that even a real job?'

We had been invited to attend the Australian ambassador's annual Bastille Day barbecue. In what I had been told was an attempt to mix up the usual embassy crowd, the ambassador had given *carte blanche* to his genial sports attaché to invite his young Aussie friends to the *soirée*.

As we emerged from the lift and were led through a vast living room onto a rooftop terrace, we were both taken aback by the view. Standing proud before us, the Eiffel Tower looked suddenly immense from such a close vantage point. Laced from top to bottom with fireworks, she would become the centrepiece of a massive pyrotechnic display for the evening's celebrations. She was the most recognisable monument in the most touristed, romanticised, beautiful city in the world. For now, in the twilight, she stood silent and still while the flashes of countless cameras flickered from the viewing platforms.

'It doesn't matter how many times you see it, it never fails to take your breath away,' I said.

James broke away from a small group of partygoers he was entertaining and bounded over, champagne flute in hand.

'Shay! So glad you could make it. Get yourselves some oysters and champagne. The barbecue is over there and that's the ambassador in the middle of that group of people there. Enjoy!'

It was always pleasant to be back in the company of Aussies: there was something easy about their manner that made me feel instantly relaxed. All the nerves caused by fronting up at an official embassy function started to slide away.

Our fellow party guests were open and friendly: a grab bag of Aussie expats similarly summoned to their Ambassador's residence to celebrate France's national day. Ricocheting politely from an insurance company executive and his wife to an art dealer and a government official, we eventually found ourselves joining a small group of people who were noticeably younger and louder than everyone else. In its midst was a curly-haired blonde guy, talking at anyone who would listen. He seemed a little overbearing and insufferably brash, but he had a fabulous smile.

'Hello, I'm Shay,' I managed to squeeze in when he paused for breath. I extended my hand.

'I know,' he replied. 'We met six weeks ago. At the embassy summer party.'

I flushed with embarrassment and cast my mind back six weeks. Lisa and I had swung by the embassy on our way into work to join the throngs at a much rowdier, less exclusive event. I recalled a raucous scene of several hundred people, long queues at the beer table, the waft of burnt sausage from the barbecue and a swift round of introductions by James to a couple of his mates. I didn't remember meeting this guy at all.

'Bryce,' he eventually offered. 'Clearly I made a huge impression on you.'

He was a journalist who had come to Paris on a wing and a prayer. A Francophile with very definite Aussie sensibilities, he seemed to have the same relationship as me with his adopted home and its inhabitants: seven parts fascination, three parts frustration. Over several more champagne top-ups, we got to talking about how we came to be in France, what was keeping us here and when or if we ever thought we might head home.

Whether it was the champagne or a pulling back of his bravado, what I had previously found abrasive I started to find mildly entertaining. He was funny, in a typically Australian, self-deprecating kind of way. We spent the remainder of the night quoting lines to one another from Australian sitcoms and comparing war stories as expats in Paris. If you could get past the hair, which bordered on blonde afro and definitely needed taming, he was okay-looking too – in a sparkling-eyed, smiley kind of way.

As darkness fell and with the best seats in the house, we stood together and watched fireworks explode over the Eiffel Tower.

# Chapter Forty-five

After an eight-year residency on the Lido stage, *C'est Magique!* was starting to look anything but. The music and choreography were dated, and the cast were increasingly hard-pressed to go out every night and give it their all. My permanent place in the Belle line and occasional stint as principal were enough to keep it all mildly varied and relatively interesting for me. But with every night that passed, the mental energy required to go on smiling and dancing through another performance became greater and greater.

Rumours had started swirling backstage that *C'est Magique!* was on its last legs, that a replacement show was already in the planning – and that an announcement to that effect would soon be made.

Having achieved my dream of dancing principal at the Lido, I had a nagging feeling that my work in Paris was done. Without a relationship tying me to the City of Light, without anything new to stretch me professionally, my thoughts started to turn to home. It felt like maybe it was time to go back to Australia and reinvent myself as something other than a Paris showgirl.

I started to scout for work in the homeland and, without wanting to get Mum's hopes up too high, began hinting to her that a permanent move back home might be on the cards. And then along came *Bonheur*.

'Ladies, gentlemen, if I could have your attention for one moment please.'

Pierre had called us all to a pre-show meeting. Waiters bustled about the *salle* setting up the dinner service as the company milled about on the stage.

'I know some of you may have heard rumours of a new show,' Pierre continued. 'Well, I'm pleased to tell you the rumours are true. *C'est Magique!* will have its last performance at the end of October, after which there will be a month of rehearsal before we open the new show, *Bonheur,* in December.'

There was a twitter of excitement.

'Auditions will be held at the start of October.'

Just as it had at the Moulin Rouge, the announcement of a new show had a polarising effect on the company. Some of the oldies knew that a show changeover would give management the perfect opportunity to dump them, and had too much pride to make it look like they cared. For us younger dancers, the prospect of a new show gave our nightly efforts an injection of energy and urgency. We knew that assessments would be being made during each performance on who should be a principal in the new show, who should be a swing and who should be cut – or worse, left to languish up the back of each number. The competitive streak that had seen all of us make it to the Lido in the first place came suddenly back to the fore, making it a pleasure to dance there once again.

The idea of heading home promptly went out the window. It would be so exciting to be part of the *montage* of a new production. And professionally speaking, to have performed in four shows on the Paris cabaret stage, working with new choreographers each time, could only enhance my C.V. I decided to stay.

The last night of *C'est Magique!* was predictably emotional. For the company members who either hadn't succeeded at *Bonheur* auditions or hadn't bothered trying, it was a bittersweet evening. Even those of us who would dance in the new show felt sad: performing a show that had become a part of each of us for the last time, farewelling colleagues who had become like family. We all invited friends and those of us who could invited relatives.

The final show was full of the usual gags and silliness. The onstage japes meant nothing to anyone in the audience, but somehow gave expression to all the mixed emotions swirling about on stage.

Rehearsals for *Bonheur* started the following morning. I had made it through the audition process in comparatively good shape: Pierre had offered me the role of swing and second captain of the nude line. The Belles were being done away with. In the *Bonheur régime* there was to be a new hierarchy, Bluebells, nudes and just one principal.

All of the dance glory now belonged to one principal dancer, instead of two – the competition among the girls to replace her when she had a night off would be keen. And finally, leading the onstage action would be a live singer – a German diva who had made a name for herself as a leading musical theatre star in her home country, and who had a powerhouse voice and a silky stage presence.

'*Mesdames et messieurs*. Listen up please!' Pierre shouted to the studio full of dancers.

While renovation work was undertaken on the Lido stage to prepare it for *Bonheur*, we were rehearsing in the ballet studios belonging to the Opéra de Paris – a set of massive brick former warehouses in the grim northern outskirts of the city. Amid the sea of familiar faces was the smattering of new blood that the changeover process had allowed Pierre and Stuart to bring in.

'I'd like to introduce you to the new *meneuse* of Lido. Will you please join me in welcoming Sabine!'

A tall woman with short-cropped blonde hair stepped forward, smiled warmly and gave a self-conscious wave.

Pierre went on to introduce the other new members of the company, before spending an hour presenting the show's concept, theme, costumes and sets. Using the elaborate sketches of the *costumiers* to fire our imaginations, he described each tableau and how it fitted into the show's overall theme of an angel coming to earth in search of happiness – hence the title *Bonheur*. Narratively speaking, it seemed to be yet another cabaret confection that drew a long and mostly unbelievable arc. But the promise of new choreography, plus the excitement of having a German musical star to set the professional tone, proved too thrilling for any of us to care.

Hanging back in the wings during Pierre's presentation were *Bonheur*'s imported duo of choreographers. Craig Revel Horwood was an Aussie from Ballarat who had danced at the Lido many moons ago and had since made a name for himself in London. Mick, his co-choreographer, was a pocket rocket from the U.S. who had earned his dancing and choreographing stripes in Vegas. Craig sat and smoked in the corner, doing his best to seem aloof, while Mick wasted no time endearing himself to us.

'I had a pair of Cuban heels made to rehearse in, so I can get a better sense of what it's like to dance in heels,' he told us with a smile as he was introduced.

'Thank you Mick,' Pierre continued. 'Now, Craig's had a lot of experience staging theatre and opera. It will be his job to draw out a full performance from each of you. I don't just want dancers up there onstage, I want you to act and to understand the motivation behind your every dance move.'

Lisa and I exchanged amused looks.

'Craig, let me hand it over to you.'

Craig unfolded himself from his chair and came to the centre of the room.

'I want you all to spread out,' he instructed. We spread ourselves about the room and looked at him expectantly.

'Now, without making a sound, I want you to either be a bird or a cat.'

There was a moment's silence as everyone pondered the instruction, unsure exactly what to make of it.

'Well? What are you waiting for? A bird or a cat. Go.'

A couple of us laughed, assuming he was joking, only to be reduced to silence by a glare that could have sunk ships. Throwing furtive looks at one another and suppressing the urge to giggle, Lisa and I sunk gingerly to the floor and tried to summon our inner felines. Around us, fellow company members were either relishing the chance to show off their method-acting skills or paralysed with confusion, unsure what to do. The Russians, for whom English was a distant third language, watched in bemusement, looking to one another for explanation. A couple of the ballet girls strutted about the stage giving it *Swan Lake*, but most of the rest of us didn't know whether to act or dance or simply lay down and hope it would all soon be over.

I went with the latter option, figuring I could say I was a sleeping cat if anyone asked. Lying on the stage, listening to Lisa guffawing into her outspread arm, I wondered if I had made the right decision to stay on in Paris for another *montage*. If it was going to be a month of this, I wasn't sure I had the mettle for it. I closed my eyes, as much to avoid making eye contact with Lisa as to pretend I wasn't in the midst of a room full of squawking and preening showfolk.

Craig walked about the room commending people on their cat impersonations. Mick lost himself in a Cuban-heeled flamenco solo in the corner. I silently steeled myself for a long month ahead.

Rehearsals were every bit as manic and exhausting as I had come to expect. True to *montage* form, we seemed to lurch from one tableau to another in a mad rush of clashing ideas and choreography. Routines we learned one day would be completely reblocked the next day. Between Craig's desire to have us acting out every scene and Mick's over-the-top Vegas showgirl schtick, we ricocheted from one distinct style to another, sometimes within the same number. With two weeks to go before opening night, we moved back to the Lido stage.

As the show's deadline loomed, Pierre's temper reached breaking point. But we had all prepared enough shows to know that it would miraculously come together just in time for opening night – just as we knew the final week would be a test of endurance and nerves. In the final days of rehearsal, when costumes were added to the mix and dancing took place in, around and on top of the brand-new sets, there were tears and breakdowns aplenty, as if on cue.

During one number, six of us nudes came rushing onstage and just stood there. Six girls, naked but for enormous pink pom-pom hats, rhinestone-studded ties and sequinned G-strings, looked dumbly at one another. The music played around us while Pierre screamed into the microphone.

'What are you doing? Dance for God's sake!'

'We don't have any choreography for this part,' I volunteered sheepishly. 'Well, we did, but then it changed and then it changed again and now we don't know what we're supposed to be doing here.'

An emergency session of all-night rehearsals was swiftly convened to salvage the pom-pom number, adding to the already packed schedule. We were all exhausted. Winter had descended on the city, wreaking havoc in the company with a blitzkrieg of fatigue-inspired colds and flu. But the show had to go on.

Drawing on reserves of energy none of us knew we had, and relying altogether too heavily on Lady Luck to make everything all right, we assembled for opening night and danced our way into a couple of standing ovations. At the end of the night, Pierre was hoarse and the company was beyond tired – and yet, the triumph left us all on a high.

On one of my nights off a couple of weeks later, I watched the show as an audience member and marvelled at how impressive it looked. Three million euros had been spent on the costumes alone. The feathers had been imported from South Africa and hand-dyed in Paris. Two different Paris-based costume houses had been employed to create the jewellery, and the famous French house of lace, Lesage, had helped to construct some of the more elaborate dresses. Altogether, the show had cost the Lido more than nine million euros, meaning it would have to run for at least five years before it recouped its investment.

Surrounded by couples and families and tour groups, their faces lit by the reflected stage light, their eyes wide with wonder, I couldn't help but feel proud. Having been involved in the show's creation, I was acutely aware of its faults, but I could see how the whole experience would come across from a punter's point of view. The *salle*, the champagne, the Champs Élysées location and the onstage pushing of all the right French-cabaret buttons (feathers, sequins, beautiful dancers in big production numbers) added up to a uniquely Parisian experience.

Sabine's voice sailed through the auditorium, pulling at heartstrings and tingling neck hairs as it went. As a *meneuse* she was a powerhouse, managing somehow to make her Dietrich-inspired coldness utterly engaging.

Some numbers held up better than others. The opening scene, in which Sabine made her angelic entrance by floating down from the heavens in a white-feathered cloud, set the tone nicely with its birds of paradise theme – the stage undulated with a thousand exotic feathers. The *défilé*, in which the nudes paraded a collection of over-the-top leather *couture*, while intoning 'I look fabulous' in several languages, was inspired for its unapologetic campness. Sabine 'jetted' into the *salle* from above the audience in a replica miniature Learjet. In another impressive tableau, a triple-tiered, rotating Hindu temple rose up from beneath the stage and disgorged a cargo of topless goddesses. The ice-skating duo who similarly emerged from the depths just before the finale elicited a gasp from the audience for their death-defying antics, including a routine which saw the beefy male skater hold his female partner by the ankles and spin her around in a wild human centrifugal manoeuvre. And the water tableau, featuring a fountain, a stage-wide rain curtain and twelve nudes in little more than golden backpacks, shimmering headgear and strings of jewels, was undeniably stunning.

But it was the Indian tableau that looked the most impressive from down in the *salle*. Opening with the appearance onstage of a full-size replica elephant, the tableau featured a dance sequence that was a joyous riot of colour and movement. The costumes were spectacular, the choreography was tight and the staging was seamless.

Meanwhile, life backstage was proving to be at least as entertaining as anything taking place onstage. As if conforming to an unwritten rule of cabaret, the new company boasted the usual number of eccentrics. No matter how long I was exposed to the entertainment business, the calibre of crazies that seemed to flock to it never ceased to amaze me. They came in every shape, from every nation and in all ages.

As a six-year veteran of the Paris cabaret scene, I became something of a den mother, doling out advice and helping new girls assimilate to life in France. These ran the gamut of experience and sanity – from the fairly low-maintenance new arrivals who just needed help connecting the gas or opening a bank account, to the young showgirls who wanted to know the French for 'morning-after pill' and whether it was okay to bury a recently deceased pet dog in the grounds of Parc Monceau.

For the most part, however, life backstage was a happy mix of *bonhomie* and camaraderie. Certainly, some girls still made it their life's work to be awful, but there were enough of us on a new-show, new-cast high to make ignoring the bad apples easier.

After work, I became part of a new band of late-night revellers. Sabrina, Lisa and I happily showed the nightlife ropes to an evolving posse that included Tobias, the toothsome Swede; Sara, the genial girl from coastal Queensland; Luke, the gentle giant Englishman; Jason, the mischievous Canadian; Andreas, the friendly South African; and Sheree, Kate and Donna, the jovial roses from county England.

It was winter in the city, meaning most of the rest of Paris was in hibernation, but, energised by the new company I was keeping, I held up my end of the revelling bargain – while being careful to avoid any open car windows.

In the early days of *Bonheur*, I found my way into a romantic entanglement or two, but nothing of any real seriousness. A date here, a mini-fling there, but for the most part, I was delighted to be single and determined to remain free and independent. Olivier had been lurking around, and though it was definitely over, he was doing his best to drag out the break-up. He would linger in the cafe on the corner of Rue de Levis waiting for me to pass or otherwise make excuses to see me. I was never sure where he'd turn up. I felt like I was constantly on guard.

With my thoughts turning increasingly to home, and with the bad taste left by the Olivier saga, the last thing I wanted was to get caught up in another relationship with a French man. But then that's the thing about life – it's nothing if not unpredictable.

# Chapter Forty-six

'Hello? Shay? It's me, Guillaume.'

It took me a couple of seconds to place him. It had been almost a year since we had last spoken.

'Oh, hey,' I replied, taken aback. 'This is a surprise.'

'I know. I've been meaning to call you for ages, but what with one thing and another, I've been a bit busy.'

There was a pause.

'So,' he continued. 'How's the finger?'

'The what? Oh, the finger. Right. Yeah, no, it's fine thanks.' I couldn't imagine he was calling just to get an update on how my hand was healing. I let the silence hang.

'So, listen,' he said. 'I thought maybe you'd like to get together some time.'

'Sure,' I heard myself saying. 'Why not?'

I hung up the phone and looked across the sofa at Willy, who was busily sucking his tail.

'So, this should be interesting.'

About a week later, Guillaume collected me from the Lido one night after work. I emerged from the stage door to see a vaguely familiar black four-wheel drive parked on the street – through the reflection of streetlamps on the windscreen, I could just make out Guillaume's face.

As I made to open the front door, the passenger window slid down.

'What? You're not going to come through the window?' His face lit up mischievously. A flash of cheeky humour – he was off to a good start. We sat for a while in the car, exchanging pleasantries.

'So, shall we maybe go for a drink?' Guillaume finally suggested.

'Sure,' I replied. 'A group of my friends are out at a bar. We could go and meet them?'

He took a moment, to make it seem as if he was considering it as an option.

'*Oui*. Or we could maybe go and have a drink just the two of us?'

Twenty minutes later we were sitting together at a table in the corner of the Chao Bar in Pigalle. Sipping on cocktails, we spent the next two hours talking. He told me about the films he had been working on and the script he had in development. He had grown a shaggy beard and long hair for a role he was about to play – a look that did a lot to counter his otherwise boyish features and gave him a definite sexiness.

He asked me about Australia and, like all French people, said it was a country he longed to visit.

'But twenty-four hours on a plane? *Ça, c'est pas possible.*'

He was still fascinated with the Lido. He wanted to know about the world of cabaret and marvelled at the hours we kept and the work schedule we maintained. He was extremely charming company: easy to talk to, funny and interesting.

Our conversation was interrupted by an incoming text message from Lisa. 'Bank card not working. Can I pls borrow some cash?'

She was with the rest of the Lido crew at Corcoran's, the Irish bar down the Boulevard at Clichy.

'Do you mind?' I asked Guillaume. 'Small emergency.'

He didn't, and so we headed off. As he stepped inside the bar, he stopped and took in his surroundings, a look of mild bemusement on his face.

'What is this place? In twenty-eight years, in Paris, I have never seen a place like this.'

It occurred to me for the first time that a typical Irish pub, with a typical Irish pub interior, was a totally atypical place for a Parisian to contemplate having a drink. I began to wonder if it had been a bad idea bringing him with me.

I introduced Guillaume to the Lido brigade. Comprised mostly of expats, none of them recognised him, and I couldn't tell whether he was secretly pleased or disappointed. Either way, he threw himself with gusto into the moment, ordering a Guinness and launching himself confidently on the crowd. As the night wore on and I watched him work the room, glancing back occasionally to make eye contact with me, I found myself feeling drunk, attracted and just a little bit reckless.

Guillaume and I became an item of sorts, and would meet occasionally when the opportunity arose. It was a wholly un-French affair, simple and without drama. Plans were never made from one *rendez-vous* to the next: we were happy to keep it all in the moment. We enjoyed each other's company, and that was enough.

For reasons that neither of us bothered to talk about, we shared a desire to keep it all in the shadows. I never met his friends and, other than that one night in Corcoran's, he never met mine. We met almost exclusively under the cover of darkness and only ever alone. If I was at a bar with the crew and received a text message, I would hop in a taxi and meet him across town.

To my mind, the whole showgirl-and-the-film-star thing reeked of cliché and could only really have one outcome. There was no point pretending it was anything other than short-term.

But if our liaison was the stuff of caricature, Guillaume was anything but. Passionate about his work and brimming with ideas and enthusiasm for future films and theatre projects, he was a delight to be around. His energy was infectious.

He had mastered enough English to be funny with it, displaying a particular flair for self-deprecation, a rare virtue among his countrymen. He told me all about himself – his childhood, his parents, his start in the film industry, his collaborations with famous names and faces.

Everything was on the table, except the particulars of who he was with when he wasn't with me.

He would appear in Paris for a week or so, then disappear for a fortnight. I only ever knew, vaguely, that he was busy working on film sets, and that was as much as I wanted to know. We both understood that this was only a friendly fling: it was best to keep it at arm's length.

Only a handful of people at work knew of the relationship, and only Lisa knew the full extent of it. I didn't want to tell everyone, thinking that to do so would only bring the silliness of it into sharp focus. But then, silliness was exactly what I was in the mood for. Compared to some of my colleagues I had been a model of showgirl sobriety through the years, lurching from one sensible (if ill-fated) relationship to the other, with only the occasional slip-up in between. I figured I could be forgiven one lapse into cabaret cliché before I hung up my sequins.

Paradoxically, it was the frivolous nature of the affair that clarified for me how much I wanted to be in a simple, normal, committed relationship again. By being charming and exciting yet ultimately unattainable, my French film star had helped heal my heart. Without even knowing it, I was ready to fall in love again.

# Chapter Forty-seven

If, when I arrived in Paris, you had taken me aside and asked me to describe my ideal love-interest, there's little doubt he would have been dark, brooding and wonderfully, mysteriously French. Like many women before me, I had come to Paris harbouring my very own French-lover fantasy.

Though things hadn't worked out with Olivier, there had been a time in our relationship when I saw a future that was firmly rooted in France. And in all the years I had been in Paris, it had never occurred to me to date a fellow Australian. It seemed somehow counter-intuitive to come all the way to France to meet and fall in love with someone from my homeland. But then that's the funny thing about life: sometimes after all your searching, you end up somewhere familiar.

Around the same time that Guillaume had suddenly reappeared, Bryce – the cheeky Australian from the embassy party – also rematerialised. We crossed paths again in December at a mutual friend's party and made vague plans to catch up. A month or so later, I invited him to join the Lido posse for post-work drinks in Pigalle, whereupon he became somewhat of a fixture in our late-night shenanigans. He professed to have a day job, though how he held it down while keeping up with us nocturnal folk I was never entirely sure. What I did know was that his energy was endless, his enthusiasm for life was boundless and his fascination with the world I inhabited seemed sincere. Where others before him had hovered on the fringes of our showbiz world, never getting much beyond the topless showgirl stereotype, he seemed genuinely interested in the machinations of my admittedly unusual existence.

At first I put it down to professional curiosity: he was a journalist who had once written a gossip column for a Sydney newspaper. But the more time we spent together in the group, the more I felt there was a connection between us. We talked so easily, riffed so effortlessly off one another's sense of humour, and seemed to share so much in the way of Australian upbringing and expat experiences. I felt like he understood me. And after years working at cross-cultural relationships, never properly understanding or being understood, it was such a relief. It wasn't long before we became firm friends.

At first, we only met during post-work drinks in bars and clubs. Occasionally, I would excuse myself from the celebrations to rush off and meet Guillaume.

I was unaware of any feelings Bryce had for me, and either in denial or unaware of any feelings I might have had for him. For a couple of months, we danced around one another. A mutual attraction started to blossom, but neither of us acknowledged it, much less dared to burst the friend bubble in the pursuit of something more.

It wasn't until we broke the daylight barrier and began meeting one-on-one for the occasional lunch that I started to wonder if we might become more than friends. There was no bolt of lightning or thunderclap of high emotion – just a gradual realisation that when I woke up in the morning and went to bed – at night, there was no-one else in the world I wanted to talk to.

The insight was driven home when I took a three-week break from work to spend time with my family in Brisbane. Ostensibly, the trip was a test to see if I was ready to move home. After all, I had achieved my professional dreams on the cabaret stage, and there was nothing particular keeping me in France.

So why, I had to ask myself, did I spend half my vacation time in Brisbane on the phone to Paris? Almost every night at the same time, the phone would ring in Mum and Dad's kitchen. 'It's your *friend* Bryce calling,' Dad would tease as I ran eagerly to pick it up.

By the time I got back to Paris, Bryce and I knew that something had changed between us. But who was going to make the first move?

# Chapter Forty-eight

I quickly checked my hair again in the mirror before answering the door. Pulling it open, there he was, looking suddenly more handsome than I had remembered. A black shirt, a pair of jeans, his hair recently cut – it gave him a boyish appearance. In his eyes was the glint I had missed so much, and in his hands, an orchid.

'This is for you,' Bryce said, stepping through the door and pecking me on the cheek as he handed me the flower. 'To welcome you home.'

Previously, conversation had flowed effortlessly between us – now every word seemed loaded. The long-distance phone line had proved a valuable medium for our unorthodox courtship, allowing us to say things we might never have ventured in person. Now here we were, sounding each other out, dancing around each other again.

'So anyway, I have to go to Marrakech tomorrow for work,' he said. 'And I know you probably can't get the time off, and tickets are probably stupid expensive – but if you wanted to come down, I've got a few free days tacked on the end of my stay.'

Was he asking me on a date? No, not a date, a weekend away, in another country? Was it an offer from one friend to another or a leap from the realms of friendship into something more? What kind of a male friend asked a female friend to Marrakech for the weekend? And if it was a romantic weekend away, what was wrong with Saint-Tropez? Or Cannes? Or Biarritz or the Loire? Marrakech was a four-hour flight away on a whole other continent.

I gave a noncommital response, confused about how to react.

Ten minutes after he had left, however, I was at the travel agency downstairs. It turned out he was right. Flights to Marrakech were definitely not cheap. And getting time off work, having just spent three weeks in Australia, was going to be nigh on impossible. And yet I found myself handing over my credit card and signing on the dotted line.

On the plane to Marrakech eight days later, I spent a good part of the flight staring out the window wondering what the hell I was doing. When I had booked the ticket, I had been sure I was simply playing my part in a two-person romantic drama, and that our getting together was just a matter of time. But what if I had gotten the wrong end of the stick? What if this courtship was only in my head? If so, with the help of Air Maroc, I was hurtling at seven hundred kilometres an hour to possibly the biggest humiliation of my life.

Things didn't look good when I emerged into the arrivals hall to see Bryce waiting to meet me in the company of a work colleague. A woman.

'This is Mary,' he said, introducing me to the affable, if unwelcome, redhead.

As we drove through the desert of western Morocco, I sat in the back of the taxi trying to work it all out. I was mortified. More than that, I was embarrassed and angry. I'd moved heaven and earth to get two consecutive nights off, and it had cost me a fortune to buy my plane ticket. This wasn't what I pictured happening at all.

The first night was spent in the company of Bryce's colleagues, all of whom were nice enough, but not worth a trip to Morocco to meet. I could see that Bryce was ill at ease. He seemed distracted and nervous – a state I had never seen him in before – and if things hadn't been so awkward, it might have been endearing. That night, we shared a room but nothing else.

But at sunrise the following day, he shook me awake to tell me we were headed back to Marrakech – just the two of us. Two hours later, we were checking into a hotel on the outskirts of the medina. It was a crumbling five-star affair that had probably once been the height of sophistication, but was now a kind of museum to seventies kitsch. Its wonderful retro hilariousness immediately reset the tone between us. We were back on common ground, finding humour in the macrame wall hangings, the poo-brown and orange furnishings and the russet-coloured plush pile in the lobby.

That afternoon, we whiled away a blissful couple of hours in the souk, getting lost in the labyrinth of stalls, soaking up the atmosphere, breathing in the exotic smells. Over dinner that night we talked and laughed, drank and relaxed. Back at the hotel, during a furtive midnight dip in the pool, under palm trees dappled with moonlight, we finally kissed.

There's no greater city in the world to fall in love than Paris. It's as if the place was built expressly to serve as a backdrop for romance. I had been there for seven years, but in all that time Paris had never looked as beautiful as it did in the first few months of our love affair.

It was summer; the days were long and hot and the nights languid. Bryce had a Vespa, and I rode on the back as we travelled all over the city. If we stayed the night at my place, we would put together a picnic from the vendors on Rue de Levis and spend the afternoon lying in the shade in Parc Monceau. If we spent the night at his apartment in the Marais, we would rise late and sit on a sunny cafe terrace, watching the world go by.

When August came and the whole of Paris fled south, it felt as though we had the city all to ourselves. He would meet me each night at the stage door after the show: I'd climb aboard the Vespa and we'd sail down the Champs Élysées and down along the *quai* of the Seine. Some nights the river was so still, the turrets of La Conciergerie reflected perfectly on its surface. I drank it all in, delirious with happiness.

I woke up on my thirtieth birthday, at the end of August, and looked across the bed at Bryce, still fast asleep. I had never felt happier.

In that moment, I knew this was the man I would spend the rest of my life with.

Of course, being male, it took Bryce a little longer to arrive at the same conclusion. But it was not a wholly unpleasant wait. Our love affair was easy, uncomplicated and fun – like being in love is supposed to be. Whereas my previous relationships had been melodramatic and complicated, this was all just wonderfully effortless.

It had never been part of the grand plan – if in fact there ever had been one – to meet and fall in love with a fellow Aussie in France. But it turned out to give me the best of both worlds. My Australian beau didn't tell me he could see the stars in my eyes, and he didn't write tortured love poetry for me, but when we were together, we laughed. And the fact that we came from the same country, had experienced the same culture shock upon moving to Paris and saw France and the French through the same Aussie prism meant that we had so much in common. No longer completely Australian, no hope of ever being completely French, we were both of no fixed address or nationality. France had gotten under both our skins and become an important part of our lives.

Just when I thought I was done with Paris, along came an Australian to help me fall in love with it all over again.

A month into our relationship, Bryce and I hired a car for a day trip out of Paris. With Lisa and Jason in tow, we drove to Honfleur, a picturesque town near the Normandy beaches, where we spent the day eating seafood and exploring the hamlets that dotted the coastline. It was a gorgeous day – and it was so refreshing to be out of the city for a change. As we drove back in to Paris later that night, I felt as though the sea air had done me good.

Bryce dropped me at his apartment and went off to return the car. As I opened the door and dropped my bag on the living-room floor, my phone rang.

'*Salut. C'est moi.* How are you?'

It took me a moment to recognise the voice on the other end of the phone.

'Guillaume? Oh hi. How are you?' I was flustered.

'I'm good, thanks. I've been pretty busy, working on my screenplay and, well, you know.' There was an awkward moment of silence. 'So anyway, I'm calling to see if you wanted to get together tonight?'

A smile played on my face. I was mildly incredulous that I had ever been involved with someone who thought it was okay not to speak or see each other for two months then call up out of the blue as if nothing was amiss.

'You know what? I don't think so,' I replied. I searched for the right words. 'Remember how I told you that I had met someone? Well, it turns out he's quite special, and I just want to be with him.'

Guillaume was silent for a moment.

'Oh really? Well, that's great. I'm happy for you.'

'Thanks.'

'But you know, I'm not the jealous type. We could still see each other if you wanted.'

I laughed. He was French to the core. 'No thanks. He means a lot to me. But it was really nice to get to know you.'

'Yeah, you too.'

'And good luck with your film. I'll look out for it.'

'Thanks. That's sweet of you. *Bisous. Ciao.*'

I hung up the phone and stood for a moment staring out Bryce's living-room window at the Sunday night parade of people down below. I felt I was exactly where I should be.

## Chapter Forty-nine

Falling in love with Bryce felt like a whole new start for me. And so it seemed only natural that I found somewhere new to live. Villiers and my little apartment on Rue Légendre was so imbued with memories of a failed romance and a difficult period in my life, I wanted a clean slate. So when I heard through the showbiz grapevine that a studio apartment on Boulevard Voltaire in the eleventh *arrondissement* had recently become available, I jumped at it.

The apartment was owned by the Bouglione family, a well-known dynasty of circus performers who owned and operated the Cirque d'Hiver, the majestic old theatre at the top of the third *arrondissement*. The place was tiny – only twenty-five square metres – but I didn't care. Located on the sixth floor of a walk-up apartment building, it required serious cardio exertion to reach, but boasted sensational views north across the Paris rooftops to Sacré Coeur. There was hardly a day I would climb my stairs and not pass one of my eighty-year-old neighbours making the ascent. Often laden with shopping bags and almost always taking a rest on every landing to catch their breath, they performed their daily exercise with impressive cheer and resilience.

Framed by my north-facing window and beautifully lit at night, the Sacré Coeur basilica, perched on the Butte de Montmartre, provided a glorious, permanent reminder that I was in Paris.

My new *quartier*, Oberkampf, wasn't nearly as pretty as the old *arrondissement* had been, but it was only a short walk to the fabulous Marais and Bryce's place.

As summer turned to autumn and autumn slid all too quickly into another winter, my relationship with Bryce went from strength to strength. When my parents came to visit in January, I couldn't wait to introduce them to him.

The city was hit by a snowstorm the night they arrived. Waiting down on the boulevard for their taxi to pull up, Bryce and I huddled under the awning of a cafe. As the cab pulled into the kerb, Mum barely waited for it to stop before leaping out and pulling me into a hug. Bryce busied himself at the boot with the luggage and helped Dad lug their two enormous suitcases up six flights of stairs.

The four of us spent the evening chatting excitedly. True to form, Mum and Dad treated Bryce like they had known him forever. They hadn't come to check him out or give him the seal of approval; rather, they had come to celebrate how happy their only daughter seemed to be. Bryce listened politely to Dad's anecdotes and laughed at his ribald jokes. With Mum he turned on the charm, asking after my brothers, my uncle and my nana as if he knew them all intimately. He gave good Mum – as I fully expected he would – and it made me smile.

'He seems lovely, Shelb,' Mum said, after he had left. 'And you seem so happy.'

The snow stayed for a week: each time it looked like thawing out and turning the white-covered footpaths into dirty grey sludge, a new burst of snow would float down and blanket the city anew. Paris in the snow is a sight to behold. A wonderful silence descends as traffic slows to a crawl, and the city's buildings and monuments are coated in a dusting of pristine white. I spent a magical week with Mum and Dad. Not even the thrice daily treks up and down the six flights of stairs could dampen my parents' enthusiasm.

They didn't say anything – it wasn't their style to try to influence their kids in any way – but I could tell they were pleased that my relationship with Bryce meant there was now a greater chance I might eventually come home.

But I wasn't ready to leave just yet. For the first time, I was dating someone who was not only interested in my work, but seemed to understand – and even celebrate – my passion for it.

To say that Bryce came regularly to see me perform is an understatement. His visits to the Lido were so frequent, he soon came to be recognised by the *maitre d*'s, who would spot him in the long queue that snaked down the Champs Élysées and spirit him to the front of the line. If he had come alone – often after an evening out on the town with his mates – he would sit on a bar stool at the back of the *salle* next to Stuart. Mostly, though, he came in the company of friends, relatives or colleagues – anyone who happened to be passing through Paris and expressed an interest in seeing me perform. He was so proud of me, of what I did and how well I did it, and it filled me with such joy. Even if his constant presence in the audience did become a running joke backstage.

'He's not in again, is he?' the girls would tease. But I couldn't have been happier. I would come out on stage, pick him out in the audience (his blond hair backlit by the spots) and see him beaming. He saw the show so many times he knew the words to every song. It got to the point where he would even begin to issue corrections at the end of the night. 'That tall girl was out of sync with the rest of the Bluebells in the Indian tableau,' he would tell me as I stifled a laugh.

He knew exactly where to find me on stage in every number, pointing me out proudly to whichever guests he happened to be hosting. I had butterflies in my stomach the first ten times he came, but after that, whenever I stepped out into the spotlight and knew he was in the audience, I would soar. I threw everything I had into every performance, feeding off the energy coming at me from that particular curly-haired bloke out in the darkness. Just knowing that among all the sleeping tourists there was one person – one very special person – enraptured by my every move and appreciating how hard I was working, made it so very fulfilling.

As much as our love affair unfurled against the backdrop of Paris, it also ventured further afield. After all, as Australians-in-Europe, we had a national duty to make the most of our new location and travel as much as possible. The world was our oyster. So I joined Bryce on jaunts to Croatia, Tunisia, London, Scotland and Rome. We took summer holidays in Cassis – the picturesque port town nestled amongst the famous Calanques of Marseille – and spent a glorious week in wintry, pre-Christmas New York, indulging a shared passion for restaurants, theatre, shopping and doughnuts.

Almost a year into our relationship, we travelled home to Australia. I met his parents: a jovial, smiling couple from Sydney whose enthusiasm for life was almost as deep-seated as their pride in their son. I sensed a relief that their middle child, the restless, wandering son, had wound up with a fellow Aussie. Now, all going well, they could rest content that whether he chose to remain in France, decided to go somewhere else or came back to Australia, the question of what constituted home was always going to be obvious.

Returning from that trip, I set to work to find a place in Paris for us to move in together. It was a formality, really – our names may have been on separate leases, but our entire lives were already spent in each other's apartments. Still, Bryce initially bristled at the prospect of giving up his bachelor pad to set up house with me. As a wily 31-year-old woman, I gave him enough space so that when he finally did come around to the prospect, he could convince himself it had ultimately been his idea.

Despite a Parisian rental crunch, I happened upon an apartment one afternoon that I felt fate had thrown in my path. It was located only a stone's throw from my rooftop studio, on the crest of the gentle rise that is Rue Oberkampf. The beautiful old stone building was smack-bang in the centre of a busy *rue commerçant* selling all manner of delicious French fare. The apartment was on the sixth floor, but mercifully this time there was a lift.

When the owner opened the front door to me, it was all I could do to maintain eye contact with her. Down the hall behind her, reflected sunlight was flooding the living room, bouncing off the polished wood floors and giving the room a honey-coloured glow. Through the living-room window I could make out the twin spires of the nearby Saint-Ambroise church jutting into the sky.

As I walked down the hall, my heart skipped a beat. The living room was huge and had the gently sloping ceilings that were the hallmarks of a Paris rooftop apartment. With mounting excitement, I turned back down the hall and into the bedroom. The view out of its window took my breath away: there, spread out before me, were nearly all of Paris's famous monuments. The Pompidou, the Tour Saint-Jacques, the Panthéon, Notre Dame and, in the west, where the sun would soon be setting, the Eiffel Tower. It was spectacular. I opened the window and propped myself on the wrought-iron railing, drinking it all in. Terracotta chimney pots and grey lead roofs stretched as far as the eye could see.

Before moving to France, I had dreamed of living in a rooftop garret like this, as a result of watching countless films set in Paris. After eight years of getting by in a succession of run-down, sun-starved Paris apartments, I felt finally as if I had a place we could happily call home.

# Chapter Fifty

When Bryce asked me to marry him, I can honestly say I had no idea it was coming. Things were so right between us I had come to consider our future together inevitable — but the how and the where and the when of his proposal still took me completely by surprise. His parents were visiting from Australia, spending the Easter holidays with us in Paris. Because of his mother's legendary restlessness and thirst for travel — a trait her son had happily inherited — it had been decided that we would take a five-day mini-break to Sicily.

For reasons that hadn't made sense at the time, Bryce had organised for the two of us to take a mini-break within the mini-break. He'd booked two nights in a boutique hotel on the Aeolian Island of Salina, a small volcanic cone on the blue waters of the Tyrrhenian Sea.

Bryce spent the day of the proposal acting strangely; I had no idea why. He was distracted, unable to maintain a conversation and agitated. I sauntered happily through the day, basking in the stunning scenery, lazing contentedly on pebbly beaches as tiny waves lapped at our feet.

As the sun set on the second and last day of our mini-mini-break, Bryce was so anxious as to be almost beside himself. He carried his camera bag with him wherever he went, refusing to put it down. I'd been with him long enough at that stage to accept that occasional lapses into eccentricity were part of the package, and so I tended to ignore them.

Dinner on that night was an intimate affair – just the two of us dining under the stars, by the pool of the hotel. A dark expanse of sea stretched out before us to the line of twinkling lights strung along the coastline of the nearby island of Stromboli. The food was delicious, though the mood had been broken somewhat by my lover's constant checking of his watch. He told the waiter we'd be passing on dessert, ordering instead a couple of glasses of champagne and a plate of strawberries to go.

Tipsy from the wine and intoxicated by the night, we wandered back through the hotel's vineyard to our room, a whitewashed stone-and-thatch bungalow perched on the side of a gentle hill. I sat on the terrace and sipped my champagne, drinking in a sky full of stars. When he pulled out his laptop and started playing a compilation of our favourite songs, I was surprised. When he moved across the terrace and asked me to dance, I was enchanted. When he got down on bended knee, pulled a Cartier box from his camera bag and opened it to reveal a sparkling diamond ring, I was rendered suddenly breathless.

'Shay, will you marry me?' he asked.

I remember his smiling eyes looking up at me. I remember starting to cry, pulling him up and kissing him then melting into his arms. We clung to each other under the stars while the music drifted out through the darkness, across the sea.

Ten feverish months of wedding planning followed, complicated by the 18,000 kilometres and ten time zones between us and the wedding venue. Because he came from Sydney and I hailed from Brisbane, we had decided to choose a venue that was neutral territory for us both. We hoped to have a large number of international guests jetting in for the occasion, too, so we needed a place that could double as a beach-holiday destination. And so we settled on Byron Bay.

We spent countless nights in Paris working the phones to Australia, sourcing caterers, hunting for venues and agonising over seating arrangements. Despite declaring at the outset that we were going to keep it simple, we found ourselves sweating over the decision between cloth-covered plastic chairs or padded wooden fold-out ones. The silliest details took on ridiculous importance.

On a trip home to Australia, made for the express purpose of nailing everything down, we took to the Byron hinterland to find the perfect venue. Among the rolling green hills of Coorabell, we discovered a little property quaint enough to suit the relaxed style of wedding we both wanted, but large enough to accommodate a big marquee for the 130 guests we were to invite. The building looked across a picturesque valley. In the sunset, beyond a massive mango tree, cows grazed contentedly in their paddocks. It was perfect.

We spent the rest of the Byron recce making the other big decisions – such as which colour ribbon would go around the base of the cake and whether the flower arrangements should be in square vases or round ones. On the final day, during a visit to the 'floral consultant', I left Bryce in the car and returned to find him slumped over the wheel asleep, mouth agape, with a wedding spreadsheet in his lap.

We had chosen early March for the wedding, figuring the northern New South Wales weather at that time of the year would be perfect. Had we bothered to check, we would have learned that March can be the wettest month of the year on the New South Wales north coast, and that the region had been subject to widespread flooding only twelve months previously.

For six days prior to the wedding, it bucketed down. Never have I been as obsessed with weather reports as I was in that week. We checked, double-checked and cross-referenced forecasts on the T.V., the radio and the internet. Not only had we opted for an outdoor ceremony, but forty of our European friends had spent a lot of money to travel to the other side of the earth for some sun and sea. The behaviour of the heavens was all-important.

Two nights before our wedding, Bryce and I slept at the house where the whole production was to take place. In all my life, even my years as a kid in tropical Brisbane, I have never heard rain fall so hard. We didn't sleep a wink. At one point, getting up to get a glass of water, I walked into the kitchen to find a family of frogs had moved indoors to shelter from the deluge.

The following morning, however, as if on cue, the clouds parted and the sun beat down. As guest after guest rolled into town, we watched with delight as they variously threw on their swimmers, wandered along the beach or took up residence in the Beach Hotel beer garden.

When the big day arrived, I woke early and went for a swim with Mum and Dad. I had asked my old schoolfriends Chick and Sandy to be my bridesmaids: The three of us had been inseparable during our teenage years. Chick, Sandy and Mum helped me into my dress. Backless, fitted ivory silk, the dress was my idea of wedding frock perfection: simple and elegant. Mum buzzed around me, taking photos on her old instamatic camera, trying – and failing – to make it look like she wasn't crying.

It was just before sunset when Dad walked me down the aisle – or rather, across the lawn. With his chest bursting with pride, he delivered me to the spot on the cusp of the valley where Bryce was standing. And there, with the last rays of a perfect Byron Bay day washing the valley in gold, we declared our love before all the people in the world who meant the most to us.

The reception that followed was a rambunctious affair: lubricated by the numerous crates of bubbly we had ordered for the night, proceedings got raucous early. The marquee looked magical. Fairylights hung overhead, candles flickered beside beautiful floral arrangements, and on each table sat a miniature, hot-pink Eiffel Tower. Determined to strip the occasion of formality and stamp it with our own personalities, we held a meat-tray raffle and commissioned our ninety-year-old grandmothers to serve as barrel girls. They gleefully obliged, pulling out tickets and hamming up the delivery of an array of cheesy prizes.

Brett performed a medley about our courtship to the tune of Barry Manilow's 'Copacabana'. *'Her name was Margaret, she was a showgirl,'* he sang to uproarious applause. Our Italian friend, Claudio, was so moved by the moment (and also, no doubt, by the copious amounts of champagne he had consumed) that he grabbed the microphone after Brett and treated us all to an impromptu operatic aria.

It was more carnival than ceremony, and it suited us both just fine.

It was also a chance to show off our homeland to a host of Parisian friends – an opportunity for them to see why, no matter how long we stayed in the 'world's most beautiful city', our country of birth and our families would always have final claim on our hearts. And they came, they saw and they understood.

Returning to Paris after our very Aussie wedding felt a little bit like the beginning of the end. Both of us knew that our Paris story was not yet fully told, but we were definitely in the closing chapters. The sunburnt country would eventually become our home.

First, though, we had another wedding to organise. Not content to have said 'I do' in English, we were determined to do it all over again in French. So many of my Lido and Moulin friends had been prevented from coming to Australia by the crushing nightly work schedule, and it was important to us to celebrate our marriage with our Paris family.

The Paris wedding took place two months later and was a much less grand, but no less meaningful affair. Becky, who had been unable to travel to Australia because of her pregnancy, was my bridesmaid. Due any day, she stood in the *salle de mariage* in the town hall of the eleventh *arrondissement* and watched as Bryce and I repeated our vows – this time in French. In front of a room full of friends, we swore to the deputy mayor of our *quartier* that we would adhere to the many clauses of the French Republic's *Acte de Mariage* and were duly pronounced *femme et mari*.

At a lunch at the nearby Hôtel du Nord on the Canal Saint-Martin, we danced our wedding waltz. I had choreograped the dance and Bryce had practised with me until he was blue in the face. Hastily downing a glass of wine for Dutch courage, he stood up before a room full of professional dancers and performed – earning a standing ovation for his efforts. We looked out across a room full of smiling faces and marvelled again at our good fortune.

# Chapter Fifty-one

I stirred restlessly next to Bryce in bed. I had already thrown open the curtains in a fruitless attempt to wake him: he still snored quietly beside me. I looked out the window at Paris spread out before me, relishing my secret.

'Are you awake?' I finally ventured, shoving my husband violently.

'I am now,' he groaned sleepily, starting to rouse. 'What time is it?'

'Eight-thirty,' I replied matter-of-factly.

'It's a Saturday, for God's sake. What are you doing? You're never awake before midday. What's going on?'

I was bursting with the news. The words seemed to tumble out of me.

'I think I might be pregnant.'

Bryce sat bolt upright with tousled hair, sleepy eyes, and a look of slack-jawed shock.

'I've done a couple of tests this morning and they've been positive. I mean, I'm not a hundred per cent sure, but I think this is it.'

A huge smile spread across his face, and he jumped on me and we tumbled about the bed laughing – overcome with joy and just the slightest hint of anxiousness. It was one thing to talk about becoming parents, but another for it to be actually happening.

We dressed quickly and rushed to the medical lab at the top of our street to ask for a blood test. I was told the results would be ready in three hours. To while away the time, we went to a cafe and wandered along the Canal Saint-Martin, trying hard to make like it was any other Saturday. But it was hard to concentrate on anything other than the prospect of impending parenthood.

After three hours had passed – almost to the minute – I phoned the lab.

'*Oui Madame, vous êtes enceinte,*' came the verdict down the phone.

It seemed scarcely real.

'Really? I'm pregnant?' I stammered.

'*Oui, oui, madame.* Pregnant.'

Having children – and relatively quickly – had always been part of our plan. As members of a generation who pushed child-rearing back to their thirties, and after decades spent studiously avoiding pregnancy, we had both decided that once we were married we would get busy straight away with the whole baby-making business. Mercifully, it had happened with a minimum of angst and effort. Now, barely two weeks into our life as newlyweds, we were staring down the barrel of parenthood.

There was excitement, obviously, but also trepidation. Were we ready for this? We decided not to tell anyone until the pregnancy had passed the traditional three-month mark. We carried the knowledge around with us: on the one hand bursting to share, on the other, enjoying the secret.

While I was dealing with the swirl of emotion that accompanies the news you are going to bring another life into the world, I had to front up every night at work and maintain the ruse that nothing had changed. Physically, it meant wading through each performance ignoring semi-constant morning sickness. Mentally, I found I had to concentrate extra hard on the job at hand. My mind, unsurprisingly, was elsewhere.

Acutely aware of the sensitive cargo I was carrying, I asked Petra if I could be written out of a couple of the more vigorous numbers, blaming my weak back to avoid arousing suspicion.

Unfortunately, none of my colleagues were buying it. If I'd had an office job – or indeed was employed in any one of the thousands of occupations that actually require you to wear clothes to work – I could have kept the secret. But my breasts had already begun to swell and my waist to thicken. They were subtle changes, but to a dressing-room full of girls who saw me naked on a nightly basis, the slightest fluctuations were obvious. I did my best to ignore the looks and whispers exchanged behind my back, but eventually there was nowhere left to hide.

'You're pregnant, aren't you darl?' asked Luke, one of the showboys who was never backwards in coming forwards. 'Everyone knows.'

Barely a month and a half into the pregnancy, I had been outed, and found myself in the awkward position of having everyone at work know before I'd had a chance to tell to my family or closest friends. Still, there was a kind of relief in having the news out there. It made it easier for me to pace myself onstage, and made me less self-conscious about the changes taking place to my body. But I worried that publicly acknowledging the pregnancy four weeks before the three-month mark was tempting fate.

When I woke one Sunday morning a couple of weeks later, I knew instinctively that something was wrong. It had been almost a week since I had had morning sickness, and though the baby was far too tiny for me to feel him or her moving, something indefinable had shifted. The low-lying sense of euphoria I had felt seemed to have deserted me, and in its place was a hollow feeling of . . . nothing.

Sitting in the waiting room of the maternity hospital an hour later, I laid my head on Bryce's shoulder and cried. I didn't need a doctor to examine me. Every cell in my body was screaming the news. It was as if I had been briefly plugged in to the vast rush of life, and now the cord had been abruptly disconnected. I felt desolate, devastated, empty.

In the examination room, an ultrasound dealt the final cruel blow.

'I'm sorry Madame. There's no heartbeat.'

I squeezed down hard on Bryce's hand, grappling for some kind of anchor – someone to rip me from this nightmare and take me back to yesterday. It wasn't until that moment that I realised how much I had wanted that baby. Every inch of my being yearned for it – and now began to mourn for it.

It would take weeks to physically recover from the miscarriage. I took time off work and spent my days floating morosely about the apartment. At first, we wanted to keep the news to ourselves. You feel oddly like a failure when you miscarry. It's irrational, but for me the feeling of failure and the devastation were all-consuming. I felt as though I was in a tunnel from which there was no escape. I couldn't imagine ever feeling happy again.

But slowly, with Bryce's support, the sadness lifted. I knew I wasn't the first person to have suffered a miscarriage. I knew the statistics. But I had been momentarily stripped of empathy. I couldn't think about others: I could only think about the baby I had lost.

Immediately after visiting the hospital, we had stopped at a *pharmacie* on our way home. The pharmacist, a kindly older gentleman with a greying beard, had taken the script from my shaking hands and looked it over.

'Some roses just aren't ready to blossom,' he had said as he handed over the medicine the obstetrician had prescribed. He touched my arm and looked me in the eye. 'The next rose will be just perfect.'

# Chapter Fifty-two

The pharmacist was right. The next rose was perfect. He arrived in the middle of an unseasonal April snowstorm the following year.

Flynn Xavier Corbett was in no great hurry to make his entrance into the world. Twenty hours of labour may not have broken any birthing records, but it was a bruising enough introduction to the not-so-gentle art of childbirth.

I had fallen pregnant three months after my miscarriage. We'd received the news one Saturday afternoon at a wedding in Montmartre, after a trip to the blood lab earlier that day. I had frocked up, Bryce had suited up and we'd trooped off to the *mairie* of the eighteenth *arrondissement*, trying to concentrate on the ceremony – but as soon as it was over and everyone was heading off to the reception nearby, we'd ducked away to phone the lab.

The pregnancy was confirmed on the steps of the Sacré Coeur basilica, with a sweeping view of Paris's rooftops for a backdrop.

In a world in which couples sometimes try for years to fall pregnant, it was another blessing from the fertility gods. Still, I spent the early stages of the pregnancy terrified. I didn't dare to dream it would all work out. Even in the later stages, the spectre of disappointment and heartbreak hung heavily in the background, despite repeated assurances from ultrasound technicians, midwives and gynaecologists that everything was perfectly normal.

Almost immediately after discovering I was pregnant, I asked my gynaecologist to write me off work. There was no evidence that my dancing had had anything to do with the miscarriage – there were already a handful of showgirl mums at the Lido, and some of them had continued to work until they were five months pregnant. But neither my doctor nor I was prepared to take any chances. And so, with a flourish of his fountain pen and the impressive weight of France's justly famous social security system behind him, my doctor signed me off work for a full twelve months. The happy combination of my chosen profession – which required nudity but discouraged the display of distended-bellied showgirls – plus the fabulously generous benefits of the French maternity leave system, meant that I had twelve months to give my tired body a break.

After eight years of dancing almost every single night, it was surprising how quickly I got used to doing nothing at all – though of course, my body was busy doing all sorts of things of a gestational nature. Freed from the rigour of two shows a night, six nights a week, I relished the opportunity – for the first time in my life – to sit back and get fat.

Unlikely as it may seem, there are many showgirl mums, dancers who raise children by day and high-kick by night. In years gone by, becoming a mother more or less meant hanging up your heels. But these days, thanks largely to work contracts that cannot be easily terminated plus changing social attitudes to working mothers, the showgirl mum has become more common. Lido management took the news of my pregnancy with an air of resignation. Pierre was genuinely delighted for me, but I could see him wondering if perhaps it wouldn't soon be necessary to set up a Lido *crèche*, so numerous were the pregnancies in his Bluebell line.

And I rested. I started to discover what it was to have a normal social life. I began to enjoy evenings with my husband, either slumped on the sofa in front of the T.V., dining out at restaurants or passing lazy hours in cafes. After eight years in the City of Light, I was finally getting a taste of the life that most of its inhabitants took for granted. I fell willingly into a nine-to-five existence, sleeping when the rest of the city slept and waking in the morning to join the queues of people at the *boulangerie* or the crowds of grannies at the market. I began to discover the joy of early-morning Paris – kids moving in noisy packs to school, street cleaners sluicing the pavements with water, *boulangers* kneading dough for the lunchtime *baguettes* and waiters bustling about sunny terrace cafes, ferrying coffee and *croissants* to their early-morning *clientèle*.

With time on my hands and armed with the best excuse known to woman for a pig-out of unchecked proportions, I ate. And ate, and ate, and ate.

The cravings were subtle at first: a squeeze of lemon in my tea or a hint of vinegar on my salad. In time, though, they morphed into full-blown pregnant-woman obsessions. As my stomach grew, I found I couldn't get through the day without at least two white chocolate Magnums. Thankfully for me – though less so for my long-suffering husband – there was a late-night *épicerie* at the bottom of our building. Bryce's nightly runs for my Magnum fix became a running joke with the store's friendly Tunisian owners.

The pregnancy passed relatively effortlessly. We attended prenatal classes, watched ultrasounds of our unborn child excitedly in darkened rooms and made a series of painful visits to Ikea to feather the nest. Injuries I had from fifteen years of nonstop dancing finally had a chance to heal. A niggling hip problem that no number of scans or X-rays or visits to sports physiotherapists could account for magically healed.

Oddly enough, though, after three weeks off work my calves became sore from a lack of high heels. The muscles had become so used to walking in heels, it was painful for me to wear flats. I found I had to wear a pair of heels for a couple of hours every day and wean myself off them. Vacuuming the house in my bathrobe and heels made for quite a sight, but it was truly more comfortable.

I loved being pregnant, not least because my body developed curves. Wanting to record and celebrate them, I asked my friend Carla Coulson, an Aussie photographer in Paris, to photograph me in costume at the Lido. In full make-up, heels and draped in jewels and feathers, I felt wonderfully, ineffably womanly.

As the due date drew nearer and we started to make plans for the dash to the hospital, I began to feel the distance between us and our families more than ever. I missed my mum and wanted her there. From a practical point of view, it would also have been nice to have back-up on hand in the event of an emergency – even if we were quietly confident of handling whatever was thrown at us. But more than that, the magnitude of what was about to happen started to sink in, and all I could think about was how much I wished our families were there to share it.

When Flynn finally came crashing into the world, he bore all the hallmarks of his Aussie lineage. At 3.7 kilograms and 52 centimetres, he was hardly the world's largest baby, but compared to the neat little French specimens who were being nursed in adjacent hospital rooms, he was a giant.

The labour had been conducted entirely in French and the whole experience, while exhilarating, had left me exhausted. The first few weeks of parenthood were terrifying. Neither of us knew what we were doing. None of the pregnancy books I had read really prepared me for the complete shock to my system that was first-time motherhood. I can honestly say I have never been so tired in my life. Days melted into nights in one great big blur of sleep deprivation, dirty nappies and anxiety – and, of course, some of the purest moments of happiness I have ever known.

Both sets of grandparents beat a path to Paris to meet their grandson. To see Mum and Dad holding Flynn for the first time brought me to tears.

Just as I started to feel I might be able to get my head around this whole motherhood thing and was finding a routine that worked for all of us, it was time to start getting ready to go back to work.

My exit from the stage had been so abrupt, I didn't feel as though I had finished on my own terms, and I wanted to step back into my dancing heels. Because I was going to be back at the Lido, dancing topless in skimpy costumes, I had to lose weight and stop breastfeeding. It wouldn't do to have a slightly chubby showgirl squeezed into an array of sequinned strings. And performing with breasts swollen with milk just wasn't going to work.

As much as my motivation to drop the extra kilos was driven by my contract, there was also no small amount of pride involved. I knew that on my first night back at work all eyes would be on me, assessing exactly how my body had been affected by pregnancy and childbirth – and I was determined to look my best.

I took to the swimming pool and swam laps like there was no tomorrow. I banished all white-Magnum family packs from the house and cut back on the after-dinner blocks of chocolate. I tried running, until I rediscovered how much I hated it. Thankfully, breastfeeding seemed to whip off the kilos as fast as I had put them on, and my naturally high metabolism – plus a body stocked with muscles that had been toned by years of twice-nightly dance workouts – meant getting back to a dance-ready body was mercifully easier than I expected.

Nevertheless, when I surveyed myself in the mirror in the days before I was to return to work, I was definitely carrying more weight than I would have liked. Worst of all were what I came to call my breastfeeding arms – a layer of stubborn flab had settled on my upper arms and refused to budge. And although to the naked eye my stomach appeared to have bounced back, it looked different to me and definitely required more concerted sucking in to give it the desired concave showgirl look. My thighs felt heavier, my skin felt looser and, distressingly, since I had stopped breastfeeding my breasts seemed to be shrinking with every day that passed.

Despite Bryce's well-meaning assurances to the contrary, I knew my body was not as it had been before. But then neither was I.

Four months and two weeks to the day that I had given birth to Flynn, I was back in the Lido dressing-room preparing to take to the stage. When I passed Pierre in the corridor he welcomed me back with a smile.

'You look fabulous darling.'

I knew it wasn't really true, but it was nice to hear just the same.

The first night was strange. Castmates were genuinely happy to see me and made a fuss of my return, but I felt self-conscious in front of them in a way I never had before. Moreover, I found myself obsessing about how thin everyone else was. Whereas before the tall, lithe, lean bodies had just been part of the nightly wallpaper, now I was acutely aware of how much thinner, younger and more toned my co-workers were.

That night, as I sat in front of the mirror applying my make-up, I distinctly remember how strange it felt to be smearing body paint onto breasts whose primary purpose three weeks previously had been to feed my child. The disparity between the two worlds I was now inhabiting became suddenly clear, and I began to wonder if I could do justice to the role of showgirl any more. I had crossed over into a universe that was at complete odds with the *demimonde* of Paris cabaret.

On stage that night I felt exposed, but I pasted a showgirl smile to my face and danced through the show.

It wasn't just a new-found sense of self-consciousness that changed my performance. I also felt different physically. For the first three weeks back on stage, I danced gingerly, feeling my hips and pelvis were dangerously loose. High kicks were performed with less vigour and backbends were executed with greater caution.

But far and away the most painful adjustment to being back on stage was the wearing of high heels. Once I'd weaned myself off them I had happily hardly gone near a pair. Strapping myself back into high-heel torture devices for two shows a night was almost more than my ankles, shins and calves could bear. The pain in the balls of my feet was excruciating. I would perform a number and, within seconds of running offstage and into the wings, tear off my heels and pad delicately back down to the dressing-room in my stockings.

Yet, bit by bit, my strength and confidence returned and I was soon performing at my pre-pregnancy level. Well, almost the same level. Truth be told, my feet were onstage and dancing, but my mind was very definitely elsewhere. In fact, the physical feat of performing each night was nothing compared to the mental feat of concentrating on performing when all I could think about was my baby boy. While my feet moved and my legs kicked, I thought about Flynn; what noises he had made, what and how much he had eaten, how many hours he had slept, whether that little cough was getting better or worse.

It wasn't that I didn't care about the show anymore, it just suddenly seemed insignificant. Most nights I performed in a funk of exhaustion.

Several times, sitting at my dressing-table to apply make-up, I had to start by picking dry baby vomit out of my hair. In the seconds before I raced up the stairs and flew onstage as a vision of Parisian showgirl glamour, I would giggle at how two hours earlier I had been in tracksuit pants and a singlet, hair unwashed, face drawn from lack of sleep, furiously rocking a small child as he drooled down my back.

Bryce and I had a system. I would spend all day with Flynn – playing, feeding, wiping his nose, changing his nappies. At 8 p.m., I would hand him over to Bryce, jump on the Vespa and rush off to the Lido to don the stage make-up and perform two shows. I would finally collapse into bed at 3 a.m., only to hear my little bundle of joy stir three hours later. Bryce would take the early-morning shift until he had to go to work, at which point I would drag myself out of bed and the routine would begin all over again. To say that it was tiring doesn't even come close to describing it. But it was a kind of virtuous exhaustion, and no matter how frazzled I got, one gummy smile from my new number-one fan somehow made it all worthwhile.

Other mums would ask how I could possibly front up to work each night after a day spent with a baby. But the truth was, it was a welcome break. It was nice to be briefly away from the nappies, to have an adult conversation and to be reminded that not everyone's universe revolved around Teletubbies and puréed vegetables. I had joined the ranks of those most incongruous of things: showgirl mums.

I would sit in the *loge* at night and smile as I listened to the younger girls talk about their wild nights on the town. Occasionally I would feel a pang of nostalgia for the nights when I could stay out until dawn and sleep all day, when first dates and spontaneous romantic encounters would add unexpected piquancy to any given week. And then, after the nostalgia had passed, a wave of relief would wash over me that I could stop moving, stop searching and stop facing up to life each day alone. I may have been exhausted, but I had also never been happier. And the more my little boy grew, the more I became engrossed in his ever-enlarging life.

Nevertheless, I still prided myself on trying to give my all in every show I performed. Whether it was a high-tourist-season first show, packed to the rafters, or a low-season second show with fifty slumbering package tourists, I did my best to perform like it was my first night on the Paris stage. I knew the clock was ticking and that my time in the spotlight was soon going to end, and I didn't want to walk away regretting that I hadn't given it everything I had.

# Chapter Fifty-three

It was neither my creaky bones nor the ranks of fresh-faced dancers nipping at my nine-centimetre heels that finally saw me take my final Paris curtain call. It was something much more special.

'Why are we stopping here?' There was an edge to Bryce's voice. Neither of us had slept particularly well the night before and our early-morning stroll through the Jardin des Plantes had been marred by a constant drizzle. We were on the Pont de la Tournelle, en route to one of our favourite little cafes behind Notre Dame for a hot chocolate and a serve of its famous *tarte tatin*. After a good thirty minutes of grizzling, Flynn was finally asleep in the pram.

'I just think it's a beautiful view. Back up the river, the flying buttresses of Notre Dame. Don't you?' I looked at Bryce hopefully, but he didn't appear to be convinced.

'Yeah, it's lovely. Let's keep walking. You know if we stop moving he's going to wake up.'

'Not yet,' I replied. 'There's something I want to tell you.'

He looked at me expectantly.

'You know how we were saying we might be ready to have another baby?'

He looked puzzled for a moment. Then a smile broke across his face. I smiled back.

When I discovered I was pregnant again, and that in nine months I would be the proud, but very busy, mother of a toddler and a newborn, I knew my Paris dancing days were numbered.

From that moment, knowing that I would soon be leaving the lights and the feathers, I made sure I savoured every second I spent onstage. I had dreamed of dancing in Paris since I was a teenager, and now it would soon be over.

I performed my last show on 27 May 2009 – eleven years and five months since I had taken to the stage at the Moulin Rouge for the first time. I was three months' pregnant. Mum flew over from Brisbane and sat in the audience with Bryce and a group of our friends.

I was the *meneuse* for my final performance, replacing the singer – one last turn as the star of the show. I made my entrance in the feathered cloud, and as I floated above the audience and was gently lowered to the stage, I looked out across the auditorium and caught Mum's eye. If she had been any more proud, she would have burst.

With so much invested in what I knew to be my last performance in Paris, every dance step, every song, every sequence was charged with emotion. The hormones of early pregnancy ensured that I was barely able to finish a number without welling up.

My cheer squad gave me a standing ovation at the end of the show. As a bemused group of tourists wondered what all the fuss was about, Bryce came walking down to the stage and handed me a large bunch of roses.

In the dressing-room after the show, I was inundated with flowers and cards and presented with a cake in my honour. Girls I had known and danced with for years hugged me to them. There were tears streaming down my face and happy laughter in the air. On my dressing-table sat the bouquet from my husband. To each rose was tied a scroll of paper - messages he had spent weeks collecting from people I had danced with since I was six. Kim Bowkett, Todd McKenney, Jeannie,

Brett, Matthew and Jenny. Chick, Becky, Lisa, Tamra, Thierry and Janet. It was all too much to take in.

I looked about the dressing-room, the place where I had spent so many happy, exhausting, exhilarating years. The place where, in some ways, I had grown up. I felt a deep affection for it. The very walls seemed soaked with memories.

And then, in the midst of it all, Cathy, the head dresser, came into the *loge*. She excused herself as she stepped into the circle of emotional dancers and reached down to grab the pair of heels at my feet. 'Shay, may I borrow these for just a minute? I need to check to see if your shoes fit Elsa.'

I looked up to see one of the most beautiful girls I had ever seen on: tall, skinny, luscious locks of long brown hair and the flawless skin of a twenty-year-old. She had big brown eyes, legs that went forever and a figure to die for. She had been chosen to fill my shoes. Literally.

As the girls began to drift away, I collared Stuart. 'I don't suppose you could have found someone younger or more beautiful to replace me?'

He smiled. 'You should see her naked.'

And there it was. I was so utterly replaceable. People would say lovely things and write lovely messages on my farewell card. Pierre would tell me the Lido was losing a little bit of class, flowers would be sent and tears would be shed. But the reality of it all was, when I walked out that door, the machine would keep turning. The show would go on.

# Epilogue

## Paris, 2009

Bryce and Flynn are asleep in our bedroom when I return home from my final show. Mum is curled up on the spare bed in Flynn's room. I set down the bag full of farewell flowers and gifts and head into the kitchen to make a cup of tea.

I love this time of the night. In a day otherwise packed with nonstop noise and movement, it's the only chance I get to stop and be still – the only time I truly have to myself. I know I should be getting to bed. I know that in four hours' time I'll be woken by a babbling toddler, but I just need a moment to wind down. I stand at the open window in the living room with my tea. In the distance, Notre Dame is floodlit dramatically and the Pantheon has a halo of soft green light. The Eiffel Tower glows orange, a silent sentinel keeping watch over the city as it sleeps. I'm going to miss it all. I'm going to miss it all so much.

When I think that I arrived as a fresh-faced twenty-three-year-old, expecting to stay a year, it boggles my mind that I have spent almost my entire adult life in Paris. And now it's time to say *au revoir*.

Piled behind me are the boxes we're shipping to Australia, a motley collection of clothes, books and keepsakes. I don't know whether to be sad or relieved at how small the pile accounting for twelve years of my life is. I remind myself that what we haven't accumulated in material possessions, we've more than made up for in memories. Too busy living to be bothered collecting.

The removalists will be here in three days, but we've decided to stay in Paris until the baby arrives. The health system in France is good and the maternity benefits are second to none, and we want to be able to offer both our kids the gift of dual nationality. Besides, many of the most important, momentous things in my life have happened in Paris. The birth of our second child should happen here, too.

When finally it came, the decision to return to Australia was mutual. Watching our son grow, we've come to realise he's too robust for the hemmed-in life on offer to kids in Paris. During winter, we've ferried him from our small apartment to the closed-in walls of his *crèche* wrapped in so many layers he could barely move. He needs space: fresh air, big skies and room to grow. I want him to have parks with grass he can actually run on and trees he's allowed to climb. I want him to have beaches, backyards and bush. Maybe some of it only exists in our imaginations, in a rose-coloured vision of our homeland, but we want to at least try to give him – and his brother or sister – a flavour of the childhood we both had.

More importantly, we want our children to know their family. For them to know what it is to have cousins, grandparents, aunties and uncles and the unconditional love that only they can offer has become more important than we could ever have imagined.

Of course, the transition is going to be tough. To leave behind a city as magical as Paris is obviously going to be hard. And not just the city, but the friends who have become like family. Just thinking about it makes me emotional.

On trips home, Australia has often felt like a foreign country, too. So much has happened in my absence, so much has changed, there are so many cultural markers that I have missed and so much to re-learn. And yet, it is still home – it will always be home – and the comfort in that is enormous.

Perhaps the toughest thing of all will be adjusting to the 'real' world. When I told Pierre I was planning to resign, he said he understood my reasons and wished me nothing but success, but asked if I was mentally prepared to stop performing. 'It's a difficult transition for people to make, you know?' he said. 'And I'm speaking from experience.'

I understand what he meant. I've been on stage for so long, it's become an extension of who I am. Even on the nights I was wishing I could be anywhere else, performing was still a buzz: the lights, the applause, the *caché* of being a Paris showgirl. Am I mentally prepared to leave it all behind? I honestly don't know. What I do know is that I don't want to be one of those tired old dancers who has to be hidden up the back. A graceful exit on my own terms is infinitely better than being slowly nudged offstage.

Still, the future is one big question mark. New baby, new country, new career, new beginnings. I'm thirty-four years old and facing the prospect of retirement. At an age when most people are only just hitting their stride, career-wise, I'm hanging up my heels and starting all over again. The prospect of having to reinvent myself is frankly terrifying.

Certainly for now, being a mum will occupy my every waking hour, but eventually I'll become restless and want to return to the workforce. But to do what? What kind of work can a former showgirl expect to find? I've been dancing professionally since I was seventeen. It's what I know.

But if I'm leaping into the unknown, at least it will be in the company of my husband and family. I feel so very lucky to have been able to do what I love for so long – in Paris, on the stage. I have no regrets about putting away the feathers.

And in the end, that's the nice thing about getting older. You are less riddled with self-doubt. I think back to when I arrived in Paris and remember how petrified I was when I first performed at the Moulin Rouge, scared I wouldn't measure up. With age comes experience and with that the confidence that you can handle whatever life throws at you. To the fresh-faced girl from Brisbane who stepped off a plane from Japan all those years ago, becoming a Paris showgirl was everything. Now it's just a job. A good job, a steady job, but a job just the same. Something I slot in between raising a child and nurturing a marriage, because those have become my priorities. Maybe not forever, but certainly for now. And that makes me one very happy old showgirl.

# Acknowledgements

First and foremost, I owe an enormous debt of gratitude to Bryce, my number one fan – for his tireless work and for believing I had a story worth sharing. When all I saw in front of me was another night at work, you saw the glitter in the grind. And now, even with a child on each hip, you manage to make me feel like a beautiful showgirl.

Thank you to my parents, Marie and Graham, for always saying 'just be yourself'; and to my brothers, John and Adam, for keeping my feet firmly on the ground.

*Merci beaucoup* to Janet Pharaoh and Pierre Rambert for giving me the opportunity to grace the Paris stage; to Thierry Outrilla, Stuart McGhee and the teams at the Moulin Rouge and Lido for their continued support and encouragement.

To photographer extraordinaire Carla Coulson, a huge thank you for your beautiful photos and your friendship.

I am grateful to my editor, Vanessa Radnidge for patiently sifting through endless pages of feathers and sequins, and to the ever generous Miranda Murphy and Helen McCabe for their keen-eyed copy-editing.

Thanks are due also to Paris for taking me in. I feel honoured and humbled to have played a tiny – if showy – part in the history of this proud city.

And finally, to all of the showfolk who were my surrogate family, this is a tribute to the hard work you do every night, on stage and behind the scenes, to create the magic that is Paris cabaret.

# If you loved *Memoirs of a Showgirl*, you can read Bryce Corbett's *A Town Like Paris*.

'A rip-roaring book . . . with widespread appeal' *Sun-Herald*

**At the end of a nine-year relationship, stuck in a dead-end job and on the run from his broken heart, Australian journalist Bryce Corbett left London for Paris, home of *l'amour* and *la vie bohème*.**

Arriving with only a suitcase and school-boy French, he finds himself an apartment and slowly launches himself into *la vie parisienne*. It doesn't take Bryce long to discover his down-home Aussie charm has no currency in France – either with Parisienne women or French plumbers.

Undeterred, Bryce is determined to make the city his own – no matter how many bottles of Bordeaux it takes. Fully embracing his newfound culture, he is exposed to some of the more unfathomable idiosyncrasies of the French, from the revealing lack of window coverings and alcohol-rationed soirées, to the exasperating non-existent customer service and the traffic black hole around the Arc de Triomphe.

Just when he thinks he knows it all and Paris has offered him all she has to give, he meets a showgirl – an Australian beauty whose sequin-clad high-kicks are the toast of the Champs Élysées.

Bryce might just discover that what he came to France looking for was a lot closer to home than he had ever imagined.

Here is the first chapter of Bryce's book.

## Chapter 1

Are you sure you've got the right person?

Outside the train window, the flat plains of Picardie flash by in a dark brown blur.

The sky bearing down on them is grey and featureless. The kind of sky that makes any Australian living in London wonder when they last felt properly warm, and why they left their sun-drenched homeland in the first place.

The last weeks of December are counting down the end of an old century. And while the world is flush with the excitement of an impending new millennium, I am crossing a continent on a day-return train ticket to do an interview for a job I'm not the least bit interested in.

On the tray table in front of me, a collection of barely opened books tell the riveting tale of European economic integration. I have fallen asleep three times in the last hour while trying to read them. I hunker down in my seat, stare out the window at a frost-bitten northern France and wonder what the hell I am doing.

A former newspaper gossip columnist turned showbiz TV producer en route to Paris to interview for the position of Director of Communications of an international business organisation. It is frankly ridiculous.

I sit and wonder if they will laugh me out of the interview – see through the sham I have made of my résumé, demand I pay back the Eurostar train fare and hound me back across the Channel.

What had possessed me to apply for this job in the first place? Ah yes, of course. Britney Spears and boredom. How could I forget?

It had all started two months before, on an unusually quiet afternoon in the newsroom of the 24-hour TV news channel I worked for in London.

As a showbiz producer for Sky News, it was my job to keep track of the tedious intricacies of the lives of inexplicably famous people.

This particular afternoon saw me flicking listlessly through copies of *Hello!*, *OK!* and assorted other quality celebrity magazines to keep across my brief.

Done with my research, and motivated by the kind of pure boredom that I felt at least seven or eight times an hour in that job, I wandered over to the nearby bank of desks occupied by the business reporters.

Movement of the financial markets commanded almost as much importance in the minds of Sky News' editors as movement of the Beckhams. Finance and showbiz therefore occupied the small portion at the end of every news bulletin not otherwise dedicated to football, royals or whatever 'shock crime wave' we were busy manufacturing on any given day.

As a result, the finance reporters were as under-utilised as we showbiz luvvies, leading to much crossing of the corridor, bored chit-chat and the occasional perusing of one another's magazine collections.

While our repository of showbiz and gossip rags were especially prized in the greater newsroom environment – and hence often stolen – their piles of *The Economist* and *Business Week* were widely neglected.

Motivated by boredom, and some perverse idea that its contents might serve to expand my mind, I picked up a copy of *The Economist* and started looking through it.

On previous sorties into the dense geopolitical realm of *The Economist*, my sense of the absurd had been piqued by the jobs section. If you've ever had the pleasure of reading it, you will know that the job listings are weekly exercises in bureaucratic nonsense.

*The Economist* is where you advertise any job that should only exist in a comedy sketch or an Evelyn Waugh novel.

It's where the Ugandan Ministry for Roads posts a half-page ad for a new Deputy Director of Road Levelling.

> The successful applicant will have at least five years' road levelling experience at an international level, must be familiar with the latest global standards for gutters, be good with concrete, a dab-hand at dealing with troublesome secessionist rebel soldiers and be in possession of a licence to operate heavy road levelling machinery. The Ugandan Ministry of Roads is a non-smoking workplace and an equal opportunity employer.

It is the favoured recruitment medium of practically every United Nations department known to Ban Ki-moon (and even, I suspect, quite a few that aren't.)

It's quite common to find within *The Economist*'s classifieds section ads for Project Directors for far-flung field-work in random West African nations, for which, mysteriously, the speaking of fluent Finnish always seems mandatory.

In between guffaws and inner-monologues on the shocking waste of money that was routinely channelled by poor governments into the creation of these absurd jobs, one advertisement caught my eye.

> The International Chamber of Commerce (ICC) is seeking a Director of Communications. The ICC is the world business organisation. The applicant will be responsible for the global communications strategy of the organisation. He/she must be familiar with the work of the ICC and have at least five years' experience as a PR and communications director of an inter-governmental or non-governmental organisation of similar international stature. He/she must have demonstrated managerial experience and at least ten years' experience in an executive role in the private or public sector. The candidate will be experienced in the creation and implementation of effective media and communications strategies. He/she will be fluent in French and English, and have excellent writing and organisational skills.

Almost apologetically, at the end of the ad it said: 'The successful candidate will be required to relocate to Paris and be expected to undertake regular international travel.'

I reflected on my work history and concluded I was hopelessly underqualified. I didn't have any of the experience they were looking for, I knew nothing about international organisations, my French was rusty from years of neglect and I neither knew nor cared what the ICC was, what it did or who it represented.

What I did know was that I had always dreamed of living and working in Paris, that I was nothing if not creative when it came to CVs, and that one more month spent in London, doing the daily early-morning shuffle out to the industrial estate in far west London that Sky News called home, was surely going to kill me.

I took to my computer and bashed out a letter of application, making a few judicious changes to my résumé.

A spot of finance reporting here, a sustained period of economic analysis there – anything to make my gossip-columnist past and entertainment-producer present seem less obvious.

Three weeks later, an in-depth editorial conversation with colleagues about the new Britney Spears single was interrupted by the shrill ring of my telephone.

At the other end of the line was an English gentleman. He introduced himself as Lionel from the ICC in Paris. He wanted to know if I was available for an interview.

'It will require you to come to Paris for the day, I am afraid,' he explained. 'It seems our Secretary-General is very interested in your résumé and she would like to meet you.'

As I frantically tried to recall the extent to which I had embellished my CV, I found myself agreeing to a rendezvous in Paris in a week's time.

What a hoot! A fully-funded daytrip to Paris – a chance to escape the office, scoff a few crêpes and sink a carafe of Bordeaux or two in my favourite city in the world.

Sure, the hour of the actual interview might prove a little awkward and the ensuing embarrassment when it was discovered I was a charlatan might be a tad uncomfortable, but for the sake of a free trip to Paris, I had decided it was a risk I was willing to take. Besides, it would make for a great story at my next dinner party.

The train crawled through the outer suburbs of Paris. Graffiti-covered walls, heavy industry warehouses and nondescript tower blocks gradually gave way to lead-roofed apartments, terracotta chimney pots and glimpses of streets lined with brasseries, boulangeries and epiceries.

I took a taxi from Gare du Nord to the Place d'Alma in the 8th arrondissement in central Paris. The interview would take place at ICC headquarters, a beautiful seventeenth-century building on the banks of the Seine, and would be conducted by the organisation's Secretary-General, a dynamo of a woman called Maria.

Maria had spent the better part of the last twenty years creating and nurturing the development of the high-powered business and political love-in that is the annual World Economic Forum in Davos.

As I sat across the table from her, she explained the ICC's history, its goals and its need for dedicated, alert, attentive personnel.

I didn't absorb a word. I was transfixed by the view from her window, taking in as it did a majestic sweep of the Seine and a stunning view of the Eiffel Tower.

With a fool's grimace pasted to my face and the presence of mind to occasionally nod in answer to her questions, I sat and stared at the *bateaux mouches* plying their way up the river. Watching them disappear from view, I imagined the route they were about to undertake, past the Louvre, under the Pont Neuf and around the flying buttresses of Notre Dame.

Paris, the old harlot, was already casting her spell, seducing me with coy flashes of her well-worn beauty.

It turned out, Maria's interview consisted more of oration than actual conversation. Possessed of a wide-ranging mind and a fierce intelligence, job interviews gave Maria the opportunity to hold forth on whatever topic of macroeconomic importance took her fancy that particular day.

They also showed off the calibre of her considerably bulging contact book. After fielding a few questions before listening to her reminisce about the time Yasser Arafat refused to use the same backstage door as Ehud Barak at the World Economic Forum, I stood to leave the room, certain I had done little to convince this woman of my suitability for the job.

Walking down the baroque staircase of the offices – the former home of a French count's mistress – Lionel, my septuagenarian interview chaperone, turned to me with a smile.

'Well, it looks like you've got the job then,' he said.

I stopped mid-stair and looked at him quizzically.

'You can't be serious,' I replied. 'I barely said a word. All I did was sit there and nod.'

Lionel chuckled. 'With Maria, as you'll soon learn, that's pretty much all it takes.'

And then, tilting his head forward to look over the top of his glasses, he looked me in the eye.

'You do still want the job, don't you?'

'Of course, yes,' I managed to stammer, not altogether convincingly.

'Good then,' he said. 'So I'll be in touch to discuss particulars.'

He walked me out to the street, shook my hand and waved me goodbye.

As I walked away the initial shock began to yield to a sense of rising panic. This hadn't been part of the plan. It was just meant to be a jolly daytrip to Paris. A brief respite from the Sky News monotony. A little jaunt to the Continent for a crepe, a carafe and a random job interview in between.

With two hours to kill before my return train to London, I decided to walk back towards Gare du Nord, to clear my head in the crisp winter air and weigh the decision I suddenly, unexpectedly, had before me.

As I wandered beside the Seine, a tour bus pulled up and disgorged an excited group of Italian tourists. They piled out of the coach and rushed in a babbling huddle towards the stone wall rising up from the riverbank. They turned to pose for a group photo. A gaggle of excited grins juxtaposed against the backdrop of an imposing, indifferent Eiffel Tower.

To my right, beyond the elegant arc of the Pont Alexandre III, and framed by its ornate lamps, Les Invalides stood proud, its gilt-edged dome glinting in the afternoon sun.

I thought of London – of the dull sky, the cold and the single mattress on the floor that constituted my bedroom in the tiny West London terrace I shared with five other people. Could it be that my time in London was finished?

But to move to Paris? Where I knew no-one. Where my university-level French, last studied eight years ago, was certain to be wholly inadequate to the task of daily living. Where I had neither lodgings nor family nor friends. To take a job I wasn't qualified for. It didn't make a whole lot of sense.

But then again, it was Paris. The world's most beautiful city. The urban embodiment of all that is chic, stylish and desirable. The most visited city in the world – rich in history, crammed with culture and chock-full of possibilities for a single guy in need of a change of scene following the recent breakdown of a nine-year relationship.

Stepping out on to the Place de la Concorde, I glanced to my left. Countless postcards, holiday snaps and picture books had rendered the scene familiar, yet its beauty still startled me. Elaborate twin fountains threw jets of water ostentatiously into the air while the majestic Hotel de Crillon kept silent watch.

It was madness, surely. What about my journalism career? What interest did I have in becoming a PR flack for an international business organisation?

But how else was I ever going to have the opportunity to live and work in Paris? I had always fancied myself doing a stint in the City of Light, and here it was being offered on a platter.

Sometimes life takes turns you cannot predict, I told myself. Opportunities are presented you could never imagine would come your way. I was twenty-eight years old, with no partner, no children and no mortgage to pay. I was as free as I was ever going to be in life. What's more I had a broken heart in need of mending and was in a dead-end job in a city I had grown to resent. Why was I hesitating? This might be my only opportunity to live and work in Paris . . . ever.

The white gravel of the Jardin des Tuileries crunched underfoot. Children dressed in immaculate woollen tunics pushed toy sailing boats across a pond. Through the skeletal branches of carefully cropped plane trees, the baroque, honeycomb façade of the Louvre loomed large. The fast-sinking sun caught the top of the glass pyramid in the museum's courtyard.

I took a seat and a very deep breath. Moving to Paris would mean starting all over again. It was terrifying.

I took my mobile phone out of my pocket and dialled the ICC.

'May I speak with Lionel, please?' I felt my heart pounding as I was put through. 'Hi, it's Bryce. Bryce Corbett. When would you like me to start . . .'

You've read the book, now join Shay online.

Visit www.shaystafford.com

... your online portal for *Memoirs Of A Showgirl*, featuring:

- an extensive photo gallery;
- video interviews with Shay;
- news and reviews;
- an online 'Guide to Showgirls';
- videos of Moulin Rouge and Lido shows;
- Shay's insider tips for the Parisian visitor;
- author contact details;
- special offers on Moulin Rouge and Lido tickets.

Be sure to also join the official *Memoirs Of A Showgirl* fan page on Facebook.

www.ingramcontent.com/pod-product-compliance
Ingram Content Group UK Ltd.
Pitfield, Milton Keynes, MK11 3LW, UK
UKHW041307180426
11947UKWH00009B/745